THE SENATOR MUST DIE

THE SENATOR
MUST DIE

by

Robert D. Morrow

ROUNDTABLE PUBLISHING, INC.
Santa Monica California

ROUNDTABLE PUBLISHING, INC.
933 Pico Boulevard
Santa Monica, CA 90405

First Printing, 1988

Library of Congress Catalog Card Number—88-061816

ISBN NUMBER—0-915677-39-3

PRINTED IN THE UNITED STATES OF AMERICA

IN MEMORIAM

This book is dedicated to the memory of two persons, without whose encouragement and cooperation it could not have been completed:

Allard K. Lowenstein,

Former U.S. Representative from the Fifth District of New York, and

"Tiny" Hutton,

Former Deputy Director of the House Select Committee on Assassinations.

ACKNOWLEDGMENTS

To my wife, Jeanne Dietz Morrow, who spent many long and suffering hours typing and editing this manuscript, as well as transcribing the hundreds of hours of interviews.

And to the many people who contributed their time being interviewed and, in many instances, risked their lives by doing so.

And, last but not least, to my agent Julian Portman, who believed in the project.

PREFACE

In 1977, just after the paperback of my book *Betrayal* was published, I started to look into the association fo the underworld with our intelligence community. The fact that this liaison existed did not surprise me. What did, however, was the extent to which the two were intertwined and the length of time this association had existed. This book is a horror story.

In the course of its writing, representing a period of ten years and over seven-hundred hours of interviews, of which only a fraction are represented here, I discovered that our government was as guilty of committing as many gross miscarriages of justice as any banana republic. It is the story of treason and conspiracy in high places, assassination plots to eliminate heads of state, the toppling of governments considered adverse to U.S. policies, and last but not least how they covered it all up.

Because of these truths, this book will be well criticized, for it portrays a portion of our historical heritage and a part of our society we would prefer to think doesn't exist. Unfortunately, the exact opposite is the case.

This book encompasses all of the above, including an extensive background into the death of President John F. Kennedy, which is necessary in order that the reader understand why and how Bobby was gunned down. For Bobby lived in the shadow of his brother from the time he was a small boy. Because of it, he was in many ways as insecure as the man who would inherit the presidency after his death, Richard Nixon. On that fateful night he won the California primary, Bobby spoke to Kenny O'Donnell, one of his brother's former aides and a long time friend of the family. "You know, Kenny," he said, "I feel now for the first time that I've shaken off the shadow of my brother."

Within hours, he was dead.

AUTHOR'S NOTE

The story behind the death of Bobby Kennedy is a complex one. Also, it did not start and stop with the discharge of a single gun in a hotel pantry by a lone deranged gunman.

Instead, I was to discover that the young senator was the victim of a carefully planned and implemented execution, followed by a conspiratorial cover-up paralleling the one that ensued after his brother's assassination.

And it was purely by accident that I uncovered how it happened and who perpetrated it. The solution came as an outgrowth of an entirely different investigation.

This is the story of that investigation.

In addition to the interviews and exhibits published in this document, there are several thousand pages of pertinent data available to the reader, that could not be published in this book due to the sheer volume it would encompass.

This data has been made available through the kind auspices of the:

Assassination Archives and Research Center
Suite 510
Washington, D.C. 20004
(202) 393-1917

Any person with the desire to review this data will, by appointment, be able to do so, at the center's offices, after November 30, 1988.

Robert D. Morrow

FOREWORD

by L. Fletcher Prouty
Colonel, USAF (Ret'd)*

The dread theme of this work is established as fact by the grim words to be found in such quasi-governmental publications of the clandestine services of the United States government as *The Clandestine Operations Manual for Central America*. Among other chilling statements appearing in this manual is one that confirms the monumental findings of this book:

> If possible, professional criminals will be hired to carry out specific selective "jobs."

Instrumentalities of the U.S. government maintain and hire professional "mechanics or hit men" to carry out assassinations and other "jobs." I know this as a result of my own longtime experience with the clandestine services. President Lyndon B. Johnson, himself, labeled it, "Murder, Incorporated."

There can be no doubt that a team of such "mechanics," with government incentives and Mafia know-how, was used to kill President John F. Kennedy. A similar team, with similar backing, carried out the exquisitely professional "job" of killing Senator Robert F. Kennedy in

---

*Colonel Prouty was, at the time of his retirement in 1964, Chief of Special Operations in the Office of the Joint Chiefs of Staff. As such, he was responsible for the military support of the worldwide clandestine operations of the CIA and the military departments.

the crowded Ambassador Hotel in downtown Los Angeles.

Murder is one thing. The ability to carry it out and to use the combined resources of the government and of the Mafia to extricate the "hit" team stealthily—and then to create and maintain the cover-up story that has blanketed the media for decades—is a task of far greater magnitude. This masterful cover-up that has endured unscathed for more than twenty-five years underscores the continuing existence of the terrible strength and vitality of that ultimate power team. It has done its job, and the threat for the future continues.

The fact that such enormous uncontrolled power has existed without challenge for more than one-quarter of a century speaks for itself. This country and perhaps the world are under the control of a High Cabal, unequaled for its magnitude and effectiveness in the history of civilization.

THE SENATOR MUST DIE

Chapter One

If anyone was destined to die by the hand of an assassin, it was Robert F. Kennedy.

His life was tumultuous, his death, tragic.

I met "Bobby," as everyone called him, in 1961, only twice. The first time was a pleasant experience; it was at his brother's Inaugural Ball. The second was not; he was then Attorney General of the United States in his brother's administration. At the time, I was thirty-four years old and a CIA contract agent working with a Cuban exile leader by the name of Mario Garcia Kohly. Kohly, who had been a prominent Cuban businessman and financial leader, was the man picked by the conservative elements in the Eisenhower administration to succeed the island dictator, Fidel Castro.

Shortly before the Bay of Pigs, Kohly had incurred the wrath of the new Attorney General by insisting that the Russians were starting to build missile sites in Cuba. Then, just about a month after the so-called "missile crisis" of October 1962, Kohly was literally thrown out of the Attorney General's office—after telling him the missiles had not been removed and demanding that the administration do something about it.

Unfortunately, I was with him.

Bobby Kennedy had a temper, an unforgiving memory, and an insatiable drive to accomplish what he believed in. Because of these traits—combined with his relentless pursuit of organized crime, his determination to destroy the Central Intelligence Agency, and his unrelenting suppression of the anti-Castro Cuban exiles—and because of his candid political ambition—he and his brother would be murdered within a period of five years.

The evidence I gathered, which eventually led to the perpetrators behind both Kennedy murders, emerged during a period when I was investigating the role of organized crime in the Cuban exile movement.

My investigation began in 1975 after the publication of a book I had written called *Betrayal*. The book was about my experiences working with the Cuban exile movement between 1959 and 1963, and it grew out of my giving evidence to a special subcommittee of the Senate Select Committee on Intelligence Matters, which had been investigating the possible tie between the CIA/Mafia assassination attempts on Fidel Castro and the murder of John F. Kennedy.

I was aware of the relationship between the underworld and the Cuban exile movement, because, in 1962, I had been introduced to two men meeting with Kohly, whom I later recognized to be Sam "Momo" Giancana and Johnny Roselli. Both men were Mafia dons, who—I subsequently learned—were working with the CIA in efforts to assassinate Fidel Castro. At the time, I was told their meeting with Kohly was to arrange for the Mafia to regain control of their property in Cuba that had been appropriated by the Castro government. It was intended that Kohly would become Cuba's new president, with the help of the Central Intelligence Agency.

The information that surfaced during that investigation left me astounded, and it answers questions that many writers and commentators either have not pieced together or have feared to divulge. I discovered:

- That President John F. Kennedy was killed in order to stop his brother from pursuing his investigation of organized crime.
- That, when he was Vice President, Richard M. Nixon sanctioned—then ordered—the implementation of political assassination and assassination squads.
- That Nixon was tied directly to organized crime and the Cuban exile movement, and these ties would lead to his resignation as president of the United States.
- That the Shah of Iran, aided by the Central Intelligence Agency, was directly involved in the assassination of Robert Kennedy and the election of Richard Nixon.
- That Sirhan Sirhan was not the real assassin of Robert F. Kennedy.
- That Richard Helms, as Deputy Director of Plans for the Central Intelligence Agency, committed *what could be considered tantamount to treason* to hide the CIA's role in the assassination of John F. Kennedy and the attempted assassinations of Fidel Castro.
- The reasons the Federal Bureau of Investigation and the Central

Intelligence Agency entered into a conspiracy to distort and hide the evidence behind the assassinations of both Robert and John Kennedy. I also discovered the name of the real assassin of Robert Kennedy.

With the uncovering of these facts, I decided to compile an account of my investigation for the historical record, explaining how it all came about and what part I played in it.

Therefore, the first half of this book deals with history. It lays out the background of how all the forces came into play that would culminate in the destruction of an era, an era known best as "Camelot." It all took place in the turbulent years between World War II and 1968.

* * * * *

When it all began, I was a *sophomore* at Pennsylvania Military College in Chester, Pennsylvania, prior to entering Pennsylvania State University. That beginning was in 1947, with the founding of the Central Intelligence Agency, an outgrowth of the Office of Strategic Services (OSS) that had been formed during the hectic days of World War II.

Working with a secret budget, the OSS had performed all types of clandestine acts, such as espionage and sabotage. Unknown to most, it had utilized the talents of the underworld to carry out many of its operations. During World War II, the OSS had made a pact with the Mafia, which was known as "Operation Underworld." It provided gangland assistance to keep U.S. and European ports operating so that Allied armies could land in Sicily.

According to the official OSS war report, declassified and released in June of 1976, the OSS/Mafia relationship began in 1943 when the Office of Naval Intelligence (ONI) secretly enlisted the services of top Mafia leaders Lucky Luciano, Frank Costello, and Meyer Lansky. The criminal syndicate agreed to direct clandestine operations on the island of Sicily in return for the parole of its incarcerated chief, Lucky Luciano, once the war was over.

But the liaison was compounded when the Office of Naval Intelligence—at the request of the OSS—employed Luciano and his deputy, Meyer Lansky, for domestic services. The Mafia leaders were asked to set up a network of underworld contacts to act as informers against potential German sabotage, particularly on the docks of New York's waterfront.

On May 8, 1945—the day the war in Europe ended—Luciano's

attorneys submitted a petition for executive clemency to Governor Thomas E. Dewey of New York, who was made aware of the Mafia/OSS involvement. According to Dewey, "Luciano's aid was sought by the Armed Services in inducing others to provide information concerning possible enemy attacks. It appears that he [Luciano] cooperated in such efforts, though the actual value of the information provided is not clear."

On January 3, 1946, the most notorious Mafia leader in the nation received his clemency—and was deported.

Later, the Kefauver Senate Committee, investigating the role of organized crime in the U.S., would discover that most of the official files on "Operation Underworld" were missing, but ultimately it concluded that Dewey's pardon of Luciano had been issued "in the national interest, at the urgent request of Naval Intelligence [OSS's partner]." Interestingly, Murray Garfein, the Assistant District Attorney in New York who played a central role in arranging Luciano's pardon, was subsequently appointed to a federal judgeship by President Nixon, in 1971.

However, with the war's end in 1945, the OSS was disbanded. It was a move that alarmed the Mafia, who, for the first time, enjoyed an official relationship with the U.S. government—a relationship that had given them a large measure of immunity from prosecution.

They weren't alone in their apprehension. There was also a circle of businessmen, politicians, and intelligence experts who felt the United States was suddenly left defenseless to a myriad of alien acts. The men who comprised this circle were, for the most part, well-bred and well-educated Easterners connected with the highest levels of government and finance. Two of the most distinguished were Allen Dulles, a Princeton graduate and former top-ranking OSS official, and the man who freed Luciano, Governor Thomas Dewey of New York.

Together they spearheaded the effort to resurrect the OSS.

Both men were convinced that the United States could not survive the political chaos left by World War II without a powerful, independent intelligence agency. In fact, Dulles so successfully championed this idea among his contacts at the Pentagon that President Truman appointed him to head a three-man commission to investigate the U.S. intelligence system. The result, after a two-year study, was the formation of the Central Intelligence Agency.

Dulles was concerned, however, that Truman would not remain a friend of the Agency when it became necessary for the CIA to bend the law. To guarantee the Agency's future, Dulles convinced Dewey to run for the presidency a second time. The former Governor had run against Franklin D. Roosevelt in 1944 and lost; after Roosevelt's death, he had become the odds-on favorite to capture the presidency in 1948. To guarantee his election, the CIA—under Dulles' direction—funneled more than one-million dollars of its unvouched funds into Dewey's campaign coffers.

Ironically, the Mafia hierarchy also supported Dewey, after being assured by the CIA that it would be to their best interests to marshal syndicate money and political clout behind the former anti-crime czar.

It was easy for Dulles to have the CIA invest in Dewey's campaign. Like the OSS before it, the CIA also was given a secret budget. It literally consisted of funds that could be drawn from various parts of the Department of Defense. Also, unlike any active U.S. agency before it, the CIA charter was drafted so licentiously that the new clandestine agency had virtually unlimited power.

Such power would be necessary, for the CIA would carry on a tradition started by the OSS. It would not shrink from making deals with organized crime to preserve its interests, which they considered U.S. interests. Under the CIA's charter, such arrangements were legal.

Once again, the intelligence community became involved with the underworld in a number of ongoing projects.

From 1947 to 1950, the clandestine agency recruited various Mafia figures to "put down" a series of leftist strikes in Marseilles, France. These strikes had seriously impeded the flow of American war materials through Marseilles to the French forces then fighting in Vietnam.

For the next twenty years, this alliance would remain quite important. The Mafia was changing its image—creating a worldwide crime cartel under the guidance of their financial genius, Meyer Lansky. The aging dons who headed the old Mafia families had been so impressed by Lansky's aptitude for business that they were letting him merge the rival groups into a conglomerate of banking, real estate, tourism, and gambling.

By 1947, Lansky would be able to claim this international crime cartel was "bigger than U.S. Steel." It would give him the resources to wield vast political power—power that Robert F. Kennedy would challenge in a massive attack on organized crime and—from the syndicate's point of view—make it mandatory that he be "removed."

The year 1947 was one of significance for Robert Kennedy, for it spawned yet another figure who would also dispense vast political power. James Riddle Hoffa had risen to become head of Michigan's Teamsters

Joint Council 43; as its president, he was undisputed boss of all of that state's locals. Like the Mafia leaders, he would become a target for Robert Kennedy, for he made an alliance with organized crime to increase his sphere of influence, and it was a partnership that worked.

By 1952, Hoffa garnered sufficient importance and friends to demand— and get—an international teamster vice-presidency.

As his puissance grew, he took control of the union's Central States Pension Fund, which in 1949 was worth over two-hundred million dollars. With it, Hoffa made loans to various mob enterprises to buy the kind of power that could not be denied. Those who tried were threatened, beaten, fire-bombed, or murdered.

Also in 1947, Richard Milhaus Nixon (then a young Republican congressman from California in his first term of office) was beginning to pay back the Mafia piper for support of his congressional campaign. As a member of the infamous House Un-American Activities Committee, Congressman Nixon was asked to use his influence to make sure a Chicago gangster would not have to testify against his peers. Nixon was successful, and the mobster was excused.[1]

Sixteen years later, this same Chicago mobster would perform an important service for the syndicate—the killing of accused presidential assassin, Lee Harvey Oswald. The mobster's name was Jack Rubinstein; later in Dallas, Texas, he would become known as Jack Ruby.

In the 1950s, this same Jack Ruby would become involved (along with an ex-Cuban president) in gambling and gunrunning to Fidel Castro— activities carried out with the full knowledge and blessing of the CIA.

Nixon's early involvement is in line with Mafia tradition. Mickey Cohen, the syndicate's southern California gambling chief in the 1940s, admitted to helping finance the early stages of Nixon's career. According to Cohen, the transactions were handled by an attorney named Murray Chotiner, who was an early Nixon campaign manager and would remain an advisor to Nixon into his presidency.

Columnist Drew Pearson reported that, in exchange for the syndicate contributions to Nixon's campaigns, Chotiner used his influence to keep bookmakers out of jail in Los Angeles. When Pearson first aired these charges in 1959, Chotiner demanded a retraction. But after Mickey Cohen offered to supply details, Chotiner dropped his demand. Between 1949 and 1952, Pearson reported, Chotiner and his brother, both lawyers, represented Mafia underlings in 221 cases and succeeded in keeping nearly every client out of jail.

In 1952, when Chotiner was called before the McClellan Senate Committee investigating organized crime (an outgrowth of the Kefauver probe of a year earlier), Pearson reported that Nixon interceded with committee member, Senator Joseph McCarthy, to tone down the investigation.

* * * * *

Cuba had entered the Mafia picture in the early 1930s, when Meyer Lansky first visited the island in search of molasses to use in making rum. Instead, he found the island brimming with other opportunities.

By the fall of 1933, he had befriended Fulgencio Batista, a chubby ex-army sergeant who had just proclaimed himself dictator. With Batista's blessings, Lansky opened several casinos, which would be the genesis of organized crime's international gambling network.

However, during World War II, when Nazi submarines prevented the tourists from coming to Cuba, Lansky had to shut down the casinos. Then, when the U.S. entered the war, the Cuban economy really started to crumble, and Batista encountered political turmoil. To stay in power, he began making concessions that increased communist influence inside his government.

U.S. corporations began to fear that their Cuban investments might be nationalized. In 1944, the OSS—through ONI—requested another favor from Lansky. They asked him to pressure Batista into stepping down in order to abate the communist encroachment.

Lansky, a staunch anti-communist himself, prevailed upon the dictator, and subsequently, elections were held. A pro-American candidate named Carlos "Prio" Socarras won. Batista left Cuba for eight years of exile in southern Florida.

In March of 1952, Batista returned to Cuba to resurrect his dictatorship in a bloodless coup, which was also arranged by Lansky, without any request from U.S. intelligence, but with a $250,000 mob payoff to Socarras. In addition, during his eight-year reign, Socarras was reputed to have funneled off at least $20 million in cash into a number of Miami bank accounts.

Socarras then retired to Miami to assess his fortune and cement his ties with both the syndicate and the rapidly expanding CIA. In the 1950s, Socarras would become a working partner of Jack Ruby. He would die mysteriously before he could testify about what he knew of President John Kennedy's assassination.

By 1952, as Dulles had feared, Congress was posing a danger to the CIA's autonomy. As a hedge against any difficulties, the Agency, under the guidance of Dulles and Dewey, began to buy congressional goodwill. Friendly congressional members found their re-election problems eased by contributions, volunteers, and endorsements. Also, their staffs were increased with the addition of bright young assistants introduced by members of the Agency. Most attention was devoted to congressional members who seemed to have a promising future—politicians who someday might be Capitol Hill leaders and White House aspirants.

Congressman Nixon was one of these. In 1946, he had been elected a member of the House of Representatives from California. The Orange County Republican party had placed a newspaper ad to solicit a token candidate in a race against the undefeated Democratic incumbent. Nixon, just out of the Navy, applied for the job. His credentials were slim: the FBI had rejected him; his law clients had found him embarrassingly naive; and his war record was mediocre. But Nixon ran with maniacal anti-communist zeal, and, slandering his opponent as a communist, he returned a winner.

Having demonstrated his ability to be politically programmed, he would be tapped by Dewey and Dulles to be the vice-presidential candidate for Dwight D. Eisenhower in 1952. It came about because Dewey liked Nixon's amoral pragmatism and his fierce anti-communism.

As part of his grooming, in 1948, Dewey had arranged a special favor for Nixon, getting him involved in the Alger Hiss case.

A magazine editor named David Whittaker Chambers had accused Hiss, a top State Department official under Truman, of having belonged to the Communist Party. The House Un-American Activities Committee (HUAC) investigated and was about to exonerate Hiss—when Nixon asked to take over. Nixon claimed the CIA had conducted an investigation of Hiss and confirmed to Dewey that Hiss had indeed belonged to the Communist Party. And Dewey had passed this information along to him. However, on August 5, Hiss appeared before the HUAC and denied that he'd ever met Chambers. Nixon, uncertain about how to proceed, held a rendezvous with Allen Dulles and his brother John, the future Secretary of State, at the Roosevelt Hotel in New York. At that meeting, Allen Dulles provided Nixon with verbal assurance that Hiss had known Chambers ten years before.

Nixon, years later, admitted that at the onset of the investigation, he had no "real facts" to prove Hiss guilty of any crime; he obviously had less than the wholehearted support of the Committee, and, as it turned out, he had his doubts about accepting Chambers' word against Hiss'. All of this made his pursuit of Hiss extraordinary and, for many, inexplicable, unless they adhered to the theory that Richard Nixon was ruthlessly ambitious to the extent that he would put an innocent man in prison to gain power for himself. Harry S Truman, would label the investigation a "red herring."

Five months later, Hiss once more appeared before the HUAC and, under Nixon's questioning, began to retreat from his earlier statements.

For example, at the start of the hearings, Nixon gave the impression that "Chambers' disclosures dealt with Communist espionage activities." But no such testimony was offered—until three months later. It was after CIA agents led the young congressman to the evidence that would eventually convict Hiss, even though the HUAC had tremendous doubts as to its value. The doubt would be understandable, the evidence was a piece of microfilm—supposedly of classified State Department documents— that was found hidden in a pumpkin on Hiss' property.

The scandal gave Nixon a national reputation as an anti-communist fighter. On the strength of it, he ran for the Senate in 1950 against popular Helen Gahagan Douglas, wife of movie star Melvyn Douglas. Nixon labeled her the "Pink Lady," and his campaign literature described her as a fellow traveler of communists. Murray Chotiner, Nixon's congressional campaign manager and attorney, wrote the smear pamphlets—all based on information in CIA files.

Predictably, Nixon won and took his seat in the Senate, thanks to the CIA—and to the syndicate, who helped finance it.

Richard Helms' career started in the early 1950s, when the CIA first adopted the policy of using covert operations to interfere internally in unfriendly foreign governments, even to the point of overthrowing them. By 1953, thanks to Allen Dulles, these clandestine activities had become the CIA's major forte, swallowing up most of the budget. CIA covert operations had planes, clandestine airfields in Greece, Germany, England, and Japan, and a cadre of U.S. Army officers with hired mercenaries trained in branches of guerrilla warfare. In Germany alone there were five-thousand men—armed, trained, and ready to go.

It was during this unstable period that the CIA would mount an operation that would set the stage for Robert Kennedy's assassination thirty years later.

The operation began after one of Helms' best childhood friends, the young Shah of Iran,[2] fled his throne in the face of threats from mobs under the leadership of communist-inclined Mohammed Mossadeq, which had seized control of Britain's Anglo-Persian oil wells in southern Iran.

The business of putting the Shah back in power and the oil wells back into the hands of the western powers was handed over to the CIA and Kermit "Kim" Roosevelt, who headed its Middle East section. Roosevelt was to be Richard Helms' original case officer.

Helms' career advanced rapidly. He was brought into the CIA fold to take over the Office of Strategic Operations (OSO). In those days the OSO was the group responsible for perfecting the Agency's direct espionage and other esoteric activities such as assassination. One of OSO's first assignments was to overthrow Mohammed Mossadeq.

The OSO group set about bribing the Iranian army and revamping the police force.

Once this was accomplished, most of Mossadeq's powerful political supporters were spirited away, their throats slit and their bodies buried in the Elburz Mountains outside of Teheran. Demonstrators were hired, and a revolt (also orchestrated by Helms) was organized. With hardly a shot fired, Mohammed Mossadeq, who had wanted simply to get the international oil cartel off his country's back, was easily toppled.

After Mossadeq fell from grace, Roosevelt made an enemy of OSO chief Helms. He started to feel sorry for the deposed leader after he had done a three-year stint in prison. Roosevelt arranged for Mossadeq's release with a comfortable pension! However, Mossadeq died soon afterward, a death engineered by Helms.

The Shah and his queen were re-established on the throne. The young Shah had learned his lesson well; to prevent another Mossadeq from appearing out of the Iranian woodwork, he established—under the influence of Helms—a secret police force to be known as the SAVAK, with its operatives trained in the U.S. in the fine arts of torture, murder, and the intricacies of covert activities.

These activities were first carried out in a building located in the 1800 block of R street in Washington, D.C. The organization formed by the CIA to do this training was called the International Police Academy. The man who ran this operation was named Joseph Shimon.

By the late 1960s, the SAVAK was performing important services for the CIA inside the U.S. Their most dramatic would be accomplished in 1968.

CHAPTER ONE NOTES

1.   A copy of the FBI memo which indicates that Ruby was to be called as a witness before the House Un-American Activities Committee, until Congressman Nixon interceded, is shown in the Appendix, Exhibit No. 1.

2.   During the early 1930s, Richard Helms and the Shah had been best friends and schoolmates together as children at the LeRosey school in Switzerland; *Faces in a Mirror,* Princess Ashraf Pahlavi, Prentice Hall, 1980.

Chapter Two

In the summer of 1952, the year Richard Nixon joined Meyer Lansky as an ardent fan of Cuban president Fulgencio Batista, I was a young man of twenty-four.

As a child, I had been keenly interested in the engineering sciences, most particularly electronics, and pursued that as a career. By 1950, I had left my studies at Penn State to form a company doing general and electrical contracting in Pittsburgh, Pennsylvania. As an outgrowth of that, I put public the first master TV-antenna system company in western Pennsylvania, and by 1952 had designed and built one of the first CATV (today commonly known as cable TV) systems in the U.S. After selling out my interest in the cable company, I went into designing automation equipment for the heavy steel industry, installing the first automated rolling mill equipment in the Clairton, Pennsylvania, works of U.S. Steel.

I knew nothing then of how my life was to be affected by various international plots and counter-plots that were already under way. In fact, even after playing a role in many of the tumultuous history-making events of the late 1950s and early 1960s, I did not, at the time, really comprehend the ramifications of them.

It was not until revelations of high-ranking wrongdoing on the part of the CIA began to emerge from the Senate Select Committee on Intelligence Matters in 1974 that I began to realize the significance of some of my acts, many of them involving Cuba, starting in 1959 with the crumbling dictatorship of Fulgencio Batista, the island republic's first partner with organized crime.

Batista had yielded to communist pressures within his government during World War II, and then he had given up his position as Cuban dictator at the request of the U.S. government. Finally, after seeing the post-war political climate of his northern neighbor, he turned into a hard-line anti-communist, once he was returned to power. With that change, his new Cuban regime provided a haven for American entrepreneurs. None were more successful than Meyer Lansky and Lucky Luciano. And they enlisted the aid of a man named Rolando Masferrer.

Masferrer was a powerful senator from Oriente Province, who had his own private army, which roamed Cuba, reportedly killing, stealing, and committing rape. To the bitter end of the Batista regime in January of 1959, Masferrer's troops safeguarded the National Crime Syndicate's illegal operations in Cuba, including its narcotics traffic.

It was during this period, according to the Federal Bureau of Narcotics, that Luciano planned for Cuba to "become the syndicate's center for all its international narcotics operations."[1] Lansky and Luciano were not the only ones interested. Two of the three men who would help finance the demise of the Kennedy brothers would also become deeply involved in Cuban narcotics. They were Mafia dons Carlos Marcello of New Orleans and Santos Trafficante of Florida.

In 1947, when Luciano had arrived in Cuba to lay the groundwork for the mob's drug operations, there were already factories that processed cocaine. With the cooperation of Cuban President Carlos Prio Socarras, Luciano added additional laboratories for the processing of heroin.

Thus, by 1952, with Batista's return, Cuba had become the syndicate's major narcotics headquarters. Santos Trafficante, Jr., would emerge as the head of Lansky's Cuban drug empire. His father, Santos Trafficante, Sr., a Sicilian born gangster, had been given the job of handling Lansky's Havana interests.

During the 1950s, the senior Trafficante delegated his Havana concessions to Santos, Jr., whom he considered the most talented of his sons. Although the son's official position in Havana was that of manager of the Sans Souci Casino, his actual position was far more important than that designation indicated.

As his father's financial representative—and ultimately Meyer Lansky's—his responsibility was to receive bulk shipments of heroin from Europe and forward them through New Orleans to New York and other major urban centers. There the distribution was assisted by the local Mafia bosses. Among the most important in the chain was Carlos Marcello of New Orleans.

Santos Trafficante, Jr., also controlled much of Havana's tourist industry. As a result, he became quite close to Fulgencio Batista and came under the protection of Rolando Masferrer's private army. This association would continue throughout the years, resulting eventually in a relationship between Trafficante, Jr., and Masferrer. Most importantly, it would continue in the United States after Castro took control.

It was also during that epic post-war period that Meyer Lansky rejuvenated gambling in Cuba and persuaded other syndicate leaders to invest heavily in the new hotel-casino concept. It would be Rolando Masferrer who would convince Batista to go along with this.

The first hotel-casino had been built in Las Vegas by a long-time associate of Lansky and Luciano. Bugsy Siegel brought in two-million dollars in syndicate money and began building the Strip. But Siegel's arrogant nature prevented him from seeing the project through. After a quarrel with Lansky in 1947, Siegel was killed by a hired gun, who shot him through his living-room window. New Lansky associates, headed by John Roselli and Moe Dalitz, replaced Siegel.

In a few years the casinos were earning an estimated annual profit of one-hundred million dollars—and the narcotics operation, four times that.

Under Masferrer's guidance, Batista arranged legislation that guaranteed a gambling license to anyone who would invest one-million dollars in a hotel. The Cuban government not only matched such investments dollar for dollar, it also waived the hotel-casino's corporate taxes.

Finally, in the mid-1950s, the Cubans, after a long battle with U.S. authorities, ousted Luciano and put him on a boat for Italy. From there, the chief of the underworld continued to monitor the Cuban operations.

By that time, the Tropicana Hotel was owned by the Lansky brothers, along with another Miami mobster, Norman "Roughhouse" Rothman. At the Tropicana, Lewis J. McWillie, a gambler whom Jack Ruby "idolized," became casino boss.

Down the Havana strip from the Tropicana was the Sans Souci, owned by Santos Trafficante, Jr., and the Mafia family of Pittsburgh, which included Johnny Rocco and the Mannarino brothers. Working there was the man who would be the future leader of Rolando Masferrer's anti-Castro mercenaries in Florida, Loren Eugene Hall.

With the exception of operating expenses and money to pay off politicians, no cash stayed in Cuba. The island was merely an enormous funnel through which the cash and dope flowed, bound for its next destination—the United States.

It would be the McClellan Senate Investigation subcommittee, of which Robert Kennedy would become chief counsel, that would first name Carlos Marcello's New Orleans as the key distribution point for heroin and syndicate cash. According to Aaron Kohn, New Orleans Crime Commission director: "The Commission had long been suspicious of the massiveness of Marcello's holdings—which were much too large to be controlled by a single don—even one as powerful as Marcello. 'There is too much money here,' said a New Orleans chief assistant district attorney. 'We feel that it's flowing in from other Cosa Nostra [Mafia] organizations in other parts of the country for investment by the local mobs. This could be their financial center, with a lot of nice safe places where campaign contributions and outright bribery have pretty well insulated them from the law.'"

Carlos Marcello, whom U.S. Senator Estes Kefauver called "one of the worst criminals in the country," was also one of the most successful. Among his holdings were hotels, restaurants, a sightseeing bus service, sixteen-million dollars worth of undeveloped land, and tourist attractions throughout Louisiana. He also controlled gambling, prostitution, and narcotics in a region stretching from Florida to California.

Also among the fiefdoms under his control were the rackets in Dallas, Texas. In 1970, the *Wall Street Journal,* in a long front-page profile, called Marcello the "undisputed patriarch of the Cosa Nostra in Louisiana and the Gulf Coast area."

With Batista in power—and Masferrer protecting their interests—it was not only the syndicate that was enjoying a wide open Cuba, but also American politicians. Not surprisingly, Richard Nixon was among Batista's frequent and well-received guests during the 1950s.

The Vice President could afford it. By 1955, Nixon was a beneficiary of billionaire Howard Hughes, owner of the country's largest privately-held corporation. Hughes considered himself a patriot; and, after feeling he had been unfairly singled out during World War II for violation practices standard to most defense firms, he turned bitter and cynical.

He needed powerful allies inside the government. The CIA was an obvious choice. According to sworn testimony in 1974 from his former aide, Robert Maheu, Hughes believed that "if he ever became involved [again] in any problem with the government, either with a regulatory body, or an investigative arm, it would be beneficial for him to be in the position of being a front [for the CIA]."

Hughes—a tough-minded opportunist and an intensely private man—

was an ideal ally for the CIA. As early as 1949, Hughes' companies were designing and manufacturing special equipment for the clandestine agency. Then, in a calculated program during the 1950s, Hughes' companies began hiring ex-CIA employees as top administrators. Within a few years, he became the country's leading CIA contractor.

In addition, Hughes, like Lansky and the CIA bureaucracy, understood the *quid pro quo* of electoral politics. He contributed up to $400,000 each year to "councilmen, county supervisors, tax assessors, sheriffs, state senators, assemblymen, district attorneys, governors, congressmen, vice-presidents and even presidents." (The man who verified both the amount and recipients of Hughes' political gifts was his close friend and most trusted aide, Noah Dietrich.)

By 1956, Hughes had established a close relationship with the White House, giving Vice President Richard Nixon a secret gift of $100,000 to help him fight a dump-Nixon move by fellow Republican Harold Stassen. In December of the same year, Hughes loaned $205,000 to the Vice-President's brother, Donald Nixon, to start a hamburger restaurant. The "loan" was never repaid.

It was worth it. In the months and years to follow, Hughes received several special dispensations from 1600 Pennsylvania Avenue. In one instance, a Justice Department antitrust suit was settled by a consent decree: the Hughes Medical Foundation (which technically owned his aircraft company) was granted a tax-exempt status, after being turned down twice before. In 1969, Congress closed the tax loopholes enjoyed by such foundations. The Hughes' organization asked for an exemption and—until Hughes' death—was able to delay compliance with the new law. It was a tactic that saved the billionaire $36 million a year.

This and other concessions rendered Hughes agreeable to provide a small island off Florida's southern coast, called "No Name Key," for the training of Rolando Masferrer's anti-Castro mercenaries—the ones, I was told, who were used in the John F. Kennedy assassination conspiracy.[2]

* * * * *

By 1956, Batista's Cuba—laced with corruption—was starting to come apart. With the Mafia operating wide open in Havana and ever increasing amounts of narcotics being delivered to American soil, the U.S. State Department was becoming less and less tolerant of the island dictator. One man in particular led the torrent of protest against the Batista regime—the man who had been American News Service correspondent in Havana in 1933 and 1934, and was now the State Department's special assistant for public affairs in its Department of Inter-American Affairs, William Arthur Wieland.

Wieland had a personal dislike for Batista dating back to his newspaper days just after the Cuban assumed power the first time. Wieland would be the one credited with ending Batista's rule.

By 1959, the time had come for a young lawyer by the name of Fidel Castro. Born on his father's sugar plantation near Biran in Oriente Province on August 13, 1926, the thirty-year-old caught the imagination of the Cuban people by launching a guerrilla war against Fulgencio Batista.

Castro attended two Jesuit schools prior to entering law school at the University of Havana. His studies were interrupted in 1947, when he joined an abortive attempt to unseat Rafael Trujillo of the Dominican Republic. This experience nurtured in him the seeds of revolution.

After graduating from law school in 1950, Castro devoted his time to defending the poor without fee, while contesting a seat in the Cuban Congress in order to give the constitutional method of fighting corruption a chance.

He was disillusioned. With Batista's overthrow of Carlos Prio Socarras in March of 1952, he abandoned all hope of bringing about change by constitutional means. Castro then dedicated himself to revolution, selling all his possessions and, with his brother Raul, raising a volunteer force of about 150 men. They had collected $16,000 for arms and uniforms.

On July 26, 1953, this small force attacked the Moncada Army Barracks in Santiago de Cuba and killed seventy-five of the one-thousand troops stationed there. He and Raul were subsequently caught and prosecuted for leading an armed uprising. They were sentenced to fifteen and thirteen years respectively.

By 1955, Batista—having crushed his opposition—felt secure enough to declare a political amnesty for the rebels. Castro took advantage. In May, he and his brother slipped out of the country and into Mexico, where he gathered around him freedom fighters from other Latin American countries. One of the most violent was "Che" Guevara, an Argentine surgeon turned revolutionary.

After training for a year under Colonel Alberto Bayo—one of the most successful Loyalist commanders and guerrilla fighters during the Spanish Civil War—they prepared to go back to their homeland. The beginning of the end for Batista's Cuba came when Fidel Castro, his brother Raul, and Che Guevara landed on the south coast of Oriente Province in December of 1956, with an expeditionary force of eighty-one men.

They were intercepted by Cuban gunboats and patrol planes, but the three revolutionary leaders and a handful of others managed to escape safely into the rugged eight-thousand-foot Sierra Maestra Mountains. For the next two years, Castro and his group prepared for their final assault on the Batista regime. Young men flocked to the Sierra Maestra. Castro promised that his revolution would transform Cuba into an independent socialist state.

With Castro successfully ensconced in the Sierra Maestra Mountains and Batista's credibility battered, Carlos Prio Socarras made a move once more to become president of Cuba. To help accomplish this, Prio was wooing governments he formerly opposed. One of them was the Dominican Republic, whose president, Rafael Trujillo, sent a special emissary to Miami to invite Prio to attend a conference with him in New York. The outcome of their meeting was that Trujillo offered the former Cuban president everything he needed in war materials and men.

Prio accepted Trujillo's offer and, according to Batista's interview with the late journalist Theon Wright, Prio, being unsuccessful in his efforts to go it alone, decided to team up with Fidel Castro. To make the alliance attractive, Prio began working with Trujillo, and elements of a radical terrorist group known as the "Caribbean Legion," to overthrow Batista. During that period, partisans of the Cuban ex-president would receive their military training from officers of the Dominican army—an operation funded by the CIA.

So, with the blessing of the syndicate and the guidance of the CIA, Prio made his deal with Castro, arranging for the Mafia (which was also supporting Batista) to supply the necessary arms and finances to make Castro's revolution successful—on the condition that Fidel would reinstate him as president once Batista had been overthrown.

Castro agreed, and Prio turned into a high-class gunrunner. One of his partners would be Jack Ruby of Dallas, Texas, then known as Jack Rubinstein.

This is supported by a Miami FBI informant named Blaney Mack Johnson, who claimed Ruby supplied arms for Castro through Prio, that he had seen Ruby around a private airport, and had known Ruby to run guns by boat.[3]

There are others who confirm that Ruby was in the gunrunning business in Florida during the late 1950s. One was Eladio del Valle, a former Cuban congressman and good friend of Mario Kohly, the man I would become deeply enmeshed with in the Cuban exile movement.

With the training given Castro by the CIA and with funds and guns funneled to him through Prio, the phantom guerrilla force moved closer to Havana, a victorious army fighting pitched battles with modern equipment. However, with each successful action, Castro's attitude towards his benefactors gradually changed. He discovered that the mob had supplied financial aid to Batista as well as to him, and he decided that they would be dealt with when he took over Havana.

Meyer Lansky fled Cuba on the same day as Batista, leaving his brother Jake behind to salvage the syndicate's gambling and narcotics empire. Castro's answer was to throw Jake in jail for twenty-five days. Santos Trafficante would later be placed under house arrest, then sent to Trescarnia Prison, and finally deported with future No Name Key mercenary, Loren Eugene Hall.

Castro's successful revolution has been attributed in large part to the terrorist tactics employed by Prio's partisans, under the direction of the CIA. Prio, in violation of the Neutrality Act, had been allowed to send arms and money to Cuba from Miami. Simultaneously, U.S. authorities, as a result of the unrelenting efforts of William Wieland and the American press, turned their backs on Batista and actively endorsed the communist guerrillas.

As history has shown, this was a mistake.

* * * * *

In 1956, after spending several years in Pittsburgh working in the commercial electronics field, I was attracted by the lure of the newly born aerospace industry—and thus enticed to Baltimore, Maryland, to work as a senior engineer for the Martin Company, which was building the first U.S. space vehicle to compete with the Soviet Union's Sputnik. Unfortunately Martin's Vanguard rocket, unlike the Russians', blew up on the pad at Cape Canaveral.

In 1958, after two years of frustration, I left to become consultant to a number of government contractors. This work brought me to Washington, D.C. There, in the course of my consulting work, I met Marshall Diggs, a prominent attorney and entrepreneur, who had been appointed by President Franklin Roosevelt, in 1941, as Deputy Comptroller of the U.S. Treasury, a position in which he served for many years, until he tangled with Henry Morgenthau in 1950. He then left government service and set up a private law practice.

It would be through Diggs that I would be swept up into a world of intrigue, conspiracy, and assassination.

CHAPTER TWO NOTES

1. Harry J. Anslinger, *The Murderers,* Farrar, Straus and Company, 1961, p. 106.

2. Interview with Oscar del Valle Garcia, April 13, 1983.

3. WCD 914; WCD 919.

Mario Kohly describing to the press missile locations in Cuba, fall of 1961. (City News Bureau)

Chapter Three

My entanglement in the incredible complexities of Cuba and their deadly reverberations in American politics began in September 1959, when Marshall Diggs introduced me to Cuban exile leader Mario Garcia Kohly and a man called Oscar del Valle Garcia, later referred to as "Oscar the Assassin." I was to discover that Oscar was the first military organizer of a group of professional mercenaries allied to Rolando Masferrer. Their headquarters was No Name Key.

Kohly, I was told, was to be the next president of Cuba. To him, I was described as the person who could solve his communication problems. Within months, I would be under an Army contract working for the CIA and, at the same time, become Kohly's chief technical advisor and consultant.

Kohly's life and career were paradoxical. He had been introduced to Diggs by the CIA as a former business associate of ex-Cuban president Carlos Prio Socarras. When I interviewed Mario Garcia Kohly, Jr., on September 26, 1975, he told me: "Before the downfall of Carlos Prio Socarras, my father had been negotiating with him to do a housing project for the poor people of Cuba. Also, Carlos Prio Socarras in the Machado time in the early '30s had been hidden by my grandmother. Machado was looking for him because he was a revolutionary at the time and she helped him out and saved his life, so he was at that time an old friend of the family."

At the time Castro came to power, Kohly was in the real-estate business in Cuba and the United States. During the course of that activity, he also founded the New York Credit Exchange. Prior to that, his business experience had been wide and varied. He had established the first milk-pasteurizing plant in Spain, had started the use of paraffin milk containers in Europe, and had been successful in financing government credits in

Cuba, one of them for the construction of the Havana Hilton Hotel.

Although not naturally inclined to be politically active, Kohly was ready to fight oppression in any form. He had been jailed in 1936 for speaking out against the Batista regime.

Then Kohly opposed Castro, even before he came to power, and was one of the first to castigate him for being a communist. For this, Kohly was imprisoned in the first days of 1959 and sentenced to be shot. But he escaped to the United States in late January, a daring act of bravery, considering that he was no longer young. Enraged, Castro maintained a reward of $100,000 for Kohly—dead or alive—through 1969.

Kohly became known as the mystery man of the Cuban exiles, always functioning behind the scenes. By the end of 1959, he had emerged as the most conservative, non-aligned exile leader in the U.S.

What I found extraordinary, as I learned more about him, was the scope of his involvement with Richard Nixon, the CIA, the mob, and the Kennedys.

* * * * *

At the beginning of my association with Kohly, I was unaware of the ties between organized crime and the Cuban exile movement. But in time it became more and more apparent that, in the era immediately following Castro's ascent to power, the two were so tightly bound that it was difficult to distinguish between them. By the late 1970s, after I was further into my investigation, I found also that there was no readily discernible source to which the funds flowing into various exile organizations in the 1960s could be traced—either the CIA or the Mafia. It was as if they were one and the same.

Bobby Kennedy could not know this until he became Attorney General of the United States. Even then, it would be a matter of two years before he would have the hard evidence of the close ties that existed between the CIA, the Cuban exiles, and the Mafia dons. Later would come the mind-boggling revelation that the three factions had joined together in a pact to commit mass murder and assassination, a pact that, a decade later, would implicate Richard Nixon, lead to the Watergate conspiracy, and result in his resignation.

To understand the intricacies of the mob/CIA association—and its relevance to both Kennedy murders—one must go back to the beginning of 1959 when Bobby Kennedy was in the middle of an intense personal duel with Jimmy Hoffa.

At that time the Teamster leader was increasing his involvement with organized crime. He began by making top union officials out of gangsters and mob enforcers. Three of them would be directly linked to Jack Ruby:

The first one, Barney Baker, described by Bobby in his 1960 book *The Enemy Within,* was one of Hoffa's key lieutenants. Baker, as the Warren Commission would find out four years later, was not only an acquaintance of Jack Ruby, but talked to him at least twice in the three-week period preceding the President's assassination.

The second, Irwin S. Weiner, the Teamsters' top bondsman in Chicago, was an integral part of Hoffa's dealings with the Mafia and another of those whom Jack Ruby is known to have talked to during the month prior to the presidential assassination.

The third was Paul "Red" Dorfman, who took over the Chicago Waste Handlers Union in 1939, after its president was murdered. At the time, the secretary of that Union was "Jack Rubinstein."

It was no coincidence that Ruby and Dorfman were in frequent touch during the month of November 1963. Dorfman served as middleman between Hoffa and the Chicago mob controlled by Sam "Momo" Giancana, the Mafia assassination coordinator for the CIA in its attempts to murder Fidel Castro.

Bobby described Giancana as the "chief gunman for the group that succeeded the Capone mob."[1]

* * * * *

While Bobby Kennedy was initiating his attack on organized crime, certain international events were also shaping our destinies.

By the middle of 1959, Castro—under the guidance of Nikita Khruschev—had engineered the first successful breach of the Monroe Doctrine since its inception in 1823. With Cuba, the Soviet Union was acquiring a satellite ninety miles off the coast of the United States. In the process, the Mafia was suffering a financial disaster. The new island dictator was padlocking all their amusement parlors and razing their narcotics labs.

Simultaneously, Batista's Mafia henchmen were fleeing for their lives. Cuban senator Rolando Masferrer escaped with Cuban congressman Eladio del Valle and showed up in Miami. Masferrer was to become the U.S. Mafia liaison to the anti-Castro movement; del Valle, Mario Kohly's right arm. Former Cuban president Carlos Prio Socarras fared no better.

Not only did Castro not honor his commitment to make him president, he canceled all elections until further notice.

Then, for a grand finale, Castro started expropriating American property, a situation intolerable to Allen Dulles.

In response to Castro's illegal seizures and reports from operatives inside Cuba, the CIA chief decided that the best solution to the problem would be to invade the island with an army of Cuban refugees. Dulles of course knew that, in order to carry out an operation involving the invasion of a foreign country, huge sums of money had to be spent that could not be traced to the U.S. government, the CIA, or any of their cover organizations.

This disassociation was necessary for the sake of our expressed U.S. policy of non-intervention, as well as for a much more serious reason.

On December 11, 1959, Dulles took the suggestion of a CIA officer named E. Howard Hunt: "To insure the success of the Cuban operation, serious consideration had to be given to the elimination of Fidel Castro." By "elimination," Hunt meant "assassination." Hunt had begun his career in the OSS in 1943, and continued with the CIA as an agent in Mexico in the early 1950s. However, he was best known to his peers for having helped engineer the 1954 overthrow of the Arbenz regime in Guatemala.

Ten months later, Dulles would allow the implementation of the CIA's notorious assassination squads. One, known as "Operation Forty," was spawned in a deal between Vice President Richard Nixon and Mario Garcia Kohly. As the plans developed by Dulles and Hunt were being actualized, Dulles—always being one to hedge his bets—elected to keep Richard Helms, his Director of Strategic Operations (OSO), out of the Cuban melee. He would need someone with Helms' talent and dedication, both to himself and the Agency, if something went wrong.

As an indication of Helms' talents, it should be noted that Dulles, in September of 1960, put the OSO chief in charge of planning the assassination of African leader Patrice Lumumba. The fringe leader of the former Belgian Congo had incited the wrath of Dwight D. Eisenhower. The President suggested to Dulles "that he be removed." Helms took this to mean assassination.

This interpretation initiated a trend in the covert agency that would become standard operating procedure. Helms' blueprint for the "elimination" was simple. A CIA employee was called back from Leopoldville, the Congolese capital, and handed a "first aid kit," as it was referred to. There were rubber gloves, a vial of lethal fever germs, a portable electric toothbrush complete with batteries, and three tubes of toothpaste. The tubes of toothpaste were to be impregnated with the germs and somehow introduced into Lumumba's toilet requisites.[2] However, Lumumba was overthrown and killed by Congolese rivals before he had a chance to use the lethal gift.[3]

During this same period, Senator John F. Kennedy, on the floor of the United States Congress, had been seeking an accounting from the Shah of Iran, whom he had accused of appropriating large amounts of U.S. AID (Agency for International Development) funds for his personal use. In revenge, the Shah would commit large sums of money to the Nixon presidential campaign the following year.

In the summer of 1959, Lee Harvey Oswald came to the attention of the Cuban movement. He suddenly started corresponding with the Cuban consulate in Los Angeles, intimating that he was prepared to desert the Marine Corps and join the Castro revolution.[4] He would be remembered, and that was the idea.

By the end of that same summer, Castro, in an attempt to reverse the trend of Cuba's financial fortunes, began seizing additional U.S. property in the name of agrarian reform. These actions prompted U.S. Ambassador Robert C. Hill to return to Washington in September of 1959 for an indefinite stay. It then became evident to Castro that there might be difficulty in working out an extension of Cuba's arrangement under the U.S. Sugar Act. The agreement—due to expire on January 1, 1960—had given Cuba virtually one-third of the U.S. sugar market.

When the date passed and the extension failed to materialize, Castro expropriated the balance of American property and threw Cuba's lot totally into the sphere of the Soviet Union.

* * * * *

Against that background of turmoil, Mario Garcia Kohly began his political career during the first week of July 1959, when his good friend, Pedro Diaz Lanz, Commander of Castro's air force, resigned and fled to the U.S., joining him.[5] Lanz became the first really important Castro defector. On July 11, before the Senate Internal Security Subcommittee, he denounced Castro, citing the mass infiltration of communists into his government.

Needless to say, the island dictator was upset. He charged the U.S. with perpetrating an unfriendly act and interfering in Cuba's internal affairs.

With Lanz's advice, Kohly formed the Cuban Liberators, an anti-Castro activist group composed of ex-Cuban army, navy, and air force personnel located both in the United States and abroad; drafted a plan for a new provisional government of Cuba; and in Cuba, organized an underground resistance movement, risking his life by making several trips to Havana. With the underground in place, he then planned an invasion called "Operation Lake," which was to be combined with a guerrilla army operating out of the Escambrey Mountains.[6]

An important segment of Kohly's underground came from the efforts of another major conservative exile leader, Manuel Francisco Artime. As a young manager of the National Agrarian Reform in Oriente Province, he became disillusioned with Castro's revolution and made plans to defect.

The decisive factor in his decision was an occurrence on October 19, 1959. One of Castro's highest ranking officers and military chief of the Camaguey Province, Major Hubert Metos, resigned, charging communist penetration of the Castro government. On December 15, Metos was arrested and sentenced to twenty years for treason, conspiracy, and sedition.

A short time later, Artime was spirited out of Cuba and taken to Miami by the CIA.

However, he had left his mark in Cuba. Prior to departing, he had taken a governmental leave of absence and begun to organize peasants into an underground, succeeding in forming a nucleus in each province by early November 1959.

Kohly had become quite powerful politically by the summer of 1960, representing the interests of dozens of U.S. companies whose properties had been seized by Castro. For this reason, Marshall Diggs introduced Kohly to Vice President Richard Nixon, who was as determined as Kohly to see Castro defeated and U.S. property returned to its rightful owners.

Kohly took the opportunity to tell the Vice President of his plans for a provisional government of Cuba, the invasion, and of his underground to support it. Nixon asked if he could submit the documentation to the National Security Council and CIA. Kohly agreed, and several weeks later was informed that it was looked upon favorably. As Diggs would put it later, "Your plans are what they're going with."

As a result of this and subsequent meetings, Nixon indicated that, once he was elected, Kohly would be his choice to head a Cuban government in exile. This was tantamount to saying Kohly would be the next president of Cuba, once Castro was overthrown. It was also during this period that

Kohly was made aware that a CIA invasion was also being planned, and he committed his underground to support it.

But in August of 1960—through the intercession of William Wieland, Fidel Castro's man in our State Department—Kohly was told to keep "hands off" Cuba regarding the property claims and other matters, until after the U.S. presidential elections in November.

Kohly refused, and Wieland started a campaign to undermine him. He was successful. The State Department officer managed to convince friends who worked for the CIA to install former members of Castro's cabinet as the leaders of a newly formed CIA-backed organization—the Cuban Revolutionary Front (FRD).

After this setback, Kohly sent word to Nixon, through Diggs, about his concern. Within a month, Kohly was called back to Washington to meet with General Cushman, Nixon's military adviser. When he arrived, General Cushman wasn't there; but a CIA man—who said he represented both the General and the Vice President—tried to convince Kohly to join the new Front, the one started by Howard Hunt.

Comfortable about his position with Nixon, Kohly refused to cooperate, because the Front was being formed primarily from the ex-Castro government hierarchy, individuals who were known socialists and communist sympathizers.[7]

After this meeting, the exile leader returned to Miami and forgot about it. He was busy getting his underground ready for the invasion. Unfortunately for Kohly's cause, Wieland and his cohorts had not forgotten.

By the end of August, with plans for the invasion proceeding at a rapid pace, Wieland acted on behalf of the State Department—against the wishes of Vice President Nixon and FRD Coordinator Howard Hunt—to exert more influence on the CIA to accept additional leftist leaders to head the impending invasion and staff the future Cuban government. His rationale: Kohly's conservative Cubans would be classified automatically as former Batistaites—not acceptable to the Cuban people.

Meanwhile, the more liberal elements in the CIA, seeing that they had obtained the upper hand, managed to outmaneuver Howard Hunt and replace the FRD with their own organization, the Cuban Revolutionary Council (CRC), formed entirely of the more extreme leftist members of the FRD. Their purpose: to counter and totally nullify Kohly's efforts.

Wieland had been shrewd. The man selected to head the newly formed CRC was Jose Miro Cardona, Fidel Castro's first prime minister.[8]

In an attempt to show the close bond that existed between Cardona and Wieland, Ambassador Earl T. Smith stated in testimony before the Senate Select Subcommittee on Internal Security that:

> ... Many of these people, who later became members of the first cabinet of Castro, were asylees in the United States. They had close contacts with members of the State Department.
>
> To name a few: Urrutia, the first President of Cuba, Agramonte, the first Foreign Minister of Cuba, and the first Prime Minister of Cuba, Miro Cardona. As a matter of fact, the first time that I met Cardona was after Batista had left the country. It was about the 4th of January of 1959 in the Presidential palace. He turned to me and said, "I am a good friend of William Wieland, a very good friend of William Wieland."

The Front, or FRD, was now under the complete control of former Castro lieutenants, leaving only two members who could be considered moderates—Carlos Prio Socarras and its New Orleans director Sergio Arcacha Smith, a man tied directly to Louisiana Mafia leader Carlos Marcello. Smith's ties to Marcello stemmed from his association with a former FBI agent, Guy Banister, who would become deeply involved in the murky world of Lee Harvey Oswald.

Banister had been special-agent-in-charge of the Chicago FBI office during the latter part of World War II and the late 1940s. Twelve years later, one of his former agents would become the CIA's assassination coordinator, working with Mafia assassination coordinator Sam Giancana. His name was Robert A. Maheu, front man for billionaire Howard Hughes in the 1960s.

Guy Banister Associates, a New Orleans private detective agency, was the employer of several of Marcello's close associates. One of them would play a role in the President's death and be positively identified as a companion of Lee Harvey Oswald.[9] He was Marcello's pilot, David W. Ferrie, a man I met because of my work for Kohly. Ferrie, known to his friends as a master of intrigue, was an active homosexual with a formidable academic background and outspoken right-wing political views.

I met Ferrie three times: first, on an operation into Cuba during the Bay of Pigs; second, in late 1961, while buying firearms for Kohly's underground; and the third time, in 1963, when Ferrie flew to Baltimore to pick up three Mannlicher rifles—supposedly to be used by his associates in a coup against Juan Bosch, successor to Trujillo as president of the Dominican Republic.

In 1960, Ferrie had become involved with Mario Kohly through his two close Cuban associates, ex-Cuban congressman Eladio del Valle[10] and Rolando Masferrer.

The association of Smith, Marcello, Banister, Maheu, and Ferrie became important in the scheme of the Kennedys' futures after the formation of the leftist CRC, because it forced Mario Kohly to take a political back seat to former members of the Castro regime, a move that not only alienated the moderate Cuban exile leader, but also put various elements of the CIA into major conflict. When the plans for Kohly's invasion and provisional government had been approved by both the National Security Council and the CIA, the Agency was committed to using his U.S.-based exile organization, his underground inside Cuba, and his guerrilla army hiding in the Escambrey Mountains.

All this was causing great problems for Nixon. Because of the impending elections and the public controversy over Cuba then being stirred up by Democratic presidential candidate John F. Kennedy, the Vice President could not take a stand on Kohly's behalf.

So the CIA Moved to rid Cuba of Fidel Castro the way Howard Hunt had recommended. They activated their program of assassination against the Cuban dictator—a program Dulles had assigned to Richard Bissell, the Agency's Deputy Director of Plans, the man in charge of all its covert activities. Bissell in turn assigned the project to Colonel Sheffield Edwards, the Agency's Director of Security.[11] Edwards, to come up with a plan for Bissell, gave the assignment to his Operational Support Chief, a former FBI man named James O'Connell.

In August, after being briefed by O'Connell, Edwards belatedly contacted Bissell, telling him he had a plan. Without informing Bissell it was actually O'Connell's idea, he told the CIA Deputy Director of Plans that Castro's assassination would best be done by Cubans who had worked for the Mafia—Rolando Masferrer's men.

Bissell bought the concept. He rationalized that the syndicate would be highly motivated to salvage their Cuban investments. Bissell told Edwards to proceed. In turn, Edwards told O'Connell to go ahead.[12]

For O'Connell, implementation of the plan was simple. He knew his old FBI colleague, Robert A. Maheu, the former FBI special agent who had worked for Guy Banister in Chicago, was tough enough to handle the mob.

Maheu, who had been running Robert Maheu & Associates—a private detective firm in Washington, D.C.—had been on a mandatory CIA retainer since 1954. His firm was used for jobs the Agency didn't want their own personnel associated with—namely domestic covert operations. Ironically, Maheu was just starting to handle extensive work for billionaire Howard Hughes,[13] who had hired him as a consultant and troubleshooter for the Hughes Tool Company.

O'Connell had been Maheu's CIA case officer[14] over the years. As a result, they had become close personal friends.

Sanctioned by Bissell to bring in the mob, O'Connell asked Maheu to contact an underworld figure named John Roselli. Known as "Don Giovanni" to his Mafia cohorts, Roselli had been the Capo Mafioso for Las Vegas since the late 1950s. After working for Al Capone in the 1940s, he had a long history of immunity as a result of ties to the CIA.

In May 1966, the FBI threatened to deport Roselli for living in the United States under an assumed name unless he cooperated in an investigation of the Mafia. Roselli, whose true name is Filippo Saco, was born in Italy and was allegedly brought illegally into the United States while still a child. He contacted CIA Office of Security Director Edwards, who informed the FBI that Roselli wanted to "keep square with the Bureau," but was afraid that gangsters might kill him for "talking." After Roselli was arrested for fraudulent gambling activities at the Friars Club in Beverly Hills in 1967, he requested William Harvey, a former top CIA agent, to represent him. Harvey contacted the Agency and suggested that it prevent the prosecution.

In a little noticed footnote in the Senate Intelligence Committee Report on Foreign Assassinations, a substantial amount of information was set forth regarding the ability of Johnny Roselli to receive various forms of "assistance" and occasional immunity from the federal government, with a little help from his former colleagues in the Central Intelligence Agency. This CIA "assistance" continued as late as 1971.

O'Connell told Maheu to ask "Roselli if he would be inclined to help in a program of eliminating Mr. Castro in connection with an invasion of Cuba."[15] At first, Maheu was hesitant; he didn't want to lose his wealthy new client, Howard Hughes, who was making more and more demands on his time.

The money that Maheu was to offer Roselli seemed adequate—$150,000. So did the cover story. Maheu was supposed to be representing businessmen who regarded the elimination of Castro as the first step toward the recovery of their Cuban investments—such as the expropriated clients originally represented by Kohly.

Maheu finally accepted the assignment. He felt he owed it to the Agency. And, as he would later claim to the Senate Select Committee on Intelligence, "we were involved in a just war."[16]

The private detective's relationship with Hughes was unhindered. When Maheu received a personal call from Hughes pressing him to come to the West Coast, he told the billionaire that the project that was keeping him busy "was on behalf of the United States Government," adding that "it included plans to dispose of Mr. Castro."

Hughes gave his blessing, and continued to provide authorization for Maheu to coordinate the conspiracy between the CIA and the Mafia all during the early 1960s. Subsequently, the billionaire sought to involve himself in a deeper relationship with the Agency. In testimony before the Senate Select Committee on Foreign Assassinations, Maheu stated: "Mr. Hughes suggested I try to work out some kind of arrangement with the CIA whereby either he or the Hughes Tool Company could become a front for this intelligence agency."

Though Maheu claims to have been disturbed over Hughes' desire to "become a front" for the CIA, there is strong documentary evidence that Maheu himself shared that desire. And, once again, relevant information dates back to the CIA-Mafia-Maheu assassination plots. In September 1975, the Senate Intelligence Committee heard the testimony in executive session of Joseph Shimon,[17] a close friend of John Roselli and Sam Giancana. Shimon testified that he had accompanied Giancana and Roselli to Miami shortly before the Bay of Pigs invasion in early 1961 and had been present when CIA officials passed the non-traceable poison pills to Roselli and Giancana for use in murdering Fidel Castro.

Shimon told the Senate Committee that Maheu indicated to him that he was letting John Roselli handle the details of the proposed Castro assassination. Shimon testified that Maheu told him, "Johnny's going to handle everything, this is Johnny's contract." In his Senate testimony of September 20, 1975 (most of which has never been publicly released), Joseph Shimon also states that Giancana had told him that Robert Maheu was using his involvement in the CIA-Mafia plot to further his own purposes, and that "Maheu's conning the hell out of the CIA."[18]

Maheu's role in the CIA-Mafia plots particularly disturbed Attorney General Robert Kennedy when he first learned of them in May, 1962. As time would tell, he would have good reason for concern.

CHAPTER THREE NOTES

1. Senate Select Committee Hearings, 86th Congress, 1st Session, February 20, 1959, p. 1704.

2. Senate Select Committee Report on Foreign Assassinations, p.37.

3. *Ibid,* p. 4.

4. Edward Jay Epstein, *The Secret World of Lee Harvey Oswald,* Readers Digest Press, 1978, pp. 88-89.

5. E. Howard Hunt, *Give Us This Day,* Arlington House, p. 98.

6. According to a memorandum of October 18, 1960, Kohly claimed to have six-thousand men organized in the U.S. and twelve-thousand inside Cuba. See Appendix, Exhibit No. 2.

7. Hunt, even though responsible for running it, completely agreed with Kohly. In his book, *Give Us This Day,* he reiterated this position continually.

8. In Exhibit Number 28 of the Senate Select Committee on Internal Security, date January 23, 1959. See Appendix, Exhibit 3; Jose Miro Cardona's name is signed as Cuba's prime minister.

9. HSCA Report, pp. 170-171, Bantam edition.

10. Del Valle's son, Alejandro, would die in the Bay of Pigs. Wyden, *Bay of Pigs,* Simon & Schuster, p. 283n.

11. Senate Intelligence Committee Report on Foreign Assassinations, 1976, pp. 94-96.

12. *Ibid.*

13. *Ibid,* p. 75.

14. "Case officer" denotes the person in the CIA to whom an operator or contract employee, such as the author, reported .

15. Senate Intelligence Committee on Foreign Assassinations, p. 75.

16.   CBS Reports Inquiry, "The American Assassins," Part Two, Dan Rather, November 26, 1975.

17.   Joseph Shimon was the man who ran the International Police Academy (IPA) for the CIA to train foreign agents, such as the Iranian Secret Police (SAVAK), in interrogation, murder, and terrorist tactics.

18.   Senate Intelligence Committee Report on Foreign Assassinations, p. 82.

Chapter Four

Maheu had known Johnny Roselli since the late 1950s and considered him well qualified to finger an assassin to hit Castro. However, when he met with Roselli at the Brown Derby restaurant in Beverly Hills, he decided to drop the cover story, after the Las Vegas Mafia don seemed reluctant to accept such an assignment on behalf of U.S. businessmen. Instead, he told him, "high government officials needed his cooperation to recruit Cubans who would eliminate Castro."

Roselli then eagerly agreed to help the CIA. He, like Carlos Marcello, was facing deportation proceedings for having entered the country illegally, due to the unrelenting efforts of Robert Kennedy.

Roselli did insist on one condition—that he could confirm his mission of murder with an official representative of the U.S. government. So, on September 14, 1960, Maheu and Roselli met with James O'Connell at the Plaza Hotel in New York.[1]

There would be no problem. Roselli knew O'Connell. They had met socially at Maheu's home in Washington.

While Roselli and Maheu were meeting in New York, Deputy Director of Plans Richard Bissell and CIA Security Director Sheffield Edwards were briefing Allen Dulles and CIA Deputy Director General Charles Cabell on the Agency's plans regarding Castro. It was a meeting that would deeply cement the partnership between organized crime and the American intelligence community, a partnership that would last throughout the 1960s.

By the end of September, Roselli—at the request of Maheu—had asked the number-two man in the syndicate, Chicago's Sam Giancana, to seek the help of Roselli's old Havana boss, none other than Florida's top mobster, Santos Trafficante, Jr.

A few days after Sheffield Edwards and Richard Bissell briefed Dulles and Cabell, Bissell and Cabell briefed Vice President Richard Nixon about the plans to assassinate Fidel Castro. Richard Nixon, unlike President Eisenhower, thoroughly understood the politics of assassination.

In a Warren Commission document (WCD 279, still classified), Marion Cooper, a former CIA operative, disclosed that on January 1, 1955, he attended a meeting in Honduras with Vice President Richard Nixon, at which the planned assassination of President Jose Antonio Remon of Panama was discussed in detail. Among those present: the hit team hired to kill the Panamanian leader.

The following day, Remon was machine-gunned to death at a racetrack outside Panama City.

I first found out about this in early July of 1975, when I was called to testify before the staff of the Senate Select Committee on Intelligence Matters to tell them what I knew about Richard Nixon and his association with Mario Kohly. During the course of my interview, I was asked whether I knew a former CIA agent by the name of Marion Cooper. I told them I didn't know Cooper, but had heard his name mentioned in reference to the Vice President on several occasions around 1960.

The Committee was interested in Nixon because Cooper had appeared on the Lou Staples talk show in Dallas, Texas, a week earlier and had told the story about the meeting of January 1, 1955.[2]

Subsequently, I was informed that Cooper's statements were validated by a polygraph examiner "of the highest rating." In addition, newsman Joe Pennington of Chicago said he had been able to verify most of the details of Cooper's story.[3]

Understandably, President Eisenhower had never been told about any of the CIA assassinations, nor about Bissell and Cabell's briefing of the Vice President regarding Castro. It was after this briefing—aware that Eisenhower was not cognizant of what was happening—that Nixon acted, ostensibly to save Kohly's position and the whole Cuban situation. In October, just a few weeks before the national elections, Nixon and CIA Deputy Director Cabell met secretly with Kohly on the golf links of the Burning Tree Club in suburban Washington, consummating a deal that finally satisfied Kohly. Less than a week later, Kohly disclosed to me the substance of that meeting. He and the Vice President had agreed that Kohly could eliminate all of the prominent Cuban leftist leaders after a successful invasion. The plot would assure Kohly of being the new president of Cuba.

From the way the Cuban exile leader related it to me, the deal was made in the belief that it would be in the best national interest and that Nixon, as the next president of the United States, would be in a position to justify such an action. At the time, it was an understandable decision. Kohly claimed that the agreement was reached only after he guaranteed the Vice President that he would still support the invasion with his large Cuban underground and guerrilla forces located in the Escambrey Mountains.

To accomplish their scheme of mass murder, Kohly told me, the leftist Front leaders were to be held as prisoners by the CIA until the landing had been secured. They were then to be delivered to the beach and assassinated by Masferrer's men—the mercenaries from No Name Key, who were at that time led by "Oscar the Assassin."

Thus was initiated Operation Forty, which assassin Oscar del Valle Garcia was asked by the CIA to help organize, at the direction of Vice President Nixon. Kohly, before his death in 1975, told me that Oscar the Assassin was to play the key role in this operation. This was reaffirmed by Kohly's son, Mario Kohly, Jr., after his father's death. His notarized affidavit is shown in the Appendix, dated July 15, 1976.[4] Air Force Colonel L. Fletcher Prouty also confirmed that the leftist leaders of the Front were to be delivered to the Cuban beachhead after seventy-two hours, if the invasion force was successful.

Kohly, in a recorded deathbed statement made in the presence of myself and my wife, said: "I had arranged to recruit or to enlist better than three-hundred boys who, on a set signal once we took over the island, would meet with me and arrange for the overthrow of the CIA-inspired council with Miro Cardona and the rest of them. If this had been successful, they would have been eliminated almost at once and I would have come into Cuba and taken over. . . . This can be confirmed through Mr. Sourwine,[5] in the U.S. Senate, who called me one day to meet with one of the troopers who had come out of the Bay of Pigs alive and back to the States. And it was this trooper who very discreetly divulged our plans to former Senator Owen Brewster and stated that each one of them [Kohly's men] was wearing a yellow handkerchief around their collar to show who was who and to know who each other was, so that at the proper time they could communicate. Yellow was chosen because it fitted in with the uniforms and would not attract attention as they wore current army handkerchiefs or bandannas, whatever you wish to call them."

Shortly after Kohly's meeting with Nixon and Cabell, I asked my case officer Tracy Barnes,[6] in the presence of General Cabell, if in fact Kohly had made a deal with the administration. Both men confirmed that an arrangement had been made for Kohly to take over Cuba once the invasion had been successful. They did not elaborate, other than to say that Kohly had made some arrangements regarding the leftist leaders.

However, Oscar del Valle Garcia, in a videotaped interview on April 15, 1983, confirmed that Cardona and the leftist leaders held at Opa Locka Air Base in Florida were to be assassinated as part of Operation Forty, confirming Kohly's story. It was to be part of his job to arrange it.

Because this deal involved Nixon in a conspiracy to perpetrate a number of political assassinations, it is easy to understand why, twelve years later, as President of the United States, he would seriously consider paying one-million dollars in blackmail to former CIA man and Watergate conspirator E. Howard Hunt to shut up, even though the CIA had tacitly been a party to it.

In an attempt to explore the potential relevance that the Nixon/Kohly deal may have had to President Kennedy's assassination, a sworn affidavit[7] was also supplied to Congressman Thomas N. Downing (D, Va.) by me in 1976. My and Kohly, Jr's, affidavits, attesting to the validity of the allegations, prompted Representative Downing to hold a press conference on August 2, 1976.

The reaction to the press conference moved the House Rules Committee to send HR 1540—the directive to reopen the assassination investigation of President John F. Kennedy—on to the full House for a vote. A month later, it passed the House by a strong vote of 280 to 65.[8]

The following is an excerpt from the statement made at that August 2, 1976, press conference by Congressman Thomas N. Downing prior to his becoming the first chairman of the House Select Committee on Assassinations.

> I would like to know what was behind the intense interest shown by President Nixon and his staff in the Bay of Pigs. Reportedly, in a memo to H. R. Haldeman, July 2, 1971, concerning Howard Hunt, Charles Colson wrote, ". . . that he [Hunt] was the CIA mastermind on the Bay of Pigs. He told me a long time ago that if the truth were ever known Kennedy would be destroyed."[9]
>
> A note made by John Erlichman after a meeting with President Nixon, September 18, 1971, reads "Bay of Pigs—

order to CIA—President is to have the full file or else. Nothing withheld. President was involved in Bay of Pigs. President must have full file—deeply involved—must know all the facts."

I find it most interesting that, according to transcripts of the conversations between President Nixon and H. R. Haldeman on July 23, 1972, five weeks after the Watergate break-in, great concern was expressed about what an investigation might divulge concerning the Bay of Pigs which took place 11 years earlier.

Downing then read quotes from the Nixon White House Tapes.

NIXON: . . . It's likely to blow the whole Bay of Pigs thing which we think would be very unfortunate.
HALDEMAN: I told Helms the problem is it tracks back to the Bay of Pigs . . .
NIXON: . . . Say, look the problem is that this will open the whole Bay of Pigs thing. . . .

The congressman then concluded his statement on Nixon with:

The association between Nixon and Kohly apparently went back at least to 1960 when Vice President Nixon had a direct role in our government's Cuban policy, particularly as it involved the training of Cuban exiles in the United States. There have been far too many allegations concerning connections between the Bay of Pigs, Cuban exiles, attempts to overthrow the Castro government, attempts to assassinate Castro, the assassination of John F. Kennedy, and an alleged conspiracy which connects some, if not all, of them. I want to see the possibility of such a conspiracy investigated fully.

Five months after the secret meeting on the golf course, on April 16, 1961, the night of the Bay of Pigs invasion, as I was saying goodbye to my case officer prior to flying to Florida to meet Dave Ferrie, I was again reminded of the Kohly/Nixon deal. Knowing of my close relationship to Kohly, Tracy Barnes made an incidental remark regarding the Cuban leftist leaders: "With the exception of those members who are actually participating in the invasion, Cardona and his crowd are being held incommunicado and are they mad! If they knew what the hell was in store for them once the boys take over the island, they'd never have left the loving arms of Fidel."

I interpreted this to mean that they would never be heard from again, once they had been delivered to the beach in Cuba.

Operation Forty was mentioned briefly during the Watergate hearings, when Howard Hunt's Mafia aide de camp, Bernard Barker, and Frank Sturgis, a self-styled CIA soldier of fortune, were testifying in front of the Erwin Committee. It would not surface again until 1975, when Sturgis again testified about it to Frank Church's Senate Select Committee on Intelligence Matters.

Frank (Fiorini) Sturgis' career began when he started flying military missions and running guns for Prio to Castro's 26th of July forces in the Oriente Province in early 1958. These flights originated in Ft. Lauderdale, Florida. Sturgis and Bernard Barker were caught together in the Watergate complex as part of Howard Hunt's operation to bug the Democratic Committee's telephones during the 1972 national elections.

Sturgis told me that Operation Forty "was a top secret government operation consisting of American and Cuban intelligence officers who worked for the CIA. This assassination section, which I was part of, would—upon orders naturally—assassinate either members of the military in a foreign country or members of political parties of a foreign country we were going to infiltrate, and, if necessary, some of our own members. . . . The training these men received from the CIA could have been used against President Kennedy."[10]

Also verifying Kohly's deathbed statement and assassin Oscar del Valle Garcia's taped interview was Pulitzer Prize journalist Tad Szulc, who said of Operation Forty: "a Bay of Pigs offshoot which allegedly included professional killers [was] recruited for assassinating Artime's [i.e., Kohly's] opponents within the Bay of Pigs' Brigade. The group was recently dissolved, after some of its members were arrested as major narcotics traffickers inside the United States."[11]

On the night of the Bay of Pigs invasion, the leftist leaders were flown to Opa Locka air base in Florida and placed under house arrest. For three days, as the invasion raged on to its desperate conclusion, the imprisoned leaders waited, incensed. Then, on April 19, one of them, Tony Verona, managed to elude the guards surrounding the house by escaping through a bathroom window. Once free, he called the White House in a frenzy.

After hearing their story of being held captive, Arthur Schlesinger, Jr., telephoned the President and advised him to see the Cubans immediately, in order to smooth their ruffled feathers.

The President dispatched Schlesinger and A. A. Berle to rescue the leftist Cubans. Within hours, they were headed toward Washington on an Air Force plane.

When Representative Thomas Downing held his press conference on August 2, 1976, to motivate the House Rules Committee to reopen the Kennedy assassination investigation, he also told the story of the CRC leftist leaders being held captive as part of the Nixon/Kohly deal. As a result, Arthur Schlesinger, Jr., was contacted and, in a statement to *Richmond Times Dispatch* reporter Eston Melton on August 3, 1976, Schlesinger confirmed the release of the Cubans from Opa Locka:

> Arthur M. Schlesinger, Jr., former special assistant to President John F. Kennedy, confirmed yesterday that he freed "six to eight" Cuban exile leaders being held "under house arrest" at Opa Locka, Fla., by the Central Intelligence Agency during the 1961 Bay of Pigs invasion.
>
> Schlesinger said "Kennedy was furious, when he discovered this," referring to the Cuban exile leaders.

It was apparent that President Kennedy, even at that fateful point in time, had not been informed by the CIA hierarchy of the Kohly/Nixon deal or Operation Forty.

But other factors came into play in the summer of 1960, months before the presidential election, that would turn the future Kennedy administration into a hated enemy of the Cuban exile community. Two of the most virulent opponents would be Mario Kohly and Rolando Masferrer.

CHAPTER FOUR NOTES

1. Senate Intelligence Committee Report on Foreign Assassinations, p. 76.

2. KRLD Radio, June 6, 1975.

3. Interview with B. Gary Shaw, February 18, 1983, in Cleburne, Texas.

4. See Appendix, Exhibit No. 4.

5. In 1961, Julian G. Sourwine was working as the chief attorney for the Senate Internal Security Committee. His name and home address appears in Oscar del Valle Garcia's confidential CIA telephone file.

6. The author's case officer, Tracy Barnes, graduated from Harvard Law School and practiced with Carter, Ledyard & Milburn on Wall Street. In the OSS, he worked with Dulles in Switzerland, parachuted into occupied France, and won the Croix de Guerre twice—once with palm, the other time with star.

7. See Appendix, Exhibit No. 5.

8. See letter of acknowledgment from Rep. Thomas N. Downing, Appendix, Exhibit No. 6.

9. Nixon was referring, no doubt, to the fact that missiles were in Cuba long before the October 1962 missile crisis and were not taken out after it, as President Kennedy had claimed.

10. Telephone interview with Frank Sturgis on February 15, 1979.

11. *The New York Times,* January 5, 1975, p. 4.

Chapter Five

Nine months after my introduction to Mario Kohly, June 1960, Russian troops and supplies were being poured into Cuba at an alarming rate. Then, ominous reports started emanating from the captive island regarding unusual construction activity.

One of the earliest came from Paul Bethel, the former U.S. Press Attache to our Havana embassy. Bethel reported that a friend of his, "a Cuban named George Fowler, invited me to his house at Saroa, where there were some famous Cuban caves. Fowler told me something was going on there because the military had taken over the whole area. Fowler claimed his house was on a hill overlooking a site where he could see all kinds of construction going on. Ostensibly under the guise of it being developed for tourism."

According to Bethel, after a supposed visit to Fowler's house, "It was missile sites under construction."[1] This statement was made by Bethel in a recorded interview with free-lance writer Dick Russell and was played for me in 1976.[2]

Bethel also testified on March 7, 1967, before a Senate Judiciary Subcommittee investigating the communist threat to the United States through the Caribbean that he had additional reports that the Russians were bringing in long-range missiles as early as February 1961.[3] I was sent into Cuba during the Bay of Pigs to verify that.

When questioned by Senator Strom Thurmond, Bethel stated:

> In February of 1963, I interviewed a defector from Castro's diplomatic service. His name is Hugo Bell Huertas. He was in Cuba at the time, and he said this, this is his testimony. I told

him about the caves, and the Poles being in there and
excavating, and he said, yes; however, the Poles were a screen
behind which Soviet and Czech and East German technicians
really did the work in preparing the caves as early as February
of 1961; in other words, that they were there at the time. He
states that the missiles were brought in Soviet oil tankers that
had no oil in them.

Six months earlier, British R.A.F. reconnaissance flights, overflying
Cuba from Nassau, had also detected unusual military construction—not
normally associated with conventional defense weaponry. They decided to
increase their surveillance.

By the end of October 1960, aerial photographs revealed sufficient data
to ascertain that offensive Russian missile installations were being
prepared for use against Cuba's neighbors. Once this conclusion had been
reached by British Intelligence, they reported the information through
diplomatic channels to the State Department. I have in my possession a
memorandum that quotes a former R.A.F. squadron leader and later
MI-6 (British intelligence) man as saying: The R.A.F. knew of the missiles
as early as October of 1960, and the British government passed the
information on to our State Department.[4]

At the same time this missile information was being evaluated by the
CIA, the country was gearing up for the upcoming national elections.
With all the anti-Castro propaganda being disseminated, there was no
doubt in Allen Dulles' mind that Richard Nixon would win the race
handily.

Unfortunately, Nixon didn't. And, the one responsible was Kohly's old
nemesis from the State Department—William Wieland.[5] The leftist Cuban
leaders—targeted for assassination by members of Operation Forty—were
introduced by Wieland to the Kennedys at the time of the Democratic
national convention. The leftist leaders then gave the presidential nominee
the details on the planned Cuban invasion.

It was a great political coup. Kennedy knew that Nixon, abiding by
security restrictions that he could not disavow, had to limit his discussion
to the official government position. There was to be *no* U.S. intervention
in Cuban affairs.

As this official policy did not publicly apply to Kennedy, he could, and
did, openly advocate the overthrow of the Castro government, calling for
an invasion—Nixon's real position. Thus, Nixon, because of the cloak of

security, was forced to rebut Kennedy's stand. Unfortunately, the Vice President's frustration and anger at his opponent's calculated disclosure was clearly evident on the TV screen.

Political strategists claim it was this ploy that gave Kennedy the narrow margin to win the election. As a result, it would ally the President behind the leftist Cuban exile leaders and cause him to defend William Wieland.

As late as January 25, 1962, President Kennedy continued to defend Wieland, even though he was considered a security risk by the Senate Subcommittee on Internal Security Matters. In a *Washington Post* article of that date entitled "President Rebukes a Reporter," the President's reply to the accusation of Wieland and a State Department associate being a security risk was:

> In my opinion, Mr. Miller and Mr. Wieland, the duties they have been assigned to . . . they can carry out without detriment to the interests of the United States and I hope without detriment to their character by your question.

In November of 1960, John F. Kennedy was elected President of the United States and would be briefed on Cuban matters by CIA Director Allen Dulles and Deputy Director of Plans Richard Bissell. This briefing took place on November 18, 1960. Because of his declaration during the debates, the two CIA chiefs indulged in one of the most infamous pieces of hypocrisy ever perpetrated on an American head of state. Not knowing that the president-elect was already cognizant of the CIA invasion plans, Dulles and Bissell informed him that "the Central Intelligence Agency had a plan to invade Cuba using Cuban exiles. A plan looked favorably upon by the National Security Council and President Eisenhower."

They went on to elaborate that exile training operations had been set up in Florida and Guatemala, then neglected to mention the secret deal made between the lame-duck Vice President and Kohly, whose underground would be essential for the success of any invasion; the suspected construction of missile sites; and information the current occupant of the White House, Dwight D. Eisenhower, was also unaware of—the CIA/Mafia assassination plans against Fidel Castro.

The president-elect's reaction to the briefing shocked both Dulles and Bissell. Kennedy told them to put a hold on the invasion.

For the next two months, during the transition of power from the Eisenhower to Kennedy administration, Washington was chaotic. It was also chaotic in Guatemala. By late January, the invasion Brigade was about to mutiny. When some of the CRC leftist leaders arrived at the military training center in Guatemala and started to assert their authority over the Brigade commander, 230 of the 500 men resigned, including the base commander.

With Kohly's blessing, the CIA turned to Manuel Artime, who was at that time in Panama taking a guerrilla course, and proclaimed him leader. This action stopped the insurrection but infuriated the leftist leaders, who now saw their chances of regaining power if the invasion succeeded becoming less and less.

In late February, when Kennedy still failed to let the CIA proceed with the invasion, Dulles warned the chief executive that to delay any longer could be fatal. The young President, after talking it over with brother Bobby, the new Attorney General, instead ordered Dulles to stop all anti-Cuban operations.

Their reason would soon become apparent. William Wieland and the leftist factions in the exile community—seeking to regain their power over the Brigade and to save their influence with the new administration—had proclaimed to the new President and Attorney General that the rightist-controlled Brigade was being funded in part by the Mafia. The leftist Cubans got their reaction, and Bobby Kennedy, at this critical point, immediately expanded his war against organized crime. He chose as his first target a close associate of Jimmy Hoffa—New Orleans crime boss, Carlos Marcello.

Marcello's Mafia empire had been identified by the McClellan Senate Committee as the key distribution point for drug shipments coming into the United States.[6] To stop Mafia funds from reaching the Cuban exile organizations, Marcello, as financial broker for the vast sums of money flowing to the various syndicate operations, would be the logical first target of the new Attorney General.

To expedite his plan, twelve days before the Bay of Pigs invasion, Bobby had Marcello seized by Federal agents as he was walking along the street. The crime czar was then driven to a waiting jet liner, in which he was the only passenger, and flown to Guatemala.

Marcello was not allowed to pack a bag, call his lawyer, or even call his wife. The deportation—or kidnaping—at the hands of Bobby Kennedy, enraged the Mafia leader, and he declared war on the two brothers. Friends and associates of Marcello stated that he spoke of little else for weeks.

With Marcello's arrest, Mario Kohly—suddenly in danger of losing the extra funding needed for his Cuban underground—made a deal with Mafia dons Meyer Lansky and Santos Trafficante to give them back their casino rights once he had taken over as president of Cuba. This deal, reached in the Washington, D.C., residence of Kohly, was consummated in the offices of attorney Marshall Diggs, through Washington mob liaison man for Lansky and Trafficante, C. H. "Jim" Polley.[7] Interestingly, several years after the Bay of Pigs failure, Lansky would again approach Kohly. It was after the exile leader was declared by the Guatemalan government to be the Cuban de facto president in exile.[8]

Although I was never introduced to Polley, I saw him with Diggs and Kohly upon numerous occasions.

With the Marcello organization temporarily immobilized, Trafficante pressured CIA assassination coordinator Robert Maheu to have the Agency convince the administration to stop delaying and invade Cuba. He figured (correctly) that it would be a last-ditch effort to save their underworld interests.

Whatever effect, if any, this had on the CIA, the President, on April 10, after another briefing from Bissell, made a complete turnaround from his position of holding back the Cuban invasion. During this briefing, Tracy Barnes, my case officer, told me that Bissell had told the President something that only he, General Cabell, and CIA Director Allen Dulles knew: The Bay of Pigs was also designed to cover a flying mission into Camaguey Province to ascertain the progress the Russians were making on their Cuban missile installations. To cover this operation, a secondary invasion was to take place simultaneously. Its purpose was to be twofold: first, to act as a diversion for the main assault; and second, to pull troops away from the site of the clandestine aircraft's landing.[9]

This diversionary force was supposed to land thirty miles east of the U.S. naval base at Guantanamo under the command of a young Cuban exile named Nino Diaz, whose men had been trained in New Orleans by Sergio Arcacha Smith, an associate of New Orleans Mafia leader Carlos Marcello and ex-FBI man Guy Banister. The pilot who would fly this mission into Cuba, with me on board, was Dave Ferrie, the Mafia don's personal pilot.

With the President's decision, the Bay of Pigs operation would proceed on the night of April 16, 1961. It was ironic. Kennedy's decision to finally launch the invasion was made just at the time his advisers, members of the Joint Chiefs of Staff and some of the CIA hierarchy, were expressing serious doubts as to its probable success. Their reason was the last-minute restrictions being imposed on the plan by the President—the requirement that no U.S. support or intervention would be provided, either prior to or during the initial landing.

These restrictions, which would ultimately cause the operation to fail, were due to a confrontation between Kennedy and United Nations Ambassador Adlai Stevenson, which occurred because Stevenson had sworn to the United Nations that President Kennedy had told him, "there would be no United States intervention in Cuban affairs under any conditions. And the U.S. government would do everything it could to make sure that no American participated in any actions against Cuba."

When Stevenson was proven wrong by our own media, in front of the Cuban ambassador and the entire U.N. General Assembly, he flew into a rage. This occurred after another diversionary operation failed, one planned to convince the world that the attacks upon Cuban airfields were being conducted by defecting Castro aircraft.

A Brigade pilot by the name of Mario Zuniga was to fly one of the planes, a World War II B-26 with Cuban Air Force markings, to Miami. His story, once he arrived, was to be that he was one of three pilots, all disenchanted with Castro, who had been planning to defect for months. And, on that particular day, he had been flying a routine patrol from his home base, San Antonio de los Banos, and decided to strafe the field. Then, after being hit by small-arms fire and low on fuel, he decided to head for Miami.

Thirty minutes from Miami International Airport, Zuniga opened his cockpit window and fired enough pistol shots into the port engine so that it had to be feathered. After landing, he gave out his cover story. In less than an hour, it was proven a hoax. Reporters noted that, not only had the plane's machine guns not been fired, but it had a solid metal nose. Castro's B-26s had plastic noses.

When the Cuban ambassador waved the damning photographs and news reports in front of the United Nations General Assembly, Stevenson acted.

He intimidated Kennedy. He claimed he would inform the U.N. that the new chief executive had lied, then resign as ambassador. Obviously, the young new President—sufficiently coerced—would not give any support orders. That included a formally pledged air strike by our navy, in the event the exile air force was unable to knock out Castro's jets.

There can be no question in anyone's mind that Adlai Stevenson, for the most part, was responsible for the failure of the Bay of Pigs. Had John Kennedy been just a little more secure after only seventy days in the White House, he would never have let the U.N. Ambassador get away with such a challenge.

At the time, according to all my Washington contacts, including my case officer Tracy Barnes, Stevenson not only knew about the invasion but had been briefed by both President Kennedy and the CIA. He would have had to have been deaf, dumb, and blind not to know all about the upcoming action against Castro. Every exile was talking about it. In fact, open recruiting stations had been operating in Miami for months. It was the poorest kept secret in the world. Howard Hunt also claimed that he knew Stevenson was briefed by Tracy Barnes and even mentioned it in his book, *Give Us This Day.*

Although Stevenson would state he had been kept in the dark about the invasion preparations, Barnes would produce a record of his briefing of Stevenson well prior to the invasion date. The Barnes-Stevenson memorandum was furnished to Lyman Kirkpatrick, CIA's inspector-general, at the time.

The one man in the CIA who would suffer the most from the President's disastrous decision was Deputy Director Charles Cabell. From the beginning, it was obvious that the Bay of Pigs operation would fail without U.S. air support, for Castro's air force had not been knocked out as planned on the first day. For that blunder, Cabell would be held accountable.

It occurred on Sunday morning when the former Air Force General decided to visit the Agency Operations Center in Washington, known as "Quarters Eye." He arrived just as the Air Operations Officer was preparing to launch the cleanup air strike. Dressed in slacks and a sports shirt, after coming directly from a round of golf at the Chevy Chase Club, he inquired about what was going on as he scanned U-2 photographs of the previous day's damage.

When the Air Operations Officer told Cabell that he was readying another strike to get the last of Castro's air force, Cabell, in doubt as to what orders had been issued from the White House, put a personal hold on the action, pending confirmation that it was all right. After realizing what a terrible mistake he had made, Cabell would repeatedly try to make up for it. He requested air cover for the invasion on four separate occasions. His final attempt was at 4:00 a.m. on the second day of fighting.

In a last desperate effort to persuade the President to reconsider his orders, the CIA Deputy Director drove through the darkened capitol to Secretary of State Dean Rusk's hotel. In Rusk's apartment, Cabell again expressed his fears. Despite the hour, the Secretary of State called the President once more. The reply was still negative. The surviving Castro jets were free to destroy the exile army and invasion fleet at will.

The final blow for the Brigade came when Kohly discovered that the air cover was being withheld. He learned it from former Senator Owen Brewster of Maine on the night of the first assault.[10]

Kohly's immediate reaction was to stop his underground from supporting the invasion force. Without air protection or internal support, the invasion failed and the Brigade was vanquished in a humiliating defeat.

Infuriated, the President promised to splinter the CIA into a thousand pieces. Kennedy would not concede that withholding the air strike had contributed to the invasion's failure, though his best military advice had been that the operation would fail without it.

However, in a bizarre twist of fate, by his action, the new President had saved the lives of the leftist exile leaders. He would also soon learn that it had aligned the right-wing elements of the CIA and the violent Cuban exile organizations against him. One of the most virulent CIA opponents of the Kennedys was Howard Hunt, who had mistrusted the administration from the very beginning. Hunt had told his assistant, Bernard Barker, several months before the Bay of Pigs that "it was becoming increasingly hard to identify the enemy." Hunt stated that the second air strike was "basic to the success of the entire operation." After its failure, he laid the blame entirely on Kennedy and his advisers.

Bernard Barker, who would be the future leader of the Watergate burglary team, served as Howard Hunt's top deputy during the Bay of Pigs. Barker was the CIA's chief liaison and paymaster for all exile work. He was connected to the Santos Trafficante mob—along with his good friend, Frank Sturgis—through ex-Cuban president Carlos Prio Socarras. In the mid-1960s, according to Richard Helms, Barker had been "fired" by the CIA because, "we found out he was involved in certain gambling and criminal activities."

Hunt was not one to contain his opinion as to how he felt about at least one of Kennedy's advisers. In his book about the Bay of Pigs, *Give Us This Day,* Hunt links Kennedy adviser Arthur Schlesinger with a member of the Fair Play for Cuba Committee, calling the historian's decisions, "the ultimate in folly." After reading what Schlesinger had to say about me in his book, *Robert Kennedy and His Times,*[11] I'm inclined to agree with Hunt's assessment.

Fortunately, the operation I was on with David Ferrie turned out to be successful. We got the evidence that a missile control center was being built in Cuba's Camaguey Province.[12] It would fall on deaf ears in the White House.

The cover-up of all CIA clandestine activities by the Agency to the new administration began when the Kennedy brothers ordered the dismissal of Allen Dulles and Richard Bissell as a first step in dismantling the CIA house. It would give the CIA Director and Deputy Director of Plans seven months to circumvent their plans.

CHAPTER FIVE NOTES

1.   In 1964, Bethel wrote the first major paper for the CIA-funded Citizens for a Free Cuba Committee, entitled "Terror and Resistance in Communist China," a copy of which is in the author's possession.

2.   Dick Russell in 1976 wrote feature articles for *The Village Voice,* one of which was about the author, entitled, "Cubans Connected to JFK Murder—But Which Cubans?" (June 24, 1976).

3.   Hearings to Investigate the Administration of the Internal Security Act and Other Internal Security Laws, Senate Judiciary Committee; March 7, 1967, Part 16, p. 127.

4.   See Appendix, Exhibit No. 7.

5.   Wieland, in August of 1960, was being investigated by the Senate Subcommittee on Internal Security for his communist leanings by chief counsel for the committee, Julian G. Sourwine.

6.   Senate Committee on Government Operations, "Organized Crime and Illicit Traffic in Narcotics," 88th Congress, pp. 800-801.

7.   This information was given to me in an interview with Mario Kohly, Jr., on October 11, 1977, and confirmed independently by Oscar del Valle Garcia on March 12, 1983.

8.   Interview with Dr. Edward von Rothkirk, August 26, 1976.

9.   Wyden,   *Bay of Pigs,* Simon & Schuster, p. 170; Johnson, *Bay of Pigs,* Norton, p. 96; Morrow, *Betrayal,* Regnery, p. 4.

10.   Kohly's deathbed statement, July 5, 1975. See Appendix, Exhibit No. 8.

11.   *Robert Kennedy and His Times,* Random House, 1978, p. 524n.

12.   Morrow, *Betrayal,* Warner, 1976, pp. 7-8.

Chapter Six

The Kennedy administration was also having other problems, precipitated by the Bay of Pigs failure. They couldn't control Rafael Trujillo, the right-wing dictator of the Dominican Republic, and the Dominican-based terrorist group, the "Caribbean Legion." Trujillo, concerned over Castro's dramatic success on the invasion beach and the possible exportation of the Cuban revolution into his own island republic, was becoming more and more oppressive.

Because of his sadistic regime, the CIA had targeted Trujillo for assassination during the Eisenhower administration, even though he had helped Carlos Prio Socarras. So, in December of 1960, Nixon, heading the special group that controlled Operation Forty, approved a program of covert support for a group of dissident Dominican generals.

Henry Dearborn, the American consul, was in charge of this operation. Dearborn claimed the generals felt that the only way to get rid of Trujillo was by assassination. Dearborn agreed, reporting it to Nixon.

By May, when rumors were abounding in Washington that Trujillo was about to be assassinated, the Kennedys instructed White House aide Richard Goodwin[1] to tell Henry Dearborn not to get involved in any assassination attempt. Dearborn's reply, after a year of dealing with the conspirators, was that it was "too late to consider whether the United States will initiate the overthrow of Trujillo."[2]

It was the opinion of William D. Pawley, former ambassador and State Department advisor, that William Wieland was the one directly responsible for the State Department dropping diplomatic relations with the Dominican Republic prior to Trujillo's assassination. It became known to those who would overthrow him that, if they took action against the "island strongman," the United States would not lift a finger.

Trujillo was assassinated on May 30, 1961, in his 1957 Chevrolet. The attack was carried out by a three-man team with backups. According to the CIA, who reported to Goodwin, the dissident generals received weapons—M-3 Thompson submachine guns—from the CIA to neutralize Trujillo. How they got there and were used is an interesting story, told to me by Oscar del Valle Garcia. I relate the following, recorded in my presence.[3]

Well, to make a long story short, after I assembled my crew together, I took them out in the Everglades and we test fired and familiarized ourselves with the weapons. There were four men counting myself.[4]

When we hit Trujillo, we lucked out. We observed him for three weeks. And on a route he chose, there was a small village he had to go through; and the road he took came into the center of this village, where there was a little square. I needed a point where I could catch him at his slowest speed. This was a small square. In other words, you couldn't whiz around it, with the narrow streets.

I set one man here [he said drawing on a paper napkin], on top of this little two story building, a cafe I think it was. There was a church on this corner—in this area, and there was a garage on this little plaza in here. This was kind of like a garage and filling station and that sort of thing.

I had one man on the roof of each building, and I was just inside the church—you know, the big double doors on churches. The plan was the man located on the cafe roof was to fire the first burst, which would trigger me, and I would make the second hit, or the killing hit; and the third man located on the garage roof would make the *coup de gras*.

What happened was, we were expecting three cars; but what happened was, there was only one—it was a '57 Chevrolet. It reached the entrance to the square . . . and the single car got to this point. The first man's gun jammed. Of course, I was under the impression that this car was the first of three cars. From my position I had no way of knowing that there weren't two cars behind it. So, actually, Trujillo's car was at the point I could see it. When I recognized him, I realized what had happened, we were dealing with a single car.

I was watching this area through the half-opened double door of the church. When the car got to this point, that's when I stepped out of the church—as close as I am to that window, about ten feet, and opened fire. The automatic fire literally tore the driver's head off. The car went past me, swerved, and hit a tree. It stopped, giving me a perfect field of fire. Then I raked the car with machine-gun fire and emptied my clip. Hurriedly I shoved in a new one. Trujillo was hit, but only wounded, sitting on the passenger side in the rear seat. A guard next to the driver had also been hit. This was the thing that totally astounded us—there were only two men with him. He was in the rear seat, alone, and I fired through the window at him. The thing I remember is his body jerking when the burst hit him; and I do admit a solid hit.

After, oh, the deed was done, the man on the garage roof opened fire; and, hell, I'm out in the open. Well, I had about a half a clip left. . . . It was only a matter of seconds before he'd have hit me; so I turned around and fired a short burst at him to tell him to quit firing at me. The man on the cafe never did fire.

The detailed story del Valle tells of this assassination was identical to the one told to me by Tracy Barnes in 1961.

In the summer of 1983, I requested del Valle to take a polygraph test on this subject. It was conducted in Chicago, Illinois. The results were termed inconclusive.

Other stories about the Trujillo assassination vary in different press and magazine articles. However, whether del Valle was involved or not, the scenario related by del Valle was corroborated by Barnes, and I believe it to be factual. I was also told by Mario Garcia Kohly that "Oscar was on a mission in the Dominican Republic" and Cuba during the spring of 1961, just after the Bay of Pigs.

It was after the Trujillo assassination that Oscar del Valle Garcia claims he discussed the attempts on Castro's life with a Cuban exile leader named Antonio Veciana in Cuba. Later, Veciana told the same story to Senate and HSCA investigators.

To complicate matters for the new administration, the Mafia, taking advantage of growing exile sentiment against the Kennedys, started taking a more active role in anti-Castro affairs. Their participation would intensify all through the summer and fall of 1961, with the full cooperation of the CIA. This activity would peak by the end of November when John

McCone, a defense contractor who had formerly headed the Atomic Energy Commission, was named to replace Dulles. Then McCone and Bissell agreed that the Deputy Director of Plans should quit in December.

At this point, the Central Intelligence Agency would embark upon its darkest period. Allen Dulles, prior to his enforced retirement, would, to the dismay of CIA Inspector General Lyman Kirkpatrick, recommend Bissell's replacement to Bobby Kennedy. It was the man whose hands he had kept from being tainted by the Cuban brush—Richard Helms.

Dulles had chosen well. He knew the Agency would need a skilled and dedicated covert operations professional. He considered Helms one of the best, and his allegiance to both the Company and Allen Dulles could not be shaken. Before Dulles himself was banished, Helms' goal was to rebuild the influence of the clandestine agency. According to Col. L. Fletcher Prouty, ret., who was an intelligence liaison to the White House during this period, Dulles accomplished this task masterfully. He made sure that Bobby Kennedy, during the congressional investigation of the Bay of Pigs failure, heard only the things Dulles wanted him to hear.

To accomplish this, he selected a string of witnesses whose testimony would present the Agency in its best light—in effect, transferring blame for the Bay of Pigs to others, such as the Joint Chiefs of Staff. In a brilliant piece of strategy, Dulles turned the hearings around by arranging for the witnesses to provide background briefings of the Agency's new policy of counterinsurgency.

In 1961-62, "counterinsurgency" was the chief strategy being pushed by both the Pentagon and the CIA. It was a plan for implementing a tactical strike force, by arranging a marriage between the CIA and the United States Army, a strategy mapped out during the last months of the Eisenhower administration.

Bobby Kennedy was taken in to the point where he met with the "counterinsurgency group" regularly. He maintained that, after the Bay of Pigs and the Berlin Wall, his brother could not afford another setback.

Dulles had done the job well. For the next decade, the CIA would have control over a large segment of the Army for special missions. Some would engage in assassinations, and others contribute to illicit trafficking in drugs.

As these events were occurring, I was in the midst of setting up the largest counterfeiting operation since World War II. It was to print Cuban pesos. The intent: to destroy Castro's economy. By August, we had succeeded, forcing the island dictator to change all his currency.

After completing that program, I was asked by Kohly to secure a load of automatic weapons for his underground. It caused me to make a second trip with David Ferrie, from Athens, Greece, to Madrid, in early November.[5]

I didn't know that Ferrie, just five months earlier, had transported Mafia chief Carlos Marcello back from Guatemala to the U.S.—in defiance of orders given by Attorney General Robert Kennedy. Ferrie, by the end of 1961, was working for Marcello, on an almost full-time basis, through New Orleans private detective, Guy Banister, former FBI special-agent-in-charge of the Chicago Field Office, where he was Robert Maheu's former boss. Maheu, CIA Castro assassination coordinator, would remain unknown to John McCone, even after McCone had taken over the reins as CIA Director.

Briefed by Allen Dulles and Charles Cabell, McCone was not told about the assassination plots against Castro. In fact, it would be months before either he or the chief executive would find out. McCone, taking Dulles' advice, elevated Richard Helms, the now outspoken critic of the Bay of Pigs, to replace Richard Bissell as CIA Deputy Director of Plans, in January of 1962.

The following month, CIA Deputy Director General Charles Cabell, by prearrangement, went to work as a consultant for a CIA proprietary company, the Pacific Corporation, which was the parent company of Air Asia and Air America. Air America,[6] a spin-off of Civil Air Transport (CAT), was the CIA-run carrier that would become heavily involved in drug traffic in Southeast Asia during the Vietnam War.

Victor Marchetti, former executive assistant to Richard Helms, claimed that Air America had been used to carry opium and that some of the highest military officers in several Agency-supported, far-eastern countries were the kingpins of this illegal traffic.[7]

During the early 1970s, columnist Jack Anderson and *The New York Times* disclosed hard information regarding CIA involvement in the heroin trade in South Vietnam, Thailand, Cambodia, and Laos through the Agency's Asian mercenary operatives. Former South Vietnamese Premier Ky was reported to be involved with both CIA elements and Corsican Mafia operatives in the drug trade. On August 30, 1971, *The New York Times* reported that the Director of Customs in South Vietnam had stated that he "believed that planes of the South Vietnam Air Force were the principal courier of heroin into the South Vietnam region."

As in the case of General Cabell, Richard Bissell did not stray far from the CIA fold. He took over as Director of the Department of Defense's

Institute of Defense Analysis, a conduit for CIA programs that the Department didn't want known to have originated with the clandestine Agency.

After an internal bureaucratic struggle, Tracy Barnes established the Agency's super-secret Domestic Operations Division. Barnes then appointed E. Howard Hunt as its Chief of Covert Activities. This new division, tailored to accept projects unwanted elsewhere in the CIA, has to this day been shrouded in mystery.

It also could not have been formed at a more propitious time; for, on May 7, 1962, the FBI discovered the CIA/Mafia assassination attempts against Fidel Castro. The leak occurred when Mafia assassination coordinator Sam Giancana became suspicious that his girlfriend, singer Phyllis McGuire, and comedian Dan Rowan were having an affair. To check it out, Giancana had CIA assassination coordinator Robert Maheu order a bug installed in Rowan's Las Vegas hotel room. It was discovered by a maid, and with the ensuing publicity, the FBI got wind of the Maheu/Giancana relationship and Castro assassination plots, through its ongoing wiretap operations against the Mafia.

All this was reported by a gloating FBI Director J. Edgar Hoover[8] to Bobby Kennedy and CIA Director John McCone. When McCone demanded an instant answer, he was told all such operations had been terminated in May of 1961, a year earlier. When Bobby Kennedy discovered that these plots also involved CIA's Maheu and Mafia chieftain Sam Giancana, he became enraged, ordering the new CIA Deputy Director of Plans, Richard Helms, to give him an immediate briefing. So, on that same day—May 7, 1962—Helms instructed Colonel Sheffield Edwards (one of the original architects of the CIA/Mafia assassination plots) and Lawrence Houston, the Agency's general counsel, to conduct the briefing. It was at that meeting, under the direct orders of Richard Helms, that the CIA officials deliberately lied to the Attorney General. They told him what they had told McCone earlier, all such operations had been terminated in May of 1961.[9]

This was done despite the fact that a new batch of poison pills had been delivered to John Roselli just three weeks earlier; and the CIA was, at that very time, providing rifles and other equipment to gunmen for yet another attempt against Castro.

The implications of Sheffield Edwards and Lawrence Houston's briefing of the Attorney General were serious. The CIA Inspector General's office was cognizant of the fact that Edwards had withheld—and thereby concealed—the ongoing attempts on Castro's life from the Director and the Attorney General. But more importantly, the Mafia execution plans were in direct contravention of Bobby Kennedy's orders.[10]

It seemingly did not disturb the new Deputy Director of Plans. Helms went on to compound his felony. In order to insure that there would be no more questions raised regarding the Castro assassination attempts, he directed a fraudulent internal file memorandum to be prepared by Colonel Sheffield Edwards, deliberately stating that the CIA had terminated the conspiracies.[11]

It worked. The massive extent of this cover-up would not surface until 1967, at a time when the two major political parties were gearing up for another presidential race and a New Orleans investigation into President Kennedy's assassination was just getting under way. Then Helms, on his own authority, made the decision to continue the Castro assassination operations. This time the new DDP worked directly with John Roselli, dumping Sam Giancana and Robert Maheu, but retaining Santos Trafficante as a consultant.

It remained a mystery why Roselli and Trafficante were kept on by Helms, until Oscar del Valle Garcia gave me a logical explanation in January of 1984. Roselli was Helms' only link to Trafficante. The Deputy Director of Plans wanted to keep that one measure of separation from the Florida Mafia don. Trafficante was using Rolando Masferrer's assassins on No Name Key, the men who comprised Operation Forty, to carry out the hits.

Ironically, the decision by Helms to use Roselli as his sole contact with Trafficante had a lethal side-effect for the Kennedy brothers. Trafficante, normally a cautious person, felt that his sudden isolation from the CIA meant he was losing his protective cover. He reasoned correctly; without the Agency shield, he would be totally open to attack from Bobby Kennedy, including electronic surveillance. Given his extensive narcotics dealings with Carlos Marcello, he couldn't survive that kind of exposure, nor could Marcello.

The Kennedy administration's drive against the Mafia was at its most intense by midsummer of 1962, and the Justice Department had all but a few of its leaders under twenty-four-hour electronic surveillance.[12]

Santos Trafficante of Florida and John Roselli of Las Vegas were partially immune because of their CIA affiliation, and Carlos Marcello was by virtue of being isolated on his six-thousand-acre Churchill Farms estate.

This wiretapping and surveillance was being accorded all top members of the Mafia families—now being referred to as the "National Crime Commission" or "syndicate"—with the exception of Johnny Roselli, Santos Trafficante, and Carlos Marcello.[13] The fact that the results of wiretapping and surveillance efforts against Carlos Marcello and Santos Trafficante yielded results less than those experienced against other targets was confirmed to the HSCA by a former official of the FBI. The official, who was second in command of day-to-day intelligence operations relating to organized crime, stated in an interview with the HSCA, with reference to Santos Trafficante: "I do feel that we were never really able to penetrate on him [Trafficante] very clearly. Certainly nothing like we were able to do in Chicago and New York."

With reference to Carlos Marcello, he said: "I certainly agree with anyone who says we never were really able to get very far with Marcello. That was our biggest gap. You just couldn't penetrate his kingdom, with the control in that State that he has. With Marcello, you've got the one big exception in our work back then. There was just no way of penetrating that area. He was too smart."

Organized crime intelligence relative to Carlos Marcello and Santos Trafficante, as well as to the Dallas area, was therefore insufficient to indicate whether they or others in Dallas may have been involved in a conspiracy to assassinate John F. Kennedy.[14]

By late summer, the two Mafia dons had made the decision to get Bobby off their backs by killing the President. By September of 1962, Marcello's concern and hatred of the Kennedy brothers prompted him to hold a highly secret meeting between himself and his top aides at his New Orleans Churchill Farms estate. It was during this meeting that Marcello divulged in a rage that plans were being developed to assassinate the President, and possibly Bobby.[15]

Invoking a centuries-old Sicilian death threat, *"Livarsi na petra di la scarpa,"* which means "Take the stone out of my shoe," Marcello then reportedly said, "Don't worry about that little Bobby son of a bitch, he's going to be taken care of . . ." He then stated that the President would be assassinated first.[16]

They would also have the support of Jimmy Hoffa.

Carlos Marcello, like the rest of the Mafia leaders, knew that killing Bobby Kennedy would not stop the attack against the syndicate. The target would have to be the President. To emphasize the genuine intent of Marcello to kill the President in order to get rid of Bobby, a Los Angeles private investigator by the name of Edward N. Becker told of a meeting he had attended with Marcello and a Carl Rappelo of Shreveport, Louisiana. In that meeting, Marcello discussed assassinating the President. Becker claimed that, around September of 1962, Marcello clearly and angrily stated, "He was going to arrange to have President Kennedy murdered in some way." According to Becker, Marcello's statement had been made in a serious tone and sounded as if he had discussed it previously.

Becker also commented that Marcello made some kind of reference to President Kennedy's being a dog and Attorney General Robert Kennedy being the dog's tail, saying: "The dog will keep biting you if you only cut off its tail, but that, if the dog's head were cut off, the dog would die."[17]

Marcello also knew that members of his own organization could not be involved in the hit in any way. Becker stated that Marcello made reference to the way he wanted to arrange the President's murder, indicating that his own lieutenants must not be identified as the assassins— that it would be necessary to use or manipulate someone else to carry out the actual crime.

Marcello and Trafficante were not the only ones who wanted Bobby Kennedy destroyed. Their good friend, Jimmy Hoffa, wanted to take matters into his own hands.

As a result of the Attorney General's maniacal zeal, a special task force was assembled to look into labor racketeering. It was headed by a former FBI man named Walter Sheridan, and it caught up with the Teamster leader in the spring of 1962. Consequently, Hoffa was indicted in Nashville for allegedly receiving hundreds of thousands of dollars in payoffs through a trucking company set up in his wife's maiden name.

When his trial ended in a hung jury, a Justice Department investigator described it as "one of the most massive jury tampering efforts in history."

Hoffa was promptly reindicted on jury tampering charges and was eventually convicted. There was also one other present from Bobby Kennedy to Hoffa: a Chicago grand jury finally managed to indict the Teamster boss for having defrauded the Teamsters' Pension Fund of almost two-million dollars.

Convicted, Hoffa would swear vengeance and let it be known.

In the summer of 1962, Edward Grady Partin, a Baton Rouge Teamster official, whose testimony eventually put Hoffa in jail, revealed that Hoffa had decided to physically take action against his persecutor, Bobby Kennedy. Partin revealed that, while he was at the Teamsters' Washington headquarters, Hoffa called him into his office and asked if he could lay his hands on some plastic explosive. "Something has to be done about that little S.O.B. Bobby Kennedy," Partin quoted Hoffa as saying. "He'll be an easy target, always driving around Washington in that convertible with that big black dog. All we need is some plastic explosives tossed in with him, and that will finish him off."

Later Partin heard that the plot had been altered to blowing up the Kennedy home—along with everyone inside. When Justice Department aides heard this story they were skeptical, until Partin took a lie detector test, showing he was telling the truth. When other elements of Partin's story checked out, the aides were no longer skeptical.

Marcello, Trafficante, and Johnny Roselli, however, were not ready to let their largest financial benefactor rashly go astray and kill the Attorney General. They needed Jimmy Hoffa for other things—to help finance the assassination of Bobby's presidential brother.

The Teamsters were vital to the Mafia. Under Hoffa, the union provided the criminal syndicate with tens of millions of dollars in loans, jobs, and respectability. Hoffa's closeness to the mob was such that his grievances automatically became their grievances; his enemies, their enemies. In New York alone, federal investigators discovered forty union "officials" who were actually members of the mob. Among them, they had seventy-seven convictions for crimes including theft, narcotics, forgery, possession of stolen mail, robbery, and accessory to murder.

The Hoffa-controlled Central States' Pension Fund—which one federal investigation characterized as a "lending agency for the syndicate"— had hundreds of millions tied up in the Mafia's Las Vegas hotel-casinos and their Florida apartment buildings, hospitals, condominiums, hotels, motels, and country clubs. In effect, the mob considered the Kennedy assault on Hoffa as an attack on a key mob subsidiary. And, the mob always defended its interests.

So, by the end of 1962, Carlos Marcello, Santos Trafficante, and James Hoffa had the motive, the desire, and the means to plan and execute a conspiracy to assassinate Robert and/or John Kennedy. By September, Trafficante, exuberantly over-confident, would let it be known that the President was to be killed and who was going to be responsible for it. In that month, he told a prominent Cuban exile, Jose Aleman, that President Kennedy was going to be assassinated.

Aleman, the son of the late Jose Manuel Aleman, who had served Batista as Minister of Education and, in the words of Mario Kohly, owned several other ministries, including the national treasury, was also a very close friend of Prio's and a senator during his regime. Aleman was best known in the U.S. for building the Miami stadium. After his death, the ownership passed to his son, Jose Aleman.

In an account of the conversation between Aleman and Trafficante published by the *Washington Post* in 1976, Aleman also stated that it was his impression that Trafficante was not the specific individual who was allegedly planning the murder. Aleman then noted that Trafficante had spoken of Teamsters' Union President James Hoffa during the same conversation, indicating that the President would "get what is coming to him" as a result of his administration's intense efforts to prosecute Hoffa.

Aleman stated that Trafficante had made clear to him that he was not guessing that the President was going to be killed, but rather that he did in fact know that such a crime was being planned. In addition, Trafficante had given him the distinct impression that Hoffa was one of the principals involved in planning the presidential murder.[18]

Their plans would be helped immeasurably by the escalation of the Cuban missile installations.

CHAPTER SIX NOTES

1.   Richard N. Goodwin was one of three men considered part of the President's personal brain trust. In 1960, at the age of twenty-eight, he was credited with a capacity for reasoning that had made him number-one man, two years earlier at Harvard Law School.

2.   United States Senate Committee on Foreign Assassinations, 1975, pp. 212-213.

3.   Recorded interview, April 14, 1983.

4.   Oscar del Valle Garcia said he had originally requested five men but instead had to go with three plus himself—three acting as gunmen, and one driver.

5.   Morrow, *Betrayal,* p. 73.

6.   Southern Air Transport, a spin-off of Air America, was the company utilized by Lt. Colonel Oliver North for the Iran/Contra operations in 1985 and 1986. (Iran/Contra Hearings, July 1987.)

7.   Marchetti, *CIA and the Cult of Intelligence,* p. 245.

8.   Senate Intelligence Committee Report on Foreign Assassinations, 1975, pp. 131-132.

9.   HSCA, Vol. X, p. 180.

10.   HSCA, Vol. X, p. 188.

11.   *Ibid.,* pp. 188-189.

12.   *Ibid.,* pp. 196-197.

13.   HSCA, Vol. IX, p. 59.

14.   *Ibid.,* p. 59.

15.   HSCA Final Report, pp. 211-212.

16.   *Ibid.,* pp. 213-214.

17.   HSCA, Vol. IX, pp. 82, 83.

18.   HSCA Final Assassination Report, pp. 214-215.

Chapter Seven

During the month of September 1962, while I was gathering communications gear for Mario Kohly's underground, the reports from Cuba had become more and more alarming. The Russians were preparing to erect secondary IRBM sites in addition to the hard sites already in place.

Once again, the CIA alerted the White House to take action. They received the same response they had gotten earlier—nothing. Robert Kennedy had taken the initiative for dictating Cuban policy in the White House and was keeping a tight rein on the administration's position.

Meanwhile, Republicans, spearheaded by Senator Kenneth Keating of New York, tried to force an admission from the White House regarding the new missile threat. On October 10, 1962, Keating stated: "100 percent reliable evidence from exiles, indicate that nuclear missile bases are under construction in Cuba."

However, Bobby—having known all about the missiles since the Bay of Pigs—elected not to inform the American public. His brother could use the information to political advantage. Just before the 1962 congressional election, the pollsters predicted the Democrats would lose extensively. Later, in 1966, journalist J. F. Stone made a point that "the nuclear menace from Cuba would certainly have cost the Democrats control of the House of Representatives," unless Kennedy forced Khruschev to back down.

Then, the polls uncovered another problem. The President had wanted to get the U.S. completely out of southern Asia, at a time the Louis Harris surveys showed Americans—by a factor of two to one—were in favor of large-scale intervention if the communist threat worsened. Simultaneously, the hierarchy of the Central Intelligence Agency, recognizing the

Kennedys' political motives and feeling they would not act, leaked the latest missile information to Washington reporter Paul Scott.

Scott, in turn, against the administration's wishes, went ahead and published the story, amidst threats of imprisonment from Bobby Kennedy. The result: Scott's story forced the Kennedy administration to finally react to a missile threat that had been a hard reality for more than eighteen months.

On October 15, a CIA U-2 got photographs of the new sites and delivered them to Bobby. It would become known as the "missile crisis" of October 1962.

Scott told me the inside story of the attempted White House cover-up during an impromptu interview with him in August of 1976. We had met in the office of Representative Thomas N. Downing, just prior to the formation of the House Select Committee on Assassinations.

Unfortunately for the Kennedys, the confrontation did not end there. Within weeks, Kohly's underground provided proof that the missiles had not been totally removed.

Kohly was concerned, and he elected to warn the Attorney General. He had an appointment with Kennedy the following week and asked me to go along. When we met with Bobby in Washington, the Cuban leader told him his underground had reported that all of the IRBM missiles had not been removed. Instantly, Bobby became incensed. After calling Kohly a liar, he literally threw us out of his office.[1]

Since 1976, I have talked to several other knowledgeable sources who have agreed to testify that the missiles of October 1962 were not all removed from Cuban soil. One of them provided me with a taped interview. His name is Dr. Herminio Portell-Vila, a former Guggenheim Fellow in the 1930s and Chubb Fellow at Yale University in 1957. Dr. Portell-Vila reveals that medium-range ballistic missiles were in Cuba as late as 1966 —four years after the so-called October 1962 "missile crisis" and three years after President Kennedy's death. Dr. Portell-Vila's credentials are unimpeachable. He was a grantee of the Rockefeller Foundation from 1960 through 1961 and is considered the elder statesman of Cuban history. He has lectured and taught at the National War College, the United States War College, the United States Defense Intelligence School, and the Inter-American Defense College.

Paul Bethel also testified on March 7, 1967, to the Senate Subcommittee on Internal Security about the retention of missiles in Cuba:

SEN. THURMOND:	Did they say they were new missiles introduced in, or did they say they were missiles that had been hidden and never taken out, or did they know?
MR. BETHEL:	Their testimony was to the effect that they were missiles which had remained there.
SEN. THURMOND:	Had remained there?
MR. BETHEL:	Yes.
SEN. THURMOND:	Their testimony was that they were missiles which remained there and were never taken out?
MR. BETHEL:	That is correct.
SEN. THURMOND:	Although Khruschev had promised that they would be taken out?
MR. BETHEL:	That is correct.
SEN. THURMOND:	I believe we had not [had any] inspection that would determine that missiles were taken out, so far as you know, did we?
MR. BETHEL:	There was no inspection.

Having IRBM missiles still in Cuba after Kennedy told the American public they had left infuriated the CIA and the military establishment. They knew Robert and John Kennedy had made a secret deal with Khruschev to trade our Turkish missiles for their Cuban ones.[2]

It didn't stop there. The Kennedys also agreed to a "hands-off," no-invasion policy toward Cuba.

This included stopping all exile activities against the island. With our missiles out of Turkey—at presidential direction—and Russian missiles still only ninety miles away, the clandestine agency set about planning another invasion of Cuba from Costa Rica.

To insure its success, in January of 1963, Mario Kohly once again approached me to ask if I could implement another counterfeiting operation, claiming the funds were to be used to bribe Castro's military leaders into not resisting an exile landing. After checking with Tracy Barnes, I was given the go-ahead, and Kohly supplied me with samples of the new Cuban currency. Supposedly, this bogus money was to be approved by the Kennedy administration for Kohly's new Cuban government.[3]

However, I sensed something wrong. Barnes was not as enthusiastic as he had been in the past. In fact, he seemed almost reticent. He claimed they were being pressured to actively suppress the exiles, as the Kennedy administration started implementing its hands-off Cuba policy.

It was during this period that New Orleans, with the second largest Cuban population in the U.S., reacted strongly to the Kennedy challenge. They, like their Miami counterparts, felt betrayed when the ongoing missile challenge was not met with force by the President.

Another factor in the President's decision was probably the fact that the Russians, who had already shown their ability to shoot down an American U-2 with Cuban-based SAMs, were now allowing U-2 overflights of Cuba.

The bitterness of the anti-Castro exiles was then heightened when the U.S. government issued a "no-invasion" pledge to Fidel Castro. As noted by Paul Bethel:

> There is no doubt that President Kennedy and his brother,
> the Attorney General, consciously set about the business of
> stopping all efforts to unhorse Fidel Castro—from outside
> exile attacks, and from Cuba's internal resistance movement.

Literally overnight, there was a crackdown on all the training camps and guerrilla bases that had been originally established and funded by the United States.

Exile raids, which once had the government's "green light," were now promptly disavowed and condemned. According to Oscar del Valle Garcia:

> You would have had to have been in Miami during this

period of time to really comprehend what was going on. We had created a Frankenstein monster, in the sense that these men were all hyped up to go. Maybe the Bay of Pigs fiasco only incensed them more to go. Personally, I had men on my hands that I had trained, and there was no way on God's green earth that I could have stopped them outside of killing them.

Oscar del Valle Garcia was back in Miami during and after the missile crisis, according to Kohly.

Kohly claimed that the special headaches his exile organizations created for the President, before and during the missile crisis, were deliberately planned by del Valle: "The timing of the raids on Cuba, at the height of the missile crisis when Kennedy was conducting his delicate negotiations with Khruschev, was Oscar's idea."

Whoever was responsible for the raids during the missile crisis, it was academic. For another exile leader, Antonio Veciana, the head of the militant SNFE/Alpha 66, kept up the pressure. On March 17, his organization attacked a Soviet military post and two Soviet freighters in the Cuban port of "Caribbean," provoking strong official protests from the Soviet Union to the United States.

Veciana claimed that, after the raid—at the CIA's insistence—he called a special press conference in Washington, D.C. Its purpose was to publicly embarrass the administration at a time when the President was making a trip to Costa Rico in an effort to gain support from other Latin American countries for the administration's hands-off Cuba policy.[4]

The Kennedys were incensed, and on March 30 they caused the State and Justice Departments to announce jointly that they "would take every step necessary to insure that such raids were not launched, manned, or equipped from U.S. territory."

Not to be deterred, del Valle told me he had arranged, the very next day, for a group of his anti-Castro mercenaries from Masferrer's No Name Key to repeat Veciana's exploit and blow up a Soviet ship.[5] Unfortunately, on the return trip, their boat was detained by the British in the Bahamas after a tip-off by the United States. The lone American in the group was a man named Jerry Buchanan, a protege of Frank Sturgis.[6]

That same night, another exile boat was seized in Miami harbor. On April 3, the Soviet Union finally charged that the United States "encourages and bears full responsibility" for two recent attacks on Soviet ships in Cuban ports by anti-Castro exile commandos.

The United States again responded that it was "taking every step necessary to insure that such attacks are not launched, manned, or equipped from U.S. territory." To make it stick, on April 5, the Coast Guard announced it was throwing more planes, ships, and men into its efforts to police the straits of Florida against the anti-Castro raiders.

Within hours, Bobby Kennedy unleashed a team to Miami, which would eventually number six-hundred federal agents——all in an effort to prevent further actions against the Castro regime.[7]

They were not intimidated, however, and the anti-Castro groups increased their activities. In April, an organization calling itself the Cuban Freedom Fighters reported bombing an oil refinery outside Havana. In May, the Cuban government confirmed that anti-Castro rebels had carried out a "pirate" raid on a militia camp near Havana, despite U.S. promises. This operation del Valle claims to have personally organized, once again utilizing No Name Key personnel.

Later that month, Kohly reported he had formed a military junta in Cuba to serve as the "provisional government of Cuba in arms." Shortly afterwards, a group of returning Cuban exile raiders claimed they had blown up a Cuban refinery, sunk a gunboat, and killed "many" of Castro's soldiers. It is not known exactly how many incidents took place during this period, but in the spring of 1963, Antonio Veciana asserted that the U.S. government knew of eleven raids on Cuba following the missile crisis.

At the same time, the pressure being exerted against the anti-Castro movement also caused considerable reaction from American right-wingers. They wanted to see the raids continue. Even the exile left became upset, provoking Miro Cardona to angrily resign as head of the former CIA-supported Cuban Revolutionary Council (CRC), accusing the United States of going back on its promise to support a new invasion. Cardona also charged that Kennedy had become "the victim of a master plan by the Russians."

To counter this move on Miro Cardona's part, Enrique Ruiz Williams, a Bay of Pigs leader and personal friend of Robert Kennedy, was trying to promote unity among Miami anti-Castro leaders, claiming he had a promise from the Attorney General of CIA arms and money for a new invasion from outside the United States—the same story Kohly told me.

Following Williams' lead, Kohly announced the formation of his United Organizations for the Liberation of Cuba (UOLC) on May 20. It numbered 150 exile leaders. Included was former Cuban president Carlos Prio Socarras.[8]

It too renounced plans for a U.S.-based military operation that—quoting Miro Cardona—had been developed with President Kennedy's authorization in 1962.

According to *The New York Times:*

> The declaration to fight for independence comes as exiles reported that a plan for anti-Castro action had emerged from conferences with United States Central Intelligence Agency agents. This action, exiles said, calls for guerrilla warfare, sabotage and infiltration of Dr. Castro's armed forces to be followed by an invasion or bombardment from an island near Cuba.

This invasion was the one Kohly said was to be mounted from Costa Rica in December of 1963. I would discover later that, like our counterfeiting operation, it would be totally funded by the underworld. And, contrary to what Tracy Barnes had claimed, it would not be approved by the administration.

However, with the increasing crackdown on anti-Castro activities by the Kennedy brothers, the feasibility of another invasion was becoming slimmer and slimmer. So, in desperation, the most militant members of the Cuban community would take action in the only way they could: they would join willingly in a Mafia conspiracy to murder the President.

Rolando Masferrer would be the financial conduit for Kohly's Miami exile groups and Mafia mercenaries from No Name Key, and David Ferrie for Kohly's exile groups at Lake Pontchartrain, Louisiana. The New Orleans branch of Kohly's CDM group, using the name "Bravo Club," was the team training along with Antonio Veciana's SNFE/Alfa 66.

Carlos Marcello, isolated on his six-thousand-acre Churchill Farms estate, could rely on David Ferrie and Guy Banister to carry out a plan to eliminate the Kennedys. Ferrie would be one of the principals to organize it. With his close association to the Cuban exile groups, through Sergio Arcacha Smith in New Orleans and Eladio del Valle in Miami, the brilliant pilot had been well aware of the CIA Castro hit teams recruited by Rolando Masferrer for Santos Trafficante.

Given the present mood of the exiles, Ferrie reasoned, along with the Cubans, that switching targets from one hated enemy, i.e., Fidel Castro, to John F. Kennedy, would be an easy task to accomplish. With that assumption, logic would dictate that the hit could also be made to appear that Castro, in seeking revenge for the CIA/Mafia attempts on his life, had ordered the presidential assassination.

It would then be an enraged U.S. populace that would demand an all-out invasion of Cuba and the overthrow of the Cuban premier. However, to perform all this chicanery, Castro would have to believe it was actually the Kennedy administration that was trying to kill him.

To execute the presidential hit, a series of teams would be chosen from CIA exile and mercenary groups from both Miami and New Orleans.

By April 1963, at the time Lee Harvey Oswald moved to New Orleans, the assassination planners had evolved their *modus operandi*. As they knew, the murder of a United States president could not resemble a standard syndicate killing. Such a dramatic undertaking should ideally be made to look like the work of a loner. Nevertheless, from a practical standpoint, this would be virtually impossible to accomplish. An operation involving only one gunman could not guarantee a sure kill. It would require a minimum of two, and an optimum of three firing sites—a massive operation and an impossible task to keep quiet.

The plan to make Castro believe that the Kennedys were out to kill him would require producing hard evidence to back it up. Trafficante could supply it. The Florida-based mobster—acting as a double agent—would arrange to inform Castro through an intermediary that the CIA, under presidential directive, had yet another assassination team after him. The Mafia chief would then send in a team of his own men to actually attempt to kill the Cuban dictator. These men, thinking they were really working for the CIA, would be caught and tortured, and would talk. As further evidence of their CIA affiliation, they would be equipped with assassination items readily identifiable with the clandestine agency.

Then, if past reactions of the Cuban leader were any indication, Castro, convinced the CIA was still out to get him, would make some kind of statement about getting even.

Trafficante's plan couldn't miss, and it didn't. As history would record, Castro believed that the U.S. was behind the attempts on his life. It came out on September 7, 1963. In an interview with Associated Press reporter Daniel Harker, Castro charged the United States with "aiding terrorist plans to eliminate Cuban leaders." Adding that "U.S. leaders could also be in danger if they promoted any attempt to eliminate the leaders of Cuba."

With the President dead, all that would be needed to pinpoint Castro as the instigator would be to provide massive amounts of data pointing to a Castro-affiliated gunman. To set up the lone gunman plan, it would be essential to find a patsy to fit the pattern, a person active in liberal political causes, not seemingly connected to any criminal organization.

The word went out to the Mafia families. As luck would have it, David Ferrie had the perfect man in Marcello's own back yard—Lee Harvey Oswald of New Orleans.

To implement the plan, Trafficante would again call upon Rolando Masferrer. He would be coordinator as well as payoff man for the hit teams. As for the bogus Castro assassination team, Trafficante would get Prio's former prime minister, Tony Verona, to arrange for it to go into Cuba. To legitimize the operation as a CIA one, Trafficante would have Roselli report to the Agency that Verona had dispatched another team into Cuba to kill Castro.[9]

To make sure the team was captured, Trafficante arranged to have a Cuban lawyer, who at one time represented the Capri Hotel and Casino in Havana, leak the information to the Cuban dictator. According to Kohly's good friend and associate, Eladio del Valle, his name was Carlos Garcia Bongo. Eladio del Valle, portrayed in the author's book *Betrayal* as Manuel Rodriguez, was introduced to the author in Cuba on the second day of the Bay of Pigs. Prior to his violent demise, del Valle was a principal source of information to the author about the inner workings of the exile groups and their close association with the Mafia.

Bongo would years later, in March 1965, admit to the CIA his representation of Trafficante. Subsequently, the Agency, either not knowing or not daring to disclose the full extent of Bongo's 1962 mission, gave out its own story. It simply said that Bongo identified himself to CIA personnel as a lawyer who represented the Capri Hotel and Casino in Havana. Bongo claimed he had been jailed in July 1962, for a period of seventy-five days, as a reprisal for representing Santos Trafficante.

The HSCA felt that Bongo's utilization of the short prison term to establish his "bona fides" was questionable. Since Trafficante had been in jail during August 1959, it seemed unlikely to the late House Select Committee on Assassinations that the Cuban government would wait three years to exact retribution for Bongo's representation of Trafficante.[10]

CHAPTER SEVEN NOTES

1.   Morrow, *Betrayal,* pp. 98-100.

2.   An admission made by presidential advisor Arthur M. Schlesinger in his book, *Robert Kennedy and His Times,* Houghton, Mifflin (paperback), pp. 562-565. It must be pointed out that Schlesinger's version puts the Kennedys in the best light. The reader can judge for himself.

3.   See Appendix, Exhibit No. 9, "U.S. Charge Bewilders Cuban Exile," Clark Mooenhoff, *Minneapolis Tribune* Staff Correspondent.

4.   *United States-Cuban Relations, 1960-1963: Neutrality Enforcement and the Cuban Exiles during the Kennedy Administration.* Congressional Research Service, Library of Congress. See Appendix, Exhibit No. 25

5.   Oscar del Valle Garcia Interview, April 16, 1983.

6.   HSCA, Vol. X, p. 13.

7.   HSCA, Vol. X, p. 58.

8.   See Appendix, Exhibit No. 10.

9.   HSCA, Vol. X, p. 177.

10.   HSCA, Vol. X, p. 184.

Chapter Eight

By the end of 1962, two disastrous decisions were made by the President and his brother. They had decided to dump Lyndon B. Johnson in the upcoming 1964 election and to force the resignation of J. Edgar Hoover as Director of the FBI. For the Texas Vice President, this was a bitter pill to swallow. Without the mantle of the vice presidency, he had an excellent chance of being indicted for political payoffs involving his former protege, whiz kid Bobby Baker.

Baker, known facetiously on Capitol Hill as the "101st senator" before his conviction in 1967 on seven counts of tax evasion, larceny, and conspiracy, had garnered for himself and Lyndon Johnson numerous ties to mob and Teamster enterprises in Texas, Nevada, and the Caribbean. That Johnson had a number of Mafia friends was apparent. When he was Senate Majority Leader, he had appeared as one of Cleveland mobster Moe Dalitz's guests of honor at the opening of his Stardust Hotel and Casino in Las Vegas.

Hoffa's ties to the Vice President became highly visible when the Teamsters' president, locked in battle with the Justice Department, had a number of Democrats from Johnson's wing of the party take the floor of the House and denounce Robert Kennedy for persecuting the Teamster leader. To make matters worse, one of the Vice President's intimate associates had gotten himself in a quagmire of trouble. He was Texas fertilizer king, Billie Sol Estes, whose investigation was spawning a rash of mysterious deaths, the following four people being killed under questionable circumstances:

1. Henry Marshall, shot to death while investigating Estes' acquisition of extensive cotton allotments.
2. George Krutilek, CPA, found dead of carbon monoxide

poisoning after undergoing secret interrogation by FBI agents investigating Estes' affairs.

3.   Harold Eugene Orr, president of an Amarillo, Texas, company, found dead of carbon monoxide poisoning; played a key role in Estes' finance frauds.

4.   Howard Pratt, Chicago office manager, Estes' fertilizer supplier, found dead of carbon monoxide poisoning.

In effect, Johnson's exploits and friendships with Baker, Hoffa, and Estes, would make the Texan completely vulnerable to FBI Director J. Edgar Hoover, who was no stranger to the power of the Lone Star State. His best friend was Texas oilman Clint Murchison, whose worldwide empire was second to none.

To Hoover, the thought of the Kennedy brothers forcing his resignation as head of the most powerful agency of the United States government was unthinkable. Yet, once their decision had been made, the thirty-five-year-old Attorney General did everything possible to intimidate the sixty-six-year-old Director—such as barging into his office unannounced, or summoning him to the Justice Department like a clerk, something no other Attorney General had ever done.

Then, to add insult to injury, Bobby Kennedy, either directly or through the men around him, started leaking derogatory stories about Hoover and the Bureau to an eager Washington press corps, creating a mythology that lasts to this day: Hoover had no interest in combating the Mafia; there were no Black FBI agents; there was no interest in enforcing civil rights statutes; and last but not least, that all agents assigned to the South were southerners.

Hoover was incensed. He had heard the rumors and Washington gossip. It was all over town. As William Hundley, head of the Justice Department's organized crime section in 1963 recalled:

> I am convinced that the thing that finally destroyed their relationship [Hoover and JFK's] was that Bobby mentioned to too many people, who complained to him about Hoover that, "Look, just wait," and we all got the message that they were going to retire him after Jack got re-elected and Hoover hit seventy. And it got back to him.

But Hoover would not be intimidated. He had survived administration after administration by having information on everybody. The Kennedys were no exception. The brothers, in his eyes, were both amoral and immoral, which, to him, was confirmed after learning the details of Bobby's intimate association with Marilyn Monroe and the President's involvement with Judith Exner, another girlfriend of Mafia boss Sam Giancana.

So, by the summer of 1963, the Kennedys were high on his blacklist. One of them had to go. It would not be J. Edgar Hoover. He theorized that the FBI was responsible for all of the country's internal security. As its patriarch, he was above the common law. Aligned with his powerful Texas friends, he could command a potent political force that would keep him as its director until he died, once the Kennedys were removed from office.

The way would then become clear for the FBI's Division Five to recapture the power it had been forced to surrender to the CIA in the domestic intelligence field. J. Edgar Hoover, named first director of the FBI in 1924, organized Division Five for espionage and counter-espionage work, an act which President Roosevelt made official in 1936. Actually, Division Five had unofficially been in existence as the General Intelligence Division of the Justice Department since 1919. After World War II, when the CIA took over all foreign espionage work, Division Five was limited to domestic activities. Once again, Hoover would be master of all the intelligence activities in the United States, now being flagrantly usurped by the Agency.

What he didn't know, however, was that William C. Sullivan, who was in charge of Division Five at the time of the President's assassination and in command of the original FBI investigation for the Warren Commission, was also a CIA informant. Sullivan's strange death just prior to testifying before the HSCA will be discussed later. Hoover knew the CIA was illegally conducting covert operations within the country, supposedly related to their overseas activities, and he was powerless to do anything about it, because the separation between foreign-oriented operations and those considered strictly domestic was vague and confusing. As a result, there was constant bureaucratic friction between the Agency and the Bureau.

In theory, compromises and working arrangements had been made to permit the CIA a certain operational latitude within the U.S. In return, special privileges abroad had been granted the FBI in the Agency's sphere of responsibility. In reality, the overall situation could most aptly be described as a standoff, with the odds slightly in Hoover's favor. This advantage was only because the Director was privy to some of the CIA's innermost secrets. One being the Mafia/CIA attempts against Castro, unearthed by the Bureau in May of 1962. Even if the President, Attorney General, and CIA Director John McCone didn't know about Richard Helms' ongoing attempts to kill Castro, Hoover did. The Bureau Director also knew about other illegal domestic activities in which the CIA was involved. One was a highly secret mail-opening program, ostensibly implemented for the purpose of gathering intelligence on Soviet intentions. At its inception, a number of former agents, suspected agents, defectors, and suspicious foreigners were placed on a "watch list," whose mail would be regularly opened. This list was soon broadened to include Americans—ones having absolutely no connection with a foreign power.

Because the mail-opening program was recognized as a clear violation of the law, a secret CIA memo was generated in 1962 on how it was to be handled if discovered by the administration. It read:

> Since no good purpose can be served by an official admission of the violation, and existing federal statutes preclude the concoction of any legal excuse for the violation . . . it is important that all federal law enforcement and U.S. intelligence agencies vigorously deny any association, direct or indirect, with any such activity if charged.[1]

The Agency also conjured up a number of cover stories in the event the word leaked out. Ironically, it was the Bureau that discovered the CIA program. It occurred when FBI officials approached the postal authorities to begin their own mail-opening operation. And, as with the CIA assassination attempts against Castro, CIA Director John McCone was never informed of the project.

With the uncovering of these illicit activities, Hoover, by February of 1963, was finally in a position to force an alliance on Helms, who then agreed to cover up any misdeeds of the Bureau if, reciprocally, no FBI information would be available on CIA mail-opening programs or Cuban assassination efforts. Evidence of this joint coverup on the part of the FBI and CIA was noted by the HSCA.[2]

For those desiring the termination of John and Robert Kennedy, this tenuous alliance between the FBI and CIA would be a gift sent from heaven, for by April of 1963, the spirit of the exiled Cubans, who had hoped to return to a liberated Cuba, had reached its nadir, after the administration, who for campaign favors had been openly subsidizing the leftist CRC, totally dropped the last of its assistance. This move, followed by the announcement of an even tougher policy by the Justice and State Departments against anti-Castro Cuban raiders such as Antonio Veciana, who were still mounting hit-and-run guerrilla attacks on Cuban and Russian targets, was the last straw. As a result, a dramatic shuffling of alliances between various Cuban exile groups occurred. Suddenly, Rolando Masferrer—since his original summons from Santos Trafficante to provide the Mafia chief with a cadre of hit men—had a wealth of Cuban exiles who would gladly see the President dead, including a number of groups in Miami and south Florida that had highly trained mercenaries— groups, like the one on No Name Key, which CIA man James O'Connell had once recommended to Colonel Sheffield Edwards and which included former employees of the Cuban syndicate. With this turn of events, Trafficante's hapless hit squad, which was to be captured and tortured into revealing that the CIA was again trying to kill Castro, was launched. Then, as planned, Tony Verona delivered the CIA poison pills to the unsuspecting team and shipped them off to Cuba to meet their unhappy demise. They would be captured, carrying the poison pills and high-powered rifles.

The action had started. It was time to activate the patsy, give him a high profile. The man was Lee Harvey Oswald. How Oswald got to be chosen is an interesting story and has a direct bearing on the assassination of Bobby Kennedy five years later.

Oswald had come to know Guy Banister through David Ferrie and the Civil Air Patrol. When the young ex-marine arrived back in New Orleans from the Soviet Union, Banister, through his CIA affiliations, found out that Oswald had been used by the clandestine Agency.

Although the CIA categorically denied any allegation that they had any involvement with Oswald because of his obvious ineptness,[3] a former Agency employee named James Wilcott, just after the assassination, claimed he was advised by fellow employees at a CIA post abroad that Oswald was a CIA agent who had received financial disbursements under an assigned cryptonym.[4] Needless to say, any files that could prove Oswald had any formal association with the Agency suddenly became non-existent.

In essence, the HSCA stated in their Final Report, that they could neither prove nor disprove that Oswald had any formal or informal ties to any government agency.

However, contradictory evidence surfaced outside of committee investigations. It started with Oswald's initial attempt to join the anti-Castro exile movement.

No Name Key mercenary Gerry Patrick Hemming told Florida reporter Bob Martin that, in 1959, Oswald, after leaving the Marine Corps, had been turned down as a member by Rolando Masferrer's group in Los Angeles. At that time, it was known as the Second National Front of the Escambre. By late 1962, it would have combined with Antonio Veciana's Alpha 66, calling itself SNFE/Alpha 66.

Oswald, or a deliberately planted twin, had been spotted in Los Angeles in late 1962 or early 1963. I found out about it on March 27, 1978, during a telephone interview with the well-known *Los Angeles Times* photographer Boris Yaro, who told me this interesting story:

> *YARO:*   Let me just throw something at you. O.K. In Monterey Park on . . . god, I've forgotten the goddamn date . . . either the early part of 1963 or the latter part of 1962, there was a big knock-down drag out brawl in a house, where shots were fired. Do you know about that?
>
> *MORROW:*   No.
>
> *YARO:*   In the city of Monterey Park, which is a suburb of Los Angeles, in the Valley, oh, about eight or nine miles from downtown L.A. . . . from the center of L.A.
>
> *MORROW:*   I don't know it.
>
> *YARO:*   No, no. Hear me out. Everybody that was . . . there were a lot of pictures made of the holes in the wall, in the furniture. And everybody that was arrested. You know, they were lined up . . . because nobody would point fingers at one another. Ostensibly, aside from the bunch of Cubans that were in this group, there was one gentleman by the name of Lee Harvey Oswald.

MORROW: Oh. I've heard about that.

YARO: I went back there in 1967, I think it was, or
. . . excuse me, no '67 . . . yeah, it could have
been '66, '67, somewhere in there, and tried to
find the negatives. And most of these departments
. . . Monterey Park's a little tiny place . . .
[change tape] There were four or five
negatives, because the photographer who
worked for them . . . a local newspaper type,
who was tied in with the police department
had, a radio in his car, and when they called
him, he could talk to them . . . he was a kind
of ex-officio cop, and, he has since died; but we
could not find the negatives of those people.
They're all gone.

MORROW: And he claimed that Oswald was there?

YARO: Somebody did. And I don't know how it was
. . . the boss that I worked for at the time,
said, get your ass over there and check it out.
And, I went over and checked it out and we
went through this thing, and he was just nice as
pie. Here they are, boom, and pulled them all
out. There was such an incident. It did occur
on such date. And, bingo, the negs are missing
and there's no sign-out form.

MORROW: And, this was in whose office?

YARO: This was in the Monterey Park Police
Department.

What can be described as the "real Lee Harvey Oswald" didn't surface
again publicly until August 9, 1963, when he would be arrested during a
scuffle while standing on the streets of New Orleans, handing out, not
anti-Castro but pro-Castro literature. The leaflets proclaimed the attributes
of the Fair Play for Cuba Committee and gave the address of the same

office-building housing Carlos Marcello's aide, Guy Banister, and the mobster's personal pilot, David Ferrie.[5] Just down the hall was another office used by a mobster associate of Santos Trafficante and Carlos Marcello named Eugene Hale Brading (a.k.a. Jim Braden), who would be arrested in Dealey Plaza minutes after the President's assassination.

Oswald had begun playing his role. The emergence of an Oswald double would enhance it.

However, the story actually began years before when David Ferrie took a fifteen-year-old Civil Air Patrol (CAP) cadet under his wing. The year was 1955, and Ferrie was the Captain of a CAP squadron.

Oswald was withdrawn and pretty much of a loner, according to all the sources the HSCA interviewed about that period in his life, the kind of boy that would immediately attract brilliant, homosexual David Ferrie. However, Ferrie denied meeting or even seeing Oswald during 1955, or for that matter anytime. Yet, a half-dozen or more witnesses put the two of them together during that era.[6]

Oswald was selected by Dave Ferrie to be the patsy for the JFK assassination. The young ex-marine had contacted him upon his arrival back in the U.S. from the Soviet Union. From this point on, they maintained contact.[7]

Then, when Oswald moved to New Orleans, he performed many services for Ferrie and his anti-Castro Cuban associates, one of which took him to Monterey, California, where he was identified during the internal shoot-out of the West Coast contingent of Alpha 66, described above by Boris Yaro and Gerry Patrick Hemming.

After the assassination, Ferrie, aside from his denials, couldn't escape some damning facts. Oswald's former landlady in New Orleans, Mrs. Jesse Garner, told the HSCA that David Ferrie visited her home on the night of the assassination and asked about Oswald's library card. Because of his manner, she refused to talk to him. A former neighbor of Oswald's, Mrs. Doris Eames, makes the same claim. She told New Orleans' district attorney investigators in 1968 that Ferrie had come by her house after the assassination, inquiring if Mrs. Eames had any information regarding Oswald's library card. Eames told Ferrie she had seen Oswald in the public library but had no other information about the library card Oswald used.[8]

Ferrie also talked with several former members of the Civil Air Patrol in an attempt to find out if any former cadet members recalled Lee Harvey Oswald being in Ferrie's squadron. Among those contacted was former cadet Roy McCoy, who told the FBI that Ferrie had come by looking for photographs of the cadets to see if Oswald was pictured in any photos of Ferrie's squadron.[9]

From the above evidence, it appears that Ferrie was quite concerned with this past affiliation. For he had been seen in the company of Oswald just a few months prior to the assassination. As the HSCA would report, in August or September of 1963, Dave Ferrie and a man known as Clay Shaw would be seen together with Oswald in Clinton, Louisiana:

> There were six Clinton witnesses who verified this story. Among them were a state representative, a deputy sheriff and a registrar of voters. By synthesizing the testimony of all of them, since they each contributed to the overall account, the HSCA was able to piece together the following sequence of events.
>
> Clinton, Louisiana, is about 130 miles from New Orleans, and the county seat of East Feliciana Parish. In the late summer of 1963 it was targeted by the Congress of Racial Equality for a voting rights campaign. Oswald first showed up in nearby Jackson, Louisiana, seeking employment at the East Louisiana State Hospital, a mental institution. Apparently on advice that his job would depend on his becoming a registered voter, Oswald went to Clinton for that purpose . . . the HSCA could find no record that he was successful.
>
> In addition to the physical descriptions they gave that matched that of Oswald, other observations of the witnesses tended to substantiate their belief that he was—in fact—the man they saw. For example, he referred to himself as "Oswald," and he produced his Marine Corps discharge papers as identification. Some of the witnesses said that Oswald was accompanied by two older men . . . whom they identified as David Ferrie and Clay Shaw. If the witnesses were not only truthful but accurate as well in their accounts, they established an association of an undetermined nature between Ferrie, Shaw and Oswald less . . . than three months before the assassination.
>
> The Committee found that the Clinton witnesses were credible and significant. They each were interviewed or deposed, or appeared before the Committee in executive session. While there were points that could be raised to call into question their credibility, it was the judgment of the Committee that they were telling the truth as they knew it.[10]

Oswald was not sighted from then until his arrest in New Orleans on August 9, 1963. The arrest was the result of a confrontation with Carlos Bringuier, the violent anti-Kennedy leader of the New Orleans branch of the Student Revolutionary Directorate (DRE). Bringuier and two of his associates, Miguel Cruz and Celso Hernandez, saw Oswald handing out pro-Castro leaflets and approached him. When Hernandez tried to take the leaflets from Oswald, a shouting match began, and the New Orleans police intervened, arresting all of them.

As he had done in 1959, trying to join the SNFE in Los Angeles, Oswald had earlier approached Bringuier, offering to help train his anti-Castro Cubans in paramilitary operations. Oswald's offer—directly conflicting with his "pro-Castro" activities during that same period—has never been explained.

The three Cubans were set free, and Oswald was detained. He obtained his release only after supposedly talking to an FBI agent. The truth, however, is a somewhat different story. It was Carlos Marcello's top lieutenant, Nofio Pecora, who provided bail for Oswald's release.[11] If in fact Oswald was a pro-Castro sympathizer, why would the Mafia chieftain want to bail him out of jail.

Based on the Clinton sighting, the above event, and several other incidents that would later be attributed to Oswald, the only logical conclusion one can arrive at is: Oswald was unknowingly being set up as a patsy, or he was enacting a part in a carefully prepared scenario, orchestrated by David Ferrie and Guy Banister.

The Oswald sightings subsided until approximately six weeks prior to the assassination, when—judging from the number of reports contained in the twenty-six volumes of the Warren Commission Report—it became apparent that one or more persons started to impersonate Lee Harvey Oswald. During the post-murder investigation by the FBI, a number of individuals came forward to tell of their encounters with the man who had been charged with the assassination. Most of the stories could not have involved Oswald and were incriminating to him.

The man or men claiming to be Oswald were trying to attract attention, repeating the name Oswald several times, as if he or they wanted it to be remembered. In addition, several of the incidents clearly indicated that someone was trying to create the image of a man who could and did plan to kill the President.

Because these stories are well documented, there is no need to elaborate on them in this manuscript. However, due to the January 1987 fire-bombing of the Dupont Plaza Hotel in San Juan, Puerto Rico, by a member of the Teamsters Union, the following story may be pertinent.

Leopoldo Ramos Ducos, a former associate of Jimmy Hoffa's in 1962, was appointed a high-level official of the Teamsters Union in Puerto Rico. Hoffa's men had taken control of the independent Hotel and Restaurant Workers Union in San Juan following the fire-bombing and subsequent demolishing of the independent union's headquarters in February of that year. An FBI report of December 2, 1963, disclosed that one Leopoldo Ramos Ducos had informed the Bureau that the secretary-treasurer of the San Juan Teamsters, Maria del Valle, had told him on November 26, 1963, that another Puerto Rican Teamster official had said to her: "We killed Kennedy and the next will be Ramos Ducos." Maria del Valle identified Teamster organizer, Miguel Cruz, as the person who made the strange statement. When the FBI interviewed del Valle about the allegation, she confirmed that Cruz had indeed made the threat "at about five o'clock p.m.," on the day of the assassination.

Neither the CIA nor FBI would bother checking to see if Miguel Cruz, teamster organizer, and Miguel Cruz, anti-Castro exile who had the confrontation with Lee Harvey Oswald in New Orleans, were one and the same.

Lee Harvey Oswald, selected by David Ferrie, having known and worked with the anti-Castro Cubans, was the perfect patsy. The Oswald impersonator(s) had done their jobs well. He or they left a public image of a man who was loud and arrogant, had defected to Russia, would soon come into a large sum of money, and displayed expert marksmanship while practicing at local rifle ranges.

But the move that would tie Oswald irrevocably into the anti-Castro Cubans was an incident where a man—strongly resembling Oswald—was seen in Sulphur, Oklahoma, five days before the assassination. With him was Manuel Rodriguez Quesada, another violent anti-Kennedy, anti-Castro exile,[12] and president of the Dallas contingent of SNFE/Apha 66/30th of November Movement. It was the same organization referred to in Monterey, California by Gerry Patrick Hemming and Boris Yaro, of the *Los Angeles Times,* who described the incident where Oswald was seen at a shoot-out in 1962.

On the evening of November 22, Dallas Deputy Sheriff Buddy Walthers submitted a report stating that Oswald had attended meetings at the group's 3126 Harlandale Street address.[13] According to Walthers, the Cubans staying there evacuated the premises sometime between November 15 and November 23, 1963.[14]

In June 1963, when the combined Alpha 66/SNFE/30th of November group was training in New Orleans, Mario Kohly was actively getting ready for his second invasion of Cuba in December. I had no idea at the time why Kohly thought another exile invasion could be mounted so soon. However, as it had been explained to me earlier, to make it work, a second major peso counterfeiting operation under my direction was to be completed by October 1, in order to buy off Castro's top military aides prior to the landing.

Accordingly, on October 1, 1963, the counterfeit Cuban plates were delivered to Kohly in New York. This operation called for the manufacture of approximately fifty-million dollars worth of the counterfeit pesos by the middle of November. The plan, once Castro was overthrown, with Carlos Prio Socarras installed as prime minister and Kohly as president, was that they would legalize the bogus currency. Understandably, it was a temptation that few of Castro's ill-paid followers could resist. However, had I known the operation was totally funded by the Mafia and possibly included a presidential murder, I would never have finished the project.

In this tumultuous atmosphere in the fall of 1963, two more ironic twists of fate occurred. After the abortive attack on Castro, engineered by Rolando Masferrer and Tony Verona for Santos Trafficante, the CIA, this time without the aid of their Mafia allies, again decided to renew their efforts to assassinate Fidel Castro. The operation involved a high Castro official named Dr. Rolando Cubelo (code name AMLASH)[15] and Bay of Pigs leader Manuel Artime. Cubelo had been a close personal friend of Castro and a commander of his army. In a meeting with case officers of the CIA in Brazil in 1961, Cubelo expressed his growing disapproval of his former friend and offered to defect and provide intelligence information to the U.S. The case officers convinced him to stay inside Cuba and provide intelligence. He agreed. Two years later he contacted the CIA. Cubelo's offer was not to provide intelligence information. Instead, he offered to assassinate the Cuban premier. The information was immediately conveyed to CIA headquarters in Langley, on September 7, 1963, to Desmond Fitzgerald's Special Affairs Staff (SAS). But there was a delay. James Angleton, Chief of Counterintelligence, suspected Cubelo of being a double agent. Therefore, the operation was not discussed until September 12, at a meeting attended by Robert Kennedy, General Maxwell Taylor,

CIA director John McCone, Lyman Lemnitzer of the Joint Chiefs, McGeorge Bundy (National Security Advisor to the President), and Roswell Gilpatric (Undersecretary of Defense).

Bobby supposedly put a veto on it. Then he set the wheels in motion to stop the exiles in their last major effort to regain their homeland. On October 1, 1963, Robert Kennedy, issuing instructions from the White House, ordered the arrest of Mario Garcia Kohly and me for conspiracy to counterfeit foreign securities and a host of other related charges.[16]

With our arrest, the Kennedy brothers had once again thwarted Kohly's conservatives from taking over Cuba, by destroying their last chance of having a successful invasion.

Then, in mid-October of 1963, without the knowledge of the President, the Attorney General, or the Director of the CIA, Richard Helms gave the go-ahead for Cubelo's assassination attempt.[17]

Then a snag occurred.

At the end of October, Cubelo made a demand of the CIA. Before he would go ahead with the plan to eliminate Castro, he wanted some sort of personal assurance or signal from the Attorney General that the administration would actively support him. Again overruling objections by James Angleton, CIA SAS chief Desmond Fitzgerald would deliberately perpetrate a fraud. He would meet with Cubelo as Bobby's personal representative.

Fitzgerald knew it would work. Although he would not use his real name, he was a well-known figure in Washington and readily identifiable. The meeting took place on October 29, 1963, with Fitzgerald assuring Cubelo that, once the coup had succeeded, the Kennedy administration would be fully prepared to aid and support a new government friendly to the U.S.

Cubelo, totally deceived, asked for delivery of specific weapons—a rifle with telescopic sight and a means to deliver poison without detection. But, at that meeting, Fitzgerald claimed he refused to discuss such specifics. He wanted Cubelo to be assured that the President himself was involved. Fitzgerald didn't want Cubelo to back out once he had started, in the event he heard from other exiles that, in reality, just the opposite was the case as far as the President was concerned.

Fitzgerald's testimony before the Senate Select Committee of that meeting is in total conflict with Cubelo's case officer. The case officer, who was also the interpreter for Fitzgerald, testified that Fitzgerald gave assurances that the U.S. not only would support the government which emerged after a successful coup, but also gave assurances that the U.S. would help in bringing about this coup. The case officer recalled no discussion that the U.S. would have no part in assassination.[18]

So, without his knowledge, Fitzgerald would involve the President in the plot. He told Cubelo he was arranging a further administrative signal, specifically for Cubelo and his followers in Cuba. Cubelo was told by Fitzgerald that he had personally written a section of the speech President Kennedy was to deliver in Miami on November 18. It described the Castro government as a "small band of conspirators" that, "once removed," would ensure United States' assistance to the Cuban nation. This passage was to be the "signal to proceed."

According to Arthur M. Schlesinger, Jr.,[19] the speech was mainly written by Richard Goodwin. How Fitzgerald or the CIA got a copy beforehand remains a mystery.

Such a sanction by the Kennedy administration would mean a 180-degree switch in policy.

The day after the President delivered this speech, Fitzgerald ordered Cubelo's case officer to arrange another meeting with him—a meeting in which specifics would be discussed. Cubelo agreed to postpone his return to Cuba if the meeting could be held that week in Paris. The date agreed upon was November 22.

November 22, 1963, was just over a month and a half since Kohly and I had been arrested by the Secret Service on the direct orders of the Attorney General. Subsequent to our arrest, Bobby Kennedy's close personal friend and advisor, Henry Morgenthau, Jr., the U.S. attorney for the Southern District of New York, had been making life miserable for the Cuban exile leader.

I was finally told by my CIA case officer, after our arrest, that the President and Attorney General had gone back on their promise to the exiles to help mount another invasion from outside the U.S. It made sense. Since the Kennedys knew that most of the missiles in Cuba were still nestled safe and sound in their hard sites, they could not let an exile invasion expose them to be liars.

For the Kennedys, getting rid of Kohly was a brilliant ploy. It eliminated a man the Attorney General hated, and yes, even feared. Kohly knew too much about the missiles in Cuba and could not be shut up.[20] He had to be discredited as a common criminal. It was the administration's ultimate act to get rid of the moderate to right-wing, anti-Castro organizations. So, by November 22, 1963, there was no further hope that exiles—supporting the 1940 Cuban constitution—could ever again regain control of their homeland or that the CIA would expose the continuing presence of Cuban missiles.

Until 12:30 p.m. CST, in Dallas, Texas.

By one o'clock, the President was pronounced dead. Both Lyndon Johnson and J. Edgar Hoover would be safe from the threat the Attorney General and President had presented. And Richard Helms was relieved, for a massive governmental conspiracy could be safely instituted covering up their misdeeds and prevent anyone from discovering who had really killed the President. It would be a story of intrigue and murder, culminating five years later in a second assassination.

CHAPTER EIGHT NOTES

1.   *Final Report of the Select Committee to Study Governmental Relations with Respect to Intelligence Activities, United States Senate, Supplementary Detailed Staff Reports on Intelligence Activities and the Rights of Americans,* Book III: "Domestic CIA and FBI Mail Opening," p. 609 (Washington, D.C.: U.S. Government Printing Office, 1976).

2.   HSCA Final Report, p. 135.

3.   HSCA Final Report, p. 249.

4.   *Ibid.,* p. 250.

5.   HSCA, Vol. X, pp. 123-124.

6.   HSCA, Vol. IX, pp. 103-115.

7.   In 1961, this author had a long conversation with his case officer Tracy Barnes about "Harvey," an ex-marine who had worked with Clay Shaw and the Guy Banister organization. "Harvey" was Lee Harvey Oswald. (*Betrayal,* Regnery, 1976, pp. 94-97.)

8.   HSCA, Vol. X, pp. 113-114.

9.   *Ibid.*

10.   HSCA Final Report, p. 170.

11.   WCV IXX, p. 44; WCV XXII, p. 504.

12.   WCD 1085U. He was also known as Carlos Rodriguez Quesada.

13.   WCV XIX, H534.

14.   *Ibid.*

15.   *Senate Intelligence Committee Report on Foreign Assassinations,* pp. 89-90.

16.   *The New York Times,* October 2, 1963.

17. *Senate Select Committee, Final Report: The Investigation of the Assassination of the President of the United States,* p. 17n.

18. *Ibid.,* p. 18.

19. *Robert Kennedy and His Times,* Ballantine, p. 598n.

20. See Appendix, Exhibit No. 10.

Chapter Nine

The question that has persisted up until this day is: why would the FBI, on the eve of the assassination, declare Lee Harvey Oswald the presidential murderer?

It is a mystery that can now be answered, and was brought about by an extreme emergency occurring between the FBI and the CIA. First, as noted earlier, J. Edgar Hoover did not know that his Assistant Director, chief of domestic intelligence operations William Sullivan, was covertly passing FBI information[1] to CIA support chief Colonel Sheffield Edwards. This in itself was bad enough; however, the most damning thing was that Sullivan also processed requests from the Agency.

So, when Oswald was being picked up as the President's assassin, it had to send Sullivan scurrying to the Agency for help. For it was under Sullivan's direct orders that the Bureau had struck Lee Harvey Oswald's name from their security-risk lists. This request—for Sullivan to delete Oswald's name—had come directly from Tracy Barnes, Sullivan's FBI counterpart, who headed the CIA's super-secret Domestic Division. From what I learned subsequently from Tiny Hutton, former Deputy Director of the House Select Committee on Assassinations, Oswald was being used by the CIA and CIA-affiliated personnel in New Orleans associated with the Mafia. Therefore, one can only assume Barnes had gotten his orders to request Sullivan to make the deletion directly from DDP Richard Helms. I was originally told the story by Washington attorney Marshall Diggs; and I asked my former case officer, Tracy Barnes, about it in February 1964, when I was asked to meet Mario Kohly by the Secret Service. Barnes would not admit it, but his smile after I asked the question was confirmation enough.

To furthur substantiate it, there were at least two disclosures in 1976

95

that indicated that the CIA may at one time have recruited Oswald for some unknown purpose. On October 1, 1976, the Associated Press disclosed a previously classified CIA memorandum that noted that several Agency officials "showed intelligence interest" in Lee Oswald sometime in 1960, and discussed the laying on of interviews. The November 25, 1963, CIA document furthur noted that the Agency had considered using Oswald for several purposes, including to "help develop [foreign] personality dossiers." The startling CIA document directly contradicts the sworn testimony of Richard Helms, who in his May 1964 Warren Commission testimony, claimed, "there's no material in the Central Intelligence Agency, either in the records or in the mind of any of the individuals that there was any contact had or even contemplated with" Lee Harvey Oswald.

So much for the credibility of Richard Helms.

Thus, Helms, honoring his alliance with the Bureau Chief (reached when Hoover discovered the Mafia/CIA attempts against Castro and the Agency's mail-opening program), would contact and warn the FBI Director about the Bureau deletion immediately upon Oswald's arrest.

The security-list deletion wouldn't be discovered until December 10, three weeks after the assassination. It was found by another FBI assistant director, H.H. Gale, who had been ordered by Hoover to investigate the deficiencies in the Oswald case. Gale reported that Oswald should have been on the Security Index; his wife should have been interviewed before the assassination; and, most certainly, the investigation should have been intensified after Oswald had contacted the Soviet Embassy in Mexico.

Sullivan knew that Hoover would not only be livid, but that the Bureau Director would also be personally forced to cover it up—to whitewash Sullivan's misdeed if it were discovered. The easiest and most propitious solution was to instantly declare Oswald the assassin.

In order to cover himself, Sullivan, who was now suffering the wrath of Hoover, authored a secret FBI memo circulated only twelve days after Kennedy's death. The memo stated there was no evidence linking Lee Harvey Oswald to pro-Castro organizations or people or to any foreign country. How this information was arrived at by the Bureau can only be speculated on. It would help substantiate Hoover's claim that Oswald was a lone gunman.

Sullivan, head of the Bureau's Division Five, had charge of domestic counterintelligence, including sabotage, espionage, and subversion, at the time JFK was assassinated. In 1977, Washington journalists David Wise and Thomas Ross wrote, "the actual field action of counter-espionage work is conducted by the FBI's hush-hush Division Five." Other journalists have suggested that Sullivan's division was also unofficially in charge of black bag, bugging, and other dirty operation jobs, including assassination. Sullivan's strange and violent death coincided with his being called to testify before the newly formed House Select Committee on Assassinations. They were getting ready to focus on any potential CIA and FBI involvement in the Kennedy murder.[2]

The former number-three man in the Bureau and head of Division Five, who had been in charge of the FBI efforts in the original Warren Commission investigation, was shot to death while hunting in northern New Hampshire on November 9, 1977.

The official reports state that another hunter, a man identified as twenty-two-year-old Robert Daniels, shot Sullivan in the neck from a distance of 243 feet. The weapon used was a .30/06 rifle equipped with a telescopic sight. Daniels claimed that he thought Sullivan was a deer.

Sullivan, reports claim, was standing in an open field at the time. According to initial reports, Daniels was charged with a misdemeanor known as "shooting a human being" by accident. He was released into his father's custody. The senior Daniels was a New Hampshire state policeman. Daniels pleaded *nolo contendre* (no contest) to the charge. His sentencing was postponed.

Verification of Sullivan's being called to testify before the House Select Committee on Assassinations came from his attorney, Joseph Casey, of Washington, D.C.

Then, just two days after Sullivan's death, a man identifying himself as an investigator for the Committee showed up at Sullivan's home to collect the late FBI official's files and papers. Gary Young, police chief of Sugar Hill, New Hampshire, Sullivan's home town, said that "a man identifying himself as Clifford A. Fenton, Jr., a House Committee investigator, tried to obtain Mr. Sullivan's papers two days after his death." In Washington, a spokesperson for the HSCA admitted there was an investigator named Clifford A. Fenton, Jr., on the staff, but would neither confirm nor deny any visit to New Hampshire or any information about Sullivan's role as a witness.

Sullivan's death came just before the release of the JFK/FBI documents, and supposedly he was the one man from the Bureau who could have filled in many of the blanks so prevalent throughout them. Sullivan had initially told the HSCA that he became disenchanted with operations after Hoover had told him personally, "I am most concerned about having something issued so we can convince the public that Lee Harvey Oswald is the real assassin."

Hoover's decision to hide the truth about Lee Harvey Oswald and make him the lone deranged gunman, was one that would plague him throughout the Warren Commission investigation. It would also come close to destroying the Bureau thirteen years later, as a result of a Senate Select Committee investigation.

The HSCA discovered that Hoover had directed his trusted aide and old friend Clyde Tolson to give special instructions to the Dallas and New Orleans field officers: "Destroy anything that could be embarrassing to the Bureau." It was a statement heard before in the FBI. After receiving his call from Clyde Tolson, Ken Maynard, special-agent-in-charge of the New Orleans FBI office, was faced with two problems. The first was with Warren deBrueys, an agent he had assigned to report on the various political groups in the New Orleans area (primarily the anti-Castro exiles). DeBrueys had an informant named Orest Pena,[3] who was active in the anti-Castro exile community in New Orleans[4] and had worked closely with Mafia Chief Carlos Marcello's associates, Dave Ferrie and exile leader Sergio Arcacha Smith,[5] the former New Orleans director of the Cuban Revolutionary Council (CRC) during the Bay of Pigs. Maynard knew from a deBrueys' report that Pena could claim that Special Agent Warren deBrueys had been involved with Lee Harvey Oswald.

The second problem also involved Pena. Because Pena was a known associate of Dave Ferrie, and indirectly of Guy Banister, he could also be indirectly associated with underworld kingpin Carlos Marcello. And Marcello, as everyone in the Bureau knew, had threatened to have the President killed. Also, for the past year, the New Orleans Special Agent had been Regis Kennedy, who was directly responsible to Bureau headquarters for reports on organized crime. Kennedy had said there was no organized crime in New Orleans.[6] As far as Regis Kennedy was concerned, Marcello was a simple tomato and real-estate salesman.[7]

In effect, Maynard's office had been generating inane reports on the New Orleans Mafia don. So deBrueys was told to shut Pena up about Ferrie, Oswald, Banister, and Marcello. He did. However, Pena did finally talk, thirteen years later, when he charged deBrueys with threatening his life in order to force him to lie to the Warren Commission.

In a CBS interview broadcast on November 26, 1975, on a program entitled "The Assassins," Pena claimed that about ten days before he went to testify before the Warren Commission, deBrueys came over, called him from behind the bar, and said, "If you ever say anything about me . . . , I will get rid of your ass." Just in those words.

Also in New Orleans, the name of David Ferrie surfaced as a man who might have aided Oswald in the killing of the President. It surfaced in the office of District Attorney James Garrison. A former friend of Ferrie's by the name of Jack S. Martin told the DA's office that he suspected Ferrie might have known Oswald a long time and that Ferrie might once have been Oswald's superior officer in the Civil Air Patrol. Three days later, Martin told the FBI he thought he saw a photograph of Oswald and other CAP members in Ferrie's home, and that Ferrie might have assisted Oswald in purchasing a high-powered rifle. Neither the DA's office nor the FBI took it seriously. It would be another mistake.

*   *   *   *   *

In Langley, Virginia, Richard Helms had problems, other than the one created by Tracy Barnes through the Bureau. It occurred two days after the President was shot. Case officers in Desmond Fitzgerald's SAS division were notified that James Angleton, chief of counterintelligence, had ordered his staff to put out a request for information on aspiring CIA assassin, Rolando Cubelo. A cable requesting this information was then sent to each CIA station in Europe and Canada.

There was immediate alarm. Fitzgerald knew that, just a few weeks before the assassination, Cubelo had received his infamous signal that Kennedy would back his plan to eliminate Castro. Now, James Angleton wanted to know about this man. Should he provide the operational file on Cubelo, listing his contacts with the CIA, his involvement in a plan to murder Castro, and the allegation that he might be "insecure" or even a double agent? Such operational files were always kept by the division handling the agent. Fitzgerald took the problem to Richard Helms. After some consideration and consultation, the SAS chief was ordered by Helms not to provide the operational file on Cubelo to Angleton or any of his staff. This left Angleton only with Cubelo's "201" dossier, which contained nothing but overt biographical data. In addition, Fitzgerald ordered the case officer, who had met with Cubelo on November 22, to omit from his report any mention of the poison to be used to kill Castro.

Helms acted quickly; the cable and all the references to the assassination plots against Castro disappeared from Cubelo's files.

It would become obvious that Helms never replaced the cable and assassination information, for none of the documents remaining made any reference to assassination or poison pens. As a matter of historical interest, the text of the 11/24/63 cable never surfaced until 1975, when it was quoted in the Senate Select Committee Final Report.[8]

Since this information was not turned over in 1963-64 to Angleton's staff, which was to serve as the liaison between the CIA and the Warren Commission, none of this would be known to the investigators of the Kennedy assassination. Had routine Agency procedure been followed, Cubelo's file would normally have disclosed operational information, such as the details of his plot to assassinate Castro and his connections with Manuel Artime, former brigade leader of the ill-fated Bay of Pigs troops.

So the FBI and CIA cover-up would deepen, and the assassination data would become buried, along with any information linking anti-Castro Cubans with organized crime. As a result, Helms and Hoover would protect Masferrer and his Mafia associates from discovery. The result: Warren Commission files would contain no evidence that any such information ever existed.

On Sunday, November 24, 1963, at 10:00 a.m., two hours and twenty minutes before Jack Ruby gunned down Oswald, CIA Director John McCone was in the White House briefing Lyndon Johnson about the Agency's operational plans against Cuba. He said nothing to the President about Rolando Cubelo or the CIA/Mafia's abortive attempts to assassinate Fidel Castro. In sworn testimony before the Senate Select Committee in 1976, McCone claimed that in 1963 he was not aware of the plots.[9]

Thus, Richard Helms, Deputy Director of Plans for the CIA, would deliberately withhold critical information from his own superior and, most importantly, from the President of the United States—an act that could be considered tantamount to treason.

However, Helms' problems regarding Cubelo did not end there. The day following the removal of Cubelo's incriminating files, he had another fire to put out. Additional disturbing information was received from overseas as a result of Angleton's cable request. It was from a European station, stating that information from a sensitive and reliable source indicated that Cubelo was "involved" in the President's assassination. Once more, Rolando Cubelo's name had surfaced, all in the space of four days.

This was just what Helms needed: another reference to an undercover CIA assassin affiliated with the anti-Castro movement, one that nobody knew existed—not the new president, not the Director of the CIA, and not

Bobby Kennedy, still the Attorney General. Helms knew, if it were discovered by Bobby, the young Attorney General would still have the leverage he needed to destroy the Company.

Couple that with the fact that the Agency could also be blackmailed at any time by members of the Mafia, and the Deputy Director was sitting on a keg of dynamite. So, along with all the other controversial material before it, any reference to the Cubelo cable would also disappear via the Deputy Director of Plans.

As for Hoover, Helms felt the FBI Director couldn't act fast enough to declare Oswald the lone deranged gunman. And, like Hoover, he was finding the situation more and more difficult to contain. For, during the early period of 1964, as he and Hoover were continuing to cover their tracks and the Warren Commission (with no evidence to the contrary) was beginning to take the heat off Cuba and the exiles, a red herring appeared out of the Kremlin woodwork. His name was Yuri Ivanovich Nosenko. Two years earlier, in Geneva, Switzerland, during a joint seventeen-nation disarmament conference in June of 1962, Nosenko contacted the CIA, offering his services as an agent when he returned home. Nosenko, who purported himself to be a member of the KGB, had his offer accepted and was given a code to identify himself when he wished to start operations. However, after months had passed and no coded signal arrived, the CIA assumed Nosenko had either been discovered and quietly assassinated or for some other reason had gotten cold feet.

Then, on January 20, 1964, just two months after the President was murdered, Nosenko sent the coded message. Two days later, the CIA shipped Nosenko's original case officer back to Geneva to meet him. What Nosenko told that case officer would start an intriguing battle inside the CIA. It was one that would last for a decade and help increase the mystery surrounding Lee Harvey Oswald.

Nosenko told a story that was nothing short of a modern-day fairy tale, that after months of indecision, he finally decided to defect, leaving his family in Russia to fend for themselves. Equally unreal, he claimed he had personally superintended the KGB file on Lee Harvey Oswald and in fact had brought it with him. If that was not mind-boggling enough, the story he told about Oswald was, because it was totally contrary to what the CIA knew about the KGB.

Nosenko claimed that, after Oswald had arrived in Russia, he was—in the words of Soviet intelligence—not worth debriefing. Equally absurd was Nosenko's claim that the KGB's First Chief Directorate, responsible for all foreign operations and espionage, did not have Oswald's name on file until Oswald contacted the Soviet embassy in Mexico City, in October 1963.

That blockbusting bit of news was incomprehensible to the case officer. But, if true, it would be a gift sent from heaven for both Helms and Hoover, for Nosenko could provide the newly convened Warren Commission with a perfect profile of an unstable, disenchanted, lone deranged gunman—exactly the same profile Hoover had given to President Johnson.

Helms, however, saw Nosenko as a fraud and, not desiring to give the FBI any ammunition that could backfire on the CIA, wanted to keep the potentially dangerous KGB agent in Geneva. That way he would be working for the Agency as an informant inside the KGB. Unfortunately, Nosenko wouldn't buy it. So, against his will, Helms ordered Nosenko to the States.

Nosenko's story also did not inspire instant confidence in other high-ranking officials of the Central Intelligence Agency. One of them was the man Richard Helms had kept in the dark about Rolando Cubelo, CIA Chief of Counterintelligence, James Angleton. Angleton didn't believe Nosenko's story any more than Nosenko's case officer. Then, in February 1964, after reading a nine-hundred-page report prepared by the CIA's Russia Division, he became even more concerned. So much in fact that he secretly told his friend Bobby Kennedy about his own doubts concerning the Russian defector.

Ironically, the Russia Division's report had concluded what both he and Helms independently suspected—Nosenko was a Soviet plant sent to the U.S. to disseminate misinformation about Oswald to the CIA, FBI, and Warren Commission. After reviewing the matter, Bobby asked Angleton to discreetly pursue it.

Angleton then asked Helms for permission to take over the CIA's investigation of the Oswald/Nosenko allegation. Helms, possibly not knowing of Angleton's doubts regarding Nosenko or his relationship with Bobby Kennedy, told him to go ahead. Richard Helms had made his first major mistake. But it was an honest one.

Later, when Helms heard about Angleton's doubts regarding Nosenko's credibility and quite aware of his close friendship with Bobby Kennedy, he immediately became alarmed. The CIA Deputy Director of Plans knew only too well that a negative resulting investigation regarding Nosenko could open up a Cuban pandora's box. One, uncovering the fact that the Mafia/CIA assassination attempts were still going on against Fidel Castro and, by extrapolation, that Mafia/CIA elements could have been involved in killing the President of the United States.

Helms' dilemma: if Nosenko's story could be made credible, the pressure would be off the Agency from the Warren Commission, and Oswald's CIA 201 file (which now contained a copy of Nosenko's KGB report on Oswald) would come to light, showing him to be deranged. It was a sticky situation, for Helms, against his better judgment, was literally stuck with validating Nosenko. It was an incongruous situation: When Nosenko lied, both he and Hoover would have to swear to it.

To insure Nosenko's compliance, Helms took desperate measures. In a December 6, 1978, letter to Louis Stokes, final chairman of the HSCA, one of the committee members, Harold S. Sawyer, stated:

> A further comment on agency performance is in order on the Yuri Nosenko (the KGB defector) episode. The taking into custody of Mr. Nosenko within the State of Virginia without resort to a court and only under the most tenuous color of authority was itself surprising. The then building of a special cell described as a "vault" by the CIA themselves and holding him there in solitary confinement subjected to continuous mental, psychological, and actual physical torture for a period of over 3 years would have been absolutely unbelievable had not the CIA themselves together with its Director, Richard Helms, fully and in horrible detail admitted it. Mr. Nosenko was paid off with a six-figure cash settlement and apparently a life-time "consulting" stipend of about $35,000 per year all surreptitiously with taxpayers' funds, as opposed to either killing him or destroying his brain with a drug ministration which were alternatives that were considered. I believe there is a need for the availability of criminal prosecution to prevent this intolerable type conduct by agencies of the U.S. Government.[10]

As can be seen from the above statement, Nosenko's ordeal would continue for several years. All in a day's work for the clandestine agency.

But back to 1964. For Helms and Hoover, the worst was yet to come. By this time, the Warren Commission was beginning to have serious doubts about the FBI's motive in wanting to terminate the assassination investigation and the CIA's reluctance to give them any information. It happened when Texas Attorney General Waggoner Carr claimed he knew for a fact that Lee Harvey Oswald was recruited as an informer for the FBI. Also, according to Carr, Oswald was assigned informer number S-179 in September of 1962 and was being paid $200 a month.

This allegation came just three days after Earl Warren told the Commission that "President Johnson's fear of wild rumors was the reason why he accepted the Commission chairmanship." The top-secret transcript of the January 27, 1964, meeting (declassified in late 1974) reveals how Commission General Counsel J. Lee Rankin informed Earl Warren about the Carr allegation.

> I called the Chief Justice immediately and went over and told him the story . . . , and it was the consensus of the meeting that we should try to get those people up here, including District Attorney Wade, the Texas Attorney General, Waggoner Carr, Special Counsels to the Attorney General Leon Jaworski and Bob Storey, and Mr. Alexander, the Assistant District Attorney in Dallas.
>
> We asked them to all come up, and they did on Friday. At that time they were—they said the rumors were constant there [in Dallas] that Oswald was an undercover agent, but they extended it also to the CIA saying that they [the CIA] had a number assigned to him connecting [Oswald] with the CIA, and gave that to him, and none of them had any original information of their own.[11]

The Commission's choice was: having the public reject Hoover's word that Oswald was not an informer or incurring the Director's wrath if they tried to conduct an independent investigation. Rankin, knowing the ramifications, told the Commission members at the same January 27, 1964, session:

> It is going to be very difficult for us to be able to establish the facts in it. I am confident that the FBI would never admit it, and I presume the [FBI] records will never show it, or if the records do show anything, I would think their records would show some kind of a number that could be assigned to a dozen different people according to how they want to describe them. So that it seemed to me if it's really happened, he [Oswald] did use postal boxes practically every place that he went, and that

would be an ideal way to get money to anyone that you wanted as an undercover agent, or anybody else that you wanted to do business that way without having [known about] any particular transaction.[12]

The transcript of the January 27, 1964, Warren Commission session leaves one with the impression that the Commission members seemed terrified of the FBI Director. For two hours they discussed possible ways of asking Hoover about the informant rumor without upsetting him. Then they spent four months debating on how to approach Hoover for a disclaimer, one that would convince the public. They decided that a formal denial from the Bureau would not suffice, after being told by former CIA Director and Commission member Allen Dulles that Hoover would probably lie under oath, if Oswald was in fact an informer.

Dulles confided that, during his tenure as CIA Director, he would have also lied under oath to anyone except the President if, in his opinion, he thought it was in the interest of the nation or the Agency. It was a policy that Richard Helms was using on his own. However, Helms went one step further: he would even exclude telling the President.

So the members voted unanimously to let General Counsel Lee Rankin approach Hoover in whatever manner he thought best. As expected, the Director flatly denied the allegation. The matter, at least as far as the Commission was concerned, was dropped. It was understandable, since each Commission member had been made aware that the Director had put together a special embarrassing dossier on each of them.

Meanwhile, back at Langley, James Angleton (who was not privy to Helms' forced backing of Nosenko) was having his own problems. Angleton had found so many obvious flaws in Nosenko's story that he would not buy it, even after Helms, backed by Hoover, tried to adamantly dissuade him. Their argument was that the KGB man's story did not change, even after long periods of intensive interrogation.

Angleton countered that he could not believe Nosenko's claims about how the KGB had handled Oswald, not bothering to debrief him upon his arrival in Russia. It was a hard argument to shake.

By the end of February, another problem confronted the Commission, making General Counsel Lee Rankin feel like he was acting more and more as the unwitting pawn of the FBI Director. Staff counsel William Coleman, in charge of potential conspiratorial relationships for the Commission, saw the possibility of an anti-Castro/Cuban involvement. It came after Coleman wrote his famous memorandum reflecting his and staff attorney David Slawson's views. The pertinent part of the Coleman/Slawson memorandum is as follows:

> The evidence here could lead to an anti-Castro involvement in the assassination on some sort of basis as this: Oswald could have become known to the Cubans as being strongly pro-Castro. He made no secret of his sympathies, and so the anti-Castro Cubans must have realized that law enforcement authorities were also aware of Oswald's feelings and that, therefore, if he got into trouble, the public would also learn of them. The anti-Castro group may have even believed the fiction Oswald tried to create that he had organized some sort of large, active Fair Play for Cuba group in New Orleans. Second, someone in the anti-Castro organization might have been keen enough to sense that Oswald had a penchant for violence that might easily be aroused. . . . On these facts, it is possible that some sort of deception was used to encourage Oswald to kill the President when he came to Dallas. Perhaps "double agents" were even used to persuade Oswald that pro-Castro Cubans would help in the assassination or in the getaway afterwards. The motive of this would of course be the expectation that after the President was killed Oswald would be caught or at least his identity ascertained, the law enforcement authorities and the public would then blame the assassination on the Castro government, and the call for its forceful overthrow would be irresistible. A "second Bay of Pigs invasion" would begin, this time, hopefully, to end successfully.

This memorandum described exactly what the Cuban exiles had hoped for and had tried to accomplish. Declassified in 1975, it is a damning indictment of the Warren Commission, in that the information they uncovered was never pursued in depth. In fact, the only attempt to get any information on anti-Castro Cuban involvement came on March 26, 1964, when, as an afterthought, Rankin made a request to the FBI about it. Rankin's primary request was that the FBI respond to fifty-two questions regarding the Bureau's handling of the presidential assassination investigation; the second, that the FBI furnish the Commission with information regarding certain pro-Castro and anti-Castro organizations.

Hoover showed it to Helms. Needless to say, the Commission request unsettled both of them to such an extent that they both testified to the Commission. Both avowed that the Kennedy assassination case, as far as they were concerned, would always be open. It was an effort on their part to assure the Commission they were not withholding information, which of course they were, and to help the Commission's chief counsel to divert efforts away from the Cuban area—one that would definitely show CIA/Mafia involvement in the assassination.

They must not have been too convincing for, on May 26, 1964, it became apparent that the Commission's Cuban investigation was still going on. The Commission made its second request to the FBI, this time for information on specific anti-Castro groups. Namely, the MRP, SNFE/Alpha 66/30th of November Movement, and the DRE.

Hoover again informed Helms, who now had real cause to be concerned. If the Commission came up with the Oswald/anti-Castro Cuban link, it would lead them directly to the Mafia, the Agency, and finally the Bureau. They decided to hedge their bets. After putting together a plan of action, Helms secretly asked to see Earl Warren.[13]

Helms told Warren about Nosenko, whose story supported the FBI's report to the Commission. Then he cited the two positions the intelligence community had taken regarding the Russian defector: the first being that Nosenko was a legitimate defector and could be believed as far as Oswald was concerned. It was another outright prevarication. The second, that Nosenko was a Soviet agent, under instructions from the Kremlin, to misinform the Commission about Oswald's activities in the Soviet Union. As for Helms' opinion, he would lean toward the first. However, he emphasized that the CIA could not say which view was correct—only that they were working on both.

Then, on June 11, 1964, Hoover, through a letter of transmittal (covering a supposed summary from all its field offices), informed the Warren Commission that either the CIA or Department of the Army would have the information they requested concerning the Cuban organizations. The response implied that the FBI had none.

So, on September 25, 1964, when the final copy of the Commission's report was delivered to the Bureau, it would be sans any questionable information regarding Cuban exiles, Yuri Nosenko, the Mafia, or the CIA. Hoover would be pleased, Helms probably relieved, Angleton frustrated, Kohly displeased that Castro was not blamed, Masferrer and the Mafia dons delighted, and a host of other U.S. citizens—such as myself—puzzled. This was a condition that would not last much longer for me.

CHAPTER NINE NOTES

1.   Victor Marchetti (former Deputy to Richard Helms), *The CIA and the Cult of Intelligence,* p. 222.

2.   Interview with Richard C. Sprague, former consultant to the HSCA, on July 8, 1988.

3.   WCD, pp. 353-362; *CBS Reports,* "The Assassins," Part II.

4.   Warren Commission, Vol. 2, pp. 357-358.

5.   *Ibid.*

6.   House Select Committee on Assassinations, Final Report, Vol. IV, p. 70.

7.   *Ibid.,* p. 71.

8.   Senate Select Committee, *The Investigation of the Assassination of President John F. Kennedy,* p. 29.

9.   *Ibid.*

10.   HSCA Final Report, p. 674.

11.   Warren Commission Transcript, January 27, 1964.

12.   *Ibid.*

13.   HSCA, Vol. X, p. 15.

Chapter Ten

My enlightenment started seventeen days after Hoover received the Warren Commission Report (September 25, 1964), when Mary Meyer, former wife of Helms' number-two man and James Angleton's deputy, Cord Meyer, was mysteriously murdered on October 12, 1964, on the towpath of the C & O Canal in Georgetown. Mary Meyer, aside from being a good friend of Angleton and Bobby Kennedy, had been the dead President's favorite mistress.

Unfortunately for Angleton, Mary Meyer had at one time also been a close friend of Ben Bradlee, editor of the *Washington Post*.

According to Tony Bradlee, Mary Meyer's sister, the friendship between Mary and Ben Bradlee ceased six months prior to her murder. It was due to an article Bradlee had published in *Newsweek* magazine alluding to her affair with the President.

Bradlee claimed he discovered Angleton breaking into Mary's studio with a lock pick in an attempt to find her personal diary. Tony Bradlee, now divorced from Ben, says she found the diary among Mary's personal papers and turned it over to Angleton. Angleton maintained that he burned it along with other personal correspondence of the dead woman.

Angleton would be forced into retirement in late 1974 as a result of his involvement in the CIA's illegal "Operation Chaos," a secret domestic spy program that had been greatly enlarged under the Nixon administration.

My involvement with the President's assassination would be through Mary Meyer, because of Marshall Diggs. Shortly after the Warren Commission Report became available to the public, I received an urgent request from Diggs to meet him for lunch. He suggested Paul Young's Restaurant in Washington.[1] I arrived promptly.

Diggs looked much older than I had remembered him. What we

discussed during the course of the next hour also aged me. After the waiter had taken our order and served our drinks, he discreetly retired. Then Diggs, without any preamble, informed me there could be a possible attempt on my life. That got my complete attention.

"There is a very prominent lady here in Washington who knows too much about the Company, its Cuban operations, and more specifically about the President's assassination."

Cautiously, I remarked, "So?"

"What she claims to know could frankly mean a lot of trouble for Kohly's people, myself, the former vice president and especially you. If you remember, the President was killed shortly after Bobby closed down your counterfeiting operation. . . ."

"I remember, but . . . Cuban involvement? We all thought that was a dead issue. Seriously, we never heard anything about such a possibility from the Warren Commission."

"Forget that," he said, shaking his hand at me impatiently, "and listen carefully. The Commission was suspicious, and had they been allowed to pursue certain leads. . . , well, it's probable you and I wouldn't be sitting here."

"Damn it, Marshall, if you're trying to frighten me, you are. It's over . . . and not one mention of Cubans, any Cubans. There isn't a hint of anything, other than that Oswald got up one morning and decided he didn't like the President."

"I wish his brother thought that," Diggs said, shifting his sad gaze from his plate to my eyes.

"You mean Bobby?"

"Yes, Bobby. Now damn it, listen. As I said, there's a certain lady in town who has an inside track to Langley, and most importantly, to Bobby. Fortunately, an intimate lady friend of mine is one of her best friends. . . ."

I later found out that he was referring to his own mistress.

I interrupted, "Marshall, who the hell are you talking about?"

I had caught him off-guard. He stopped for a moment, pondering. Then he replied, "The woman in question is Cord Meyer's ex-wife, Mary."

"Mary Meyer. . . ." At first it didn't ring a bell, then it struck me. "You mean Cord Meyer of the CIA?"

"The same," he replied. "Except Mary divorced Cord in 1956. Then, after Jack Kennedy was elected, she started spending nights in the White House."

"Well, well, well," was all I could remember saying.

"To get to the point, Meyer claimed to my friend that she positively knew that Company-affiliated Cuban exiles and the Mafia were responsible for killing John Kennedy. My friend immediately called me. Knowing of my association with Kohly, she was concerned."

Trying to curb the fear that started my stomach churning, I tentatively asked, "Well, Marshall . . . , did Mario have anything to do with it?"

Soberly, he answered, "I don't know about Mario. If I were to hazard a guess, I'd say del Valle . . . , possibly Prio. I do know Mario had a lot to do with trying to pin the blame on Castro."

"Un huh, which del Valle. . . ?"

"Oscar and Eladio, both were Kohly's friends."

"Well, it doesn't surprise me. So, why don't you warn him about Meyer?"

"That's the whole point. I don't know where he is and don't want to know. He jumped bail and disappeared."

"What?" I exclaimed. "Jumped bail? Christ! If he's caught, they'll put him away forever."

"Not necessarily. I have a friend working on it."

I just looked at him, wondering if his friend was the ex-vice president of the United States. However, I didn't pursue it. The waiter had appeared with our meal. After he left, Diggs continued.

"Now, getting back to the subject at hand; I can't place myself in a position of actually knowing where Kohly is and chance perjuring myself to either the Attorney General or a federal marshall."

"I see your point. So, why this meeting?"

"Because Mario told me before he left he was going to contact you. He needs a favor."

Now, I didn't want to know where Kohly was any more than Diggs, and my stomach had actually started to ache; but I still hesitantly asked, "What kind of favor?"

"Mario wants you to call a Judge Murphy in New York, tell him what kind of person he is, explain how you worked for the CIA and that you were saved from going to jail by them, that. . . ."

I quickly interjected, "Damn it, Marshall, you know I can't do that! I told Mario how he could save himself back in February. He wouldn't listen. . . ."

Diggs threw up his hands and said, "I know, I know. But that's not important now. Someone's got to tell him about Meyer, and I'm sure he'll call you before he calls me."

"Hell, I don't want to talk to him either. Like you, I don't want to get any more involved."

The expression I got from Diggs could have frosted a bonfire. "Obviously you have forgotten about the Mannlicher rifles you bought. The rifles that were picked up by Ferrie."[2]

I know I paled, as he continued, "Kohly also was dealing with underworld figures—one, I understand you met and others you have seen. The house on 32nd Street, Mr. Gold and Mr. Rawlston."

After the Bay of Pigs, I met Kohly at the house I had rented for him in Washington and found myself looking at the faces of two men who would later be identified as Mafia dons, Sam Giancana and Johnny Roselli, working associates of the CIA.

Sitting across from Diggs, it all seemed so long ago. Reluctantly, I asked, "So, what do I tell Kohly?"

"Tell him what I told you—that as soon as the Meyer woman has the whole story, Bobby Kennedy is going to be told that CIA-affiliated Cuban exiles and the Mafia killed his brother. Tell him, for God's sake, to make sure he has us covered, or Miami and New Orleans will be down the drain."

"My God, Marshall, you're serious?"

He signaled the waiter for our check and said grimly. "Believe it."

After we parted, I was in a quandary. How far should I go about telling the authorities what I knew? If I did, could I be setting myself up? However, what if I didn't and the authorities found out? The Warren Commission said that the President was killed by a lone deranged gunman named Lee Harvey Oswald. But I had to admit I knew it was wrong, based on my association with the Cuban exiles.

Diggs was not paranoid, nor completely off his rocker. I remembered that a few months before the assassination, a number of CIA people had expressed concern about something being planned in New Orleans.

A few days later, when I had almost given up hearing from Kohly, I received a call from a Spanish-speaking voice. It asked if I could meet a mutual friend in New York the following day. When I said, "Yes," I was given an address on the upper West Side and told to be there by three o'clock.

The following day, in a state of depression, I drove to New York and met with Kohly. After I told him the story of Mary Meyer, he looked very concerned and didn't bring up or even mention my calling Judge Murphy.[3] He said, "Just tell Diggs I'll take care of the matter." Then he told me to stay away from him and not tell anyone I had seen him or where he could be found. I don't know why, but I urged him to give himself up. Smiling sadly, he just shook his head and offered me his hand. That evening I drove back to Baltimore and forgot the matter.

A week later, Mary Meyer would be dead and her personal diary given to another friend of Bobby Kennedy, James Angleton. The diary's contents, according to those who have claimed to have read it, contained cryptic memories of Mary's relationship with JFK. If Diggs was right, it possibly contained a lot more. It wouldn't be until the 1976 Senate Select Committee hearings that Angleton would admit knowing that the CIA had been dealing with the anti-Castro Cubans and Mafia in 1963 and 1964.[4]

But what happened to Kohly after his conviction in March of 1964 staggered my imagination. I found out that, while the exile leader was appealing his sentence, Richard Nixon, after unsuccessfully trying to influence Judge Henry Wienfeld to acquit him,[5] advised Kohly to jump bail.

In retrospect, the only reason for such a move was to preclude the possibility of having Kohly available to testify before the Warren Commission. This would effectively prevent Kohly from divulging any information about the exile/CIA/Mafia assassination plots or the deal he made with Nixon prior to the Bay of Pigs involving Operation Forty.

Confirmation of Nixon's participation in Kohly's decision to go underground was told to me by Kohly himself, shortly before his death in 1975. It was also confirmed by a man who used to work in Marshall Diggs' office, journalist Edward von Rothkirch.

In a taped interview on August 26, 1976, with me, my future wife and research associate, Tiny Hutton, and other staff members of the first chairman of the House Select Committee on Assassinations, Representative Thomas N. Downing, Rothkirch stated:

HUTTON:[6]   Do you think it was on the basis of that meeting with Nixon?

ROTHKIRCH: [Nixon advised Kohly] that if he could stay clear for a while that they [the Nixon law firm] could do something. But, of course, he couldn't stay clear as long as they wanted him to stay.

HUTTON: All right. On what do you base this?

ROTHKIRCH: Well, Kohly came to me on the Thursday or Friday before he disappeared and told me he was going underground; and I pointed out the dangers of going underground unless he was absolutely sure.

MORROW: So . . . jumping bail. Right?

ROTHKIRCH: Right. And I pointed out the dangers unless he was absolutely certain he could be hidden; and he claimed that he could be hidden. [Kohly also said] . . . as a result of his trips to New York and his meetings with Nixon, that this was [the] advisable situation if he could stay underground for a certain period of time [that] everything would be all right and he would be vindicated. Now, Kohly believed, up to the time he was brought into custody, that he was going to be vindicated—that mysteriously that [something] was going to occur and that would wipe the slate clean and that he wouldn't have to go [to prison].

Slightly later in the same interview Hutton asked:

HUTTON: Well, basically, is it after his [Kohly's] trips to New York and his visits with Nixon that he was convinced that going underground was the thing to do and that [he, Kohly] would eventually be vindicated?

ROTHKIRCH: Yes.

HUTTON: Did he ever indicate actually that Nixon
                     himself had advised him to do this?

ROTHKIRCH: He indicated that Nixon himself had
                     counseled him on the course of action he
                     was taking. Whether that was the only
                     specific action or the counseling included
                     a group of collateral actions, this I do not
                     know.

Nixon's advice resulted in sending Kohly to Allenwood Prison. During Kohly's original trial, I was told by government people to tell Kohly he could get off with a simple slap of the wrists if he would promise to stop his anti-Castro activities. Kohly refused and was convicted and sentenced to two one-year concurrent terms in federal prison.

Kohly told me, after he was finally taken into custody by federal marshals, that Nixon told him again he would take his case and pay all Kohly's legal fees[7] if he would not divulge any of their past relationships or deals regarding the Bay of Pigs, for he, Nixon, was going to be the next president of the United States.

According to Kohly, after a long conversation with Prio and Masferrer, he agreed to go along with the former vice president.[8]

Richard Nixon went on to become the GOP presidential candidate in 1968. Kohly made a mistake. He relied on the assurances of Prio, Masferrer, and Nixon, a man he would call Cuba's greatest friend.

Nixon's continuing ties to the Cubans and Mafia wouldn't start surfacing until the Watergate investigation, with the discovery that a Miami-based business having underworld connections, Keyes Realty Co.,[9] had helped both Nixon and his best friend Bebe Rebozo, owner of the Key Biscayne Bank, to transact various land deals. One included the securing of land for the future president's winter White House. Keyes Realty was reported to have collaborated in the transfer of southern Key Biscayne to a Cuban investment group known as the Ansan Corporation.

As early as 1948, an Internal Revenue Service investigator reported that he suspected Ansan of having a fund belonging "to Luciano or other underworld characters."[10] Ansan's visible partners were Kohly's friend, Carlos Prio Socarras, and the ex-Cuban president's former Education Minister, Jose Manuel Aleman,[11] father of Jose Aleman, the man whom Santos Trafficante told that Kennedy was going to be hit.

It should not have been surprising that the senior Aleman's wife, Helena Santiero, was the daughter of Luciano's Cuban attorney, Anselmo Alliergro, Batista's Finance Minister and investment counselor.

From the Ansan Corporation, control of the Key Biscayne real estate was later passed on to a company known as World Wide Realty, described by federal investigators as Meyer Lansky's real-estate front. World Wide Realty was headed by Arthur Desser, a close friend of Jimmy Hoffa. The Key Biscayne property was then routed through Meyer Lansky's financial conduit, the Miami National Bank, where it finally ended up as property of the Cape Florida Development Corporation, headed by Donald Berg.

Berg, an acquaintance of Richard Nixon and a business and personal friend of Lou Chesler (Meyer Lansky's front man) caused a flap with the Secret Service. After the 1968 presidential elections, they advised the new president to stop frequenting Berg's Key Biscayne restaurant because of Berg's background. Prior to the 1968 election, Berg sold some of his Cape Florida land to the future president at bargain rates.

Nixon's concern about the relationship must have been great. After he became president, he delayed registering the purchase of one lot for four years, until the final payment had been made on the Cape Florida mortgage. Nixon's links with Desser and Keyes Realty had been kept relatively isolated by dealing through Bebe Rebozo.

I was intrigued to discover that another Cuban exile (and future Watergate alumni figure), Eugene Martinez, was a vice president of Keyes Realty until 1971. Then, Martinez and Bernard Barker (E. Howard Hunt's former aide-de-camp and underworld link to Rolando Masferrer) set up their own realty office under the name of "Ameritas."

Ameritas, located in the same office building as Keyes Realty, would be the firm that made the reservations at the Washington Howard Johnson's Inn for the Watergate burglars. According to Washington columnist Jack Anderson, some of Barker's real-estate ventures involved Bebe Rebozo.[12]

* * * * *

By the end of 1964, as the Warren Commission submitted its report naming Lee Harvey Oswald as the sole assassin of President Kennedy, the Vietnam war was rapidly escalating into the main issue in the country.

In 1966, the Cuban exiles were struck their death knell. Richard Helms, critic of the volatile Cuban exiles, was appointed Director of the

CIA by President Johnson. After his appointment, Helms immediately chose to replace the capricious Cubans as domestic bad guys with specially trained elite members of the Iranian secret police.[13] These members of the Shah of Iran's torture squads were highly disciplined operatives known as the SAVAK.

Their allegiance to Richard Helms, the man who engineered the coup d'etat for the Shah in 1953, was unquestioned. Helms, who would control the Shah through his position as director of the CIA, suddenly would have at his beck and call a worldwide, covert strike-force of dedicated, trained, professional agents and assassins.

It would not be until 1977, eleven years later, that I would realize the significance of Helms' move.

CHAPTER TEN NOTES

1. Paul Young's was located directly across Connecticut Avenue from the Mayflower Hotel and is no longer in business.

2. *Betrayal,* pp. 125-126.

3. Robert Kennedy was adamant about Kohly going to prison. It is the author's opinion he knew members of Kohly's JGCE participated in the assassination of his brother.

4. Senate Select Committee to Study Governmental Operations with Respect to Intelligence Activities, Vol. V, p. 69.

5. Letter from Richard Nixon to Judge Henry Wienfeld, dated March 6, 1965, on Nixon, Mudge, Rose, Guthrie & Alexander stationery. See Appendix, Exhibit No. 11.

6. Hutton was Deputy Director of the House Select Committee on Assassinations up until June 30, 1978.

7. Letter to Mrs. M. G. Kohly from the law firm of Nixon, Mudge, Rose, Guthrie & Alexander, dated April 29, 1966. See Appendix, Exhibit No. 12.

8. Doris Kohly, informal interview, August 1975.

9. Kefauver Crime Hearings, Part I, p. 716.

10. IRS Report, February 20, 1948.

11. It was reported in the March 24, 1950, *The New York Times,* p. 92, that Jose Manuel Aleman had defrauded his government of tens of millions of dollars.

12. *Washington Post,* June 26, 1972.

13. Jack Anderson, 1/19/75, 1/20/75, 11/4/76, 5/3/77, 6/11/77, 9/20/77.

Chapter Eleven

The CIA started training many of the SAVAK members here in the U.S. as early as the late 1950s. Some of the first were trained at the International Police Academy (IPA) in Washington, D.C., an organization run by Joseph Shimon.[1] In an interview with Shimon on Saturday, January 24, 1981 he admitted that the IPA started training personnel from the Middle East and specifically Iran as early as the mid-1950s. Shimon said that he left the IPA in 1960 to pursue other activities.

One would be to accompany his good friend, CIA/Mafia assassination coordinator Robert Maheu to Miami, along with Mafia chieftains Johnny Roselli and Sam Giancana. It was the infamous trip made to ask Santos Trafficante to arrange Fidel Castro's assassination.

After the appointment of Helms as CIA Director, the SAVAK would also be trained in all forms of terrorist tactics at the Naval Weapons Center at China Lake, California. By 1968—the year Robert F. Kennedy would be cut down by assassins' bullets—the SAVAK would be operating in the U.S. with the complete cooperation and protection of the CIA.

I wouldn't become interested in the Bobby Kennedy assassination until the beginning of 1977, when, in the process of my investigation into the Cuban exile movement and organized crime, the SAVAK surfaced.

Because of it, after I had read several books on the assassination, one name stood out. It was an Iranian named Khyber Khan. Then on March 6, 1977, I saw a segment on CBS's *60 Minutes,* entitled "SAVAK."[2] The program intrigued me to the point that I sent for a transcript. From it, the names of two individuals emerged whom I would later interview. One was a former CIA station chief in Teheran named Richard Cottam, the other an Iranian businessman named Nasser Afshar. These interviews would become critical, once I had discovered that the SAVAK was the track to the real story behind Bobby Kennedy's assassination.

* * * * *

So it came to pass that, in 1968, a threatened mob would again call upon their beholden champion, Richard Milhaus Nixon, to take up the Republican Party banner. With the 1967 Tet offensive in Vietnam, Lyndon Johnson decided to step down and not go for a second term. This made Nixon an "odds on favorite" in 1968. The only declared candidate on the Democratic side with any real chance, other than Johnson, was Eugene McCarthy.

Then, on March 16, 1967, after much soul searching, Bobby Kennedy declared his candidacy. It had been a tough decision; McCarthy had already won 42.2 percent of vote in the New Hampshire primary, which meant he could not ask McCarthy to withdraw. But, the declaration was enough.

I would discover ten years later that, within hours, SAVAK agents were put in touch with the mob in Washington, D.C. The purpose: to coordinate the removal of Bobby Kennedy if he stood a chance of winning the Democratic nomination.

Ironically, Bobby's declaration came at the same time the Garrison investigation into his brother's assassination was making daily headlines. Because of it, Bobby felt forced to reaffirm his belief in the Warren Commission Report. In view of how the Garrison affair was progressing, his staff knew it would be damaging to his campaign to publicly express doubts about who killed his brother.

Anything less than absolute proof would leave him open to accusations of irresponsibility and rumor-mongering. Bobby knew the only practical course to avenge his brother's death was to attain the presidency and again control the Justice Department.

Jim Garrison had dropped his inquiry into the President's assassination in 1964, immediately after the FBI had given David Ferrie a clean bill of health. Then, in January of 1967, the New Orleans DA once more started to investigate the President's murder. His stated reason: he felt compelled to, after former Warren Commission member, Senator Richard B. Russell, told Garrison that members of the Commission had expressed serious doubts about the Commission's findings.

However, one can judge for oneself the real reason why Garrison reopened the Kennedy assassination investigation. In January of 1967, a Washington attorney named Edward P. Morgan broke a blockbuster of a story to Washington columnist Drew Pearson. Morgan told Pearson of the CIA/Mafia plots to assassinate Fidel Castro.[3]

Suddenly, the story the FBI and CIA had desperately tried to cover up had surfaced—in the hands of a news reporter. Ten years later, Las Vegas don John Roselli would be verifying the same story to Washington, D.C., reporter Jack Anderson.

In the course of my investigations, I interviewed Garrison on August 18, 1977. Knowing of his association with Carlos Marcello and his abortive attempt to reopen the presidential murder investigation by accusing David Ferrie, Clay Shaw, and a number of anti-Castro Cubans of complicity, I questioned him about his feelings regarding a possible CIA involvement. His assessment was surprising:

> But I make the point of the way the Warren Commission looked into it so . . . well, on purpose. Because they had to be well aware that it was a segment of the Agency, although I think quite obviously, what you would call a marginal segment—contract employee type. I find the best way to describe them, the cluster involved, as those involved in the Bay of Pigs, so to speak.

Later, Garrison explained specifically that:

> The type of individual that's involved is definitely rabid characters who were trained to assassinate even before the Bay of Pigs, and after the Bay of Pigs were used on raids.
> That's the group that we're dealing with here.

It was obvious whom Garrison was talking about. It was Rolando Masferrer and Mario Kohly's men on No Name Key, originally commanded by Oscar del Valle Garcia prior to the Bay of Pigs. In effect, Garrison was naming anti-Castro mercenaries and also verifying Johnny Roselli's accusations.[4]

When I asked Garrison if he felt anyone in the CIA had knowledge of the assassination beforehand, he replied:

> I think, if we had a magic eye and could see clearly at this moment, we'd find that there'd be some that had knowledge beforehand and, for one reason or another, did nothing. And afterwards, I think virtually all of them had to sense what happened. And, by now, most of them would have to know. I mean people in the position let's say of a Richard Helms.

He then went on to include my former case officer, Tracy Barnes, saying:

> It wouldn't be too many weeks afterwards before he knew
> with some precision.

Finally, I asked Garrison how he felt about the allegation made by Victor Marchetti that the CIA under Helms helped undermine his investigation. He said:

> Well, they interfered with me pretty good, there's no
> question about that. But, my position about that with regard to
> the Agency and the federal government at large is . . . I might
> have done the same thing if I had been in their place.

Thus, with Garrison directly confirming the anti-Castro Cubans' role in the President's assassination, it was easy to see how the third sacrificial lamb had been added to the mob's list. (The first two were Jack Ruby and David Ferrie.) It was Kohly's friend, former Cuban congressman and close associate of Rolando Masferrer, Eladio del Valle.

Three days before David Ferrie's death on February 22, 1967, Garrison's men were in Miami, Florida, seeking to question the wealthy Cuban exile about his association with Ferrie. Garrison's men and the Miami police were unable to locate del Valle until the early morning hours of February 23, when a Miami police officer discovered the exile's badly mutilated body in a parking lot.

So all the information del Valle possessed about the presidential assassination and his part in it died with him. It was just hours after Ferrie had been found dead.

It goes without saying that the Miami police never solved the murder. I would also point out that Oscar del Valle Garcia was working in the Miami area, in 1967, with Masferrer and Veciana. It is rumored that del Valle's murder was perpetrated by Oscar.

Also, Garrison's conviction that CIA contract people were involved in the Kennedy assassination (and someone in Richard Helms' position would know about it) was another reasonable explanation for Helms' actions following the President's murder. Today, I can understand why in the 1960s Helms and his close associates would withhold evidence, perjure themselves, change records, and cooperate in a cover-up with J. Edgar Hoover. It was simple: Bobby Kennedy suspected that a conspiracy involving CIA/Mafia-related people killed his brother.

Then, on August 19, 1977, I would seemingly have some confirmation of the Company's involvement in the President's assassination. I received a mysterious phone call to meet with the son of a former high-ranking member of the intelligence community.

We met the following day for lunch. In our initial conversation, the young man claimed his father, an ex-Air Force colonel, and others working for the Central Intelligence Agency had prior knowledge that President Kennedy was going to be assassinated in Dallas on November 22, 1963. It was a statement I had heard on many occasions and was beginning to believe.

He also claimed that, through his father, he learned that the CIA hierarchy had done everything in their power to thwart the Warren Commission investigation, including the suppression and destruction of evidence—evidence that could prove that a conspiracy existed.

The intelligence officer's son then made a wild accusation. He asserted that his father had been tied into organized crime and had been a bagman for at least one of the payoffs relating to the presidential assassination, transporting a large sum of money to Haiti for payoff purposes during the summer of 1963.[5]

It seemed uncanny that the young man would tell me a story so bizarre about his own father, and I took it as the wild imaginings of a deranged kid—until he said his father and another intelligence officer (also an ex-Air Force colonel), who from this point on will be referred to as the "SIO," had been closely associated with a Mafia courier. I was not shocked. I knew the ex-Air Force colonel he was referring to and also the Mafia courier. The courier's name was Mickey Wiener.[6] And no one but certain Washington parties and Mafia insiders knew what he really was.

Suddenly, the seemingly wild accusations he made against his father took on a whole new perspective—particularly after he served up another piece of information involving the SIO, information I also knew to be correct.

He said that both his father and the SIO were very closely tied to the Shah of Iran, citing that close relatives to each of them had married directly into the Shah's family, and because of it, he was now afraid that he was in danger from the SAVAK.[7]

Although I didn't know it at the time, this meeting would start me on the circuitous path to solving Bobby Kennedy's murder. It had stemmed from an interview I had on April 12, 1977, with an old friend by the name of Albert Moakler, who had introduced me to the SIO in Mafia courier Mickey Wiener's office in the summer of 1964. Moakler had told me that the SIO had a possible involvement in the President's assassination.

This interview and one that followed with another friend, Ms. Frances Russell, also gave me the link to Mickey Wiener's Mafia activities.

The following is an excerpt from the Moakler interview:

MOAKLER: One of the things that worries me about this situation is what they are doing with some of the events that took place approximately what—ten, twelve years?

MORROW: Fourteen.

MOAKLER: Fourteen years ago. Serious consideration in this is the fact that the background of Mickey Wiener. . . .

MORROW: Mickey Wiener? Is he the one that was tied up with Bobby Baker and tied up with Colonel [name deleted] of the White House?

MOAKLER: That's right. During that time period, there was quite a bit of—you might say— corroboration or mutual trading of knowledge, facts and figures and so forth between obviously Mickey and Bobby Baker. Another individual, Colonel [the SIO], was a close participant.

MORROW: What about Colonel [the SIO]?

MOAKLER: Well, basically, you might say in a generalized term that Colonel [the SIO] has always represented Mr. Clean and certainly had a most distinguished war record and served a few. . . .   His basic career has, in a sense, been quite outstanding. He served more than one Secretary of the Air Force and, up until his retirement, I believe he was a great asset to the community, etc.

MORROW: The Washington community?

MOAKLER: The Washington community. He was very closely tied to Lyndon Johnson, who was then our president, and, in fact, had the equivalent of a White House office.

. . . . .

MORROW: Are you saying there could be a right-wing connection there that he could be concerned about?

MOAKLER: That's very possible. I personally have no indication that this is it; but it's just very curious to me that an individual, after this length of time, would have become or would have been recently so vehement about . . "there's nothing there; don't bother; don't disturb; don't make waves [meaning the JFK assassination]; and so forth and so on." And, as I said, the fundamental approach to Colonel [the SIO] is that he was and reputedly is Mr. Clean. However, there is the ancient or years ago situation where Mickey Wiener was quite a close associate of Colonel [the SIO]; and this is the equivalent of black and white, in essence. It was never understood by myself or any other people of what the association or tie-in was.

. . . . .

Moakler went on to say that somehow Wiener got close to Bobby Baker.

MOAKLER: Now, Mr. Wiener showed up [at the suite in the Plaza] and during our preliminary conversation [told me] about what he could do to help our little company with government contracts and so forth and so on. [During the course of the conversation,] he mentioned that he was literally as close to Bobby Baker as he was to his mother type of thing or some other similar expression. Now this grated on my nerves a little bit because, while I was not [personally] a confidante or friend of Bobby Baker's, through some other people in the Washington area I had not only met the gentleman but had conversed with him and so forth. And this worried me a little bit, so that I, upon the departure of Mr. Wiener, picked up the phone [and] from [the suite in] New York, called Washington, D.C., and requested that the individual I was talking to—who is no mystery, it was Miss Frances Russell, who was a very close friend of Bobby Baker's—and I said, "Frances, I'm worried, this guy's shown up out of the woodwork, and he says he knows Bobby Baker this well and so forth and so on." Within thirty minutes I had a call back from Washington from Bobby Baker to me at the Plaza Hotel saying he had never heard of the SOB and had nothing to do with him. So, as far as I was concerned, that ended it. However, in subsequent months, I find that Mr. Wiener is a complete user of Bobby's [Baker's] office, of all the [Baker] facilities on the Hill, etc., etc., and they [Baker and Weiner] are thick as thieves. And, of course, further discoveries which are public knowledge—such as the testimony in the [Baker] trial and everything else; the fact that they're working on one particular lobbying bill, and so forth and so on. But the thing that [was] striking in later association with Mickey, who basically utilized me for technical knowledge where he was fundamentally lacking, indicated that he was operating under tremendous pressure, and one of the pressure points was obviously Las Vegas and the gambling. His income was great enough that he could not have had any financial problems; but his requirement to pay off in Vegas was substantial, and the proof of the pudding on this situation is when I was associated with Mickey we had an appointment in California with North American Aviation.

MORROW: [name deleted] company that he represented?

MOAKLER: That's right. Now, that particular weekend or the days involved in Vegas—which was a stopover point—we also had in the party, you might say, one Senator Williams.[8]

MORROW: Williams?

MOAKLER: From New Jersey. Now—which is completely innocent—it had nothing to do with our visit to California. But the big point is, catching an early flight from Vegas from the Sands Hotel to Los Angeles, we were up a great deal earlier and the gambling session you might say at that early hour [was normally], basically empty. However, there was one crap table. And, having about an hour to waste after coffee and doughnuts, we [Wiener and I] started shooting craps and—as will sometimes happen—in the process, Mr. Wiener happened to accumulate in about forty, forty-five minutes, a rather substantial amount of markers or chips, whatever you want to call them.

MORROW: What do you consider substantial?

MOAKLER: I'd say about thirty-six thousand.

MORROW: That's substantial.

MOAKLER: Now, my particular forte at this was to go for maybe fifty bucks as a loss, something like that. In other words, you might say I'm a nickel and dime player. However, a run of numbers and so forth had worked out that, in the post-breakfast period before the flight, Mr. Wiener made what you might call a killing. And one of the strong indications is that, rather than cashing the chips in when we left, he put them against his account that he owed.

MORROW: Against the account that he owed?

MOAKLER: Against the account he owed. Now, I was never curious enough or ascertained how much he owed the Sands, amongst other places, but it was quite obvious that he was one under their jurisdiction in certain areas, there was no question about it; because his method of paying and operating his business and so forth, the funding was such that there were large sizable sums disappearing, being paid out.

MORROW:	Would you say this was true in respect to, in conjunction with Bobby Baker? Did you ever hear of a fellow by the name of Cliff Jones?
MOAKLER:	Yes. From the ancient days. I think Bobby Baker and that situation was pretty well uncovered and explored with the vending machines and so forth.
MORROW:	Servu Corp. and that?
MOAKLER:	Yes. But the big thing here is there is nothing definite in this sense; but here is a situation where you have a—you might say—a presumably quite sharp, New Jersey attorney [Wiener] who admittedly lied to the FBI and IRS. . . .
MORROW:	When was this?
MOAKLER:	On national television; he did it very nicely. Don't ask me; I don't know what the exact date was.
MORROW:	What was it in regard to?
MOAKLER:	The Bobby Baker situation. He'd been perhaps subpoenaed or interviewed in the spring of whatever year it was, and that fall was when it came up again. And he admitted that he had lied to both these government groups. Now, the big point is that here we have this individual who was running an operation that could basically be compared to our current man, Tongsun Park. Not that there's any connection; but Tongsun Park, wining and dining and socializing and so forth, was the forte of Mr.

Wiener.

MORROW: He was of course familiar with Colonel [name deleted] of the White House staff?

MOAKLER: That's right. And he was also very familiar and very close to Colonel [the SIO], who was in essence, while perhaps not on the government payroll per se or perhaps he was a dollar a year man, but in essence he was pretty much of a staff person to the President. The facet here, the involvement, this is of course a personal viewpoint and has nothing to back it up; but I still feel it's valid. Going back and reiterating on this thing when Bobby Baker called me at the Plaza Hotel, I'm definitely sure he had never heard of Mickey Wiener. And, in a short period of time, for Mickey to gain access to Bobby Baker's office was a very big steppingstone. Also for Mickey Wiener to get himself well acquainted, you might say, with somebody such as Colonel [the SIO], [name deleted], Adam Clayton Powell—all of this indicates to me a very close tie-in to what we would term the Jersey gambling, drug interests, Vegas, Cuba, Bahamas . . . . Now back to Mickey Wiener and 1028 Connecticut Avenue.

MORROW: That's the LaSalle Building?

MOAKLER: The LaSalle Building, that's correct. His new connections were obviously fairly good from past statements with respect to Senator Williams, to Frances Russell and her contacts, to the SIO, to [name deleted], to Adam Clayton Powell, and others that escape my memory, but who you might say were in and out of the operation. Now, when Mr. Wiener testified, in a sense, against himself by admitting his prevarication to the two prior-mentioned government agencies on national television, this resulted in a loss of many of his so-called clients and his retainers.

MORROW: Was one of these North American Aviation in conjunction with [name deleted]?

MOAKLER: That's right. The other major one, you might say, was (the) Whittaker Corp. Now, when this occurred, of course, I guess you would say in the vernacular they felt Mr. Wiener was a hot potato, and they dumped him. This again brought about a financial hardship to the extent that Mr. Wiener retreated back to New Jersey and [resulted] in the closing of the so-called office/residence of Mr. Wiener in Washington in the LaSalle Building, [where] I acquired a certain number of LP records which were strictly operatic and one suitcase that was left over.

MORROW: This was in his LaSalle apartment, right?

MOAKLER: Correct. Now, inadvertently with the records were some cassette tapes that we had used trying to record music and so forth and since this apartment had to be cleaned out and Mr. Wiener was not coming back to it and was having a bit of a problem with the building owner.

Subsequently, in going through these acquisitions, I found some tapes that were in certain cases identifiable because I recognized the voices. One, of course, was Colonel [the SIO]; one that I believe was [name deleted], but I can't be positive because I didn't know the gentleman that well. Part of the conversation was concerned with a conspiracy facet. What the whole point of this [conversation] was, they were trying to cover or protect some situtation in Jersey which I had no knowledge of. I never listened to all of them.

.   .   .   .   .

But they [the tapes] were indicatvie that there was a conversation going on which was more than idle gossip. It definitely concerned Jersey and Miami . . .

MORROW: Jersey and Miami what?

MOAKLER: The areas; people in the areas. Something concerned with the assassination.

MORROW: Of John F. Kennedy?

MOAKLER: Yes. Of John F. Kennedy. Now, it was tied strictly to that era. As I said, it didn't mean anything, because my god we theoretically had everybody and their brother looking into the incident and so forth and so on. And, this, of course, occurred quite a while after the assassination.

MORROW: Approximately what year, do you know?

MOAKLER: Well, I would say this must have been approximately a year. . . .

MORROW: Late 1964?

MOAKLER: Yes. Now, I had no reason to question the tapes. And there was no way at the time to, say, return them presumably to their rightful owner, Mr. Wiener, because nobody knew where he [Wiener] was and subsequent to that through all the intervening years I have not ever seen Mr. Wiener [again] nor has he ever adjusted various financial affairs between us and so forth and so on. Basically how much [more] happens to be on those tapes I don't know. At the point of time it did not interest me to hear Mr. Wiener's comments, voice, and other people's that just had no real meaning to me. . . .

Well, let me clear this up. There was [on one of the tapes] a conversation held between Mr. Wiener and two other people whom I couldn't identify at all. However, in that conversation, they were talking about [name deleted]. . . . Now, at the time, one whom I would consider a friend of mine, Dick Connally. . . .

MORROW: That's the governor's cousin?

MOAKLER: Cousin. John Connally's cousin. Dick was, what you would say, still active in Washington, and he was, to my knowledge, quite close to [name deleted] or utilized his office and so forth.

MORROW: He was also close to Frances Russell, wasn't he?

MOAKLER: Oh, yes, very [close].

. . . . .

MORROW: Why would Mr. Wiener have made these tapes in the beginning?

MOAKLER: This I don't know. Possibly for a record to keep his skirts clean; possibly to make use of them for additional favors.

MORROW: Are you talking about blackmail?

MOAKLER: Harsh word, but it's possible. In other words, I can't put myself in his thinking.

MORROW: All right. In your opinion, he wasn't above it though?

MOAKLER: I don't think so. No. If push came to shove, he definitely would utilize any means available, and it's quite apparent to me that there had to be some means just for the record. If somebody gets up on national TV and says they've lied to the FBI and the IRS and there's nothing ever done [to him]— they've [the Wiener crew] never even had their wrists' slapped—obviously, there's some pressure or a sell-out here someplace.

· · · · ·

MORROW: Did they mention the FBI or anything like that? To your recollection?

MOAKLER: No. The only thing I can say, there was no mention of any agency. But there were comments regarding the areas I mentioned such as Jersey and Miami that somebody or something could not stand an investigation and that something would have to be done.

MORROW: Were the names mentioned?

MOAKLER: No. No names. Just in general . . . They all knew each other and knew what they were talking about. The thing is, the silly thing could have applied to Mickey's crazy bank loan out of Miami.

MORROW: What bank was that with, do you know?

MOAKLER: I don't know. You'd have to get that from Frances; she did the paperwork for him; but the bank was perfectly happy with Mickey's loan and so forth. However, the bank was being examined.

MORROW: How much was the loan for?

MOAKLER: Twenty-five-thousand.

MORROW: Which was nothing very much.

MOAKLER: Nothing very much, no. But, what it was, without having any paperwork or anything else—basically this was like a short-term loan that was renewable, O.K.? For twenty-five bills. It was supposed to be like for six months. And, of course, it wasn't repaid. When push came to shove, we [Frances and I] kept paying the interest, and the bank got to the stage where this loan was not in limbo really, but the bank examiners, in the normal course of events, if something should happen to the loan. . . .

MORROW: Was it secured by anything?

MOAKLER: No. Signature loan only, which was the problem. There was no security involved.

Moakler told me to interview Frances C. Russell, who as Lyndon Johnson's protegee spent several years as legal counsel to the House Ways and Means Committee. I had known Fran since 1959 and was her guest at

Wilbur Mills'⁹ table during Jack Kennedy's Inaugural Ball at the Mayflower Hotel in 1961, the first time I met Bobby Kennedy. After John Kennedy was elected, Fran quit the committee and, by the following year, had gotten involved with Wiener. In 1964, he would be the cause of her financial ruin.

Exactly two weeks later, Wednesday, April 27, 1977, I would be on an early morning flight to Boston. It would be the first time I had seen Fran in over twelve years.

However, prior to Fran's interview, I was given a lead to the SAVAK's connection to the assassination of Bobby Kennedy, which would start my investigation into it. This would occur through an old friend I had arranged to meet for cocktails after the Moakler interview. His name was Berry B. Rogers, and at the time he was associated with a company in Arlington, Virginia, named Systems Technology Laboratory.¹⁰

CHAPTER ELEVEN NOTES

1.   Ross Schoyer Interview, November 17, 1977. See Appendix, Exhibit No. 13.

2.   See Appendix, Exhibit No. 14.

3.   Senate Committee Report on the Investigation of the Assassination of President John F. Kennedy, June 1976, *The Performance of the Intelligence Agencies.*

4.   Jack Anderson, *Washington Post,* September 7, 1976.

5.   In former CIA agent, Hugh McDonald's book, *Appointment in Dallas,* a man known to him as Saul reported he had received his payoff for the Kennedy assassination in Haiti. (Interview with Hugh McDonald, Tuesday, February 1, 1977.)

6.   Wiener's roommate during this period was none other than Congressman, now ex-Senator, Harrison O. Williams, Jr., of New Jersey. Williams was indicted and convicted in the ABSCAM scandal of a few years ago.

7.   Interviews with intelligence officer's son, August 20 and 27, 1977.

8.   Former U.S. Senator Harrison O. Williams, Jr.

9.   Former chairman of the House Ways and Means Committee.

10.   Systems Technology Laboratory was for years suspected of being a CIA proprietary company.

Chapter Twelve

As I pushed my car into the chaos of Georgtown's M Street traffic, I couldn't help wondering why a man of the SIO's stature would have been involved with Mickey Wiener. Moakler said he would go down to Virginia to pick up the tapes. It had been obvious to me that he had been extremely nervous about what was on them. In retrospect I could see why. One does not intimate that a person like the SIO could have been either privy to knowledge regarding a presidential assassination or have been a part of it without some trepidation.

So I decided to wait and see what was on the tapes. Then I could make my own decision. Until then, Fran Russell might be able to shed more light on the subject.

It had taken me almost half an hour to negotiate crossing the Key Bridge into Rosslyn. Berry Rogers was living in an apartment owned by Systems Technology Laboratory on the outskirts of Arlington. After spending ten minutes trying to park in the lot of the Arlington Towers, I pulled onto the street. The trip to the twelfth-floor penthouse was much easier.

After I had a drink in my hand, the course of our conversation turned to what I was doing. I told him about my interview with Moakler and for some reason mentioned seeing the TV show *60 Minutes* the previous month, commenting on how it appeared that the CIA was using the Iranian secret police, the SAVAK, for some of their local operations.

Rogers immediately registered recognition. He had heard of the SAVAK from a man who was closely associated with Tongsun Park, a young Korean named J. S. Kim. At that time, Tongsun Park was being investigated for buying congressional influence. I had met Kim on several occasions at the STL facility.

As I was driving back to Baltimore, I remembered the mysterious Iranian, Khyber Khan, who had been referred to in one of the books about the RFK assassination. Something intuitively told me to follow this up.

Upon arriving home, I gave Kim a call.

Kim told me that he had heard the name of SAVAK from a man named Alexis Goodaryi, an Iranian who was maitre d' of the Rotunda Restaurant[1] and self-styled playboy of Capitol Hill. I told Kim I needed to talk to Goodaryi to ask about possible tie-ins between organized crime and the SAVAK. Kim gave me the telephone number at the restaurant, and I had my appointment made within hours.

Goodaryi and I met at his restaurant on Thursday, April 14, 1977. He was at first reluctant to talk, but he acquiesced after I put away my tape recorder. To try to set him at ease, I told him about my association with Representative Thomas Downing and about my book *Betrayal*. I then expressed my interest in the SAVAK's relationship to the mob, telling him I wondered if there could be a connection between the SAVAK and the death of Bobby Kennedy.

He became quite nervous, asking, "Are you associated with the government in any way?"

When I said, "No," he relaxed somewhat. Then I told him what I was really after—information on the SAVAK operating in this country for the CIA. Goodaryi paled. I had hit a sensitive nerve.

I didn't want to get Kim into trouble, so I explained that, earlier that week, a number of names including his had been given to me as possible sources of information on SAVAK members—and one in particular, Khyber Khan.

Goodaryi's expression became opaque.

I had to jar him, to let him think that I knew that he knew who I was talking about. So I fabricated, slightly. "I was told by a mutual friend . . . ," and casually dropped a name, one I was told he was familiar with, the former high-ranking intelligence colonel associated with Mafia courier Mickey Wiener. "The SIO said you could give me some information about Khan and his relationship with the SAVAK."

For a moment the silence was deafening. I could hear the kitchen help all the way down the hall, cleaning up after lunch. Finally Goodaryi spoke. "What relevance did Khan have to the Kennedy assassinations?"

I took a shot in the dark and said, "He was involved in Bobby's."

Goodaryi once again became silent. After what seemed like hours, the Iranian spoke. "What assurance can you give me of not having trouble if I gave you some important information on the assassination of Robert Kennedy?"

Hesitantly, not to show my excitement, I told him, "If the information is truly important and would have a bearing on either Kennedy assassination, it might be possible to arrange congressional immunity." Then I assured him I would see Tiny Hutton, the HSCA Deputy Director, and use him as a sounding board. Seemingly satisfied, Goodaryi leaned back in his chair, took off a pair of aviator style glasses, and began to wipe them off with a Kleenex. After putting them back on, he told me a story.

"Khan was a man, how shall I put it, a man much taken by himself, a man with an ego. In Iran, he was quite wealthy and during the late 1950s wished to build an athletic stadium in Teheran. He managed to interest members of the royal family, but they eventually backed out after Khan became overbearing. About that same time, the new Kennedy administration accused His Highness of stealing money given our country for development programs. To get even, Khan came over to the United States claiming to have proof of these charges. As a result, he got himself in trouble with His Highness." Goodaryi then went on to tell me the story of Khan suing the royal family and how, after they made their peace, he was catered to at the Iranian embassy and began a close relationship with Colonel Mansour Rafizadeh, head of the SAVAK in the U.S. "For years Khan and Rafizadeh worked together. When Rafizadeh worked at the United Nations, Khan went to live in New York. They became very close.

"In the mid-1960s, Khan was sent to your West Coast by Rafizadeh to recruit and set up student organizations friendly to His Highness. He was quite successful, and in 1968 he was entrusted with the job of setting up the assassination of Senator Kennedy. To do this, he staffed the Kennedy campaign headquarters with his people, selected the assassins, and set up the plan." Khan then went into what specifics he had gotten from members of the SAVAK in Washington. Because they are similar in detail to a scenario related to me some time later by another Iranian, they will be described together in Chapter Fourteen. Goodaryi then said, "And that is that. Other people know it. People close to the royal family and associated with your Central Intelligence Agency. People in big positions."

I unfortunately discounted the whole story as pure fiction. As I would learn several years later, this was a serious blunder on my part. I should have sensed something more serious and sinister was happening when I found out that Goodaryi was murdered just a few weeks later.

* * * * *

The trip to Boston was uneventful, and Fran Russell was waiting for me in the lobby of the airport Hilton. After I told her what I was looking for, we decided to rent a room for the interview. After breakfast we started. Fairly far into the interview we got onto the subject of Mickey Wiener and the SIO:

MORROW: What ties did Mickey Wiener and the SIO have together?

RUSSELL: It was something I couldn't quite figure out. How a man of the SIO's background, obvious social position.

MORROW: Mr. Clean, in other words.

RUSSELL: Yes, Mr. Clean . . . would be having anything to do with Mickey. They weren't cut out of the same cloth. Nor could I see how the SIO would have his wife involved in the operation. At first I figured Mickey was pursuing the SIO and was trying through him to buy a certain amount of social prestige, have him "open doors" so to speak. But then I realized there were actual business dealings between them, such as oil wells, which the SIO was selling.

MORROW: Mickey bought oil wells from the SIO?

RUSSELL: Mickey bought oil wells from the SIO.

MORROW: That would have taken quite a bit of money.

RUSSELL: I don't recall now . . . I would have to give it some thought. I know that he gave checks to the SIO which I made out and had knowledge of to pay for the oil wells. There were more people than Mickey involved in the oil wells. Later, it developed these were not actual wells, but rather speculative drillings on fields around active gushers, the land itself being originally owned by the SIO's friends. . . .

MORROW: Getting back to our friend Mickey Wiener. He had offices in the LaSalle Building. You were involved with him to a certain extent. In fact, I think to be perfectly frank about it, he was instrumental in ruining you.

RUSSELL: Well, I don't know how much he did try and blacken my name. Let's say it that way.

MORROW: Did he ever try and blackmail you?

RUSSELL: No. Never to my face. I do know that he made a phone call to one of my former employers and said you can't trust Frances. Because Leo immediately called me.

MORROW: I'm going to cut this off for a second.

[Conversation off tape.]

MORROW: The SIO's office was in the Executive Office Building?

RUSSELL: At no time. . . . Is that thing going?

MORROW: Yes.

RUSSELL: O.K. At no time, to my knowledge, did he have an office in the White House.

. . . . .

RUSSELL: Now, Albert mentions Dick Connally. Dick Connally was completely shocked at the relationship between the SIO and Mickey Wiener. Because the SIO and Mickey were not cut out of the same cloth at all. As Al says, Mr. Clean and Mr. Black. Dick, many times, puzzled over that association.

. . . . .

But the fact that these two [the SIO and Mickey] associated, Mickey being the type of person he was, which was obvious on the surface; although not necessarily a bad person, but socially you would not elect to be with him. . .to me the SIO was more or less a pragmatic, secure person, almost naive in some things. He neither cared very much nor hated very much. He was a smooth, easy-going guy. He never got upset about anything easily. He did get upset, however, at one time when Mickey was in dire trouble because of his lying on the stand; that Mickey would have the gall later to try and associate with him in public or at any time, because he had tried to wash his hands of Mickey, ruffled him. I never could figure out that relationship. I could figure out why Mickey would buy a case of Chateau Lafitte Rothschild 1918, which then was about thirty-two dollars a bottle so that the SIO could have a drink of wine when he came in. That was the only purpose for the case being there. I could have a drink of the wine if the SIO was there.

MORROW: Did it surprise you that they're back together?

RUSSELL: The SIO and Mickey?

MORROW: Seeing each other again.

RUSSELL: It amazes me. Tremendously shocks me. Because I thought perhaps his original acceptance of Mickey came at a time when the SIO was going to be looking for a thing to do. Felt with his experience Air Force-wise, he might be able to be . . . also with his connections with the Johnson administration . . . could be helpful on defense contracts. I thought that the SIO figured it was to his advantage to get mixed up with what he thought was the Washington lobbying scene and this was part of the Washington scene. But there's . . . I can't understand why at this point he would have anything to do with Mickey, knowing Mickey's gross mistake at the time of the Bobby Baker investigation. It just thoroughly shocks me, because it shows to me that he has little or no good sense.

MORROW: Maybe he's being blackmailed.

RUSSELL: It could well be. I can't believe that at any time he's trying to get money out of Mickey because Mickey never got money from the SIO, to my knowledge . . . he couldn't have owed the SIO money. Maybe Mickey owed the SIO. Anything is possible. But I still think the SIO maybe just puts up with Mickey.

MORROW: O.K. Let me ask you a question. During the Bobby Baker investigation, did [name deleted] ever allude that he knew the people behind the Kennedy assassination?

RUSSELL: I've heard that's been said.

MORROW: Did you ever hear it in your presence?

RUSSELL: I have never heard it in my presence. I've heard that statement attributed to [name deleted] from Mickey.

MORROW: What about Mickey's Mafia connections?

RUSSELL: Here is one that I want to bring up now. It's one that you may want to ask Al about. There was a fellow by the name of Brown, who was in Applied Electronics, who was a Jersey gangster. I do not know of my own knowledge what was said . . . I heard it from Mickey that Brown had good connections in Las Vegas. He was on the board of Applied, with Warren Wilentz.

MORROW: Applied Electronics?

RUSSELL: Repeating, I do not know how they became so close—the SIO and Mickey, that is. For example, the SIO and Dick Connally . . . let's put it this way, Dick didn't care if the SIO saw him with Mickey; the SIO cared that Dick should not see him with Mickey. Because Dick, being an outspoken sort of guy, would say, "why you son of a bitch; how in the hell did you ever get tied up with this guy?" He was just strange, foreign. I don't mean foreign-ethnic group; he was just not the kind of person you would expect the SIO to be with. This is the mystery . . . Dick Connally was very close to [name deleted].

MORROW: Dick Connally was?

RUSSELL: Dick Connally was. And he never could understand how [name deleted] and Mickey Wiener got so close. Because Dick's conversations with me about it were that Mickey's got a nothing operation. He's got a big front and all he needs—and he told me this—all he needed was an office, a telephone, an answering service, and a girl. He didn't need that showplace. And I always figured this was a kid who didn't know how to handle money, which he didn't know how to handle.

MORROW: How in God's name did he have so much power and was in with so many people?

RUSSELL: I believe that his entree, you might refresh Al on this, to Bobby Baker—which we know did not exist at the time of the IRE convention at the Plaza. However, it was firmed up so quickly. It was perhaps through Senator Pete Williams of New Jersey, who lived at 1028 for a period of time, in Mickey's apartment.

MORROW: Is he still alive?

RUSSELL: Very much alive; he just remarried. He's quite young. He's about your age.

MORROW: Thank you. He's not still a senator?

RUSSELL: Yes. He is still a senator, still in the United States Senate. Senator Harrison Williams. And Al can tell you; if you called there at night and Mickey was not in, the phone would be answered by a man saying "Pete Williams speaking." He lived in the back bedroom of the first apartment Mickey had, which was on the ninth floor before he moved to the penthouse.

· · · · ·

RUSSELL: Going back to the SIO. He then set up an office, having gotten a contract with Dexter [?] Engineering of Pennsylvania—which Albert may have forgotten—on Connecticut Avenue right around the corner from Mickey. It was on the first floor of the building that housed

Air Transport Command . . . I've forgotten the number; but he had the kind of office you would expect of someone in business as distinguished from Mickey's type of operation. The SIO's office was just a functional office, and there was office-type equipment there.

I also want to bring up in this connection, something that we all may have overlooked, but since we've brought up Mickey's gambling—his frequent trips to Switzerland. . . .

All right. Well, Mickey flew back and forth frequently. Now there is a tie-in to Switzerland . . . On his return trip to Switzerland, he always stopped by Miami. He would fly from Switzerland, usually stopping at the George Cinq on the way back, fly into Kennedy, and never from Kennedy to Washington, but always direct from Kennedy to the Bank of Miami Beach.[2] The guy's name was Carl Epstein, and the president of the bank . . . I can't think of his name . . .

MORROW: Well, we can dig it up.

RUSSELL: But Carl Epstein and Phil are the ones who, on his signature alone, gave him what I consider a substantial—it was a demand note—a substantial loan, unsecured. Well, I frequently covered the interest on that loan, and Carl Epstein knew I did.

MORROW: How about the Miami National Bank?

RUSSELL: Miami National Bank, no. The only dealings he had to my knowledge in Florida were with the Bank of Miami Beach . . . , and I have been to the Bank of Miami Beach.

MORROW: Well, we get back to the same thing. He's back [meaning Wiener]. . . .

. . . . .

RUSSELL: You see, I don't understand how the SIO and Mickey could be together again. It's something that would just. . . .

MORROW: You must understand, the Kennedy investigation has resurfaced. . . .

RUSSELL: I know that he did tape conversations. There's one area that really sent Mickey into panic and that was about certain dates, and it had to do with his trips to Las Vegas. Because the FBI had questioned him rather extensively about [name deleted].

MORROW: [name deleted]?

RUSSELL: Yes. And he was also terribly concerned . . . , and Torby was also involved. Of course, Torby died about six months ago.

MORROW: Who was he?

RUSSELL: Torbert McDonald . . . Congressman McDonald. He was Jack Kennedy's roommate at Harvard. Mickey was always fearful that his dates wouldn't be quite right as far as his Las Vegas dealings were concerned, and he would also use a great deal of doubletalk on the telephone.

MORROW: Would this be before or after the assassination?

RUSSELL: This would be before.

MORROW: The assassination occurred in '63.

RUSSELL: In '63. Well, I was out of there in late '64.

MORROW: Lyndon Johnson wasn't even president yet.

RUSSELL: Right. I was out of there . . . Mickey's office was closed in the fall of '64. Mickey didn't survive. Mickey didn't survive long in that upstairs office.

MORROW: I remember being in it in 1964 . . . the latter part of '64.

RUSSELL: Now I'm talking about . . . in '63, at the time of the assassination, he was on the ninth floor. . . .

MORROW: He had a double. . . .

RUSSELL: No, the double floor was on the tenth floor. That was his second move in the LaSalle Building.

MORROW: I was in that suite in the late summer or early fall of 1964. The reason I remember it is because I have articles that were in *Popular Mechanics* of that year, showing the previews of the '65 automobiles of that year. So it had to be something like August, September, October of 1964.

Because of the Moakler and Russell interviews, I had to give credence to the story told me by the intelligence colonel's son, for my interviews with Moakler and Fran Russell had occurred four months prior to my receiving the call from him.

And the young man had mentioned the SAVAK, claiming he would be in serious danger if they found out I was talking to him.

Even after the Goodaryi interview, and the fact that the Capitol Hill playboy had been murdered (allegedly by the mob), it still seemed incomprehensible to me that there could be a SAVAK connection to Bobby Kennedy's assassination.

I was still pursuing the allegations the intelligence colonel's son had given me about his father and the involvement his father and the SIO might have had to the President's murder.

Instead, after what Goodaryi had told me, I should have been investigating the mob and CIA's next logical step. To insure both their futures, they had to have Nixon in the White House. And, if it appeared that Bobby Kennedy had a chance of becoming president, they had to eliminate him.

With the Shah of Iran's vast resources to help fund the Nixon campaign and the monarch's secret police force coordinated with the Mafia, both could be done with ease.

Nixon was the perfect foil for both the Syndicate and the CIA, since his early career had been substantially financed and promulgated by both the Mafia and founders of the clandestine Agency. It was time for both of them to call in their markers.

With Nixon in the White House, Jimmy Hoffa could be pardoned, and the mob could once again enjoy unlimited privilege. They, as well as the covert Agency, knew the ex-Vice President's major weakness—the fear of losing an election.[3] They would play upon it unmercifully.

It was this paranoia about elections that would manifest itself all during the first four years of his administration and allow Nixon as president of the United States to cause a myriad of illegal acts to be perpetrated in order to assure his re-election.

Millions would be committed by the Shah of Iran to Nixon's 1968 campaign, arranged by members of the CIA. The money was routed through Zurich and sent into Mexico via the Banco Nacional de Mexico. There, it was picked up and hand-carried to Washington by Iranian Ambassador Hushang Ansary,[4] in diplomatic pouches.[5]

CHAPTER TWELVE NOTES

1.   The Rotunda Restaurant is today the site of the National Democratic Club.

2.   In 1967, the Bahamian Royal Commission of Inquiry examined a man by the name of Max Orovitz, a prominent trustee and director of the City National Bank of Miami during the mid and late 1960s. Orovitz's troubles began in the early 1960s with a real-estate company of which he was a principal owner, the General Development Corporation (GDC)—a supposedly respectable company, but with "Trigger" Mike Coppola and Lansky-associate Lou Chesler as its principals. Worse for Orovitz was the fact that in 1961 he committed an elaborate securities fraud involving GDC stock and some fancy Swiss-bank maneuvers. His 1968 conviction was part of U.S. Attorney Robert Morgenthau's war on organized crime.

Orovitz hasn't been able to rid himself of some of the friends of his GDC days. In 1963, Meyer Lansky and his key lieutenants planned the installation of gambling casinos in the Bahamas in Orovitz's office, and Orovitz was later put on the payroll as a "consultant" of the company that controlled the first casino on the island. Orovitz's role in handling stateside money transfers and manipulations for the Lucayan Beach Casino, including some large transactions between Orovitz and Lansky couriers—which produced unauthorized signatures on checks after they were cashed—gave rise to the suspicion that tainted money was being laundered. At the time of the transactions, Orovitz was using the mob-controlled Bank of Miami Beach. A Justice Department memo was later to offer "proof of a collection account in the Bank of Miami Beach with Max Orovitz taking millions of dollars out of the account for the benefit of Lansky and Chesler."

Orovitz began to feel the heat, and in 1965 he transferred the casino accounts to the City National Bank of Miami, of which he, together with another Lansky associate, had become a director. Orovitz and the casino accounts remained at City National.

By 1970, Orovitz set his sights on Israel, and when Meyer Lansky took refuge in Tel Aviv that year, federal investigators, who consider Orovitz a "respectable associate of Lansky," were not surprised to see Lansky, the aging but still active financial wizard, take up residence at the Orovitz-owned Dan Hotel in Tel Aviv.

The Bank of Miami Beach is most interesting. As noted, the bank was originally set up to service Cuban casinos operated by organized crime and continued to perform laundering services through the 1960s—and was still considered mob-connected. It was considered a sister bank of the Miami National Bank in the 1960s, sharing many of the same directors and performing many of the same services.

3. Interview with Nasser Afshar, February 13, 1981.

4.   *Ibid.*

5.   A similar scenario revealed by the Watergate investigation would take place in the 1972 presidential race. As with the money from Iran, which went through the Banco Nacional de Mexico, corporate funds—$100,000, illegally contributed on April 3, 1972, to the Committee to Re-elect the President from Gulf Resources and Chemical Corporation of Houston, Texas—also took the Mexican route, according to *The White House Transcripts* (Bantam Books, 1974).

Chapter Thirteen

All through the latter part of 1977 and into the early part of 1978, I went about the task of trying to confirm the allegations the intelligence officer's son had given me. The Wiener tapes had mysteriously disappeared from the place Moakler said he had hidden them. He was very nervous after his trip to Stafford, Virginia, where he said they were in storage. I had no choice but to believe him. However, several interviews I had made were worthless without this backup.

At this point I had the choice of looking into the allegations made by Goodaryi, who by this time was long buried, or pursuing leads the intelligence colonel's son had given me. I chose the latter—spending tedious months tracking down names, relationships, and dates regarding the alliance between the Cubans, CIA, and Mafia, my original quest.

The pattern that started to emerge was exactly the one that the intelligence colonel's son, Fran Russell, Al Moakler, and others had implied, i.e., that many high-ranking intelligence officers during and after the Kennedy administration appeared to have had close ties and dealings with organized crime—dealings that not only involved the CIA and Cubans, but also the SAVAK—beginning in the mid-1960s. More importantly, because of these ties, they would have been forced to involve the CIA in a cover-up of the President's assassination, a role that could later force the clandestine agency to make their SAVAK resources available for the elimination of Bobby Kennedy.

Exploring this avenue, I would interview a young lady who had lived with the intelligence officer's son over an extended period of time. The gist of information Didi Hess provided, combined with all the other pieces of the jigsaw I had gathered through the years, did seem to confirm his story. She also told her story to the HSCA. It was about a meeting and

155

subsequent telephone conversations between her and the intelligence colonel. Unfortunately it occurred just two months before the committee would submit its report, and because of this timing, no action would be taken. Here is a short excerpt from my interview on Tuesday, September 27, 1977, in Pittsburgh, Pennsylvania. (The intelligence colonel's name has been replaced with "Intellfirst" and his son's name with "Intellson".)

HESS: What he said to me over the phone [after a Sunday meeting at the Naval Academy's Officers' Club in Annapolis, Maryland] was simply this. From what he said to me when I first met him and what Mrs. Intellfirst said to me, the whole conversation was [that] he was trying [testing] me. In other words, he was trying to feel me out as far as I was concerned and as to whether I had believed what Intellson had told me. But when I talked with him on the phone, he admitted to me that it was all true.

MORROW: What was all true? What Intellson had talked to him about that afternoon? [referring to Intellson's accusations of his father's being bagman for the Kennedy assassination]

HESS: Right.

MORROW: He told you about the assassination?

HESS: Right.

MORROW: His personal involvement?

HESS: Right.

MORROW: How did he say it?

HESS: He said, well . . . something about, "The whole thing's true, Didi." He said, "Intellson doesn't understand. He understands bits and pieces. He doesn't understand how serious it is." He said, "It is for me."

· · · · ·

MORROW: That's when he admitted what to you?

HESS: He said, "It's all true." He said, "What Intellson heard, Intellson has magnified the bits and pieces and he can't put the whole thing together." He said it was true. He said, "I did it for the total good."

MORROW: O.K. . . .

· · · · ·

MORROW: All right. Tell us what the Colonel said in Annapolis that day.

HESS: All right. He took me aside and was telling me all this stuff about Intellson and everything else . . . and he was so. . . . The first thing you know . . . he started to ask me . . . he was trying to feel me out as to how much Intellson had told me about . . . obviously what he knew.

MORROW: O.K. I'll buy that. It makes sense.

HESS: And I was trying to say . . . hey . . . you know. I said, you know, I had taken it with a grain of salt, whatever. [She starts sobbing.] I said whatever Intellson has told me I have taken with a grain of salt. I understand . . . I was trying to be nice. [She also admitted later to being terrified.] And he took my hand, and the trouble is you can't really look into his eyes unless you're telling the truth. You really can't.

MORROW: Sure. I'll buy that.

HESS: He said, "Didi," he said, "whatever I did, it was because I had to do it." He said, "You understand that, don't you?"

MORROW: All right. What was your interpretation [of that statement] . . . or did he go any further than that?

HESS: Yeah. I asked him . . . I mean, we both knew what each other knew. It was obvious. He knew goddamn well that I couldn't live with Intellson for over a year and not hear the whole thing . . . .

MORROW: Did you ask Intellfirst . . . remember, I asked you, did you ask Intellfirst if he would take congressional immunity? Did you mention it to him at all?

HESS: Yes.

MORROW: What did he say?

HESS: He said he thought he could do it.

MORROW: Intellfirst said he thought. . . . Did you tell him I asked?

HESS: Yes, I did.

MORROW: O.K. Was he sad?

HESS: No. He was just going to call me. He really was; he was going to call me.

MORROW: I don't want to put any words in your mouth, but do you think he felt relieved?

HESS:　　　　　　Yes. Because I think he'd worn the burden for
　　　　　　　　　a long time . . . .

Like the intelligence colonel's son, her story would later also include many people I had met or known through Capitol Hill connections, names that had never been publicly connected to either murder. As of 1986, Ms. Hess held an important government position in the Reagan White House.

* * * * *

By the end of 1967, the Garrison investigation had turned into a fiasco. Its failure was primarily due to the New Orleans DA's association with Mafia don Carlos Marcello, with a helping hand from CIA Director Richard Helms. Politically, Bobby Kennedy had been right to once again assert his belief in the Warren Commission.

There was no question now that Bobby Kennedy would have to become president in order to unearth the true story behind his brother's murder—a fact that the mob was keenly aware of. They were also keenly aware that, if RFK did get into the White House, their financial empire would be doomed.

After John Kennedy's assassination, the Justice Department's Nevada project against Las Vegas racketeering had been abandoned. Within four years of the murder, the number of field days spent by agents of the Justice Department's organized crime division had been cut in half. Their time before grand juries and court appearances declined by seventy-two and fifty-six percent respectively, and the number of federal court briefs filed in organized-crime cases reduced by eighty-three percent.

What these statistics added up to was a surrender by Lyndon Johnson of the war Robert Kennedy had declared. It had cost only one casualty— the life of his brother. They also knew, if Bobby became president, he would restart the war with a vengeance.

Another decision had to be made.

In the beginning, Bobby was not running strongly. However, on the off-chance he did win the 1968 Democratic nomination for president, he would handily beat Richard Nixon, the silent partner and beneficiary of organized crime. Instead of being pardoned, Jimmy Hoffa, still in control of millions in Teamster Pension Funds, would not only rot in jail, but key mob figures would probably join him.

The California primary was the key. If Kennedy lost it, his life could be spared. If he won it, *the Senator must die*. And, by 1968, organized crime knew—via their associates in the CIA—the most efficient organization to set up and carry out Bobby's execution would be the SAVAK.

* * * * *

By the middle of 1978, I had almost given up on finding the true facts behind Bobby's murder. All the data I had gathered was tantalizing, yet remained disconnected. However, by this time one thing seemed certain; it all seemed to track back to the Shah of Iran. Two former intelligence officers, supposedly tied to the mob, were also related to the royal family. Alex Goodaryi, the SAVAK's liaison to the mob in Washington, had been murdered within weeks of my interviewing him. It was all too coincidental, but I couldn't seem to move one step closer. Richard Helms, now the U.S. ambassador to Iran, had apparently removed any loose ends that could tie the SAVAK to the mob or CIA.

Then, in late 1979, after the Shah was deposed and more of the misdeeds of the SAVAK began to surface, I pulled out the CBS *60 Minutes* transcript and decided to try to reach Richard Cottam and Nasser Afshar, men who supposedly knew all about the SAVAK's activities in the U.S. After spending a month tracking them down, I reached Cottam first through the University of Pittsburgh. When I called, he was in.

On the phone, Cottam was quite pleasant but guarded when I asked him some leading questions about the SAVAK. I could understand that, so I made an appointment to see him the following week.

When I got to Pittsburgh, I called Cottam at the home number he had given me, and we arranged to meet at a friend's house in the Shadyside section of the city. Cottam, although quite willing to talk, refused to let me tape the interview. Sensing that this might occur, I had taken the precaution of bringing along Jeanne "Hap" Dietz, my research associate.

It was a revealing interview.[2] The former foreign service officer at our United States embassy in Tehran (I was to discover later he was a CIA intelligence officer) told me in essence what he had revealed on *60 Minutes*, years earlier—that "SAVAK assassination squads were operating freely in the U.S. during the 1960s and 1970s." According to Cottam, "they were also operating with the full knowledge, cooperation, and protection of the CIA." Cottam also claimed, "while the CIA and State Department would vehemently deny it, the Shah and therefore the SAVAK was, by the mid-1960s, under the absolute control of the CIA." Which, in effect, was the same as saying, under the direct control of Richard Helms. Cottam elaborated on several instances where the SAVAK actually "terminated" individuals in both Europe and the United States. However, as much as I pressed him, Cottam would not reveal specific names. In late 1979, when I asked another supposed foreign service officer (he had just retired after thirty years with the CIA) about the SAVAK, he—like Tracy Barnes had earlier with regard to the Cuban exiles—just smiled.

Cottam, whose credentials are impeccable, was asked by the U.S. government to contact Iranian Foreign Minister Sadegh Ghotbzadeh, in 1979, after fifty U.S. diplomats and citizens were taken hostage by Iran, to attempt negotiations for their release. Ghotbzadeh, who was a close personal friend of Cottam's, was himself targeted for assassination by the SAVAK.[3]

Ghotbzadeh's assassination story was disclosed in a bizarre account given to Mike Wallace—by the intended SAVAK assassin—on *60 Minutes,* aired on Sunday, March 6, 1977.

As a sad aftermath, Ghotbzadeh, trying to help release the hostages, came into disfavor because of being a moderate. He was then accused of being a traitor and, as a result, was executed shortly after as an enemy of the revolution.

Because of the extreme nature of the information revealed on *60 Minutes* about the SAVAK, I have chosen to include part of its transcript in order to show how I came to seek out and interview Cottam and a man named Nasser Afshar—the man who would be one of the key sources about how the SAVAK was involved in Bobby Kennedy's assassination.[4]

> *WALLACE:*   SAVAK is the Iranian counterpart of the FBI and the CIA—the Iranian secret police, which has a fearsome reputation inside Iran—tales of torture, repression, denied by the Shah of Iran, but substantiated by Amnesty International and the International Commission of Jurists. In an interview with the Shah of Iran, last October, he acknowledged to me that the SAVAK does operate in the United States.

After the Shah disclaimed any wrongdoing on the part of the SAVAK, Wallace continued, interviewing one of their assassins. He was a man named Jules Kahn Pira. According to Wallace:

[Pira] spent a decade living clandestinely in Western Europe, a stateless man, in and out of prison several times, until finally he was granted an Iranian passport and went to work as a journalist. Actually he had another mission—political assassination.

Wallace then interviewed Pira and one of Pira's intended victims, a man named Sadegh Ghotbzadeh, who shortly after the Ayotollah came to power, was named Iran's Foreign Minister.

After interviewing Ghotbzadeh, Pira described another of his intended victims, a man by the name of Nasser Afshar. Afshar would become the main key to my solving the Bobby Kennedy assassination.

KAHN PIRA: [In French] Yes. Next on his hit list was to be a man called Afshar, about whom I ·knew nothing.

WALLACE: This is Afshar—Nasser Afshar—a wealthy businessman, formerly an Iranian citizen, now an American. He commutes between Geneva, Switzerland, where Kahn Pira says he had been assigned to kill Afshar, and Alexandria, Virginia, where he now publishes the *Iran Free Press,* a paper for which Afshar claims a circulation of twenty thousand, including many prominent Americans. The paper is filled with attacks against the Shah, his regime and his family.
         Why would the SAVAK want to kill you, Nasser Afshar?

AFSHAR: Because I'm the publisher of *Iran Free Press.*

WALLACE: As simple as that?

AFSHAR: As simple as that.

Wallace then went on to interview a former United States foreign officer, who would later attest to what Afshar would tell me about the workings of the SAVAK assassination teams operating in the U.S.

WALLACE: In the United States we found more— apparent confirmation from this man, Richard Cottam, who worked in Iran for the U.S. Government in the 1950s, he says for the State Department, but we hear it was for the CIA. He is a professor of international relations at the University of Pittsburgh and a close observer of the Iranian political scene. Cottam says a trusted friend in the U.S. Government told him that SAVAK had indeed dispatched assassination squads to the United States and Europe.

COTTAM: I was told by someone in government—a friend of mine who I trust very much—that this was the case. He told me that it was absolutely true. And—

WALLACE: That *what* was absolutely true?

COTTAM: That assassination squads had been dispatched to both the United States and to Europe by SAVAK. And that this individual wanted me to inform some of the possible victims.

WALLACE: Who told you, if you can tell us?

COTTAM: Well, I can't tell you.

WALLACE: Do you know a man by the name of Sadegh Ghotbzadeh?

COTTAM: Yes, I do.

WALLACE: He told us that he was on the hit list, and

indeed introduced us to his supposed— presumed—assassins.

COTTAM: If I were to work up a list of—of people who the Shah would like to kill, I would put Ghotbzadeh up near the top.

WALLACE: Nasser Afshar was also on that list. Does that make sense?

COTTAM: Yes, it does.

WALLACE: Various inquiries have been put to various people in the U.S. Government, and they claim that they have been able to find absolutely no evidence that such squads entered the United States, existed then, or exist now.

COTTAM: Or that they ever were intended to be sent in? That's included? Well, I just plain don't believe that. I just simply believe the person who told me. I don't—I don't have, in my own mind, one—one iota of doubt that this information was correct.

WALLACE: You believe that the CIA has the information?

COTTAM: Yes, I do.

WALLACE: Your familiarity with Iran—does it come from service in the CIA in Iran?

COTTAM: I was with the Foreign Service.

The third and most important name to surface from this show was a man named Mansour Rafizadeh.

WALLACE: One of those agents, said the Ambassador, is Mansour Rafizadeh, a member of Iran's U.N.

Delegation. Others say he is the head of SAVAK in the United States. He would not talk to us.

At the end of the segment on the SAVAK, Wallace made a point of the close ties the Iranian Secret Police maintained with the CIA and FBI. It appears that they all worked happily together. After all, former CIA director Richard Helms did become ambassador to Iran.

WALLACE: The Chicago Police regularly traded their information with the FBI, which also has its own informants among Iranian students. And some of that FBI information is said to be passed on, through the CIA, to SAVAK.

For example, through a court suit, Nasser Afshar, publisher of the *Iran Free Press,* obtained possession of a confidential FBI memo transmitting information about him to the CIA. And the memo indicates that that information was passed on one step further.

And then on the next page it says: "The FBI interposes no objection to the passage of the above information"—deleted—[and, that, I would imagine, is to the Government of Iran, "G-O-I"]—"provided the FBI is not identified as the source." Would you like the United States Senate Committees to investigate the activities of the SAVAK?

After concluding my interview with Richard Cottam, I sensed I might now be on the right track about who might have killed Bobby Kennedy. So, I sent for and got a Los Angeles Police Department report on Khyber Khan. Then after spending more fruitless months, I caught up with Nasser Afshar. The explanation of why his phone didn't answer: he goes overseas on business for months at a time.

CHAPTER THIRTEEN NOTES

1.   See sworn affidavit of Didi Hess, Appendix, Exhibit No. 14.

2.   Interview with Richard Cottam, Pittsburgh, Pennsylvania, June 26, 1980, at the home of Mrs. Margo Kamin.

3.   Sadegh Ghotbzadeh was, in 1962, the subject of a National Student Association "White Paper" involving the Iranian Student Association in the United States. During the months of May and June 1961, the Iranian Embassy in Washington, D.C., concentrated an attack upon the president of the ISA, Mr. Ali S. Fatemi, and its secretary-general, Mr. Sadegh Ghotbzadeh. At the time, Fatemi was a graduate student at the University of Columbia and Ghotbzadeh was studying in the School of Foreign Service at Georgetown University.

A complete review of their plight was included in the *Working Papers on Iran,* and a "White Paper" addendum (Book III, *International Student Relations, Working Papers 1961-1962,* U.S. National Student Association). Both Mr. Fatemi and Mr. Ghotbzadeh were, in 1962, in immediate danger of deportation because of this political activity against the Shah while studying in the United States.

4.   *60 Minutes* © copyright CBS News, 1977. All rights reserved.

Chapter Fourteen

Cottam's description of Nasser Afshar matched his voice, which was nervous but vibrant and extremely rushed, as if he were out of breath. I introduced myself, telling him that Richard Cottam recommended my talking to him.

He asked what I wanted, and I said, because of the sensitive nature of the topic, I had better write him a letter outlining the subject matter and talk to him after he had read it. It could be possible he might not wish to discuss the matter over the phone. He agreed, and I sent him a brief summary of my conversation with Alexi Goodaryi about Khyber Khan and Bobby's assassination.

Eleven days later, on February 13, 1981, I called him back. The following is a transcript of this telephone conversation.

> *MORROW:*   Mr. Afshar?
>
> *AFSHAR:*   Yes.
>
> *MORROW:*   Mr. Bob Morrow. How are you?
>
> *AFSHAR:*   Fine, thank you. I read your paper, and I found that the [unintelligible] concern that Khyber Khan. . . .
>
> *MORROW:*   Excuse me, sir. I didn't understand you.
>
> *AFSHAR:*   I found the man named Khyber Khan you have in the paper [referring to the letter I had sent him].

MORROW: Yes?

AFSHAR: He was . . . mentally, I think he was a little ill.
But, at any rate, he had some arrangement
years ago, in the 1950s, to build a stadium in
Iran with some of the Shah's relatives. And
that went sour, and he came back to the
United States; and he brought a suit against
the royal family here. And then he disclosed
some information, in the 1950s, that some of
the aid to the Shah—American foreign aid—
went to his personal account in the Pahlevi
Foundation. And then he had some documents
from the Union Bank of Switzerland showing
that the money was paid to different members
of his family and came from American aid. Of
course, the Senator Mc. . . .

MORROW: McClellen?

AFSHAR: Yes, that's right. His committee asked the
question if the information was not correct
according to that time.

MORROW: McClellen asked Khan?

AFSHAR: Yes. And then after that, he [Khan] brought a
suit. And, in connection with that suit, he had
been in touch with some members of the royal
family[1] after that, and they settled the case with
him. And the payment he supposedly got . . .
from that moment he became an Iranian
secret-police agent. And it was well known. I
mean, he was working for the SAVAK, and
there was no question about that part.

MORROW: What year was that, sir?

AFSHAR: That was early . . . it was in the late 1950s. And

so, as I recall it—I have to look . . . I have this
file completely. But it is my recollection that it
was the late 1950s. . . . No, early 1960s, I would
say. Because I was in Teheran at the time, I
remember. The early 1960s . . . 1963, '64, '65.
That's it.

MORROW: Then he would have been ripe.

AFSHAR: Yes. So, he brought the suit in the late 1950s
and early 1960s, and 1964, '65, '66, '67, he
became an agent of the Iranian secret police.

MORROW: And this was in the Los Angeles area?

AFSHAR: He was in Washington in the beginning part of
it, and he was in New York, he claimed . . . As
I said, he's mentally ill . . . showing some
newspaper he has 280 shoes . . . He's supposed
to be the best-dressed man . . . something like
that.

MORROW: Did he have any connection with organized
crime, do you know?

AFSHAR: He was connected with those people in
Washington who were running some restaurant
or something. . . .

MORROW: The fellow at the Rotunda?

AFSHAR: Yes . . . something like that. He was working
with them . . . , and there was some woman
involved. As I said, I have to . . . it was some
years ago. I have to look into it, to get more
details . . . exact dates.

MORROW: You see how important it is?

AFSHAR: Yes. Oh, definitely he was involved, that I know. But . . .

MORROW: Involved in the assassination?

AFSHAR: Yes. Yes. I think one thing you should . . . Do you have any connection with Jack Anderson's office?

MORROW: Yes, I do. Very close.

AFSHAR: It was Joe . . . Joe something that was his assistant . . . I call him always Joe. In Jack Anderson's file you will find the connection of the payment to Nixon's campaign in the '60s. . . .

MORROW: This is 1968?

AFSHAR: Yes. If you get this information from them, which is from Mexico . . . and the money was transferred from Zurich to Mexico, and from Mexico it disappeared . . . , assuming . . . I mean, the indication was Ambassador Ansary at the time . . . he went to Mexico every week.

MORROW: The Iranian ambassador?

AFSHAR: That's right. And, he brought lots of money— cash, over a million dollars each trip, according to Mexican banking authorities.

MORROW: Do you know who in Mexico would know that?

AFSHAR: The Bank of Mexico. The bank . . . I do not have the name, but Jack Anderson has the name of the bank, because he wrote the name of the bank.[2]

MORROW: Then the SAVAK were in the Nixon campaign very heavily?

AFSHAR: Very much so.

MORROW: Do you think they had a deal to knock out Bobby Kennedy?

AFSHAR: Definitely. That was Mansour Rafizadeh. Mansour Rafizadeh was . . . . When the assassination of Bobby Kennedy was completed without any difficulty, that man from a rank of . . . a very low class of SAVAK became the highest one in the United States. He is the one you should look into his past.

AFSHAR: Rafizadeh was the head of the Iranian secret police . . .

MORROW: In the U.S.?

AFSHAR: In the U.S. He lived in New Jersey. . . .He was the one involved with Khyber Khan. . . . He had a half a dozen different names[3]. . . . But part of the settlement that they paid him. . . . I do not know what they paid him, but his case was dismissed by settlement, and part of that he began working for Rafizadeh and the Iranian secret police for the assassination of Bobby Kennedy.

MORROW: Let me ask you some questions, if I may.

AFSHAR: Please do.

MORROW: You, of course, were aware of SAVAK assassination squads operating in the United States?

AFSHAR: Yes.

MORROW: Were they Iranian SAVAK personnel or hired by the SAVAK to carry out these assignments . . . , such as this chap in Paris . . . , or was it both?

AFSHAR: Both. Always both. They had both, but the management of all of them was done between Tehran and in the United States.

MORROW: Did you know any SAVAK members in Los Angeles? . . . Yourself?

AFSHAR: Oh, there were. . . . We had approximately in the United States . . . it would be very difficult to say, because in the early 1970s, they had by '75 . . . or '74, they had at least about three-thousand here. But most of them were students.

MORROW: Did you ever hear of this chap . . . or recognize the fact that the SAVAK had several members in Bobby Kennedy's campaign, under Khyber Khan.[4]

AFSHAR: Well, that we know definitely. They were telling us at that time that . . .

MORROW: Who was telling you, sir?

AFSHAR: The Iranians . . . that there are very close connections . . . that John F. Kennedy against the Shah was not true. John F. Kennedy, when he became president, the first head of state to come here was the Shah in February of that year. And the oil companies met his father . . . John F. Kennedy's father, and made all the arrangements . . . and there is no difficulty between Kennedy's family and the Shah's family. But that was not true. Because we knew from Tehran that, on many occasions, that the Shah said that . . . very bad things about the entire Kennedy family. And the influence of the SAVAK in the camp of Bobby Kennedy was trying to tell us how close they are with the Kennedy family. But, in reality, they wanted to get even with them. You understand what I mean?

MORROW: I understand the philosophy. Was this talk by the Central Intelligence Agency?

AFSHAR: That is really difficult to say, because some of the documents released even show that Rafizadeh was working for the FBI and was receiving some money from the FBI, as well as salary from the FBI. The documents released by mistake to American Civil Liberties Union on my behalf, show that Rafizadeh not only was the head of Iranian SAVAK according to their own documents but liaison man for the FBI and working for them for some time. It is really difficult to say some of them . . . they say that Khyber Khan was working with the CIA. Whether this is true or not, I cannot verify, but they were always saying that they were very close to the Kennedy family.

MORROW: In reality they were not, however . . .

AFSHAR: This we knew was not . . . [true].

MORROW: Because the Nixon campaign was being supported by the Shah . . .

AFSHAR: This is exactly true, all of it. We have all the information, which we can prove . . . We have many information, cash payment, even when Nixon was in Tehran.

MORROW: Let me ask you some questions, if I may. Did you know of an organization called the International Police Academy in Washington . . . supposedly who trained SAVAK members. They were formed around 1950. Did you ever hear of the China Lake, California, facility that trained the SAVAK in terrorist tactics?

AFSHAR: I heard about that, yes. You see we knew that SAVAK agents, as a matter of fact, some of the people coming over here to the United States had been seen. For example, if you see Rafizadeh in demonstration in front of White House for Iranian students, you will see two CIA men with him all the time.

MORROW: Now, did you know anything or get any information regarding this young Jordanian, Sirhan Sirhan's relationship with the SAVAK, possibly, or Jordanian students out there in the Los Angeles area?

AFSHAR: The only thing we knew, and we had information that he was a member of an organization in Jordan which was supposedly financed by the SAVAK completely . . . in Lebanon, and in Jordan, and in the United States.

MORROW: Is there also one in Pakistan, just out of curiosity?

AFSHAR: That's right. That's right.

MORROW: Do you have the names of those organizations?[5]

AFSHAR: No, but I can find out for you if you want.

MORROW: Well, I think for documentation sake . . . we are going to have to, so if you'll keep that on your list . . . and as much information on Sirhan Sirhan as you can relating to Khyber Khan.

AFSHAR: That I have to contact some of the people in Tehran. They own some of the documents that have been captured by some of the people now in power. Of course, they don't understand what they [the documents] are talking about.

MORROW: Yes.

At this point Afshar and I discussed certain references made to a communication center that the SAVAK had set up in New York state and certain Iranian students who had been murdered.

The conversation with Afshar left me in a quandary. It was obvious that Goodaryi and Cottam had been right. There were SAVAK assassination squads operating right here in the United States. And they not only worked for the CIA, they also worked for the FBI and mob.

But it was my personal meeting with Afshar in Washington a month later that left me with little doubt that the SAVAK had indeed murdered Bobby Kennedy. And had done it in conjunction with organized crime, the CIA, or both. We met at the same restaurant where Marshall Diggs and I had had our infamous conversation a decade and a half earlier. It was under a new name. Even so, I still got a cold chill as I walked in.

Afshar's appearance matched his voice. He was small and dynamic and seemed high-strung. An hour and a half later, I could understand why. He told me about himself, his experiences of being hunted by the SAVAK in Europe, and about how Bobby Kennedy was killed. It was almost identical to the story related to me by Alex Goodaryi four years earlier.

During the last two weeks of May 1968, Khyber Khan, apparently an Iranian playboy, was in reality a high-ranking member of the Shah of Iran's SAVAK. In addition to himself, he had a number of his operatives working at Senator Kennedy's Wilshire Boulevard headquarters.[6]

According to Afshar, after Khan was taken into the SAVAK, he operated out of New York and Washington, D.C., under the supervision of Alexis Goodaryi, the former maitre d' of the Rotunda Restaurant who, according to Washington, D.C., police was murdered by the mob a month after our interview in April 1977.[7] Afshar claimed Goodaryi was killed under orders from Colonel Mansour Rafizadeh, head of the SAVAK in the U.S.

Both Afshar and Goodaryi's stories about Khan started out basically the same. In the late 1950s, after the Shah of Iran had been handed back his throne by the CIA, a rich Iranian by the name of Khyber Khan put together an Iranian group to build a sports stadium in Tehran. This group, consisting primarily of members of the Shah's immediate family, intended to fund the project with expropriated AID money, loaned to Iran by the U.S.

In 1968, it was disclosed by California Deputy Attorney General, Charles A. O'Brien, that the Office of Public Safety of the Agency for International Development (AID) had long served as a cover for the CIA's clandestine program of supplying advisors and instructors for national police intelligence services, known to insiders as the "Department of Dirty Tricks," and one of its specialties was teaching foreign "intelligence apparatus" the techniques of assassination vis-a-vis the International Police Academy, operated in the late 1950s and early 1960s by Joseph Shimon.

The Shah, having given up eighty percent of his personal land-holdings, on the advice of his CIA advisors, and having helped fund Nixon's 1960 attempt at the presidency, felt he was owed the AID money. This money was funneled through the Pahlevi Foundation and deposited in numbered Swiss accounts by the Shah's relatives. The Shah's actions were so blatant that Khan easily discovered it was AID money being used to fund the stadium project. According to Afshar, one of the AID checks was simply endorsed over to the Shah by the manager of the Omran Bank and deposited to the monarch's account.

When John Kennedy, then a U.S. senator, discovered this misuse of AID funds, he launched an attack against the Shah from the Senate floor. By 1960, just after John Kennedy was elected president, feelings were so bad between the Shah and the Kennedy brothers that both American and British oil interests sent their top executives to see the President's father, Joseph Kennedy. They asked the elder Kennedy to intercede on the Shah's behalf in order to keep the monarch from resigning, an act that would eventually destroy their vested interests.

About this time, Khan's stadium deal went sour, with the Shah's relations pulling out, claiming lack of funds due to pressure being exerted by the Kennedy brothers. Later, when Khan found out that the Shah was still misappropriating AID funds and that he still refused to go ahead with the stadium project, he became enraged.

Seeking revenge, Khan came to the U.S. with the evidence of the royal family's continued misappropriation of AID funds and turned it over to Bobby Kennedy, then the Attorney General. Bobby, furious by this additional evidence, then chose to bypass Iran and snub the Shah on his goodwill trip around the world.

The Shah, incensed, demanded a state invitation to visit Washington for a showdown. The President refused. Then, using a maturity the President had yet to acquire, Joseph Kennedy, the Presidents' father, personally invited the Shah and his wife to the U.S.

The royal couple arrived in Washington on April 11, 1962, and immediately started exerting pressure for more U.S. aid. With this overt insult, a serious confrontation occurred between the President, the Attorney General, and the Shah. They wanted to cut off all U.S. support to the Persian nation. Again, the President's father intervened, and with a helping hand from the CIA, an unhappy truce was negotiated. By CIA influence and Joseph Kennedy, the resultant truce would allow the Shah to keep on receiving AID funds—but with more stringent conditions attached. Needless to say, the monarch's attitude toward the Kennedys' did not improve. According to Nasser Afshar, the Shah was privately delighted when the President was assassinated. And, like the mob, let it be known that Bobby Kennedy was dangerous to him as long as he remained the Attorney General.[8]

Khan, meanwhile, after provoking the Shah's anger by his disclosures to the Kennedys, fled arrest in Tehran and became an alien resident of the United States.[9] He then added insult to injury by proceeding to enter suit for damages against the royal family.

Within days of filing suit, the irate Khan was approached by Goodaryi, claiming he was a representative of the Iranian government (in reality, the SAVAK).

Goodaryi told me that he was instructed by his superiors to make an offer of restitution for Khan's losses. Afshar claimed that Khan was threatened with death if he didn't comply with their wishes.

Then, according to Goodaryi, Khan insisted on receiving the offer from Goodaryi's superior. Goodaryi told me he agreed to Khan's request and drove him over to the Iranian embassy. Afshar claimed that Khan was kidnaped and taken to the Iranian embassy.

Goodaryi told me he then introduced Khan to Colonel Mansour Rafizadeh, who had just come from Teheran and was stationed in New York. The meeting between Khan and Rafizadeh was obviously successful. Khan withdrew his suit against the royal family—according to Goodaryi, after Khan accepted a large cash settlement; according to Afshar, after he was given back his life. At any rate, Khan began working for the SAVAK.

After Khan was taken into the fold, Goodaryi told me he introduced him to a number of Mafia figures friendly to the CIA.[10] One would be Kohly's old Washington, D.C., mob liaison, Jim Polley.

Goodaryi told me he was also charged with providing the now thoroughly indoctrinated Khan with large amounts of female companionship. Before he knew it, Khan was under the absolute control of Rafizadeh, whose authority he did not question, for he personally saw how Rafizadeh cooperated both with the FBI and CIA.

After that, Goodaryi said he only saw Khan from time to time, that he mostly traveled around the country for Rafizadeh. Things were going along just fine, until Bobby Kennedy declared he was going to make the run for the White House.

By early 1968, according to Goodaryi, his mob contacts made it known that it would be to the Shah's distinct advantage to have Richard Nixon in the White House. Here, Goodaryi's story differs somewhat from Nasser Afshar's, who claimed that the Shah was so concerned about Bobby Kennedy that he personally ordered Rafizadeh to eliminate the aspiring senator and started funding Nixon's campaign to the tune of several million dollars.

Goodaryi's version, although similar overall, stated: "The mob claimed, with Nixon as president, the Shah would be in a position to eventually raise oil prices. Then, with U.S. backing, control the whole Middle East—a fact that did occur. However, if Kennedy won, the Shah would be totally isolated from any further U.S. aid and military support and be subject to worldwide censure.

Whoever was right, the result was the same. When Goodaryi reported this to Mansour Rafizadeh, who supposedly checked with the Central Intelligence Agency, millions began to flow from the Shah's coffers into Nixon's 1968 campaign. Then plans were implemented by the SAVAK to murder Bobby, if he won the California primary.

According to both Goodaryi and Afshar, the man selected by Rafizadeh for that task was Khyber Khan. Khan had, at Rafizadeh's request, set up SAVAK operations on the West Coast in 1963.[11] Khan was a perfect choice. He would be considered a trusted friend of Robert Kennedy. It had been his evidence of the Shah's continued misappropriation of U.S. foreign aid that had triggered the Attorney General's anger at the monarch. Khan could staff Kennedy's California campaign with SAVAK agents and never be questioned. Bobby would never suspect that the turncoat Iranian was totally under the control of the SAVAK—and that the SAVAK was out to eliminate him.

It would be Khan's assignment to coordinate Bobby's assassination in Los Angeles. Accordingly, Khan set up permanent residence on the West Coast.

After surveying the various pro-Shah organizations in the Los Angeles area and checking with Rafizadeh, it was decided to select agents other than SAVAK members or Iranians to perform the actual murder. Two would be Sirhan Sirhan, a Jordanian, and Ali Ahmand, a Pakistanian. According to Afshar, Sirhan and Ahmand were recruited from the General Union of Jordanian Students and the National Union of Students (Pakistan). They both had large organizations in Los Angeles and were staunch supporters of the Shah. Concurrently with this decision, Khan started staffing Kennedy headquarters with members of the SAVAK. Within a short period of time, they were manning a sizeable portion of the Kennedy election staff in their Los Angeles Wilshire Boulevard headquarters.[12]

Thus the ensuing drama of assassination and cover-up would once more be carried out with the highest degree of skill and expertise. As a reward, Rafizadeh would become director of all SAVAK and CIA assassination operations in the U.S. within weeks of Bobby's death.

When Alexis Goodaryi told me this story during our interview on April 18, 1977, he did so under duress. He knew of my association with former Representative Thomas Downing and the House Select Committee on Assassinations, talking to me only after I voiced the hope that I could get him immunity from the HSCA. He desperately needed it in order to take off the heavy pressure being exerted by the Tongsun Park investigation. However, before I could approach Tiny Hutton, the HSCA Deputy Director, Goodaryi was murdered. According to Afshar, it was done personally by Rafizadeh. Later, when I asked Hutton about telling the Committee the story, he replied, "Forget it. They won't believe you."

From what I know today, it all seems so obvious that the SAVAK perpetrated the murder of Bobby Kennedy. Sirhan Bishara Sirhan, a young Jordanian student, was the accused murderer. Only he couldn't have done it by himself, as the evidence will prove.

As far as the investigation was concerned, Sirhan had a number of Arab friends who quickly exited the U.S. after the assassination and returned to the Middle East. Strangely, neither the Los Angles Police Department nor FBI had enough interest to expeditiously interview them. One young Arab man stood out in the photographs I subsequently got from "Photoreporters," the people who took the pictures of the Embassy Room stage used by *Time* magazine.[13] His name, according to Kennedy workers, was Ali Ahmand. They claimed he worked for the Microdot Company in Pasadena.

Microdot had never heard of him.

In fact, by the time the last shot was fired from Sirhan's gun, he had dropped out of sight, never to be seen again. Ali Ahmand was standing to Jesse Unruh's left in the photographs, wearing a yellow sweater (a fact that will become quite significant later), and had a camera hanging from a strap around his neck.[14]

According to Goodaryi, and confirmed by LAPD report I-21,[15] Khyber Khan made out twenty-four volunteer cards with the same address. It was the address of his ex-wife. Khan was also in the Ambassador Hotel the night Bobby was assassinated. He was carrying a briefcase with the name "Goodarzian" stenciled on it.[16]

I don't know how many other Americans were up at 3:17 a.m. on the morning of June 5, 1968, but, for some reason, I had been restless. The California election returns had started coming in around eleven on the East Coast, and I decided for the first time in months to watch the late late show and see the results. Finally, after listening to Bobby Kennedy's speech, I felt tired enough to switch off the set and head upstairs. As I reached for the knob, all hell broke loose. It started with someone screaming, "Bobby . . . , Bobby's been shot. . . ."

Suddenly I was wide awake. As I watched the chaos of the crowd and heard the reports unfold from the terrified witnesses, I experienced the same cold chills that had gripped me five years earlier when I had watched Lee Harvey Oswald die at the hand of Jack Ruby.

A decade later, I would vividly remember both scenes as I launched into my investigation of the deaths of John and Robert Kennedy.

CHAPTER FOURTEEN NOTES

1. It was apparently one of the Shah's sisters. (See Appendix, Exhibit No. 15, LAPD Report on Khyber Khan, and Exhibit No. 27, Khaiber Khan Settlement Letter.)

2. I subsequently found out through Jack Anderson's office that it was the Banco Nacional de Mexico.

3. See Appendix, Exhibit No. 15.

4. *Ibid.*

5. These organizations are listed in a later chapter.

6. See Appendix, Exhibit No. 29.

7. Jack Anderson, June 8, 1977.

8. Interview with Alex Goodaryi, Thursday, April 14, 1977.

9. As of June 8, 1968, Khan was out on $4,000 bail for alien registration violations. (See Appendix, Exhibit No. 15.)

10. Although I asked, Goodaryi refused to tell me any of the mobsters' names. When I asked if one was Jim Polley, he reluctantly admitted it was. When I asked Afshar, he claimed he didn't know any by name.

11. According to Goodaryi, Khan was under investigation by the Senate Rackets Committee from 1963 through March 1965. According to Jerry Alderman, counsel for the Rackets Committee and U.S. attorney John van de Kamp, Khan was considered a con man.

12. This would be a fact that the CIA operatives running the Los Angeles Police Department's investigation of Bobby's murder would be careful to discount or ignore.

13. *Time,* June 14, 1968.

14. See Appendix, Exhibit No. 16.

15. See Appendix, Exhibit No. 15.

16. *Ibid.*

Chapter Fifteen

Sirhan Bishara Sirhan was out early Tuesday morning. The election precincts were just beginning to open as he left his house at 7:00 a.m. and headed his pink and white 1956 DeSoto toward Alhambra, for a meeting with his SAVAK case officer, a man reported to be an Iranian named Goodarzian, a pseudonym for Khyber Khan, also known as Kibar Khan and Khaiber Khan. As Sirhan passed through Pasadena, he stopped and bought a newspaper at the corner of Washington Boulevard and Lake Avenue. Perusing it while he waited for a red light, he noted it was mostly full of stories on the candidates, primarily on the chances Bobby Kennedy had against Eugene McCarthy.

By 8:45, Sirhan was parked and waiting for his contact in Alhambra. Spotting him forty-five minutes later, he got out and followed him into a restaurant. For the next hour, they pored over plans of the Ambassador Hotel, plans which Sirhan had gotten the previous Sunday. In the LAPD Investigation Summary (1,500 pages), the whereabouts of Sirhan between 8:00 a.m. and 9:39 a.m. has been discreetly noted as "Unknown" (page 616).[1]

Sirhan cased the hotel well on Sunday, the second of June. Campaign plans called for Kennedy to appear at the Cocoanut Grove Room of the Ambassador Hotel that evening. Sirhan and a girl arrived about 7:30 p.m. She would be the same girl described by Khan on the day of the primary as being twenty-three to twenty-six years of age, Caucasian, wearing a short dress with polka dots and accompanied by a man named Michael Wayne.[2]

Within minutes of their arrival, Sirhan and the girl had worked themselves into a front-line position on an aisle. Once he got her in place, he told her to observe what security measures the Kennedy campaign had mustered. Then he headed for the lobby.

Mr. Paul Redding said Sirhan stood in place for an hour. Mrs. Susan Redding would remember seeing Sirhan and the girl. They pushed their way in front of her before she really noticed them. "Sirhan stood out from the others gathered in the room." The LAPD Report discreetly deleted Redding's comment about Sirhan being with a girl.[3]

Sirhan's mission was to map out the areas of the hotel where the presidential candidate might be making appearances.

That Sunday evening the Senator was late. He had decided to take several of his children to Disneyland.

After Sirhan left the girl in the Cocoanut Grove, the room became so crowded that the doors were closed. Then he discovered that Kennedy planned to appear at a reception in the Palm Court after his Grove speech. So he walked to the other side of the lobby, wandering around the big marble fountain separating the Embassy Room from the Court's open area.

It was while Sirhan was in the lobby that Bert Blume, a boy who worked in a Pasadena liquor store where Sirhan hung out, noticed him. Blume had come to the Ambassador with a friend to hear Kennedy's speech. Both were active in the Pasadena Youth for Kennedy group. When the Grove talk ended, they rushed to the Palm Court for the reception and, on their way across the lobby, they passed within a few feet of Sirhan. Blume recognized him.[4]

Sirhan's next objective was to survey the Embassy Room, where the celebration was to be held on primary night. If Bobby won the primary, he would die before leaving the hotel. If he lost by a large enough margin, the plans to kill him could be canceled.

As Sirhan stood in the Ambassador's lobby looking down the corridor leading to the Embassy Room, he could see waiters entering and exiting from another corridor off to the right. Sirhan knew all about that corridor. It led to a kitchen pantry, and would most certainly be used by the presidential candidate for access to other rooms where he would be speaking or holding press conferences.

The plan was simple enough. It called for two possible assassination sites,[5] one in the Embassy Room and the other in the relatively confined pantry. Depending upon the Senator's exit route, either Sirhan or his partner were to wait for Ahmand to be in a position directly behind the Senator before firing their diversive fusillade.

With Ali Ahmand behind Kennedy for the kill, and he or his partner creating a rapid-fire diversion to his front, the result would be the same.

The primary site was the pantry, where Sirhan would be stationed. The secondary was the Embassy Room.

The diversion was to make sure that Ahmand got away, for Ahmand could be identified as a member of the SAVAK, and his weapon recognized as one made by the CIA. Sirhan must have thought it unfortunate that his SAVAK partners didn't manage to get waiters' jackets earlier that morning. They would have made a perfect disguise. After the assassination, Juan Romero, the little busboy who would hold Kennedy's mortally wounded head, would tell the police about the two strangers who had come to the Ambassador's kitchen on Sunday, looking for white coats similar to those worn by the waiters.[6]

On Sunday night, after leaving the girl to observe for him, Sirhan left the Ambassador and headed for his rendezvous at Kennedy headquarters on Wilshire Boulevard. A short time later, he and two companions would be overheard speaking loudly in Arabic by a man named W. L. Wood. "There were three men," Wood would tell police, "and they began speaking a distinct Arabic dialect, one saying, 'He won't be in the hotel tomorrow night, but we can get him the next night.'"[7]

By eleven o'clock election morning, as Sirhan headed toward the Valley Gun Club in San Gabriel, the car radio in his DeSoto indicated the voting was still very light. After several days of practicing on pistol ranges, he had felt confident he could do his part to get off a full volley before he was subdued. But, to make sure, he decided to have one more practice session. He arrived at approximately 11:30, and as he signed in, he was noticed by Range Master, Everett Buckler.

Ali Ahmand was also checking out his weapon, loading it for the last time. The following description of Ahmand's assassination weapon is based on Los Angeles County Coroner Thomas Noguchi's description of Bobby Kennedy's autopsy finding and test firings of Sirhan's weapon. These findings and conclusions are described later.

The camera strapped around Ali Ahmand's neck was a highly unusual one. Nested within its body was a four-shot, mechanically fired .22-caliber weapon. A weapon that, within half a dozen feet, could fire soft-nose slugs, which would fragment upon impact and be extremely lethal.

I have fired weapons of this type built within a Nikon SLR (single lens reflex) camera body. It is truly ingenious. Made from a solid cylinder of high-carbon steel, approximately three inches in length, four barrels are drilled out to the caliber of the desired cartridge (usually .22 or .25). The overall effect is similar to extending a conventional revolver cylinder two additional inches. In some cases, depending upon the sophistication desired, each of these drilled barrels can be rifled. However, because of the close range intended for their use, they rarely are.

Once the cartridges are in place, the cylinder is fitted with an end piece that is screwed on. Rim activated firing pins are located in another drilled chamber alongside each barrel, each with its own spring and release mechanism. This release mechanism is usually operated mechanically from the camera's spring-loaded shutter control.

The whole device is then placed within the camera body with its fake lens and connected to the firing control. A mass of steel-wool wadding is then placed in front of the barrels to act as a silencer. Then a gelatin filter is screwed onto the front of the lens body to hold the wadding in place. Once set, it can be aimed through a modified view finder with little or no trouble.

If Ali Ahmand was properly trained, he could hit any target within a half a dozen feet with pinpoint accuracy. The weapon's intended use was the assassination of Robert Francis Kennedy. The target date, as history has shown, had been set for the night of the fourth of June. The success of Ahmand's mission depended only upon how much of a diversion either of his partners could create with their cheap Saturday night specials.[8]

Khan's plans had been perfectly worked out. With his crew of people inside Kennedy headquarters, they could monitor every move the candidate made.

At 7:00 on that primary morning, Bobby Kennedy was in a deep sleep at the Malibu Beach home of his good friend, John Frankenheimer, recovering from an exhausting previous day. His campaign schedule had called for him to be in three cities in twelve hours, all by plane—San Francisco, San Diego, and a number of spots around Los Angeles. He would have nothing to do until early evening, until the returns started coming in at the Ambassador Hotel victory headquarters. Relieved, he would spend the rest of the day playing in the Malibu surf with four of his children.

Ali Ahmand, in order to insure his physical location behind the presidential candidate, had made very sure to be in the Embassy Room early. He was confident Sirhan or his other partner could create enough of a distraction, enough for him to get off his four rounds into the back of the unsuspecting Senator.

The plan was to wait until he and the girl could make a clean getaway. That would be most likely if Kennedy was to go through the corridor or pantry area. No one would detain them in the pandemonium that was sure to follow Sirhan's fusillade. Whoever spotted them running would think they, like everyone else, were trying to escape Sirhan's bullets.

Everything was proceeding on schedule. The Embassy Room was beginning to fill, and Ahmand started working his way up to the podium. No matter which way Bobby Kennedy elected to leave the stage, he would be able to kill him. The only thing of concern was to make sure he himself was not gunned down by either of his companions.

Earlier, while Bobby Kennedy was playing with his children in the Malibu surf, Sirhan was winding up his pistol-shooting session at the San Gabriel Valley Gun Club. During the course of the afternoon, he had purchased several additional boxes of ammunition from the Range Master. As a result, he would fire over four-hundred rounds in his little Iver Johnson. Psychologically, he had made the gun an extension of himself. Aside from two minor breaks, he constantly kept firing. By the time the Range Master shouted for everyone to stop, it was after 5:00.

He was ready. Picking up his shell cases, he took off in his aging DeSoto and headed for the campus of the Pasadena City College. It was there that he had been recruited by Iranians working with the SAVAK,[9] who were actively trying to drum up support for the Shah. Because he was a Jordanian, no direct finger could be pointed at the Iranians.

According to Sirhan's own testimony, given after the assassination, he had decided to eat prior to heading for the Ambassador. So, when he spotted a Bob's Big Boy Restaurant adjacent to the campus, he pulled his car into the lot and went in. As he entered the door, he spotted Gaymoard Mistri, an Indian student friend of his, drinking a cup of coffee at the counter. At 6:45, Mistri and Sirhan left the restaurant and walked to the Pasadena City College campus, where they met some Arabs from the Organization of Arab Students.

These organizations consisted of many groups both pro and alien to U.S. interests in the Middle East. In 1968, the pro-Shah Iranian students' organization on California campuses, controlled by the SAVAK, was the "Tehran University Students Union." The anti-Shah group was known as the "Conference of Iranian Students" (CIS), which evolved from the Iranian Student Association of the U.S. The CIS was also infiltrated by the SAVAK.

The Jordanian group, which in 1968 was openly divided in its east/west affiliations, was the "General Union of Students" (Pakistan), also divided in allegiance between east and west. All these organizations were, up until 1965, known to have members receiving funds from the CIA through the coordinating body of the "International Student Conference" (COSEC).[10]

After a few minutes of conversation Sirhan and Mistri left the group. As the sun began to set, Sirhan and Mistri walked back to the restaurant parking lot. After wishing each other luck, Sirhan left, pointing his DeSoto downtown towards the Ambassador Hotel.

The time was 7:15 p.m.

At the same time Sirhan pulled out of the restaurant parking lot in Pasadena, movie director John Frankenheimer, along with Bobby Kennedy and Fred Dutton, pulled his big Rolls Royce away from his Malibu home. Turning north via the Malibu Canyon, Frankenheimer headed toward the Ventura Freeway, which would take them downtown to the Ambassador Hotel.

Although the early voting turnout had been unexpectedly light, the recorded voting level of the 1964 presidential campaign had been surpassed by 4:00. In the final four hours of the primary balloting, a million voters would go to the Los Angeles County voting booths to register their choice on the new IBM ballot computer.[11] The voters of California's most populous county were to have the final word in what suddenly had grown to be a hotly contested campaign.

By 6:00, the crowds had begun to assemble at the Ambassador. As a result, the horseshoe drive of the hotel's main Wilshire Boulevard entrance was fast becoming clogged with an endless stream of traffic. Three candidates had chosen the Ambassador for this campaign. There were, of course, the Kennedy people; Allan Cranston, now a U.S. Senator, a special candidate for the district; and Max Rafferty. Each one had staked their claim to a section of the Ambassador's main lobby.

At 6:15, the Cranston band started playing in the hotel's Palm Court, just off the lobby. As could be expected, the Ambassador had been a madhouse the whole day. Aside from the election parties, there had been several business meetings, and to add to the confusion, people were starting to check in early for a Pacific Telephone Systems seminar scheduled to start Thursday. In the vernacular, the hotel was full. Even the usual few percent reserve held for VIPs was sold out.

By 7:00, Judy Royer, who had been secretary to the former governor of California, Pat Brown, had stationed herself in the anteroom corridor behind the Embassy stage.[12] Her job was to keep the area cleared of anyone not specifically connected with the Kennedy entourage.

On the fifth floor, Jesse Unruh, head of the California delegation, and his staff had taken over the Presidential Suite for their hotel headquarters. And just around the corner was the Royal Suite, which was being held for the Senator, his family, and personal staff.

At 8:00, the polls closed and the bars opened, catering to the thousands of people converging upon the gaily lit hotel. Along with the masses, however, came the problem of the air-conditioning inadequacy. The day had been quite humid, and the Mardi Gras atmosphere had sent the inside temperature skyrocketing, estimated by some to be over ninety degrees.

Television cameras from the various networks were being set up, along with their bright lights, as the crowd anxiously watched the TV monitors awaiting the returns from southern California.

At 8:15, Sirhan reluctantly pulled his old DeSoto into an illegal parking spot, approximately two blocks from the hotel. After cruising the whole area, he discovered it was the only place he could find. Parking, he carefully took out his wallet and slipped it into the glove compartment. Then he systematically checked the chambers of his Iver Johnson. Satisfied everything was all right, he tucked it into his waistband, carefully making sure it was not detectable.[13]

Anyone observing him as he walked the two blocks to the Ambassador would have said that Sirhan appeared to be in a state of grace. He had to figure his chances of getting out of the hotel alive were minimal. He also knew that his counterpart was stationed in the Embassy Room. So, if Ali Ahmand elected to hit the Senator there, it would be Sirhan's counterpart who would receive the bulk of the reward. According to Alexis Goodaryi and Nasser Afshar, the successful perpetrators of Robert Kennedy's assassination were amply rewarded.

If he was captured and acted the way he was programmed to do, he would be a free and extremely wealthy man under forty by the time he was paroled in the mid-1980s. In addition, from his own admission on the stand during his trial, Sirhan felt he would be considered a super-hero in the Middle East. At that time, Jordan was very anti-American, siding with the Pakistan cause. It was well worth the risk, even though he must have been psyched to a point where he would have done it for nothing, and even though it was obvious he expected some kind of reward. Sirhan never could or would explain the reference to "Pay to the order of . . . of this or that 80000," in his notebook. Although I do not believe Sirhan was programmed to assassinate Kennedy, in my conversations with ex-FBI man William Turner, who explored the Manchurian candidate theory as it possibly related to Sirhan's participation in the RFK assassination, he cited several instances when similar psychological programming had been successful. Because I'm familiar with an experimental, CIA-sponsored, mind-altering program, known as Operation Artichoke, I cite one case that occurred just a year prior to Bobby's murder.

It occurred in the Philippines, when the Philippine National Bureau of Investigation (NBI) suspected that a man they had in custody had been hypno-programmed to assassinate President Ferdinand Marcos. The NBI called in a hypnotist to try to deprogram him. In his report, the hypnotist asserted that "it is firmly accepted that a properly hypnotized subject can be made to send out a post-hypnotic instruction during his normal, waking state with the use of prearranged key words or devices . . . the remarkable character of the zombie state in our subject is its deeply ingrained and systematic presentation, indicating a certain disturbing degree of conditioning." The subject exhibited a "deep-seated resistance due to the presence of a post-hypnotic block. . . ."

What the hypnotist did draw out of the suspect was that he used the name Luis Castillo and had been trained by the CIA for activities against Fidel Castro. After six months, the deprogramming was discontinued and the subject deported to the United States.[14]

Sirhan had been cautioned to arrive early in case the returns came in sooner than expected. When the Senator was assured of victory, he would appear in the Embassy Room. Sirhan had been told that, after his appearance, the Senator could leave by one of three ways: The first was by way of the anteroom, which was behind the gold curtain at the rear of the stage. It was the most likely alternative, and as history would record, the one actually used. The second was down the stage stairs and through the kitchen corridor. Both this route and the one through the anteroom were covered by Sirhan. The third would have been through the crowd and out to the main lobby, the area covered by Sirhan's counterpart.

In both cases, Ali Ahmand would be the actual assassin, firing the camera gun from directly behind the candidate. The assassination had to take place before Bobby Kennedy left the area. The three Middle Easterners knew, if Kennedy won, the candidate would be surrounded by Secret Service agents within minutes.

By 8:30, the Embassy Room, where Bobby Kennedy was to speak, was rapidly filling to its legal limit. Anyone approaching its main doors was being screened for their Kennedy badges in order to get in.

CHAPTER FIFTEEN NOTES

1. See Appendix, Exhibit No. 17, LAPD activity list for Sirhan.

2. Wayne, strangely enough, would be in the kitchen pantry area and actually get Kennedy to give him his autograph just prior to his last speech. (See Appendix, Exhibit No. 15.)

3. LAPD Summary Report, p. 1123.

4. *Ibid.,* p. 886.

5. As with the JFK assassination scenario, at least two sites were planned to cover all last-minute contingencies.

6. *Ibid.,* p. 1132.

7. *Ibid.,* p. 1219.

8. Terminology for an inexpensive small caliber gun, usually purchased illegally.

9. Nasser Afshar Interview, Thursday, March 26, 1981.

10. Sources: Foreign Policy Research Institute, University of Pennsylvania, Philadelphia, Pa.; U.S. National Student Association documents.

11. Everyone anticipated "early returns" that night. Los Angeles County had just joined the electronic age, with the new Fotoramic IBM data-processing tabulator installed and ready to replace the antiquated method of hand counting. The new computer was credited with being able to count fourteen-thousand ballots a minute. Theoretically, enough votes could be tabulated in a single hour to predict the winner.

12. LAPD Summary Report, p. 1137.

13. Robert Blair Kaiser, author of *RFK Must Die,* claims that Sirhan did not originally take his gun into the Ambassador, but left it in the back seat of his car, then came back for it.

Other than Kaiser's reference, I could find no evidence for this in any police report. However, it could explain how Sirhan would be seen with the actual assassin, Ali Ahmand, and the girl in the polka dot dress climbing up an outside fire escape prior to the assassination.

14.   Report of Victor R. Sanchez, September 1, 1967; copy in possession of William Turner.

Turner also cited the CIA's MK-Ultra Mind Control Program, which included a study called Operation Artichoke to determine if a person could be induced to involuntarily commit an assassination. (*Washington Post,* September 2, 1977.)

I am familiar with this program, which dates back to the late 1950s, having met it director, Dr. Joseph Geshicter of Georgetown University, during that era.

Chapter Sixteen

As Sirhan surveyed the masses entering the hotel, he kept reminding himself that, when he saw Bobby Kennedy and a man directly behind him wearing a gold sweater holding a camera, he was to start firing. It was a foolproof plan. That afternoon, Ahmand had been given a Kennedy workers blue badge. He would have no problem maintaining his position behind the Senator.

Since all the weapons were to be of the same caliber and use the same ammunition, it would be difficult to determine that the bullets found had not come from one gun, particularly since Ahmand's gun-camera barrels were also rifled.

Shortly after 9:00, Sirhan stood at the end of the lobby, amidst the excitement and anticipation emanating from all three political camps. After a few moments, he wandered into a party being held for Rafferty supporters and got himself a free Tom Collins. Then he again surveyed the lay of the land.

At the meeting in Alhambra, he had studied the probable route from the Senator's suite to the Embassy Room. The problem was that no one would know the actual plans until the last minute. The most logical route would be through a back freight elevator in the kitchen, which also gave direct access to the back of the Embassy Room stage.

It is here that I would like to point out another reason one can conclude Sirhan was part of a conspiracy.

If Sirhan was a lone deranged gunman, it would be much easier to achieve a positive kill by firing at the Senator as he was entering the pantry on the way *to* the Embassy Room, because there would be far fewer people around. Not only would this increase his chances of a lethal hit, but it would also infinitely improve his chances of escape.

Instead, like his counterpart in the Embassy Room, his job was to create a diversion, one that would allow Ahmand to get within inches of the rear of Bobby's head, as the autopsy would later show.

Sirhan's progress through the evening was well charted. After finishing his Tom Collins, he walked outside the Venetian Room, where the Rafferty crew was celebrating, and spotted an electrician working in a sound booth. He made his way to it.

Walking in, he stuck out his hand and asked the startled technician, who had just finishing hooking up cables, "Are you done?" Evidently harassed, the electrician answered with a simple nod. Then Sirhan asked what floor the Senator was staying on. The electrician replied that he wasn't sure.

When Sirhan pushed it, asking if the Senator kept any bodyguards, the now curious technician said he had no idea. Just then, a fire inspector entered the booth.

The man in uniform startled Sirhan, and he jumped up, asking the newcomer what his job was. After being told, he breathed a sigh of relief, and apparently sensing discretion was the better part of valor, he hurriedly left, not bothering to say goodbye.[1]

Still shaken from his experience at the electrician's booth, Sirhan cautiously worked his way through the lobby toward the Embassy Room. As he crossed the lobby, he would make himself highly visible, when a man in work clothes addressed him in Spanish. Before Sirhan could reply, the stranger asked in English. "Hey, are we winning?"

When Sirhan replied, "Yeah," the stranger queried, "But McCarthy's ahead, he's winning, no?"

With a shrug, Sirhan exclaimed. "Don't worry. If Kennedy doesn't win, he's a millionaire. If he does win, I don't think he'll do anything for you, for me, or for any of the poor people." Then, in an arrogant tone, he continued spouting deprecating remarks about the presidential candidate. Turned off, the stranger and a man beside him walked away.[2]

Abruptly, Sirhan, realizing he may have spoken out unwisely, got himself another drink. Then, peering around to see if he had been noticed, he walked off towards the Colonial Room, where the press had set up their facilities. The room was jammed with teletype machines, TV network monitors, and communication links to all the primary campaigns throughout the country.

Once inside, he stood behind Western Union telex operator, Mary Grohs, who was typing out a message on her machine. After he had been standing behind her for several minutes, she got nervous. Thinking he might be looking for Kennedy returns, she pointed to another machine. This broke Sirhan's concentration, and he walked away without addressing her.

The briefing he had gotten earlier in Alhambra must have been thorough. It appeared Sirhan had access to all the locations on the Embassy Room floor. It also confirmed what he and the others had observed of the area Sunday while looking for waiters' coats.

At 9:30, a fire inspector from the Los Angeles Fire Department directed hotel security guards to shut the main doors of the Embassy Room, with orders that no one could enter unless someone came out. This move had evidently been anticipated and presented no problem for Sirhan. Half an hour later, he slipped into the tightly packed Embassy Room via the kitchen.

There, he was observed standing on his tiptoes trying to get a good view of the room. It was probable that he was attempting to spot Ali Ahmand in the gold sweater. As he twisted around, he inadvertently brushed the backside of a woman who turned to face him, telling him to stop pushing. Startled, Sirhan mumbled a half apology and quickly moved out of the room and into the lobby.

* * * * *

Before heading back to the corridor, he wended his way over to the Palm Court. There, the Cranston party was going in full swing. He got himself another Tom Collins. Then he walked across the lobby. At a men's room, he asked a waiter if he would mind holding his drink. When the waiter nodded affirmatively, Sirhan handed it to him and took a chair from a stack piled in a nearby hallway. Muttering to the waiter, "It's sure hot and crowded in here," he retrieved his glass and sat down.[3]

At 10:30, the computer centers started pumping out the election returns, and on the fifth floor, Bobby Kennedy, who was about to inherit the Democratic nomination for the presidency, had just finished taping four interviews for the media. In the staff suite, its atmosphere full of anticipation, the presidential candidate invited the press in for a drink. Of course, the real party wouldn't begin until after the victory speech, at Hollywood's newest "in" discotheque, The Factory, where the presidential hopeful had invited all his friends to join him.

Five stories below, Sirhan had once again started his vigil of the pantry area. With his bright blue velour shirt, he looked out of place around all the white uniforms. However, with all the well-wishers from the Kennedy camp wandering through, he remained relatively unnoticed.

Around 11:00, the noise from the Embassy Room abruptly increased, indicating some good news had been heard from the returns trickling in. Out of curiosity, Sirhan walked through the pantry into the corridor. As he attempted to enter the anteroom, he was stopped for the first time by a young female Kennedy worker, asking if he had a pass.[4] Sirhan shrugged his shoulders and returned to the pantry.

He then took up a position next to the ice machines. When a busboy stopped to fill a pitcher, Sirhan asked, "Is Kennedy coming through the pantry?" He replied, "I don't know."

Sirhan began to foresee a problem. His instructions to cover the whole area behind the Embassy Room stage would be severely limited without the girl as a lookout. If Kennedy did come through the anteroom, he wouldn't know it until the Senator actually appeared through the doors. For the next half hour, he would not be observed in the pantry.

At 11:00 p.m., on the basis of a fraction of the votes tabulated, CBS projected Bobby Kennedy as the winner. Inside the now steaming ballroom, the news was greeted by a jubilant roar, which prompted Sirhan to check the anteroom, still looking for the girl.

Sirhan found his lookout. She was dressed in a polka dot dress. They were observed by Booker Griffin, head of the Los Angeles Chapter of the Negro Industrial and Economic Union. It was after 11:00 when Griffin noticed Sirhan and a girl standing in the pantry corridor.[5]

The next time Sirhan would be seen would be with both the girl and Ali Ahmand, this time by a young Youth for Kennedy volunteer named Sandra Serrano. At 11:30, Serrano bought a screwdriver at a temporary bar set up in the southwest corner of the Embassy Room. Because it was hot and crowded inside, she stepped out through an emergency-exit door that had metal stairs leading to the ground.

As she sat on a step halfway down, sipping her drink, a girl and two men climbed up and brushed by her. "Excuse us," the girl said and continued on. The description Serrano would later give to the FBI was of Sirhan, Ali Ahmand, and a female companion wearing a polka dot dress. She stated that one of the men was a white male of Latin extraction, five feet, five inches tall, twenty-one to twenty-three years of age, with olive complexion, black hair, long and straight, hanging over his forehead, needing a haircut. He wore dark pants, light shirt, and a gold or yellow cardigan-type sweater.[6]

Her description of Ali Ahmand coincides exactly with the picture taken just minutes later by P. Gonzales of Photoreporters. This picture appears on page 17 of the June 14, 1968, issue of *Time* magazine.

To those gathered outside the swinging pantry doors, it became evident that the Senator would be taking that route from his suite on the fifth floor to the Embassy Room.

Half an hour later, as Kennedy's lead increased, an excited, cheering crowd started screaming, "We want Bobby! We want Bobby!" Jesse Unruh, leader of the state's Democratic party and of the California Kennedy delegation, was sent down from the Senator's suite to placate the crowd, now raising pandemonium throughout the hotel's first floor.

As Unruh got to the lectern, the clamor of the crowd screaming "We want Bobby" amplified tenfold. Unruh immediately sent his administrative assistant back to the fifth floor, urging the Senator to come down.

So, at 11:45 p.m., Bobby collected his wife Ethel and, after observing the crowded corridor, said to his assistant Frank Mankiewicz, "Let's not go down through the crowd." He headed for the freight elevator.

Meanwhile, a number of Bobby's inner circle, including George Plimpton and his new bride Freddie, went down the regular elevator.

Others, like reporter Constance Swann, raced down the back stairs and beat the slow-moving elevator. As she hurried through the kitchen and passed through the pantry, someone yelled, "Which way is he coming?" When she replied loudly that she thought through here, she noticed Sirhan—because, as she would later remark, "He was so out of place."

Suddenly, the man of the hour, the man who now according to all the political analysts would be the next president of the United States, appeared calmly walking through the kitchen corridor into the pantry opposite the ice machines.

Strangely, just inside the pantry doors leading to the back of the stage, the Senator would autograph a poster for Michael Wayne,[7] a man whom Khyber Khan admitted giving a ride to the afternoon before.[8] A coincidence—perhaps yes, perhaps no.

Sirhan, now standing by the warming tables, observed Bobby Kennedy with complete detachment, as the Senator walked quickly through the pantry, shaking hands with cooks and waiters. Then, just as rapidly as he had appeared, he passed through the pantry's double doors into the corridor behind the lectern, now blazing with the lights of television cameras shooting.

As Robert Kennedy's countenance flashed across millions of TV screens throughout the country, he scribbled his autograph for a young election worker and waved to the cameras. Then, as rapidly as he had swept through the pantry, he stepped into the ballroom, where he was greeted by an honor guard of Kennedy girls. With the young Senator hurrying up the few stairs to the lectern, the screams and yells of "We want Bobby" were deafening.

It took five minutes before his voice could be heard above the continuing roar. Then, as it became quiet enough for his voice to be heard, Bobby Kennedy started the last speech of his life.

It was an ad lib victory speech containing some amusing remarks about his entourage. Then, with the magnetism of the great and loved, Bobby finished with his exhortations:

"I think we can end the divisions within the United States. What I think is quite clear is that we can work together in a great country, in a selfless and compassionate country. In fact, Mayor Yorty has just sent me a message that we've been here too long already. So, my thanks to all of you, and on to Chicago, and . . . let's win."

The time was 12:14 a.m., June 5, 1968.

CHAPTER SIXTEEN NOTES

1. The electrician was Hans Peter Bidstrup, and the fire inspector was Michael Miherton, both of Los Angeles. (LAPD Summary Report, p. 882.)

2. The man speaking to Sirhan was Enrique Rabago. His silent friend was Humphrey Cordero, both of Los Angeles. (*Ibid.,* p. 1119.)

3. The waiter's name was Gonsalo Cetina. (*Ibid.,* pp. 905-906.)

4. *Ibid.,* p. 1137.

5. *Ibid.,* p. 977.

6. *Ibid.,* pp. 408-417. See Appendix, Exhibit No. 26.

7. *Ibid.,* p. 144.

8. See Appendix, Exhibit No. 15.

Ali Ahmand, in sweater next to Robert Kennedy minutes before Kennedy was assassinated. Note SLR camera. (Photoreporters)

Chapter Seventeen

As the presidential candidate concluded his speech, Ali Ahmand, who was standing next to Jesse Unruh,[1] turned behind aides Fred Dutton and Bill Barry as they got ready to pull the curtain aside to let the presidential candidate slide through. Moments before, he had watched intently as Barry and Dutton left the stage briefly to ask Bobby's campaign manager and security men the fastest way to the Colonial Room, where the presidential candidate had agreed to give a short impromptu press conference.

When Dutton and Barry walked through the pantry, they observed it was much less crowded than any other passageway, and they agreed that it was the best route for the Senator.

Jesse Unruh had asked Bobby to take a few minutes to speak to the overflow crowd waiting in the Ambassador Ballroom on the floor below, but Dutton decided against it. It was far too crowded. Besides, another jubilant crowd of stars and celebrities were waiting excitedly at the plush discotheque in Beverly Hills.

Unfortunately, neither Dutton nor Barry noticed the small, crouching figure of Sirhan lurking next to the noisy ice machines. Nor, after they returned to the stage, did they notice the dark-complexioned young man holding a reflex camera tightly against his gold sweater. Ali Ahmand, beads of perspiration coursing down his face from the heat of the packed room, was waiting to follow the triumphant presidential candidate.

As Bobby finished speaking, the screams of adoration once more filled the huge ballroom, and advance men Jack Gallivan and Richard Rosen rushed off the stage, headed for the Colonial Room. When Bobby started to leave via the lectern steps, a voice said, "This way, sir," and he turned and exited quickly through the gold curtains. In the crush, Ali Ahmand hurriedly followed.

Meanwhile, Bobby intimates Rafer Johnson and Rosie Grier didn't know about the decision to go through the pantry. Expecting the Senator to leave by the lectern stairs, they instantaneously found themselves separated from their idol by a thick crowd immediately following the victorious candidate. One of the closest was Ali Ahmand, who had his camera at the ready, anxiously awaiting the pandemonium that would shortly begin.

As the noise reaching the pantry intensified, Sirhan, partially hidden behind one of the ice machines, knew the speech was over. The girl, in her high-profile outfit, the polka dot dress, moved away from him to the pantry doors. Looking through, she signaled. Sirhan meanwhile had rolled up a Kennedy poster and slipped the Iver Johnson into it.

His act was about to begin.

A slight chill passed up his spine when, all of a sudden, the pantry doors swung open and Bobby Kennedy appeared, being led by a hotel assistant maitre d' named Karl Uecker and a hotel staff man named Edward Minasian.[2]

Due to the mass of humanity surrounding them, Barry and Dutton were unable to flank the Senator as was their normal practice.

In spite of the multitude, Barry had managed to keep fairly close to Bobby's right-hand side as he passed ABC press man Larry Johnson and *Los Angeles Times* photographer Boris Yaro.

Yaro was holding his camera up, getting ready to shoot a picture, when his viewfinder was blocked by a woman pushing in front of him. His friend, Dick Drew, also taking pictures, yelled, "Boris, you missed him." Mad, Yaro pushed the interfering lady aside, trying to get a picture. He missed.

Sirhan meanwhile, now crouched and ready to spring, watched Kennedy, flanked with bodies, shaking hands, as he walked toward him. From his position, all he had to do was jump forward and fire point-blank.

When the Senator was halfway to him, Sirhan spotted the gold sweater. It was in a wedge of people just passing photographers who were shooting pictures inside the pantry doors. Ali Ahmand was within a foot of the Senator, aiming through the viewfinder of the gun camera.

Then, when Bobby, with Ahmand following, was almost to the ice machines, Sirhan darted towards the Senator, pulling his Iver Johnson out of the rolled-up poster.

Uecker, who had hold of the Senator's hand, dropped it and lunged for the young Arab, as Sirhan's gun flashed *twice* in rapid succession.[3]

Behind and to Bobby's right, Ali Ahmand had held his position, closely following the Senator, when Sirhan's gun went off, sounding like *two* firecrackers.

Ahmand watched through his viewfinder as the startled and dodging presidential candidate tried to back away from the wild-eyed gunman. Then, as Bobby literally backed into him, Ahmand pushed the lethal camera up behind the Senator's ear and pulled the release mechanism.

The soft-nose lead projectile made virtually no noise as it exited the camera and tore through Bobby's right mastoid, the force of the shell literally stopping him in mid-air. As Bobby started to collapse, Ahmand followed him with his camera, pulling the trigger three times more.

Holding on tightly to the lethal weapon, Ahmand pulled back as the crowd started screaming, "Get him, get his gun," referring to Sirhan, whose arm was being slammed down on a steam table by Uecker.

Then all hell broke loose, as another series of shots spurted in quick succession from Sirhan's gun. They echoed throughout the small pantry, amidst the screams and yells of, "I've been hit."

In the pandemonium of people diving for cover, Ali Ahmand spotted a path made by bodies falling to either side of the small room. Motioning for the girl to follow, he dove through the screaming mob. In the crush, he almost lost the gun camera as he struggled into the outside corridor.

Booker Griffin, who had spotted Sirhan with the girl earlier, was standing in the corridor outside the pantry. He saw Ahmand and the girl making their exit. After shouting "They're getting away," he rushed into the pantry to help subdue Sirhan. Kennedy campaign worker George Green and press photographer Evan P. Freed also saw the girl and Ahmand exiting the pantry.

One can only speculate as to who changed their original stories, for—as in my interview with Boris Yaro (Exhibit 19)—what ended up in the LAPD and FBI Reports bore no resemblance to the original testimony. According to the LAPD, Griffin would declare himself a bald-faced liar by later retracting his story, claiming it was a total fabrication on his part.[4]

As for Green's and Freed's story, the LAPD Summary Report indicated Green was drunk and told conflicting stories regarding the girl in the polka dot dress.[5] Poor Freed just saw people running around him.[6]

Once past the screaming crowd, now exiting in a panic from the anteroom, Ahmand and the girl ran down the opposite corridor. Because of the confusion, it had relatively little traffic. Hurriedly, they headed for the same fire exit they had entered a short time earlier with Sirhan.

Still sitting halfway down the steps was Sandra Serrano, now holding an empty glass. Suddenly, the girl in the polka dot dress and the man in the yellow sweater, whom she had encountered earlier, appeared, running down the stairs. As they came toward her, Ahmand's female partner shouted, "We shot him! We shot him!"[7]

Astonished, Serrano asked, "Who did you shoot?"

The girl in the polka dot dress replied, "Senator Kennedy!" Then, after she and Ahmand reached the ground, they ran down a service driveway toward a parking lot, passing a startled elderly couple named Bernstein, who had witnessed the exchange. Within minutes, Ahmand and the young girl were in a shiny black car[8] speeding down Wilshire Boulevard away from the Ambassador.

They hadn't gone more than a block before the screaming sirens of police units converging on the hotel could be heard. The first to arrive at the parking lot was veteran LAPD Sergeant Dave Sharaga, who was timidly approached by the elderly Bernstein couple telling him their story.

It would be ignored.[9]

Serrano would later testify that she thought she heard gunfire. It was on this basis that the LAPD discredited all of her testimony. She would explain it was probably a car backfiring, to no avail.

Meanwhile, Sirhan had fared far better than he could have expected. He had been grabbed by Uecker just after firing his second round, at what he estimated had been little more than a yard from the Senator. From Sirhan's actions, it was apparent he had to keep firing. After his first glimpse, he probably lost sight of Ahmand. So, he kept pulling the little gun's trigger. As he did, people fell around him.

Uecker, with Sirhan's neck in his right arm, grappled for the gun with his left hand. But it took the gargantuan effort of Edward Minasian, the hotel employee, to slam the small Arab forward against a stainless steel serving table and grab his gun hand, pounding it again and again onto the steam table. Even so, Sirhan kept firing until all eight chambers were empty.

George Plimpton and Jack Gallivan had been ahead of the Senator, and as the little weapon erupted, they also converged on Sirhan. Frank Burns, who would have been next to Ali Ahmand, also lunged for Sirhan, grabbing his legs a second before Bill Barry finally locked his hand over Sirhan's clenched gun hand.

Then, with a desperate surge, Uecker and Minasian managed to push Sirhan hard into another serving table. At that point, six-foot-five, three-hundred-pound Rosie Grier broke through the screaming mob, covering all of the combatants with his immense body.

Finally, Bill Barry managed to slash Sirhan's gun from his hand. This statement is in direct contradiction to the official LAPD reports and FBI reports. In my recorded interview with Boris Yaro, on March 28, 1978, he had this to say as a direct eyewitness and participant:

> There's no more firing, and two guys went for him; and I moved; and they hit him and pushed him kind of spread-eagled on the counter; and they were trying to slam the gun loose; and the gun came loose and I took it. I picked it up [obviously from the floor]. And I picked it up and I'm thinking that the son of a bitch [referring to Sirhan's gun] doesn't have any knurls on the grip. This gun is still warm and it . . . when the gun is warm, the grip is warm. Not the barrel or the cylinder; but the grip is warm. And it's a smooth grip. And I'm thinking this. And, all of a sudden, wham, the gun goes over my shoulder. Somebody pulled it out of my hand. As it later turned out, it was apparently Rosie Grier.[10] But the first thing I said when I came into our office, where I'm on a dead run, and I hollered at Bill Thomas who is now the editor of the *Los Angeles Times,* and I said, "My fingerprints are on that gun. "

Minasian managed to slide free from Grier's crushing figure and ran for a phone. Maitre d', Angelo DiPierro, also ran to the nearest phone to call for help, as TV cameraman Jim Wilson dropped to his knees and began pounding on the floor, shouting, "My God! No! No! No!"

Backup camera operator Bob Funk screamed at him, "You've got to shoot, Jimmy, you've got to shoot." Finally Wilson stood up, switched on his camera, and moved forward. Wilson would provide invaluable coverage. However, he had missed the exit of Ali Ahmand.

The crowds were starting to push in from the ballroom at the end of the pantry, where, just moments before, Ali Ahmand and the girl had exited. Then, the press started piling in from the Colonial Room.

The carnage that greeted them was a shock to all.

Paul Schrade, a regional director for the United Auto Workers, was lying on his back on the concrete floor, a sea of blood spilling from a head wound onto the brim of a styrofoam campaign hat.

In a corner, William Wiesel, an ABC-TV unit manager, sat on the floor, moaning in agony from a hole ripped in his abdomen.

Elizabeth Evans had staggered and fallen, blood streaming down her face onto her light print dress.

Nineteen-year-old Ira Goldstein sat in a chair holding his side from a bullet that had torn open his thigh, pitifully asking for help from people ignoring him in their rush to get to the Senator.

Another stray .22 mini-mag had caught seventeen-year-old Irwin Stroll in the calf of the leg and spun him down.

With those *five shots,* there was blood everywhere.

And, in the midst of it all lay the man who might have been the next president of the United States, Robert Francis Kennedy, his eyes fluttering open and shut, hit by four slugs, three of which entered or passed through his body from the rear and the fourth passing through the shoulder of his suit coat.

Ahmand's first slug, the lethal one, had smashed into Bobby's mastoid from less than an inch away, atomizing into tiny fragments that angled through his brain.

The distance of Sirhan's gun from the Senator would become the subject of great controversy.

Some of Robert F. Kennedy's last words would be heard by busboy Juan Romero, kneeling beside the young Senator, cradling his head in one hand and giving him his crucifix with the other.

The mortally wounded Bobby asked, "Is everybody safe?" Romero in tears blurted out, "Yes, yes, everything's going to be okay." Then, clutching the beads, Bobby's lips moved once more, but no one could hear what he was trying to say.

Fred Dutton reached the Senator moments later and managed to get his tie and collar loosened. Frank Mankiewicz took off his own coat jacket and, after folding it, placed it under Bobby's head. Then he removed the Senator's shoes.

At the edge of the crowd, Ethel Kennedy, with tears of frustration, was begging for help to get to Bobby. When the crowd finally realized who she was, they literally propelled her over their heads so she could drop to her knees beside her husband.

Roger Mudd of CBS-TV was next to Ethel as she knelt by Bobby's side. As she held his hand, he whispered his last words: "Oh, Ethel."

Aides fought the crowd now ringing the stricken candidate, pleading, "Give him air . . . For God's sake, please give him air."

The Embassy Ballroom had become a sea of panic; men, women, and children, hands wringing helplessly, were weeping, "Oh, God . . . It can't be . . . Not again."

The Senator's brother-in-law, Steve Smith, managed to get a live mike on the lectern. Seizing it, he asked the crowd to leave quietly so that the doctors could get in. Then, as the crowd became silent, three doctors materialized. They would be too late.

Back in the pantry, the first wedge of uniformed police appeared. They had missed Ali Ahmand and the girl, but wasted no time buffeting their way through the crowd to spirit Sirhan from the clutches of Rosie Grier and the others. What no one could believe was the vacant smile on the little Jordanian's face.

Sirhan had a lot to smile about. He was still alive. Now, if everything went well, he would be paroled in 1984. Coupled with the money deposited in the numbered account, it had been well worth the risk.

CHAPTER SEVENTEEN NOTES

1. See Appendix, Exhibit No. 16.

2. LAPD Summary Report, p. 1075.

3. Boris Yaro Interview,(See Appendix, Exhibit 19).

4. LAPD Summary Report, p. 977.

5. *Ibid.,* pp. 975-976.

6. *Ibid.,* pp. 957-958.

7. See Appendix, Exhibit No. 26, pp. 408-409.

8.   LAPD witness reports (not included in the Summary Report) seeing a man matching Ali Ahmand's description enter a shiny black car accompanied by a girl, then leaving rapidly.

9.   Sharaga's report on the Bernstein couple and Sandra Serrano does not appear as described in the LAPD Summary Report. See Appendix, Exhibit No. 26.

10. According to the official eyewitness statements, it was Rosie Grier who seized the weapon from Sirhan. See Appendix, Exhibit 19, p. 10.

Chapter Eighteen

Robert Francis Kennedy would die at 1:44 a.m. on the morning of June 6, 1968. His death would trigger the start of a massive official cover-up, second only to the one following his brother's assassination. The key to thwarting the investigation would be that there was a CIA-controlled operative in a high police position, high enough to manage witness testimony and censor what could be placed into evidence.

A LAPD task force was set up called "Special Unit Senator" (SUS), and a former LAPD officer named Lt. Manuel Pena was chosen to head it. Pena mysteriously appeared back at LAPD after having retired from the force in November 1967.[1] Pena's official retirement from the LAPD was noted in an newspaper article uncovered by William Turner from the *San Fernando Valley Times*. It revealed:

> Pena retired from the police force to advance his career. He has accepted a position with the Agency for International Development Office of the State Department. As a public safety advisor, he will train and advise foreign police forces in investigative and administrative matters. After nine weeks of training and orientation, he will be assigned to his post, possibly a Latin American country, judging by the fact that he speaks Spanish fluently.

According to Turner, reporter Fernando Faura, whose by-line appeared on the newspaper story covering Pena's farewell banquet, recounted that, in April 1968, five months after Pena's departure, he was sauntering along a corridor in the Los Angeles Police Center when he

209

spotted a familiar figure. According to Faura, "the square face and fireplug frame seemed to belong to Manny Pena, now sporting an expensive dark blue suit, a black handlebar mustache, and heavy horn-rimmed glasses."

"Manny?" Faura probed.

The figure stopped and looked sheepish as the reporter approached with hand extended.

"Hey, Manny, I damn near didn't recognize you with that disguise!"

According to the story, the detective was not amused, and Faura asked what he was doing back in Los Angeles. Pena claimed that the AID job wasn't quite what he had expected, so he quit and resumed his duties with the LAPD.

It is important to note that the Office of Public Safety of the Agency for International Development (AID) had long served as a cover for the CIA's clandestine program of supplying advisors and instructors for national police and intelligence services.

FBI agent Robert LaJeunesse, whom Turner had known years before in the FBI, confided to him that Pena had left the LAPD for a "special training unit" at a CIA base in Virginia—Camp Peary, Virginia, known inside the Agency as "The Farm." In fact, said LaJeunesse, Pena's departure in November 1967 had not been a one-shot deal. The detective had already performed some special assignments for the CIA in Central and South America, working with CIA operative Dan A. Mitrione, a former Indiana police chief.

Further confirmation of Pena's CIA involvement came from his brother, a high-school teacher, who casually mentioned to television newsman Stan Bohrman how proud Manny was of his services for the CIA over the years.

To help him manipulate sensitive areas of the RFK investigation, Pena selected another CIA compatriot, Sgt. Enrique "Hank" Hernandez, to work the background/conspiracy team, ostensibly assigned to dig into Sirhan's past. Hernandez did his job well. After the investigation was completed, he was promoted to lieutenant in recognition of his performance on the SUS. After his retirement, Hernandez touted his past CIA affiliation. In a resume offering his services as a private investigator Hernandez claimed that he played a key role in the CIA's "Unified Police Command, a training operation for Latin American countries. He received a medal from the Venezuelan government, for his efforts in helping prevent Fidel Castro's "exportation" of the Cuban Revolution onto its soil.

So, with their ducks in a row, Pena and Hernandez embarked on their campaign to make sure nothing surfaced during the Robert Kennedy assassination investigation pointing to a CIA, FBI, or mob involvement.

The first major problem was that too many witnesses remembered the girl in a polka dot dress, who was seen with Ali Ahmand as the pair made their getaway. To eliminate any areas of investigation that could lead to the actual assassin, the investigation team had to destroy the credibility of any witness who reported seeing the escaping pair.

These witnesses were press photographer Evan P. Freed and Kennedy campaign workers Booker Griffin, George Green, and Sandy Serrano. The most critical of these, with good reason, was Sandy Serrano, the girl who had been sitting on the steps of the fire escape. Serrano's account of the couple's exodus was confirmed by the excited report of the elderly Bernstein couple to Police Sergeant Paul Sharaga, an independent report that included the same exact language heard by Serrano, "We shot him! We shot him!" The Bernsteins had been within a hundred feet of Serrano. At the time, Sharaga put out an APB (all points bulletin) on the pair, but at that point, a police radio blackout commenced—which, according to Sharaga, lasted between fifteen and twenty minutes.[2]

When the blackout ended, as inexplicably as it had begun, communications kept broadcasting the APB at fifteen-minute intervals. Then, at about 2:30 a.m., the first in an series of inept moves began that would protect the perpetrators of Robert F. Kennedy's murder. It started when Detective Inspector John Powers came by Sharaga's command post, demanding, "Who's responsible for the description of the two suspects that's going out over the air?"

When Sharaga admitted that he was briefing Powers on the report of the Bernstein couple, Powers ordered, "Let's cancel that description. We don't want to make a federal case out of it. We've got the suspect in custody."

Sharaga reluctantly agreed to cancel the APB on the male suspect, since he considered it possible that the man might have been taken into custody. However, he continued the APB on the polka-dot-dress girl in defiance of Powers. Nevertheless, Powers did have the last word. After leaving Sharaga, he personally contacted Communications and ordered the entire APB discontinued.

Sharaga shut down his command post shortly after noon and sent a detail of officers to guard the hotel floor that housed the Kennedys. Then he drove to the LAPD Rampart Division and dictated a detailed report of everything that had occurred over the past twelve hours, giving special emphasis to the Bernsteins' sighting of Ali Ahmand and his female companion. The report was taken by Captain Floyd Phillips' secretary.

Five days later, a second event occurred that, subsequently, would immeasurably shake Sharaga.

The veteran sergeant was instructed to prepare a second report covering his command-post activities of June 5, "from beginning to end." He again complied and personally delivered the report to SUS. "There was a deadline on it," Sharaga said, recalling a brief conversation with Manny Pena.[3]

Fortunately, this time Sharaga made three additional copies, in the event they were needed. Routinely he put one in the Watch Commander's drawer, another in the inter-office mail, and kept a third copy for himself. Approximately two weeks later, while at work, Sharaga wanted to refer to something in the report. The office copies were gone. When he asked what had happened to them, his superior, Lieutenant William C. Jordan claimed he didn't know. Then he asked SUS if there was some reason why they had disposed of the copies. Their posture was they didn't know what he was talking about.

Suppressing Sharaga's report was vital, for it provided independent corroboration of Sandy Serrano's story of Ahmand and the girl. However, with Sharaga's report buried, Serrano was on her own and her testimony unverifiable. As may be surmised, Sharaga's report never officially surfaced.

By this time, rumors had started flying that Sirhan was tied in with an Arab extremist group contemplating the assassination.

It wouldn't be until 1970, when LAPD chief of detectives, Robert A. Houghton, wrote a book on the investigation entitled *Special Unit Senator,* that Sharaga knew his report had been suppressed.[4] By then, it was too late.

Unfortunately for the cover-up team, after repeated interrogations by the LAPD and FBI, Serrano's story could not be shaken. The problem of eliminating her testimony remained high on the SUS priority list. Therefore, on June 29, 1968, Manny Pena dispatched LAPD criminologist DeWayne Wolfer to the Ambassador Hotel to prove scientifically that Serrano could not have heard gunfire emanating from the pantry. He figured, if he could prove her a liar on this one point, he could discredit everything else she had said. Mounting a sound-level meter on the stairway where Serrano had been sitting, Wolfer had assistants fire test shots in the pantry. His meter supposedly registered no higher than one-half decibel—below the minimum that a person with sharp hearing might pick up.

As a former engineer of some repute developing acoustical equipment for the aerospace and commercial industries, I can state positively that no such differential readings could be reasonably taken of gunshots with the commercial metering equipment available to the LAPD in 1968.

In an ordinary case, Pena might have been able to close the book on Sandy Serrano. But, as they knew, this was no ordinary case. As long as Serrano stuck to her story, no amount of superfluous evidence would serve to dispel it. So Serrano was handed over for the special ministrations of Hank Hernandez. According to Houghton,[5] Pena asked Hernandez what he was doing for dinner that night, suggesting he might like to take Sandra Serrano out for a SUS-bought steak.

Hernandez then supposedly wined and dined the young lady but was unable to break her story. So, after dinner, he took her to Parker Center (LAPD headquarters) for a polygraph test. There, according to Houghton, he intimidated Serrano unmercifully, getting her to change her story. After characterizing her testimony as a "pack of mistruths," Serrano quit her job in Los Angeles and returned to her parents' home in Ohio.

Satisfied that they had managed to discredit Serrano, the operatives next turned their attention to busboy Vincent DiPierro, who was the only other publicly-known witness to accurately describe the girl seen with Ali Ahmand, i.e., the polka-dot-dress girl. On July 1, eleven days after the polygraph interrogation of Serrano, Hernandez summoned DiPierro to Parker Center for an equivalent grilling. The detective got what he wanted. After a distorted session, DiPierro identified a different girl from the one described by Serrano.

Vincent DiPierro appeared as scheduled at the Sirhan trial, where he readily identified the girl Hernandez insisted he had seen. No attempt would be made to impeach his testimony by comparing it with his earlier statement to the grand jury.

Young DiPierro evidently regretted his about-face. On April 20, 1969, he wrote a congratulatory letter to Art Kevin, then a reporter with radio station KHJ, who was doing a series on the Robert Kennedy assassination, lauding him on his extensive research and brilliant job of reporting a factual story. DiPierro said that, since the question of the polka-dot-dress girl "concerned my character personally, I was deeply interested in hearing the facts straight for a change." Then he offered Kevin his assistance on "this controversial issue," terming that segment "the first real true report."

This appeared on a series Kevin was broadcasting on unanswered questions in the RFK assassination. The operatives had to be worried. Before the series was aired, LAPD Inspector John Powers, visited Kevin and put pressure on him not to raise the question of the polka-dot-dress girl. Kevin declined.

Then came a surprising change of events. Due to the pressure of work, it was several days before Kevin could drive out to the DiPierros'. His father, a maitre d' at the Ambassador Hotel, answered the door, while Vincent stood in the background. Kevin immediately got the impression that they looked shaken.

It was for a good reason. The senior DiPierro said that the FBI had come by and explained how painstakingly the police and the Bureau had reconstructed the events in the pantry. They actually said that his son's life might be in danger.

When Kevin pressed on, DiPierro shoved the door shut.

After Kevin aired the segment on the girl in the polka dot dress in December of 1974 (which included an interview with ex-LAPD Sergeant Paul Sharaga) on KMPC Radio, Inspector Powers stormed into the studio and threatened to get the newsman's job. However, when KMPC management backed Kevin, the LAPD backed off.

Art Kevin's experience was not unique among the media who tried to force the "polka-dot-dress girl" issue into the open. Reporter Fernando Faura, who had written the story of Manuel Pena's retirement from the LAPD, was commissioned by *Life* magazine bureau chief Jordan Bonfante to pursue it. He interviewed both DiPierro and Sandy Serrano, using an artist to draw a composite sketch of the girl they had seen. Then Faura interviewed other witnesses, prevailing upon them to submit to polygraph tests by an operator not associated with the police. All passed, identifying the same girl.

At this juncture, the LAPD contacted Bonfante. After a six-hour conversation with the police, Bonfante still refused to call off the investigation.

Then, powerful forces acted. Within a week, Bonfante was told by his editors that the story would never make print. Someone powerful had gone over his head.

In the wake of the carnage, there would also be the red herrings spread by Khyber Khan's Iranian group, much the same as had been done by the anti-Castro exiles after the President's death. Typical of these was the investigation conducted by Sergeant Philip Sartuche of the LAPD. It concerned the story emanating from Khan's Iranian volunteers at Kennedy's campaign headquarters.

They claimed Sirhan had entered the front door of Kennedy headquarters during the afternoon of June 4 with "a girl in a polka dot dress."[6] The various descriptions of the couple, given by the Iranians, created total confusion. They were supposed to.

Sartuche's investigation of the Iranians consisted mostly of an inquiry into the activities of Khan, which revealed nothing of the actions of Ali Ahmand. The following is Sartuche's official police report. It speaks for itself:

LAPD REPORT ON KHYBER [KHAIBAR] KHAN

Subject's first visit to the Kennedy Headquarters was on 6-1-68 in the afternoon hours. On this date subject registered under his true name Khaibar Khan. He also met a Marguerite Sweeney (I-59) who was in charge of volunteer workers. Subject was then assigned to answering phones and at this time he volunteered numerous names of Tribal Chiefs who were to be in the USA during the month of November 1968. Also the other volunteers who appeared at his desk he would claim as being part of his group and would register them under his address. When individuals would call to volunteer, he would follow this same procedure. It was discovered there was a total of 24 volunteer cards which were made by Khaibar Khan. The majority of these cards were in the same handwriting and contained the same address. The 24 names are listed on the interview of June Isackson (I-80a).

Mr. Khan's second visit took place on June 2, 1968, at approximately 2:00 p.m. At this time Mr. Khan was accompanied by his sister (so-called), Maryam Kouchan alias Khan (I-361). Both parties assisted in doing various campaign tasks and left the headquarters at approximately 6:00 p.m.

He returned on June 3, 1968, at approximately 3:00 p.m. with his daughter, Shirrin Khan. Shirrin Khan was assigned to the answering of phones and general type clerical work. During the day's activities Mr. Khan was at the rear exit of the headquarters when he observed a male and female seated in a blue V/W. He states that he also observed a male leaning inside the right window talking to the couple who were seated. At approximately 7:00 p.m. Mr. Khan and his daughter left the headquarters walked toward the parked V/W. Upon approaching the vehicle Mr. Khan noticed that the male who was standing outside walked across the street and walked out of sight. When he passed the vehicle he glanced inside, and he noticed that the girl who was seated inside the vehicle turned her head as if she did not want to be seen.

On June 4, 1968, Mr. Khan arrived with sister Maryam Khan (I-361) and son Felipe Khan (I-292) at approximately 2:00 p.m. During his activities Mr. Khan was located near the drinking fountain where the coffee stand is located. At this time he observed a female, Cauc, approximately 23/6 years, wearing a short dress with polka dots.[7] He described the dress as white in color and the dots to be the diameter of pennies or smaller. This female appeared to be talking to a male described as male, Cauc, dark complexion, short in height, wearing a jacket described as blue "McGregor" type (windbreaker). He was wearing a white shirt underneath and tight trousers. It appeared that the two parties were talking as they were facing each other and that he noticed movement of their mouths, but due to the distance Mr. Khan could not overhear any conversation. Upon approaching the parties he noticed that the female turned her head and looked in the opposite direction. Mr. Khan then recognized this couple as being the same as seen on 6-3-68 in the blue V/W. At approximately 8:00 p.m. on 6-4-68 Mr. Khan and Miss Kouchan left the headquarters. Upon exiting the rear of the headquarters Mr. Khan and Miss Kouchan got into their vehicle and drove to the front of the headquarters where they stopped and Mr. Khan re-entered. While Mr. Khan was inside a male Cauc, early 20s, approached Maryam who was still seated in the vehicle and the male asked for a ride. Miss Kouchan, recognizing the male as being in the headquarters earlier, agreed to give the person a ride. When Mr. Khan returned to the vehicle he noticed the male seated in the rear seat. Enroute to Santa Monica the conversation between Mr. Khan and the male consisted of the male asking for campaign literature of press type passes. Mr. Khan refused the male any literature since he had none, but informed him that if he left his name and address he would furnish him with some at a later time. The male wrote his name and address on a piece of paper and gave the paper to Mr. Khan. The male was Michael Wayne (I-1096).

BACKGROUND

Mr. Khan became active in the campaign due to his involvement with Robert Kennedy at the time Robert Kennedy was Attorney General.

Mr. Khan is an exile from the Country of Iran. He came to the attention of Robert Kennedy through law suits which were filed against the Family of the King (Shah) of Iran. These suits resulted from 1959 when Mr. Khan was involved in a construction job with the United States. Mr. Khan states when he returned to Iran he was swindled out of money and material by the King. Upon returning to the United States Mr. Khan was made a political exile by the King.

Upon returning to the United States Mr. Khan started a group named "The United Patriots for Justice." He started a campaign against the King of Iran accusing him of mis-use of foreign aid money. He supposedly is assisted in this venture by various members of the tribes which make up part of Iran.

OFFICERS' STATEMENTS

Officers first came in contact with Mr. Khaibar Khan as a result of checking volunteer cards at the Kennedy Headquarters. It was brought to officers' attention that numerous volunteer cards were made by the same person due to handwriting. It was also found that the cards (24 in all) had the same address listed on them as Mr. Khan's. Upon checking this address it was found that Mr. Khan's ex-wife resides at this location.

Mr. Khan's ex-wife (Talat Khan I-314) was contacted by Sgt. Sartuche and he was informed that Mrs. Kahn had been separated for some time and that she was not involved in politics as was her husband. Mrs. Khan contacted Khaibar and he in turn notified our department of his whereabouts. An appointment was made for an interview on 6-18-68.

On June 18, 1968, officers met Mr. Kahn in the lobby of the Miramar Hotel located on Ocean Avenue in Santa Monica. He informed officers that he was staying at the Ocean Palms Hotel located at 1215 Ocean Avenue Apt #201 and that he was registered under the name of Mr. Goody. During the interview Mr. Khan stated his distrust of the present administration and the immigration department. It was evident that Mr. Khan didn't want his whereabouts known. He stated that his life was in danger as someone was attempting to kill him. While living in the West Los Angeles area he was leaving his ex-wife's apartment when unknown suspects jumped him and Mr. Khan received various injuries. Due to this incident Mr. Khan received surgery and had to wear a cast on his arm. This incident was reported to the West Los Angeles Detectives. In April 1968 he and his sister, Maryam Kouchan, were horseback riding in Griffith

Park at which time his sister got shot in the leg by an unknown assailant and required surgery. This disabled Miss Kouchan, and it was necessary for her to use crutches in able to walk.

Due to the above, both Sgt. Sartuche and Officer Miller were given nicknames (golfer and tennis player) to use when further contacting Mr. Khan by telephone. On further meetings, in person, officers were to meet Mr. Khan at other places than at his residence. These places were coffee shops, parks, beaches, etc.

Officers' first interview with Khaiber Khan was on June 18, 1968, and the last contact was made on July 27, 1968. During this time five contacts were made and officers learned that Mr. Khan is involved in law suits with the King of Iran. Because Mr. Khan had numerous papers from the United States Senate, United States Department of Justice along with letters from an organization called the United Patriots for Justice. Officers found that the United Patriots for Justice is an organization headed by Mr. Khan and is made up of different tribes located in Iran. Mr. Khan gave his permission for officers to make copies of these documents, which we did.

After the first visit officers found through the Immigration Department that Khaibar Khan, alias Goodarzian, had a Immigration Warrant outstanding. The warrant was for Illegal Entry (remaining beyond specified time), Warrant #A-11-01142, no bail. It was also found out through R 7 I that Mr. Khan was using the alias of Mohammad Ali and had an arrest on 1-13-67 for 647F in Hollywood. (LA#825 805A).

The only information received which is relevant to the Kennedy assassination was that on June 3, 1968, Mr. Khan observed a male and female sitting in a blue V/W at the rear of headquarters. He described the female as Fe, Cauc 23/6 years, 5-5 and the male as dark comp, short.

On June 4, 1968, Mr. Khan as a telephone operator at the headquarters again observed the male and female that he had seen sitting in the V/W. The couple was observed standing near the coffee shop area. The male and female were facing each other and it appeared to Mr. Khan that the couple were talking to each other as their mouths appeared to be moving. At this time girl was described as wearing a white dress with dark polka dots about the diameter of a penny. The male was described as wearing a blue jacket (McGregor type) with a white shirt and light colored tight trousers.

Due to the people seen on two different occasions by Mr. Khan he was shown mugs of suspect Sirhan B. Sirhan and asked if he could identify him as being the male seen. Mr. Khan stated that he could not be sure until he could actually see the male in person. Mr. Khan was asked if he would attend a show-up if it could be arranged and would he then take a polygraph test to verify the truthfulness of his statements. Mr. Khan refused to take a polygraph test or attend a show-up and stated that he wanted to be 100% sure before he accused anyone. During all the interviews with Mr. Khan he was always unsure of his identification of Sirhan B. Sirhan.

Due to Mr. Khan refusing to attend a line up or take a polygraph test it is very doubtful or simply a mistake in identity.

It was later found out by officers that Mr. Khan was arrested by Immigration authorities and is presently on $4,000.00 bail pending a hearing.

END OF REPORT[8]

One of the most glaring omissions in the report is the lack of meaningful background data on Khan. Or was it deliberate? Nasser Afshar and Alexi Goodaryi carried Khan's story 180 degrees. He was in the end working for the Shah, not RFK, or he would have been dead. Sartuche did not report that Khan deposited millions of dollars in checks for transfer to overseas accounts, signed by the Shah's sister (not the settlement funds paid by the Shah and his sister in March of 1965), or that Khan was seen in the Ambassador Hotel the night Bobby was shot. Serious omissions.

Then, as the investigation began to get too close, the Iranians, as had Ali Ahmand, mysteriously disappeared into the night. Ali Ahmand in fact was not even referenced in any LAPD files. They couldn't locate him—or didn't want to. Instead, on August 1, 1968, they came up with a free lance writer named Khalid Iqbal, from Pakistan, to interview as Ali Ahmand.

CHAPTER EIGHTEEN NOTES

1.   Interview with William Turner, February 16, 1981.

2.   In 1977, Los Angeles Assistant District Attorney, John Van de Kamp announced that there had been no blackout, because the LAPD radio logs didn't indicate one.

3.   Art Kevin's taped interview with Sharaga, KMPC radio, Los Angeles, California, December 20, 1974.

4.   *Ibid.*

5.   *Special Unit Senator,* Houghton, 1970; LAPD Summary Report, pp. 408-417.

6.   See Appendix, Exhibit No. 20.

7.   It was obvious that Khan was bringing attention to Sirhan's lookout and a man named Michael Wayne to place her identity with someone other than Ali Ahmand. Wayne, who was in the kitchen area as Kennedy made his way to the Embassy room, got Bobby to sign a poster for him as he passed through. (LAPD, Summary Report, p. 144.)

8.   Spelling corrected from the original. See Appendix, Exhibit No. 15.

Chapter Nineteen

Once the conspiracy angle had been dealt with, another major hurdle had to be confronted—the fact that the Senator's murder was actually accomplished with a weapon other than Sirhan's gun. The parties responsible for the cover-up would succeed in suppressing the evidence at the Sirhan trial—with intimidation, attempted blackmail, and outright perjury on the behalf of LAPD officials.

It began after the autopsy on Robert Kennedy's body was performed by Dr. Thomas Noguchi, the L. A. county coroner, in the early morning of June 6, 1968. It was accomplished with the help of two assistants, in the presence of at least a dozen people.[1]

Noguchi found that Kennedy had been hit by three bullets. One had struck his head just behind his right ear and fragmented in the right-hand side of his brain—the bullet that killed him. A second bullet entered his back near the right armpit—traveling along the muscle structure of his back, then lodging at the base of his neck. A third entered the back of the right armpit and exited in the front of the right shoulder. This bullet had left no fragments and was listed in the police accounting as having been "lost somewhere in the ceiling interspace."

All of this evidence was mysteriously missing from the LAPD final report. In April 1988, an official of the LAPD claimed that all of this evidence was inadvertently burned or destroyed. Several days later, it was claimed that the destroyed papers and photographs were mere copies. So much for the credibility of the LAPD.

Noguchi retrieved the second bullet, the only one striking Kennedy remaining in good enough condition for constructive forensic examination. After inspecting it closely, he scratched his initials on its base and handed it over to the police. Noguchi also found that a fourth bullet

221

had passed through Kennedy's right shoulder pad, without actually touching his body.

With four bullets hitting Kennedy—from the rear—and five bullets hitting other subjects—from the front—it would seem rather difficult for Sirhan's eight-round pistol to have done all the damage.

In fact it would be impossible, although the LAPD would claim that one of the four bullets hitting the Senator also hit Paul Schrade.

But most important, Noguchi found that, on the basis of the powder tattooing and the experiments he performed with respect thereto, that the muzzle range in relation to the Senator's head was about one inch. Thus, L.A. coroner Dr. Thomas T. Noguchi to the dismay and detriment of the conspirators, determined that it would have been impossible for Sirhan to have fired the shots that struck the Senator,[2] a fact that would be later confirmed by LAPD officer DeWayne Wolfer, who conducted a test firing of a .22-caliber Iver Johnson to verify Noguchi's autopsy report.

The cover-up conspirators knew that any report Noguchi would generate saying Robert Kennedy had been hit from behind by bullets fired from a distance of a few inches or less would completely contradict all the witness testimony given to both the grand jury and at Sirhan's trial. They did their job well, for this fact would not really come to light until 1975, when William Harper, an expert in the technical and forensic investigation of firearms, claimed that, after comparing a near perfect bullet found in a victim hit by Sirhan's gun with a near perfect bullet removed from the back of Bobby Kennedy, they were not fired from the same gun.

Harper's conclusions were confirmed by another expert in the forensic sciences, Herbert MacDonell, who, after an extensive review of the 1970 findings, also concluded that the near perfect bullet removed from William Weisel, could not have been fired from the same gun that fired the bullet taken from the Senator.

Armed with what I knew about the assassination and subsequent investigation, it didn't surprise me that these findings would be found inconclusive.

On August 14, 1975, Superior Court Judge Robert A. Wenke ordered a re-examination of the evidence relating to Sirhan's gun. It was in response to a petition filed by former Kennedy aide Paul Schrade, CBS, and others. A panel of seven experts, acceptable to all parties, was appointed to conduct the re-examination, which began in late September. The panel could not agree on anything. However, on December 28, 1975, William Harper swore out an affidavit reaffirming his 1970 findings, after an intense re-investigation of the physical evidence.

The plan utilizing Sirhan as a diversion had worked perfectly. Now all that was needed was to change or smokescreen Noguchi's testimony regarding his autopsy report. They tried.

According to the Los Angeles *Herald Examiner* of May 13, 1974, Noguchi revealed that, before he entered the grand jury room, he was approached by an unnamed deputy DA, who pressed him to revise his estimate of the firing distance from inches to feet.

Noguchi refused to suborn perjury and, suspicious of a cover-up, decided to conduct an inquest. Accordingly, he requested the bullets previously submitted into evidence in order to perform a Neutron Activation Analysis. Suddenly, he was denied access to anything by both the LAPD and the DA's office.

As the summer of 1968 wore on, Noguchi found his attempts to subject his official conclusions to formal scientific review rebuffed at every turn. He also found himself the target of an insidious campaign that questioned both his competency and character. The crux of these "rumors" centered on Noguchi's handling of the RFK autopsy. Word was being passed around (and outside) of his office that he had "bungled" the examination of RFK's body. It was blamed on his alleged propensity to "take drugs."[3] Before the year was out, Noguchi found himself suspended from his position as coroner of Los Angeles County.

In this tenuous situation, Noguchi was summoned to testify at Sirhan's trial. The DA's careful questioning of the coroner kept away from any conflict whatever with their shaky account of the assassination. Sirhan's attorney didn't help. He cut short Noguchi's answers, claiming it was "not necessary" for the coroner to go into "gory detail" about the nature and location of RFK's various wounds.

As a result, Noguchi's actual findings never saw the light of day.

Noguchi was reinstated after the trial when, during a public hearing on the issue, his lawyer, Godfrey Isaac, pressed for a complete review of the RFK autopsy.

A visibly nervous Deputy County Counsel Martin Weekes shouted, "This is a terribly serious matter!" He then urged that no further discussion of the RFK case take place in public. Weekes reasoned, "It might trigger off an international incident." Weekes didn't elaborate. He couldn't; the Iranian SAVAK was involved. Instead, he sheepishly stipulated that Noguchi's autopsy had been "superior," and the hearing was called to a close.

So, with Sirhan in jail branded as the lone assassin, the cover-up succeeded in closing the second avenue of possible discovery.

However, as the years wore on, the "second gun" controversy showed no signs of abating. One of the proponents of this theory was a friend of my wife's by the name of Allard K. Lowenstein, an attorney, a former member of the U.S. House of Representatives, and a good friend of the Kennedys.

Lowenstein told me during a lengthy interview in August of 1979 that, after he himself had conducted an investigation of the Senator's murder, he agreed with the coroner and not with the police report. Lowenstein claimed that he carefully scrutinized the grand jury and trial records, searching for testimony that placed Sirhan's gun to the rear and within inches of Bobby. There were none.

"The distances mentioned most frequently were two to three feet." Then, Lowenstein said, "Eyewitnesses can be depended on to be unreliable, but this information was unsettling. It seemed unlikely that everyone could be wrong about something as significant as the difference between inches and feet."

Lowenstein said that he talked to the same eyewitnesses in person, thinking that the transcripts were misleading or possibly that the witnesses were uncertain or confused. However, he claimed that the stories of everyone he talked to were consistent with their earlier testimony. "They were all unequivocally in agreement about what they had seen, i.e., Kennedy was shot by Sirhan from the front at a distance of several feet. "Everyone I talked to contended there were only *two shots fired,* before Sirhan was subdued and firing wildly." This is consistant with Boris Yaro's statement to me.

I must add here that the LAPD Summary Report is contradictory and totally supports Lowenstein's contention. On page 9, entitled, "The Shooting,"[4] it says:

> Kennedy stopped to shake hands with a hotel waiter and then with Di Pierro. As he let go of the hand of Jesus Perez, another hotel employee, a man moved toward Kennedy; his right arm fully extended, *he fired four shots quickly at the Senator*. Kennedy raised his arms over his head and two of the shots entered under his right arm. The first shot had struck him in the head behind the right ear; the second went through the padding of Kennedy's coat and struck Paul Schrade, United

Automobile Workers Union official, in the head.

Again, so much for the official version.

Lowenstein went on to say, "My eyewitnesses also told me it was wacky to doubt that Sirhan had killed Kennedy. That was before they heard what was in the autopsy report.[5] Few of them thought so afterward.["6]

Lowenstein then said that, because he didn't want to add any more flak surrounding the case, he had submitted a list of questions to Joe Busch, the Los Angeles County District Attorney, in 1976.

From then on, he claimed, the official response to his questions were as peculiar as the contradictions in the evidence. Every official he saw at the DA's office was polite and talked about cooperation, but nobody did anything with his list, except to ask for another copy.

However, when a question was answered, he said, "It turned out to be untrue. Not marginally untrue, but totally untrue."

Then, as time wore on, he found that propaganda campaigns were being fabricated to deliver information that was the exact opposite of the facts. In his opinion, two of these campaigns were quite effective. He explained: "They continually repeated that every eyewitness had seen Sirhan kill Kennedy, and almost as frequently there was only one gun in the hotel pantry where Kennedy was shot.

"Busch simply took to announcing the opposite of facts that didn't fit. It was ridiculous," Lowenstein said. "When we were together on the *Tomorrow* show, Busch asserted: 'There is no eyewitness that you talk to, no eyewitness that disputes that Sirhan put his gun up to the Senator's ear and fired.' When I asked him to name one such witness, he replied: 'Would you like Mr. Uecker, the man that grabbed Sirhan's arm?'

"At the time, I said nothing. Later, when John Howard became acting district attorney, I asked for the name of any substantiating witness who claimed Sirhan put his gun to the Senator's ear and fired. He was reluctant. But when I pressed him, he also cited Uecker. Why Busch selected Karl Uecker as his *star witness* totally baffled me. Uecker's testimony, as had the other eyewitnesses', clearly supported the official autopsy report."

I had to agree with Lowenstein; Karl Uecker was a key witness, the only one standing between Kennedy and Sirhan when the shooting began, the man who—as Boris Yaro put it—had grabbed Sirhan's gun arm after two shots. Uecker had gone back to Germany some years before. As Lowenstein would sarcastically remark, "Perhaps, they felt with distance he would be unavailable. So after being jerked around, I decided to make the trip."

When Lowenstein located him, he said Uecker turned out to be an intelligent man with explicit recollections, consistent with his grand jury and trial testimony:[7]

Uecker told Lowenstein, "I told the authorities that Sirhan never got close enough for a point-blank shot, never." Lowenstein then went on to say, "It irritated Uecker that he was being misquoted, and he felt that nothing could come of my efforts."

Quoting the German, Lowenstein said that Uecker felt the investigation "was to stop with Sirhan, and that is what will happen."

Then Lowenstein said Uecker reconstructed the sequence of events in the pantry for himself and two reporters from the West German magazine *Stern*. Uecker (like Yaro) was utterly certain that Sirhan had fired only *two shots* when he pushed Sirhan down onto a steam table. And that was that.

As noted earlier, Uecker's statement was consistent with the one made to me by Boris Yaro in our interview on March 28, 1978.

Lowenstein then pointed out the obvious, "If three bullets hit Kennedy, as the *official* autopsy reported, and if Sirhan was on the steam table after firing two shots, he could *not* have fired four shots at the Senator.[8]

That would have required him to put the other two bullets into Kennedy from behind, at point-blank range, while he was struggling on a steam table several feet in front of the Senator, with a distraught crowd flailing around and between them."

Because Uecker's statements had gone virtually unreported except in Germany's *Stern* magazine, they had no impact in the United States. They also had no impact on officials in Los Angeles, who still maintain Karl Uecker is their star witness. But then, as Allard Lowenstein put it, they have been unable to find another credible witness to quote, and it is unlikely that anyone else would go to Germany to check with Uecker.

As for Ali Ahmand, when the LAPD finally got around to investigating him, they discovered that he had not only fled the country, but that the name of Ali Ahmand (the one he had given the Kennedy staff) was false.

Thus, the LAPD's SUS team, with its two CIA operatives, Manny Pena and Enrique Hernandez, had done their job superbly. They had finally succeeded in cutting off all avenues of investigation that could lead to anything other than another "lone deranged gunman." So, with the help of the Shah of Iran, Rafizadeh engineered the death of another Kennedy for the mob, and the FBI and the CIA covered it up, with the same expertise as they had done in the President's assassination.

Rafizadeh would continue working in conjunction with the FBI and CIA until 1979, when the Shah of Iran would be deposed by the Ayatollah Khomeini. His last known address (as of 1988) was France.

CHAPTER NINETEEN NOTES

1. See Official Autopsy Report, Exhibit, 21.

2. See Appendix, Exhibit No. 20.

3. *Los Angeles Times,* May 27, 1969.

4. See Appendix, Exhibit 19.

5. See Appendix, Exhibit No. 21.

6. Interview with Allard K. Lowenstein, former U.S. Representative from New York, Fifth Congressional District, August 1979.

7. From this point on Lowenstein said he was referring to his notes, taken during his interview with Uecker.

8. See Appendix, Exhibit 19, p. 9.

Epilogue

From that fateful day Jack Kennedy was murdered, I spent my time consulting with various companies on the design of their electronic devices, as well as developing my own line of products for the commercial market. Then, at the peak of my engineering/executive career, I was again thrust into the maze of political intrigue—intrigue that would cause me to write my first book *Betrayal* and drive me to find out who murdered Bobby.

In 1970, two years after Bobby Kennedy was assassinated, I was asked by a prominent surgeon in Baltimore, who was running for Mayor on the Republican ticket, if I would join his campaign as a candidate for President of the Baltimore City Council. I agreed, also warning him about the controversy it might engender, due to the counterfeiting operation I had been arrested for eight years earlier.

At the time it didn't seem to disturb him, and his offer seemed innocuous enough until the local newspaper, the *Baltimore Sun,* started making a major issue out of my having been charged with a felony and pleading nolo contendre. The fact that I had been working to overthrow Fidel Castro at the express desire of my government had no bearing on the case. The resulting publicity was, to say the least, disturbing, and the outcome, a personal disaster.[1] I was asked to resign as president of a company I had spent years building, which had just completed a public offering. Worse, my running mate, who had been so blase earlier, wanted me to drop out of the race. Needless to say, I became obstreperous. I refused to quit my executive position or to drop out of the race.[2] The net result was that, to vindicate myself in the eyes of the public, I called upon Mario Kohly to join me in a press conference to explain what had transpired. It didn't win me the election, but it sure made me feel better.

One year later, as a result of the showing I had in the city council race, I was urged by friends to go for a congressional seat in the newly gerrymandered Baltimore third district. Because of it, I wound up in the strange position of being on the same side as Richard Nixon in the 1972 campaign. Then, as luck would have it, I got involved in the Watergate fiasco.

I had kept in touch with Mario after the city council race. He was still trying to get recognition for his Cuban government in exile and, as would be expected, was interested in my obtaining a congressional seat, so I didn't think twice when he called me just two weeks before the election with an urgent message.

We met at my office, where he told me a wild story. Kohly said that he had been approached by two men who identified themselves as working for the Committee to Re-elect the President (CREEP). They told him that the National Democratic Committee had some damaging information about Nixon and the Bay of Pigs, which they were going to release just prior to the election. Kohly went on to say that, if he could arrange for some of his people to recover the data, it would earn the undying gratitude of Mr. Nixon.

They wouldn't identify what the information was. However, Kohly, putting two and two together, figured it had to be about Nixon agreeing to the slaughter of the leftist exile leaders once they had been deposited on the beach after the Bay of Pigs invasion.

Kohly said he declined the offer after discovering, several weeks later, that the men who had approached him were instead working for the Democratic party. By that time the Watergate break-in had occurred. After thinking about it, he decided to come to me in order that I might be able to make some use of it.

Stunned by what he had told me, I called Senator Charles Mac Mathias. Mac said wait, don't do anything until you are contacted. The following day, I received a phone call asking if I could attend a meeting in Washington with Paul O'Brien, the attorney for CREEP. I said yes, and the meeting was set for Saturday, one week before the election.

Then, less than one hour after our conversation, I received a phone call from a man representing Resorts International.[3] They claimed they were interested in funding a last-minute push on my campaign, and asked if I would be interested. We met in my office the following day. Unfortunately, we could not arrive at an agreement. The contribution would have been in the form of a substantial loan. I was glad I had turned it down. I discovered years later that Nixon, as well as the Mafia and CIA, were tied to Resorts as early as 1961.

Resorts began with organized crime's beachhead in the Bahamas, following their large losses after the Castro revolution. By 1966, the syndicate had control of three casinos through a front company known as the Bahamas Amusement Company, figureheaded by two of Meyer Lansky's associates, Lou Chesler and Wallace Groves. Meyer Lansky being the silent partner and spokesman for the syndicate.

Two of the casinos involved the Mary Carter Paint Company, in conjunction with Bahamas Amusement, to purchase the highly desirable Paradise Island, just off of Nassau. A Justice Department memo of January 1966 stated that the "Mary Carter Paint Company will be in control of Paradise Island casinos with the exception of the one which Groves will control. The atmosphere seems ripe for a Lansky skim." The details were handled by a consultant named Seymor Alter, a man who had known his way around the Bahamas for a long time. Alter had been the man responsible for hosting Richard Nixon on the first of his many visits to the islands.[4]

Alter was also reported as being investigated for allegedly "skimming" funds from the Paradise Island Casino through Nixon friend Bebe Rebozo's Key Biscayne Bank.[5]

As late as 1970, there was solid evidence of Lansky's presence in the Bahamas—and specifically the Paradise Island Casino. A June 1972 federal indictment in Miami of Lansky and an associate, Dino Cellini, alleged that in 1968 Lansky maintained some control over running junkets to the island casino.

In 1969 the Mary Carter Paint Company—by then known as Resorts International—released Dino Cellini's brother Eddie from his post at the casino. After his dismissal, the Dade County sheriff's office placed both Cellinis in the Miami office of Resorts, checking credits and booking junkets.

As late as 1970, newspapers were quoting government investigators as believing that "Lansky is still managing to get his cut out of the Bahamas."

However, the damning part about Nixon's connection to Resorts International is that James Crosby, the head of Resorts, had donated $100,000 to Nixon's 1968 campaign and had raised again that much from friends.[6]

While much more can be added to support Nixon's connection to the syndicate network, such as Lou Chesler's $14,000 contribution to his 1960 campaign, we will never know for sure. All avenues to his murky past were closed with his pardon by Gerald Ford. At any rate, my having no commitment to Resorts, I naively prepared for my meeting with Paul O'Brien that Saturday, a week before the election.

We met at the Columbia Country Club in Chevy Chase, Maryland, at eleven o'clock. With me, I took my campaign manager, Mr. Brent Kansler.

Paul O'Brien listened to my story without comment. When I asked him if I should hold a press conference regarding the story, he replied, "Let me see what kind of statement you'll be making. I'll let you know then."

The following Tuesday, I sent O'Brien, by messenger, a copy of the proposed statement.[7] When we talked later, O'Brien told me, "Do what you think best." Meaning, CREEP had no objection.

I held the press conference that Friday. Only one TV station, Channel 13, ABC, showed up.

Evidently, by not accepting a substantial *loan* from Resorts, I was *persona non grata* with the powers that be. I lost the election.

From that point, things started to deteriorate rapidly. I lost my company, my personal fortune, and eventually my wife and family. At that point, I decided to write *Betrayal.* If nothing else, it would help explain the counterfeiting operation.

After it was published, I became very much aware of the hornets nest I had created and decided to follow it up by providing the evidence necessary to prove the allegations set forth in the manuscript. I started by looking for the ties I knew existed between the Mafia and the Cuban movement, which also meant in part the CIA.

After the HSCA came to the inane conclusion that no one, or group, or government, or government agency was involved in the conspiracy, which they say existed, I felt cheated. Somehow the CIA had pulled it off again—another cover-up.

I had been looking forward to being of help to the committee and was politely told that I wasn't wanted. A blow certainly, but from what I learned after the cover-up of Bobby Kennedy's assassination by the "Company," I'm certinly glad I didn't participate. I would never have been able to publish this manuscript. For, as I suspected, the CIA, in a brilliant ploy, took control of the HSCA in early 1977.

It happened this way. In the fall of 1976, with Tom Downing as chairman, the HSCA selected Richard A. Sprague, from the Philadelphia District Attorney's office, to be chief counsel. Sprague hired four professional independent investigators and criminal lawyers from New York—ones who had no affiliations with the Federal government, i.e., the CIA or FBI. With this team, headed by Bob Tanenbaum as chief attorney and Cliff Fenton as chief detective, Sprague was going after the real assassins and their bosses, no matter where it led. Upon joining the committee, Sprague, who politically was irascible, unwisely made it clear that he would investigate the CIA and FBI, and in the process, subpoena CIA and FBI records, documents both classified and unclassified, and people.

To get an immediate start, he contacted Jim Garrison in New Orleans and informed him he would like to follow up on all of the data Garrison felt had been pertinent in his investigation. Sprague and Tanenbaum were cognizant that individuals with CIA connections were, in all probability, involved in the JFK assassination from New Orleans and the Florida Keys. They had, in November 1966, shown photographs to the entire HSCA staff of some of these people in Dealey Plaza and elsewhere.

They initiated searches for the real assassins.

To accomplish this in the most efficient and propitious manner, Cliff Fenton had been appointed head of a team of investigators to follow up on the New Orleans part of the conspiracy, which he felt included CIA agents and people such as Clay Shaw, David Ferrie, Guy Banister, Sergio Arcacha Smith, and others—ironically, all people mentioned in this book.

They were also going to contact others they felt had attended assassination planning meetings in New Orleans.

From the photographic evidence surrounding the sixth-floor window, as well as the grassy knoll, Sprague, Tanenbaum, and most of the staff suspected Oswald had not fired any shots.[8]

Using common sense, they concluded that the single-bullet theory was not feasible, and there had been a crossfire in Dealey Plaza, the same kind used by Oscar del Valle Garcia against Rafael Trujillo.

In effect, they were not planning to waste time covering the same old ground reviewing the Dealey Plaza evidence, unless it might give them a lead to the real assassins. Accordingly, they set up a Florida investigation, especially looking at the No Name Key group, from evidence and leads developed by Garrison in 1967. Gaeton Fonzi, whom I had consulted with prior to his joining the committee, was in charge of that team. They were going to check out the CIA people who had been running and funding the No Name Key and other anti-Castro groups. Jerry Patrick Hemming, Loren Hall, Lawrence Howard, Rolando Masferrer, and Carlos Prio

Socarras were to be found and interrogated.

Tanenbaum and his research team had seen the photo collection of Dick Billings, from *Life* magazine, which by 1976, was part of the JFK assassination collection in the Georgetown University Library. No Name Key personnel, along with others from the Garrison investigation, appeared in those photos along with high level CIA agents. Then came the disaster. In 1976, Tom Downing did not run for re-election and was retiring. At that point, Henry Gonzalez, a Representative from the state of Texas, took over the chairmanship. Fortunately, Gonzalez and Sprague could work together, and both believed that, if challanged by the CIA, they could expose the Agency's involvement in the JFK cover-up.

With this potential threat, the CIA knew it was up against a much more serious opponent than it had ever had before. With the HSCA's present posture, they could not control the investigation or, for that matter, even cover it up.

They had easily discredited the Garrison investigation through a number of moves, which, as the reader saw earlier, was acknowledged by Garrison himself.

Thirteen years earlier, the clandestine Agency had been able to control the Warren Commission. It was a much simpler job; they had several members beholden to them.

But with Sprague, backed by Gonzalez, they faced a crisis. They had to get rid of them. It was relatively easy. Both men had outstanding egos and violent tempers. Over a course of several months, the ensuing battle created by congressional members in the CIA pocket and a vociferous media, caused both Sprague and Gonzales to resign in disgrace. In the wake of their departure, the door was open to supress any and all evidence of CIA involvement. They managed to do it quite successfully.

By March of 1977, Lewis Stokes, a champion of Martin Luther King, was installed as chairman. He was a good political, if not practical, choice. The next step was to replace Sprague. The man selected was Professor Robert Blakey, a scientifically oriented, academic person, with a background of work against organized crime. To clear the decks of all the previous in-fighting, he asked for and got Bob Tanenbaum, Bob Lehner, and Donovan Gay's resignations. Blakely, unfamiliar with the involvement of the CIA in the JFK assassination, not wishing to perpetrate the bad scene created by the press of the committee, took a piece of bad advice, suggested and drafted by someone who had a proprietory interest in the clandestine agency.

He instituted a personnel "Non Disclosure Agreement."[9]

This agreement was to be signed by all members of the committee, all consultants, and all independent researchers. Signing it was a condition for employment on the committee staff or for consulting on a contract basis.

When Tiny Hutton, the newly appointed Deputy Director of the committee, showed me a copy, I blanched. If I was to be able to continue my own research into areas covered by the committee, I would not be able to publish. I declined, but as described earlier, still provided pertinent information to Tiny to pass on.

The particular non-disclosure agreement adopted by the committee was insidious: First, it bound outside contractors to silence (see paragraph 13). Second, it prevented for perpetuity the signer from revealing or using any information garnered as a result of working for the committee (see paragraphs 2 and 12). Third, it gave the committee and the House, once the committee terminated, the power to take legal action against the signer, *in a court named by the committee or the House,* in the event either body had reason to believe the signer violated the agreement. Fourth, the signer had to agree to pay the court costs for such a suit in the event he lost (see paragraphs 14 and 15).

As if these four parts were not bad enough, to silence any potential malcontent, paragraphs 2, 3, and 7 gave the CIA control over what the committee could and could not do with any information they considered "classified."

The director of the CIA was given the authority to determine what information should remain classified or unavailable to nearly everyone. In effect, the signer, including congressional members, had to agree not to reveal or discuss any information that the CIA decided should not be discussed.

Because of the past disarray during the Gonzales era, Lewis Stokes did not attempt any final decisions. The net result was that Blakey, in a sense of harmony, elected to keep nearly all of the CIA sensitive information, evidence, and witnesses away from the committee members. It was all that was necessary. Stokes never had anything to argue about with the CIA director.

The CIA controlled the HSCA.

Typical of what then happened is how the New Orleans information was handled. As mentioned earlier, an investigating team headed by Cliff Fenton had already been hard at work tracking down leads to conspirators generated by Jim Garrison's investigation in New Orleans.

This team had four professional investigators, and their work led them to believe that CIA people, affiliated with the mob in New Orleans, and a splinter group from No Name Key in Florida had been involved in a conspiracy to assassinate JFK.[10] As Tiny Hutton eventually told me, after reading the first draft of this book, Fenton's team found a CIA man who attended the New Orleans assassination meetings, a man who was willing to testify before the committee.

According to Tiny, the evidence was far more convincing than any of the testimony Garrison presented at the Clay Shaw trial, and Shaw, David Ferrie, the man I flew into Cuba with on the night of the Bay of Pigs, and others were involved.

Fenton's team evidently uncovered a lot of other facts about how the CIA people planned and carried out the assassination. It was, Tiny exclaimed, "almost a replay of your book *Betrayal.*"

Their report was clearly solid and convincing. Yet, Robert Blakey buried the Fenton report. Committee members were never informed about the CIA involvement.

Thus, the evidence was not included in the HSCA report, nor was it even referred to in the ten supplementary volumes. The witnesses in New Orleans were never called to testify, including the CIA man who had attended the meetings and was willing to talk. To this day, Fenton and his team refuse to discuss anything with anybody. Of course, they are well aware of the myriad of peripheral assassinations that occurred to persons prior to their testifying before the committee. They included: William Sullivan, the FBI deputy who headed Division V; George deMorenschildt, Oswald's alluded-to CIA contact in Dallas; John Roselli, the Mafia man involved in the CIA plots to assassinate Castro; Regis Kennedy, the FBI agent who called Carlos Marcello a tomato salesman and knew a lot about Clay Shaw, alias Clay Bertrand, and was said to be one of Lee Harvey Oswald's FBI contacts in New Orleans; Rolando Masferrer, Mario Kohly's friend, murdered in Miami; and Carlos Prio Socarras, killed in his garage in Miami.

When the committee finally wound down to its inevitable end, all avenues to the real truth about the CIA involvement had been covered.

As for the inscrutable Khaiber Khan, the LAPD and FBI would collect a raft of background material on him,[11] showing he still maintained a pretense of hating the Shah's family, even after receiving a two-and-one-half-million-dollar settlement.[12] Making matters more interesting, Khan was identified by at least three independent people at the Kennedy campaign headquarters in the company of Sirhan Sirhan. One of them, a Larry David Strick, was interviewed on July 7, 1968. When the statements made by Strick were unsatisfactory, Lieutenant Manny Pena had the young man re-interviewed on August 19. He totally retracted his statement.[13]

In some ways this book is a part of my chagrin over what has been perpetrated on the American public for over four decades. There is no question that we need a CIA, and that it will still continue doing what it has always done—whether right or wrong. However, one has to say sometimes, wait a minute. The people have a right to know.

EPILOGUE NOTES

1. See Appendix, Exhibit No. 22.

2. *Ibid.*

3. The predecessor of Resorts International was a company known as the Mary Carter Paint Company of Florida. Carter Paint was originally an active corporation set up by Thomas Dewey and Allen Dulles to use as a CIA front. In 1958, Dewey and some friends had bought controlling interest in the Crosby Miller Corporation, with two million dollars in CIA money—authorized by Allen Dulles. Then in 1959, the Crosby Miller Corporation was merged with the CIA-owned paint company. As an example of one of its early activities, it provided laundered CIA money for the Bay of Pigs army. In 1963, Mary Carter Paint spun-off its paint division, after a Florida land scandal, and became Resorts International.

4. *The New York Times,* January 21, 1974.

5. *Ibid.*

6. *Ibid.*

7. See Appendix, Exhibit No. 23.

8. The author made this same contention in his book *Betrayal,* based on information he had garnered during his association with the Anti-Castro Cuban movement.

9. See Appendix, Exhibit No. 24.

10. A belief that Garrison reiterated to me in our interviews.

11. See Appendix, Exhibit No. 26.

12. See Appendix, Exhibits No. 27 and 28.

13. See Appendix, Exhibits No. 29 and 30.

Appendix

Exhibit 1
HUAC Release for Jack Ruby to Testify

UNITED STATES DEPARTMENT OF JUSTICE

FEDERAL BUREAU OF INVESTIGATION

WASHINGTON, D.C. 20535

NOTE: Extra copy. Inclosure not verified by official report. Return to file. This is sensitive.

LS   JS

It is my sworn statement that one Jack Rubenstein of Chicago noted as a potential witness for hearings of the House Committee on UnAmerican Activities is performing information functions for the staff of Cong. Richard M. Nixon, Rep. of California. It is requested Rubenstein not be called for open testimony in those aforementioned hearings.

Sworn on this day, 24 November 1947

Staff Assistant

Exhibit 2
Kohly's October 18, 1960, Memo on Cuban Liberators

<u>M E M O R A N D U M</u>

Gentlemen:

After having organized the CUBAN LIBERATORS, composed in its majority of ex-Army, Navy and Aviation men, all of them Cubans residing in exile and a large underground in Cuba, also among the ex-Army, I came to Washington, D.C. on the tenth of June this year in the vain hope of being able to obtain the arms necessary with which to equip my men and overthrow the communist regime of Fidel Castro.

Since the above date I have been told that this support would come at once as there was the desire on the part of various government members to have the Cuban situation cleared up before the elections. As of two weeks ago I have been told that nothing can be done until after the elections but I have been given to understand that immediately after the elections I would receive the necessary support and help to oust Castro.

I have been advised that the major companies whose properties were confiscated in Cuba have been told by the State Department to keep hands off Cuba until after the elections.

Mr. Thompson, representing the C.I.A. and upon request of Mr. Nixon through his military aid, General Cushman, called on me at Marshall Diggs' office and requested or at least suggested that I join with two communist front organizations operating now in Miami whom he claimed were well financed. I explained to Mr. Thompson that I could not join with either organization as they were both communist fronts organized in part by Castro himself, by the Communist Party and by the President of Venezuela, Romulo Betancourt.

Since that date after such an offer was made to me I have felt completely ostracized here in Washington while these communist fronts continue to receive the direct support of the C.I.A. and the State Department and the American Embassy in Havana as proven by the following facts:

"The FRONT, as this communist organization is known, has been receiving arms and money on their own admission from C.I.A. and the State Department. They have allowed to recruit openly in the City of Miami without ever being molested. Arms have been dropped in Cuba to particians of this communist Front. At the request of Tony Varona, coordinator of the Front, the American Embassy in Havana expedites the issuing of visas in hours that normally would take a year. Men belonging to my organization have been contacted by the American Embassy in Havana and have been issued special passports to come to the United States and told to contact the C.I.A. office in Miami. Upon doing so, they have been told to join the FRONT and later to return to that Office where they will be given the instructions as to whom to see in the State Department so they may receive the funds and coordinate their return to Cuba as an invasion force".

242

M E M O R A N D U M

There is only one reasonable explanation to Fidel Castro's actions and his attitude towards the United States, his constant agressions and insults, his many threats to take over the U.S. Base in Guantanamo and his executions and imprisonment of American citizens: his desire to achieve fame and glory.

According to Castro's own remarks he would consider he had failed miserably as the new Bolivar if he should be put out of Cuba by Cubans in open revolt against his regime. It is his greatest desire and ambition to provoke the United States by all means possible into armed intervention by the U.S. Marines.

Castro will continue his harassment of Americans until such time as American public opinion will force the President of the United States to declare open warfare or intervention in Cuba. By so doing both Castro and his communist organization will be able to claim before all the Latin American countries and the world in general that the Cuban does not repudiate communism or the 26 of July Movement that brought communism in Cuba but that it was the American Imperialism that overthrew his regime against the will of the Cuban people. This he will be able to prove because it is a well known fact to any observer of Latin American psychology that the strong nationalistic feeling which has been whipped up against the United States by Castro will make the Cubans fight and resist any direct intervention by U.S. Marines, thus, another "Hungary" will have been provoked and Khruschev will have been justified in the massacre of the Hungarian people.

There is only one way in which this can be prevented and that is to have a force of Cubans, preferably a force of ex-Army men who are already trained (such as we the CUBAN LIBERATORS have) so they be thrown into Cuba at a moment's notice thus avoiding the need of United States direct intervention.

Of the approximate six thousand men which CUBAN LIBERATORS can now count in the United States and over 12,000 men in Cuba, I am afraid we are going to lose a great many who are falling into the hands of COMMUNIST ORGANIZED FRONTS in Miami for the sole purpose of dispersing them into camps in Mexico, Guatemala and other Latin American countries so as to make it impossible for us to strike with sufficient power in the short time that we may be called to do so once Castro's provocations cause a further worsening of relations and a wave of public indignation in the United States.

In order to keep our Organization together fund should be made available at once so as to keep the key men in eating money and in touch with their subordinates and in a position to help those more needy. Men must be brought back from their camps in Latin America and kept under control in Miami. Their families must be fed. The hunger and misery of these men who want to fight for freedom are undergoing is appauling. Immediate help must be obtained.

Mario Garcia Kohly
Executive Director
CUBAN LIBERATORS

Washington, D. C.
18 October 1960

Exhibit 3
Miro Cardona's Name
on Document of House Select Committee
on Internal Security

Mr. NORTH. No, no other capacity except as a writer and newspaperman.

Mr. SOURWINE. You did not attend the convention as a representative of the Communist Party, U.S.A.?

Mr. NORTH. There was a newspaper—I was there as a newspaper writer solely.

Mr. SOURWINE. You did not attend the convention as a representative of the Communist Party?

Mr. NORTH. As a newspaperman, I attended that convention.

Senator HRUSKA. And as a newspaperman only?

Mr. NORTH. That is right.

Mr. SOURWINE. Do you consider the withdrawal of the Cuban Confederation of Labor from the Inter-American Regional Organization of Labor as constituting a Communist victory?

Mr. NORTH. Are you interested in hearing what the Cuban people feel about it as I spoke to them?

I will tell you. I regard that withdrawal in the viewpoint of what they said about it and why they withdrew.

They felt that since there was no support given them at the time that Mujal was the chivato, the stool pigeon turning over the best fighters in the trade union to torture and death and since ORIT always seemed to be lined up with the policy of the State Department as well as Ambassador Smith during his tenure there, they felt that they should leave it.

That was the statement made in the press from the convention.

It was a victory of the Cuban people and a victory for labor everywhere throughout the world.

(The following translation of the order as printed in "Gaceta Oficial" for January 23, 1959, was later ordered into the record as exhibit No. 28 and printed at this point in the proceedings:)

EXHIBIT No. 28

TRANSLATION

Law No. 22 [Gaceta Oficial, Havana, Cuba, January 23, 1959]

Doctor Manuel Urrutia Lleo, President of the Republic of Cuba, notifies That the Council of Ministers has approved and I authorize the following:

Whereas the deposed tyranny made use of all resources within their spurious power to adulterate the union elections and to place in the Labor Center, and in Federations and Unions, delinquents alien to the people, servants of interests contrary to said class;

Whereas it is necessary to endow the Cuban workers with provisional directives to govern union organizations, accepting the enforcement of revolutionary acts which liquidated the former fraudulent administration, even if only for the period necessary to call and hold free elections;

Whereas it is necessary to safeguard the property of the working class;

Therefore by virtue of the powers vested in the Council of Ministers, it has agreed on and I have approved the following:

LAW NO. 22

Article 1.—To declare as removed from their posts and as having terminated their functions all persons who, as of the thirty-first of December of nineteen fifty-eight, formed part of the Boards (Administrators) of the Confederation of Labor of Cuba, of the Labor Federations for Industries, Provinces and all Syndicates, Unions, and Guilds all over the Republic of Cuba.

244

Article 2.—For the purposes of reconstructing and functioning of the Confederation of Labor of Cuba the following persons appointed to the corresponding posts shall be recognized as the provisional committee for administration:

In Charge of General Matters: David Salvador Manso
In Charge of Organization: Octavio Louit Venzán
In Charge of Finances: José Pelló Jaén
In Charge of Representation before Official and Employer Organizations: Antonio Torres Chedebau
In Charge of Documents and Correspondence: Conrado Bécquer Díaz
In Charge of Propaganda: José María de la Aguilera Fernández
In Charge of Foreign Relations: Reinol González González
In Charge of Internal Relations: Jesús Soto Díaz
In Charge of Legal Matters: José de J. Plana del Paso

The Committee for Provisional Administration of the Confederation of Labor of Cuba, above mentioned, shall have legal personality (corporate) adequate to govern and administer said confederation and to represent it before Official and Employer Organizations, all in accordance with the rights and powers conferred by the By-laws and Regulations of the said Confederation of Labor of Cuba upon its board of administration.

Article 3.—The Committee for Provisional Administration of the Confederation of Labor of Cuba shall appoint provisional revolutionary administrative committees for the Federations of Industries and Provincial Federations, the Provisional Administrative Committees of the same to be composed of the following officers: In Overall Charge: In Charge of Organization; In Charge of Finances; In Charge of Representation before Official and Employer Organizations, and In Charge of Documents and Propaganda.

The persons who are appointed to perform the mentioned offices in the Federations of Industries and Provincial Federations, and in the Syndicates, Unions and Guilds, shall be endowed with adequate legal personality to govern and administer said labor organizations, and to represent them before Official and Employer Organizations. All of this in accordance with the powers conferred upon the Administrative Boards by the By-laws and Regulations.

Article 5.—The persons in charge of Organization and of Documents in the Confederation of Labor of Cuba shall file with the Office on Labor Organizations in the Ministry of Labor, through certified document, the legal status of those persons holding offices on the Provisional Administrative Committees of the Federations of Industries and Provincial Federations and of the Syndicates, Unions and Guilds, and shall issue the credentials for these persons, to be communicated to the respective employers.

Article 6.—The provisional administrative committees for the Syndicates. Unions and Guilds shall not call general elections until a period of ninety business days has elapsed from the date of effectiveness of this Law, after which they will have a period of forty-five days in which to call and hold said elections.

Article 7.—A period of ten week days, which cannot be extended, computed from the date of publication of this Law in the OFFICIAL GAZETTE of the Republic, is granted to all administrators and officials of Labor Organizations who functioned as such on the thirty-first of December of nineteen hundred fifty-eight, in order that they may return and deliver all documents and property of any kind, belonging to the labor organizations in which they held office.

Article 8.—The Minister of Labor is charged with the execution of the present Law and of enacting interpretative and regulatory resolutions regarding same. All laws and decrees contrary to its observance are repealed.

Therefore I order that the present Law in all of its parts be observed and executed.

Issued in the Presidential Palace, in Havana, on the twentieth of January of nineteen hundred fifty-nine.

(Signed) MANUEL URRUTIA LLEO.
JOSÉ MIRÓ CARDONA.
Prime Minister.
MANUEL FERNÁNDEZ GARCÍA.
Minister of Labor.

Mr. SOURWINE. While you were attending the convention of the Cuban Confederation of Labor in Havana last month, did you meet any delegates from the German Democratic Republic?

Exhibit 4
Kohly's Affidavit on Kohly/Nixon Deal

AFFIDAVIT:

IN OCTOBER 1960, IN A CONVERSATION BETWEEN MY
FATHER IN WASHINGTON, D.C. AND MYSELF IN MIAMI BETWEEN
TWO PREDESIGNATED PAY TELEPHONES, I WAS TOLD THAT VICE
PRESIDENT NIXON HAD AGREED TO THE ELIMINATION OF THE
LEFTIST APPROVED CUBAN REVOLUTIONARY FRONT LEADERS
AT A TIME WHEN THE ISLAND WOULD BE INVADED BY THE
EXILE GROUPS TRAINED UNDER THE DIRECTION OF THE
CENTRAL INTELLIGENCE AGENCY. THIS PROMISE WAS MADE IF
MY FATHER WOULD GUARANTEE THE USE OF HIS UNDERGROUND OR-
GANIZATION INSIDE CUBA AND HIS 300-400 MAN ARMED
GUERRILA FORCE IN THE ESCAMBREY MOUNTAINS.

JUST PRIOR TO THE INVASION IN APRIL 1961, MY
FATHER AGAIN NOTIFIED ME BY TELEPHONE TO EXPECT NEWS-
PAPER PUBLICITY REGARDING THE CUBAN REVOLUTIONARY FRONT
JOINING THE UNITED ORGANIZATIONS AS AN INTEGRAL PART
AND THAT THE INVASION WAS TO TAKE PLACE WITHIN THE NEXT
FEW DAYS AND TO CONTACT COLONEL PEPE PINERO AND COLONEL
SANCHEZ MOSQUERA (WHO LATER BECAME AN AGENT FOR THE
CIA) AND TO TELL THEM THEY WERE NOT TO WORRY ABOUT THIS
ACTION AND INSTRUCTED ME TO EXPLAIN WHY, I.E., THEY
WOULD BE TAKEN CARE OF IMMEDIATELY UPON THE SUCCESSFUL
TAKEOVER OF CASTRO'S GOVERNMENT BY MY FATHER. I WAS

AFFIDAVIT
MARIO GARCIA KOHLY, JR.
PAGE TWO

ALSO TOLD THAT MANUEL ARTIMES AND AURELIANO SANCHEZ
ARRANGO WERE TO BE SHOT AS SOON AS THEY HAD WORD THAT
MIRO CARDONA AND THE REST OF THE CUBAN REVOLUTIONARY
FRONT GROUP BEING HELD IN COMMUNICATO AT OPA LOCKA HAD
BEEN ELIMINATED. WHEN KENNEDY CALLED OFF THE AIR
COVER FOR THE BAY OF PIGS INVASION, THESE PLANS WERE
ABORTED. LIKEWISE, WHEN SENATOR OWNE BREWSTER
INFORMED MY FATHER THAT THERE WOULD BE NO AIR COVER,
I WAS INSTRUCTED TO IMMEDIATELY PULL THE UNDERGROUND
AND ARMED FORCE FROM TAKING ANY SUPPORTIVE ACTION.

MARIO GARCIA KOHLY, JR.

STATE OF VIRGINIA

COUNTY OF ARLINGTON, SS:

I HEREBY CERTIFY THAT ON 15TH DAY OF JULY, 1976, BEFORE
ME, THE SUBSCRIBER, A NOTARY PUBLIC OF THE STATE OF
VIRGINIA, PERSONALLY APPEARED MARIO GARCIA KOHLY, JR.
AND ACKNOWLEDGED THE FOREGOING AFFIDAVIT TO BE HIS ACT
AND HAND.

WITNESS MY HAND AND NOTORIAL SEAL, THE DAY AND YEAR LAST
MENTIONED ABOVE.

My commission expires on
May 27, 1978.

NOTARY PUBLIC.

Exhibit 5
Morrow's Affidavit on Kohly/Nixon Deal

<u>AFFIDAVIT</u>:

On or about the third week of October, 1960, I was with Mario Garcia Kohly when he informed me that he had met with Vice President Nixon about a week before. He stated to me that an agreement had been reached between he (Kohly) and the Vice President for the elimination of Miro Cardona and all the leftist Cuban Revolutionary Front leaders in order that Kohly could immediately take over the reins of power in Cuba, once a successful invasion by exiles being trained by the Central Intelligence Agency had been accomplished. He stated that this agreement was made once he had pledged to have his underground inside Cuba support the invaders as well as committing his 300 to 400 man guerrilla army located in the Escambrey Mountains to attack Castro's forces if necessary to support the landing. He claimed Manuel Artimes and his followers were to be assassinated by this force once a successful landing had been completed. He also stated that the balance of the Front leaders would be held incommunicado and turned over to Kohly's exile groups for elimination once the invasion had been successful or Kohly's guerrilla army had joined the invasion forces. After this meeting between Kohly and myself, I inquired of my case officer in the presence of General Cabell if this was true and they confirmed it to be so.

On the night of April 17, 1961, en route from Opa Locka to Buckingham Field, I was told by my case officer that the Front group was being held incommunicado at Opa Locka pending the outcome of the invasion. The inference was that they would never be heard from again.

ROBERT D. MORROW

District of Columbia, ss:

I HEREBY CERTIFY that before me, the subscriber, a Notary Public in and for the District aforesaid, personally appeared ROBERT D. MORROW, who acknowledged the foregoing statement to be true to the best of his knowledge, recollection, and belief.

WITNESS my hand and Notorial Seal this 19th day of July, 1976.

My Commission Expires October 31, 1976   NOTARY PUBLIC

248

Exhibit 6
Downing Letter to Morrow on *Betrayal*

COUNTIES:

ACCOMACK   MATHEWS
CHARLES CITY   MIDDLESEX
ESSEX   NEW KENT
GLOUCESTER   NORTHAMPTON
JAMES CITY   NORTHUMBERLAND
KING GEORGE   RICHMOND
KING AND QUEEN   WESTMORELAND
KING WILLIAM   YORK
LANCASTER

CITIES:

HAMPTON   POQUOSON
NEWPORT NEWS   WILLIAMSBURG

E. M. TINY HUTTON
ADMINISTRATIVE ASSISTANT

THOMAS N. DOWNING
1ST DISTRICT, VIRGINIA

Congress of the United States
House of Representatives
Washington, D.C. 20515

November 4, 1976

COMMITTEES:

MERCHANT MARINE AND
FISHERIES

SCIENCE AND TECHNOLOGY

OFFICES:
1 COURT STREET
HAMPTON, VA. 23669
722-2888

2135 RAYBURN BUILDING
WASHINGTON, D.C. 20515
(202) 225-4261

For some time I have been concerned, as have many Americans, about the unanswered questions regarding the assassination of President John F. Kennedy. Along with other individuals and groups I have pressed for the reopening of the investigation.

In the spring of 1976, Robert Morrow brought me an advance copy of his book, "Betrayal," a fascinating account of events leading up to that assassination, which concludes with a remarkably plausible reconstruction of what could have happened on that dreadful day in Dallas.

It is no exaggeration to say that the information in this book, coupled with additional confidential material supplied to me by Mr. Morrow, helped make the creation of the House Select Committee on Assassinations possible.

Where the committee's investigations will lead, of course, remains to be seen. But I am confident that investigation of the information supplied by Mr. Morrow in "Betrayal" and the additional sources to which it will lead the committee investigators will help to put to rest once and for all many of the questions about the Warren Commission's investigation that have disturbed the nation for many years.

Thomas N. Downing, Chairman
Select Committee on Assassinations

Exhibit 7
Tony Eaton's Affidavit on Missiles in Cuba

7/15/76

[handwritten signature]
notary public

Memo

TO: Robert D. Morrow
FROM: Anthony M. Eaton
DATE: 3 June 1976
SUBJ: Cuban Missiles and Their Relevant Dates

     As I told you during our recent conversations, my knowledge of the missiles (USSR) existance in Cuba began in late 1960, either September or October of that year when overflights were made from the Bahamas by the R.A.F. and pictures taken which clearly indicated IRBM implacements being set up in several locations. This information was passed by the Joint Services Committee of the SIS to the Joint Services Intelligence Bureau in Northumberland Avenue and then to the Foreign Office for passage to the U.S. State Department. I am informed by the British Embassy that the matter is one upon which there can be "No comment" and that any such information would still be covered by the Official Secrets Act under which, as a British subject, I am still liable.

     At a future date, shortly after the "missiles of October," I was approached by one of the staff of "Jane's Fighting Ships" and informed that by his calculations, the ships provided by the USSR for the ostensible removal of missiles, were not loaded with missiles. His calculated results rested on the ship displacement, weight and dimensions of the missiles, and the likely ballast loading when the ships reached Cuba. These results were checked by several other authorities using news and military photographs and they also decided that few, if any, missiles were, in fact, removed.

     Several sources of such evidence can still be reached; but, due to the Official Secrets Act, great care will have to be exercised as no one wants to be charged under the various provisions therein.

[handwritten signatures]

AFFIDAVIT:

I, Anthony M. Eaton, presently residing at 710, Park
Avenue, Baltimore, Maryland,21201.,U.S.A., do hereby
attest and affirm, in support of the confidential memorandum
hereto attached and witnessed, that, to the best of my
knowledge and belief the facts stated therein are correct
and factual, and further, that I shall be prepared to provide
further details, together with the reasons for such knowledge
on my part to any properly constituted body in closed session
bearing in mind the currently enforceable Official Secrets Act
extant in the United Kingdom. I shall hold myself at the disposal
of Mr. Robert D. Morrow and any other person who he shall
designate as being the proper authority to which to provide
such information and shall use my best efforts to provide
other persons with relevant testimony at such time as they may
be required.

ANTHONY M. EATON.

STATE OF MARYLAND.
County of Baltimore   ,ss:

I HEREBY CERTIFY that on July 1976., before me, the
subscriber, a notary public of the State of Maryland, in and for
the County of Baltimore personally appeared Anthony M. Eaton and
acknowledged the forgoing Affidavit and the attached, witnessed
memorandum to be his act and hand.

WITNESS my hand and notorial seal, the day and year last mentioned
above.

Notary Public.

My commission expires 7/1/78

Exhibit 8
Kohly's Deathbed Statement

EXCERPT OF STATEMENT MADE BY MARIO KOHLY, JULY 1975.

Summary

        The tape you are about to hear is the last statement
made by Mario Garcia Kohly, Sr. It is one side of a half hour
tape that he made just four weeks prior to his death. On it you
will hear Kohly state that the understanding he had with the
Central Intelligence Agency was that Miro Cardona, Tony Verona,
Manuel Artimes, and the rest of the Cuban Revolutionary Front group
that was being held incommunicado down in Miami would be eliminated
after a successful invasion at the Bay of Pigs. He made this deal
with then Vice President Nixon who was the CIA Action Officer in
the White House and whom the Bay of Pigs was originally developed
under.

        For this agreement that Kohly would take over the
island after a successful invasion, Kohly pledged his 42,000 man
underground internal Cuban organization as well as his 300 to 400
man guerrilla army which was fully armed and ready to go in the
Escambrey Mountains and which was to join up with the Bay of Pigs
invaders. In addition, he was to supply all the necessary information his underground had gained on the missile installations then
being installed in Cuba. When the Front group realized they were
being held incommunicado at Opa Locka, one of the members, Tony
Verona, climbed through a bathroom window and called Washington
and the Administration.

        Kohly states in this last statement of his that Castro
was responsible for the death of John F. Kennedy. This statement
is designed to completely smokescreen the fact that the Cuban
exiles had a participation in the assassination. This will come
out at a later date, but it is not relative to the fact that the

Kohly
2.

CIA was deliberately condoning the assassination of as many as
five people which they held prisoner in Miami on April 17, 1961.

Kohly Transcript

On the other tape I started to give an account of how
I learned that the treacherous action had been played upon us by
President Kennedy in stopping the air support after the boys had
already started for Cuba. There was no way of advising them
because there was radio silence at all times. The true account of
how I learned is this.

I was working at Marshall Diggs office at ten o'clock
at night preparing some reports to be transmitted to Cuba which
we had made arrangements with my son in Miami to transmit messages
from myself here to him and from him to the underground in Cuba.
We did this through portable radios -- he's quite a radio expert.
And I ran out of cigars -- out of smokes -- while I was in Marshall
Diggs office that night. Just before returning home, I stopped by
the Mayflower to buy some. I went in there to the cigar stand and
who did I run into but ex-Senator Owen Brester of Maine who had
been introduced to me sometime previously by Marshall Diggs and we
had become pretty good friends. Brewster had been trying to get me
on the phone, but I had refused to answer the phone just figuring it
was my wife calling me to get home early or some of my girl friends
and not my wife.

Then, Brewster was very angry and said, "Why don't you
answer your phone? I've got a most important message for you.
I've been trying to get you all evening."

Kohly
3.

So after due apologies and so forther, I asked what
the message is.

He said, "Mario, quick, have you any way of contacting
the underground in Cuba?"

He knew that I was working very closely with them and I
said, "Yes. I have ways of contacting them."

He said, "Look. Tell them right away that the air
support has been called off. Kennedy has double crossed the Cuban
exiles."

I was shocked also to a point of immobility for a
second. Then I excused myself, thanked him, and went to the phone
and called my son up long distance from the office of Marshall Diggs
and told him that the message must go through to Cuba at once,
saying 'do not cooperate in operations unless you see the eagle
flying.' The boys would know what that was because it was a prearranged signal in case of any such events. We had taken every
precaution. I had been somewhat suspicious of the Kennedy Administration's sincerity, while at all times under the CIA's operations
most of the time. So I had made contingency plans to communicate
to the underground in case we did get double crossed. Thus, in
effect, the message was sent and the lives of better than 42,000
men were saved who would have cooperated with the invasion and who
would have been slaughtered -- which apparently was exactly what
was intended to happen. So the Cuban people are eternally grateful
to Owen Brewster (of late) as well as myself for having given them
the advance information which saved the lives of the Cuban underground.

My part in the Cuban invasion plans were limited to some

Kohly
4.

extent. I had arranged to recruit or to enlist better than
300 boys who on a set signal once we took over the island would
meet with me and arrange for the overthrow of the CIA inspired
council with Miro Cardona and the rest of them. If this had
been successful they would have been eliminated almost at once
and I would have come into Cuba and taken over.

This can be confirmed through Mr. Sourwine in the U.S.
Senate who called me one day to meet with one of the troopers or
rather a group of troopers who had come out of the Bay of Pigs
alive and to come back to the States and it was this trooper who
very discretely divulged our plans to Owen Brewster and stated that
each one of them was wearing a yellow hankerchief around their collar
to show who was who and to know each other so that at the proper
time they could communicate. Yellow was chosen because it fitted
in with the uniforms and would not attract attention as they were
current army handkerchiefs or bandanas, whatever you wish to call
them.

Comment

The excerpt you have just heard was from the last
statement made by Mario Garcia Kohly, president de facto in exile
of Cuba and leader of the United Organizations for the Liberation
of Cuba, less than four weeks before his death on August 5, 1975.
The original of this tape is in the safety deposit box of the law
firm of Adelberg, Adelberg & Rudow, 10 Light Street, Baltimore,
Maryland.

Exhibit 9
Clark Mollenhoff Press Story on Kohly

U. S. CHARGE BEWILDERS CUBAN EXILE   April 12, 1964
By Clark Mollenhoff   Page One
Minneapolis Tribune Staff Correspondent

Washington. D. C.

When he was arrested last October 1st, anti-Castro Cuba
leader Mario Garcia Kohly thought there had been some bureaucratic blunder in the U. S. Government.

Last week he found out that he was in deep trouble and
that every effort of the Justice Department was being made to
jail him on a charge of the counterfeiting Cuban 50-peso bills.

His trial was set for April 27th in Federal District Court
in New York, N. Y., and Asst. U. S. Atty. Charles Fanning was
pushing the case as if it were vital to put Kohly out of circulation.

Until a week ago Kohly hadn't taken the charge seriously
enough to get himself an experienced criminal lawyer. He was
certain that there had been some scrambling of red tape, and
that somehow it all would be straightened out before the matter
went to trial.

On October 1st, 1963, Treasury agents walked up to Kohly
in the lobby of the Waldorf-Astoria Hotel in New York and
arrested him. He had the counterfeit Cuban plates in his
overnight bag.

The head of the United Organization for the Liberation
of Cuba was surprised, for he thought he had the approval of
the United States government.

He had co-operated with the FBI on investigations, and
with the Central Intelligence Agency (CIA). He had even notified the White House of his plans to flood Cuba with counterfeit money.

Two of his representatives, Washington lawyer Marshall Diggs
and Col. William Hoover, a retired Army Officer, had discussed
the entire plan with an assistant to Gen. Maxwell Taylor, the
chairman of the Joint Chiefs of Staff and a special adviser to
President John F. Kennedy.

His lawyer had obtained a note from an aide to Taylor ack-
nowledging receipt of a sample of a counterfeit Cuban 10-peso
bill. The plan had been to print a large amount of Cuban money,
worthless in the United States, and to distribute it to 11 Cuban
refugee groups to smuggle into Cuba to finance the fight against
Castro and to undermine the economy of the country.

256

U. S. CHARGE BEWILDERS CUBAN EXILE   Page Two
By Clark Mollenhoff
Minneapolis Tribune Staff Correspondent

Diggs and Hoover had reported to Kohly that the idea was regarded as a sound one, and Kohly proceeded with it.

As the plan developed, the original bill similar to the counterfeit bill given Taylor's assistant was taken out of circulation by Castro. The next plan was to print a 50-peso note that conformed with the new money.

Kohly and his companions proceeded with the plan. Arrangements were made with a Baltimore man, Robert Morrow, to make the plates.

In the course of the conversation, Kohly asked Morrow if he was certain that he wanted to undertake the counterfeiting project, since it was a technical law violation.

Kohly says that Morrow, who had considerable government business, in the electronics business, assured him that he wouldn't undertake it unless he was sure it "was cleared'.

The plates were delivered to Kohly's home in Alexandria, Va., and a man sent by the government to Kohly's home said he would do the printing in New York. It was to be financed without initial cost to Kohly. Payment was to be made later.

Kohly had taken the plates to New York with him and was in the process of making a delivery to a man named Harris, who was to do the printing. At the request of Harris, Kohly opened his overnight bag in the lobby of the Waldorf to show him the plates. Two Treasury agents walked up and arrested Kohly.

At this point, Kohly said he learned that Harris was a Treasury agent. However, he assumed that this was a great mistake and that the Treasury Department simply hadn't received the word on the counterfeiting plans.

For the last four months Kohly, his lawyer and friends have been contacting the White House, the Justice Department and other agencies.

They have pleaded that the charges against him are unjust, even though he was in technical violation of the law. They have pleaded that he did not intend to distribute any of the money in the United States, and have said that it would be ridiculous to believe it would be done because it is worthless here.

Article from Minneapolis Sunday Tribune
of April, 12, 1964.

Exhibit 10
UOLC Membership List Showing Prio

PAWLEY, WILLIAM D.

2157 LAKE AVE.
SUNSET ISL. #2
MIAMI, FLA
EX-U.S. AMB. TO CUBA.

PRIO, CARLOS (SOCORRAS)

MIAMI, FLA.   home VN 67277
EX-PRESIDENT CUBA

ALEX (ATT. FOR PRIO) home MO 7994

DR. LEW (FRIEND)   HOME FR 32478

PERNA, SANTIAGO REY

SDO. S.W. 6 ST.   FR-10735
MIAMI, FLA.
THIS MAN POSESSES AN UNUSUAL high iq t
t consider him EXTREAMLY DANGEROUS

found in desk in
1966 No Name

PORTER, JOHN (JACK)

1000 N.W. 61 ST.   PL 46639
MIAMI, FLA.

PIAD, CARLOS

ROOSEVELT HOTEL   HF3 4819

PORTUONDO, EMILIO NUNEZ

                          667-7842

258

Exhibit 11
Nixon Letter to Judge Weinfeld on Kohly

NIXON, MUDGE, ROSE, GUTHRIE & ALEXANDER
(MUDGE, STERN, BALDWIN & TODD)

20 BROAD STREET

NEW YORK, N.Y.

JOHN F. ALEXANDER
CARL RUSSELL
R. LE M. ASHER
ARTHUR M. BECKER
MILTON BLACK
JOHN F. BUCHMAN
GEORGE B. O'CONNELL
GEORGE E. BUCHANAN
GOLDTHWAITE H. DORR
ELLIOTT W. CAYLE
JOHN M. FREY
LEONARD GARMENT
RANDOLPH H. GUTHRIE
MATTHEW C. HEROLD, JR.
JOSEPH V. KLINE
WILLIAM B. LANNIS
PAUL B. MILLER
RICHARD M. NIXON
RICHARD C. RIEGEL
MILTON C. ROSE
NORMAN H. SEGAL
JOHN J. SILLECK, JR.
JOHN WALLIS
ROBERT E. WALSH
GEORGE W. WHITTAKER

ALFRED B. MUDGE
(1900-1945)

HIRAM E. TODD
COUNSEL

HANOVER 2-0707
CABLE BALTIMORE

WASHINGTON OFFICE
839-17TH STREET, N.W.
WASHINGTON, D.C.
STERLING 3-0778

EUROPEAN OFFICE
62, RUE DE LA PAIX
PARIS 2E, FRANCE
7 42-05-60

March 9, 1965

The Honorable Edward Weinfeld
United States District Judge
Federal Courthouse
Foley Square
New York, New York

Dear Judge Weinfeld:

I am writing, at the request of his counsel, in behalf of Mario Kohly who, I understand, has been convicted of violating a statute prohibiting the unauthorized printing of foreign currency and sentenced to a one year term of imprisonment. While I have no personal knowledge of the particular circumstances of the case, I am advised that Kohly is a person of good repute and believe that the acts which led to his conviction, although unlawful, were not motivated by any desire for personal gain but rather from a dedication to his country.

As one who has followed the Cuban problem closely, I believe it is possible that, in the face of a difficult, dangerous and changing situation, the complexities of United States policy toward the Castro regime, particularly as it has affected the exiles, might well have created an atmosphere in which a person such as Kohly could honestly, though mistakenly, believe that actions such as those for which he was convicted were not contrary to the interests of the United States. The situation of the Cuban exiles in this country in the years since the communization of Cuba has been in many ways unique in our history. Their presence here cannot be disassociated from the active hostility of the Castro regime towards the United States, and the resulting antagonism on the part of the public, the press and

259

The Honorable Edward Weinfeld   -2-   March 9, 1964

the government here towards Castro. The exiles have, in
consequence, from time to time, as your Honor knows, been
encouraged and aided by the United States in efforts to
overthrow the Cuban Government, and such efforts, in the
nature of things, have been covert and sometimes extra
legal. The patriotism, courage and energy of the exiles
in attempting to mount a counterrevolution have been in
the past, and may in the future again be regarded as
advantageous to the interests of the United States as well
as those of Cuba.

        It appears to me that to the extent compatible
with the public interest, these unique circumstances ought
to be taken into account in determining the severity of the
penalty to be imposed on Kohly.

        I trust that your Honor will understand that my
purpose in writing this letter is to aid the Court in its
consideration of the defendant's application for suspension
or reduction of the sentence imposed.

                            Very truly yours,

RMN:AGA

CC: Robert M. Morgenthau, Esq.
    United States Attorney

Exhibit 12
Letter from Nixon Firm to Doris Kohly

NIXON, MUDGE, ROSE, GUTHRIE & ALEXANDER
(MUDGE, STERN, BALDWIN & TODD)

20 BROAD STREET

NEW YORK, N.Y.

JOHN N. ALEXANDER
BLISS ANSNES
PETER W. ASHER
ARTHUR M. BECKER
MILTON BLACK
JOHN F. BROSNAN
GEORGE E. BUCHANAN
GOLDTHWAITE H. DORR
RICHARD B. FARROW
LEONARD GARMENT
RANDOLPH H. GUTHRIE
MATTHEW G. HEROLD, JR.
JOSEPH V. KLINE
WILLIAM B. LANDIS
RICHARD M. NIXON
RICHARD B. RITZEL
MILTON C. ROSE
NORMAN M. SEGAL
HARRY G. SILLECK, JR.
JAMES P. TANNIAN
JOHN WALLIS
ROBERT E. WALSH
GEORGE W. WHITTAKER

HANOVER 2-6767
CABLE "BALTUCHINE"

WASHINGTON OFFICE
838-17TH STREET, N.W.
WASHINGTON, D.C.
STERLING 3-8775

EUROPEAN OFFICE
12, RUE DE LA PAIX
PARIS 25, FRANCE
742-05-99

April 21, 1966

Mrs. Margarita Garcia Kohly
730 Pennsylvania Avenue
Miami Beach, Florida

Dear Mrs. Garcia Kohly:

I have your letter of the 19th. I have also received your earlier letter, with which you enclosed a copy of Judge Murphy's decision, dated April 4, 1966, denying the applications for reduction of the sentence recently imposed on Mr. Kohly. I have also received a letter from your sister-in-law.

As I advised you I would, I attempted to talk to Judge Murphy about the case, but was advised by his staff that any applications to him should be made formally in accordance with the Rules of Criminal Procedure. My original purpose in attempting to see the Judge was of course materially changed by the fact that he had determined to consider the letters sent to him by you and by Mr. and Mrs. Kohly as applications for reduction of sentence and had denied them. In light of that fact, I was attempting to ascertain whether the Judge would entertain an additional application for reduction of sentence.

You may well imagine that the Court would not normally permit a succession of such applications after having denied the first. However, in view of the unusual circumstances in this case generally and of the informal nature of your personal applications to the Judge, it may just be possible that the Judge in his discretion would give consideration to a more formal application which we might now make and I am prepared to make such an application. However, I want to make it perfectly plain to you that Judge Murphy, having imposed the sentence and then having denied your applications after reconsidering the

Mrs. Margarita Garcia Kohly   -2-   April 21, 1966

matter, is unlikely to change his decision. Furthermore, it would be within his discretion even to refuse to consider a further application which we might now make.

    To set your mind at rest regarding the press of time in this matter, the Rules of Procedure provide that reduction of sentence may be granted within a period of 60 days after sentence is first imposed. Therefore, we are still well within the period if Judge Murphy should in his discretion determine to consider a further application.

    From your letter I gather that you may be under a misapprehension as to the procedural steps which are possible. As I informed you when you were here in New York, there is no question of an appeal being taken to the Court of Appeals or to the Supreme Court in this matter. The only remedy available is the application for reduction of the sentence imposed on the bail jumping charge.

    Before I undertake to make such an application as I have discussed above, I will need direct authority from Mr. Kohly himself to represent him. If he wishes that I do so, will you please inform him that I would require a letter from him to that effect. It may also be necessary for me to visit him before making the application to the Court. Therefore, I would like to know where he is and when he can be seen.

    As I have already informed you, Mr. Nixon has authorized me to offer my services in this matter without charge to Mr. Kohly.

                                Very truly yours,

                                Robert R. Thornton

                                Robert R. Thornton

RRT:jg

AIR MAIL

Exhibit 13
Ross Schoyer Interview 11/17/77 on IPA

<u>TELEPHONE INTERVIEW</u>

<u>WITH</u>

<u>ROSS ALLEN SCHOYER</u>

<u>17 NOVEMBER 1977</u>

Morrow: What was the purpose of the International Police Academy on R Street, Washington, D.C. ?

Schoyer: The ostensible purpose was to train....

Morrow: Run by Joe Shimon?

Schoyer: Right.

Morrow: You knew him /Shimon/ ?

Schoyer: Yeah.

Morrow: When did you meet him /Shimon/, Ross?

Schoyer: Oh... 58, 59. Somewhere in there. George Keenan was one of -- well, he may be dead by now, but he was one of the leading forensic photographers in the country. And, particularly on gunshot wound identification and ballistics, etc.

Morrow: Did you know it /the I.P.A./ was a CIA front?

Schoyer: No. I was always a little curious about the fact that the number of students they had, and the equipment they had,

263

Schoyer/2

didn't seem to jibe quite.

Morrow: What did you do for them?

Schoyer: Oh, this and that. Improve their security and design
           some equipment for them.

Morrow: This was in the late 50's?

Schoyer: Uhum.

Morrow: Before you came to work for me?

Schoyer: Right.

Morrow: O.K.

Schoyer: And the ostensible purpose, as I said, was to train police
           officials of foreign and/or emerging countries in investi-
           gative technics, crowd control, administrative procedures,
           etc.

Morrow: Do you know if they ever carried any of their operations
           out in Washington?

Schoyer: No. Not specifically of my own knowledge.

           /Tape recorder trouble/

           Most of their personnel were ex-FBI agents. And it was
           Bill... something... I can't think of, who was the admin-
           istrator of the school or director of cirriculum or some-
           thing of this sort.

Morrow: How did you meet Shimon to begin with?

Schoyer: Through... I knew George Keenan. He lived in the same
           building I did. He was the former chief of detectives... I
           think with the Buffalo, New York, police force.

Morrow: I'll be darned.

Schoyer/3

Schoyer: And a very capable man and, as I say, in identification and....

Morrow: Forensic stuff.

Schoyer: Right.

Morrow: Well, that's interesting. Anyway, his name /Joe Shimon/ came up... he apparently was a good friend of Johnny Roselli's and Sam Giancana's.

Schoyer: That wouldn't be surprising.

Morrow: And, ironically enough, Robert Maheu.

Schoyer: Uhum.

Morrow: Who, as you know, was the Deputy Coordinator of assassination plans for the CIA and the one that worked for Howard Hughs.

Schoyer: Yeah. Right.

Morrow: All right. I appreciate the call.

Schoyer: O.K. I'm trying to think... they originally were located in a building which has since been torn down at Thomas Circle... where they built the motel with the big rotunda on it.

Morrow: Oh, yeah. Yeah. Right across the street... from your old place.

Schoyer: Right. They had a three story building there.

Morrow: Uhum.

Schoyer: And then they moved across to R Street when that building came down.

Morrow: Yeah. Well, that's interesting.

Schoyer/4

Schoyer: A lot of their students were from the Middle East.
             Iranians that were housed in a hotel I think was owned by
             the I.P.A. on 16th Street.

Morrow: Do you mean they trained the Savak, better known as the
             Iranian secret police?

Schoyer: It wouldn't surprise me. Also, their classes were top
             secret and guarded like you wouldn't believe.

Morrow: O.K., Ross. I appreciate the info. I'll get this call
        .   transcribed and you can sign it for me.

Schoyer: All right. See you later.

Exhibit 14
Didi Hess Affidavit

AFFIDAVIT

COMMONWEALTH OF PENNSYLVANIA)
) ss:
COUNTY OF ALLEGHENY)

         BEFORE ME, the undersigned authority, personally appeared
DIANE (DIDI) HESS, who being duly sworn according to law,
deposes and says as follows:

         1) That she lives at 9873 Edisto Drive, Baltimore,
Maryland 21220;

         2) That in the presence of J. Harriet Dietz of 710
Park Avenue, Baltimore, Maryland 21201 and Frank H. Stephens, Jr.
of 8 Raleigh Court, Morristown, New Jersey 07960, I did submit
to a taped interview on September 27, 1977, with Mr. Robert
Morrow of 110 Brandon Road, Baltimore, Maryland 21212 for the
following reasons:

                 a) To describe the circumstances surrounding
the admissions of former Air Force ███████████████████

████████████████████████████████ to me of his personal participation in the
assassination conspiracy of President John F. Kennedy on
November 22, 1963.

                 b) To state the desire of Colonel ███████
to convey this information directly to the proper authorities
upon being granted immunity from prosecution.

         3) I further swear the details of the said involvement
are described at least in part in another interview transcribed
with Mr. Morrow on September 1, 1977.

         4) The above statements are true and correct to the
best of my knowledge, information and belief.

Didi Hess

Sworn to and subscribed before
me this 22nd day of September,
1977.

Anna Lee Daw
otary Public

ANA LEE DAW, NOTARY PUBLIC
PITTSBURGH ALLEGHENY COUNTY
MY COMMISSION EXPIRES JAN 26 1981
Member, Pennsylvania Association of Notaries

Exhibit 15
Khyber Khan LAPD Report

Subject first visit to the Kennedy Headquarters was on 6-1-68
in the afternoon hours. On this date subject registered under
his true name Khaibar Khan. He also met a Marguerite Sweeney
(I-59) who was in charge of volunteer workers. Subject was
then assigned to answering phones and at this time he volunteered
numerous names of Tribal Chiefs who were to be in the USA during
the month of November 1968. Also the other volunteers who
appeared at his desk he would claim as being part of his group
and would register them under his address. When individuals
would call to volunteer, he would follow this same procedure.
It was discovered that there was a total of 24 volunteer cards
which were made by Khaibar Khan. The majority of these cards
were in the smae handwriting and contained the same address.
The 24 names are listed on the interview of June Isackson (I-80a).

Mr Khan's second visit took place on June 2, 1968 at approximately
2:00pm. At this time Mr Khan was accompanied by his sister
(so-called), Maryam Kouchan alias Khan (I-361). Both parties
assisted in doing various campaign tasks and left the headquarters
at approximately 6:00pm.

He returned on June 3, 1968 at approximately 3:00pm with his
daughter, Shirrin Khan. Shirrin Khan was assigned to the answering
of phones and general type-clerical work. During the days
activities Mr Khan was at the rear exit of the headquarters
when he observed a male and female seated in a blue V/W. He
states that he also observed a male leaning inside the right
window talking to the couple who were seated. At approximately
7:00pm Mr Khan and his daughter left the headquarters walked
toward the parked V/W. Upon approaching the vehicle Mr Khan
noticed that the male who was standing outside walked across the
street and walked out of sight. When he passed the vehicle he
glanced inside and he noticed that the girl who was seated inside
the vehicle turned her head as if she did not want to be seen.

On June 4, 1968 Mr Khan arrived with sister (Maryam Khan (I-361)
and son FElipe Khan (I-292) at approximately 2:00pm. During
his activities Mr Khan was located near the drinking fountain
where the coffee stand is located. At this time he observed a
female, Cauc, approximately 23/6 years, wearing a short dress
with polka dots. He described the dress as white in color and
the dots to be the diameter of pennies or smaller. This female
appeared to be talking to a male described as male, Cauc, dark
complexion, short in height, wearing a jacket described as blue
"McGregor" type (windbreaker). He was wearing a white shirt
underneath and tight trousers. It appeared that the two parties
were talking as they were facing each other and that he noticed
movement of their mouths, but due to the distance Mr Khan could
not overhear any conversation. Upon approaching the parties he
noticed that the female turned her head and looked in the opposite
direction. Mr Khan then recognized this couple as being the same

as seen on 6-3-68 in the blue V/W. At approximately 8:00pm on
6-4-68 Mr Khan and Miss Kouchan left the headquarters. Upon
exiting the rear of the headquarters Mr Khan and Miss Kouchan
got into their vehicle and drove to the front of the headquarters
where they stopped and Mr Khan re-entered. While Mr Khan was
inside a male Cauc, early 20's approached Maryam who was still
seated in the vehicle and the male asked for a ride. Miss Kouchan
recognizing the male as being in the headquarters earlier, agreed
to give the person a ride. When Mr Khan returned to the vehicle
he noticed the male seated in the rear seat. Enroute to Santa
Monica the conversation between Mr Khan and the male consisted
of the male asking for campaign literature of press type passes.
Mr Khan refused the male any literature since he had none, but
informed him that if he left his name and address he would durnish
him with some at a later time. The male wrote his name and
address on a piece of paper and gave the paper to Mr Khan. This
male was Michael Wayne (I-1096).

BACKGROUND

Mr Khan became active in the campaign due to his involvement with
Robert Kennedy at the time Robert Kennedy was Attorney General.

Mr Khan is an exile from the Country of Iran. He came to the
attention of Robert Kennedy through law suits which were filed
against the Family of the King of Iran. These suits resulted
from 1959 when Mr Khan was involved in a construction job with
United States. Mr Khan states when he returned to Iran he was
swindled out of money and material by the King. Upon returning
to the United States Mr Khan was made a political exile by the
King.

Upon returning to the United States Mr Khan started a group
named "The United Patriots for Justice". He started a campaign
against the King of Iran accusing him of mis-use of foreign
aid money. He supposedly is assisted in this venture by various
members of the tribes which make up part of Iran.

OFFICERS STATEMENTS

Officers first came in contact with Mr Khaibar Khan as a result of
checking volunteer cards at the Kennedy Headquarters. It was
brought to officer's attention that numerous volunteer cards
were made by the same person due to handwriting. It was also found
that the cards (24 in all) had the same address listed on them
as Mr Khan's. Upon checking this address it was found that Mr
Khan's ex-wife resides at this location.

Mr Khan's ex-wife (Talat Khan I-314) was contacted by Sgt. Sartuche
and he was informed that Mrs Khan had been separated for some
time and that she was not involved in politics as was her husband.
Mrs Khan contacted Khaibar and he in turn notified our department
of his whereabouts. An appointment was made for an interview
on 6-18-68.

On June 18, 1968 officers met Mr Khan in the lobby of the
Miramar Hotel located on Ocean Avenue in Santa Monica. He
informed officers that he was staying at the Ocean Palms Hotel
located at 1215 Ocean Avenue Apt #201 and that he was registered
under the name of Mr Goody. During the interview Mr Khan stated
his distrust of the present administration and the immigration
department. It was evident that Mr Khan didn't want his whereabouts known. He stated that his life was in danger as someone
was attempting to kill him. While living in the West Los Angeles
area he was leaving his ex-wife's apartment when unknown suspects
jumped him and Mr Khan received various injuries. Due to this
incident Mr Khan received surgery and had to wear a cast on his
arm. This incident was reported to the West Los Angeles
Detectives. In April 1968 he and his sister, Maryam Kouchan,
were horseback riding in Griffith Park at which time his sister
got shot in the leg by an unknown assailant and required surgery.
This disabled Miss Kouchan and it was necessary for her to use
crutches in able to walk.

Due to the above, both Sgt. Sartuche and Officer Miller were
given nicknames (golfer and tennis player) to use when further
contacting Mr Khan by telephone. On further meetings, in person,
officers were to meet Mr Khan at other places than at his residence.
These places were coffee shops, parks, beaches etc.

Officers first interview with Khaibar Khan was on June 18, 1968
and the last contact was made on July 27, 1968. During this
time five contacts were made and officers learned that Mr Khan
is involved in law suits with the King of Iran. Because Mr
Khan had numerous papers from the United States Senate, United
States Department of Justice along with letters from a organization called the United Patriots for Justice. Officers found
that the United Patriots for Justice is an organization headed
by Mr Khan and is made up of different tribes located in Iran.
Mr Khan gove his permission for officers to make copies of these
documents, which we did.

After the first visit officers found through the Immigration
Department that Khaibar Khan, alias Goodarzian had a Immigration
Warrant outstanding. The warrant was for Illegal Entry (remaining
beyong specified time), Warrant #A-11-011142, no bail. It was
also found out through R & I that Mr Khan was using the alias
of Mohammad Ali and had an arrest on 1-13-67 for 647F in
Hollywood. (LA#825 805A).

The only information received which is relevant to the Kennedy
assassination was that on June 3, 1968 Mr Khan observed a male
and female sitting in a blue V/W at the rear of headquarters.
He described the female as Fe, Cauc 23/6 years, 5-5 and the male
as dark comp, short.

Page #5   Khaibar Kha.   ⊥ ⊥₀

On June 4, 1968 Mr Khan as a telephone operator at the headquarters
again observed the male and female that he had seen sitting in
the V/W. The couple was observed standing near the coffee shop
area. The male and female were facing each other and it appeared
to .iz when that the people were talking to each other as their
mouths appeared to be moving. At this time the girl was described
as wearing a white dress with dark polka dots about the diameter
of a penny. The male was described as wearing a blue jacket
(McGregor type) with a white shirt and light colored tight trousers.

Due to the people seen on two different occasions by Mr Khan
he was shown mugs of suspect Sirhan B. Sirhan and asked if he
could identify him as being the male seen. Mr Khan stated that
he could not be sure until he could actually see the male in
person. Mr Khan was asked if he would attend a show-up if it
could be arranged and would he then take a polygraph test to
verify the truthfulness of his statements. Mr Khan refused to
take a polygraph test or attend a show-up and stated that he
wanted to be 100% sure before he accused anyone. During all
the interviews with Mr Khan he was always unsure of his identification of Sirhan B. Sirhan.

Due to Mr Khan refusing to attend a line up or take a polygraph
test it is very doubtful or simply a mistake in identity.

It was later found out by officers that Mr Khan was arrested
by Immigration authorities and is presently on $4,000.00 bail
pending a hearing.

Exhibit 16
Photos of Ali Ahmand

Ali Ahmand, in sweater, next to Robert Kennedy minutes before Kennedy was assassinated. Note SLR camera. (Photo Reporters)

Exhibit 17
Sirhan LAPD Activity Check

ACTIVITY 72 HOURS PRIOR TO ASSASSINATION

The following is a chronological hourly account of Sirhan's known activities for the 72 hour period preceding the shooting of Senator Kennedy, commencing with 12:01 a.m., Sunday, June 2, 1968.

DATE	TIME	ACTIVITY/LOCATION	SOURCE
Sun. 6/2/68	12:01 a.m.-8:00 a.m.	Bedroom, 696 E. Howard St., Pasadena	Mary Sirhan
.	8:00 a.m.-9:00 a.m.	Drove mother to church, 1757 N. Lake, Pasadena	Mary Sirhan
.	9:00 a.m.-11:00 a.m.	UNKNOWN	------
.	11:00 a.m.-	Home, 696 E. Howard St., Pasadena	Mary Sirhan Trans. #50 Line 1 thru 12
.	11:15 a.m.-5:00 p.m.	UNKNOWN	------
.	5:00 p.m.-6:00 p.m.	Home, 696 E. Howard St., Pasadena.	Adel Sirhan Trans. #52 Lines 12 thru 26
.	6:00 p.m.-8:30 p.m.	UNKNOWN	------
.	8:30 p.m.-9:10 p.m.	Seen at Kennedy Rally Ambassador Hotel, 3400 Wilshire Blvd.	Bert Blum, Susan Redding,

DATE	TIME	ACTIVITY/LOCATION	SOURCE
Sun. 6/2/68	9:30 p.m.-10:30 p.m.	UNKNOWN	------
.	10:30 p.m.-11:00 p.m.	Home, 696 E. Howard St., Pasadena	Mary Sirhan
Mon. 6/3/68	11:00 p.m.-8:00 a.m.	Bedroom, 696 E. Howard St., Pasadena	Mary Sirhan
.	8:00 a.m.-8:15 a.m.	Drove mother to work	Mary Sirhan
.	8:15 a.m.-10:30 a.m.	UNKNOWN	------
.	10:30 a.m.-10:40 a.m.	Purchased gas at Richfield Gas Station, 2529 E. Foothill Blvd, Pasadena	Sidney McDaniel
.	10:40 a.m.-12:30 p.m.	UNKNOWN	------
.	12:30 p.m.-1:00 p.m.	Home, 696 E. Howard St., Pasadena	Mary Sirhan Trans. #50 Page 19 lines 19 thru 26 Page 20 lines 1 thru 15
.	1:00 p.m.-4:30 p.m.	UNKNOWN	------
.	4:30 p.m.-5:00 p.m.	Watched Television at home, 696 E. Howard St., Pasadena	Mary Sirhan Trans. #50 Lines 1 thru 3

DATE	TIME	ACTIVITY/LOCATION	SOURCE
Tues. 6/4/68	11:00 a.m.–5:00 p.m.	San Gabriel Valley Gun Club, 4001 Fish Canyon Rd.; Monrovia Practiced - fired his gun	E. C. Buckner, Henry Carson, D. Montellano, Claudia Williams, Ronald Williams, Robert Grijavia, J. Thornbrugh, Charles Kendall, Mike Saccoman, Corliss Edwards, George Mioch
	5:00 p.m.–6:00 p.m.	UNKNOWN	
	6:00 p.m.–6:40 p.m.	Bob's Restaurant 1601 E. Colorado Blvd., Pasadena	
	6:40 p.m.–7:05 p.m.	Pasadena City College Cafeteria, 1570 E. Colorado Blvd., Pasadena	
	7:05 p.m.–7:15 p.m.	Enroute from Pasadena City College to Bob's Restaurant	
	7:15 p.m.–7:30 p.m.	Bob's Restaurant 1601 E. Colorado Blvd., Pasadena	

DATE	TIME	ACTIVITY/LOCATION	SOURCE
Mon. 6/3/68	5:00 p.m.–6:00 p.m.	At home, eating, 696 E. Howard St., Pasadena	Mary Sirhan Trans. #50 Page 17, Lines 10 thru 26
	6:00 p.m.–9:00 p.m.	At home reading in his room, 696 E. Howard St.; Pasadena	Mary Sirhan Trans. #50 Page 18, Lines 1 thru 22
Mon. 6/3/68 Tues. 6/4/68	9:00 p.m.–8:00 a.m.	Bedroom, 696 E. Howard St., Pasadena	Mary Sirhan Trans. #50 Page 18, Lines 23 thru 26, Page 19, Lines 1 thru 5
	8:00 a.m.–	Drove his car from 696 E. Howard St. to purchase a newspaper	Mary Sirhan Trans. #50 Page 19, Lines 2 thru 12
	8:00 a.m.–9:30 a.m.	UNKNOWN	------------
	9:30 a.m.–11:00 a.m.	Home, 696 E. Howard St., Pasadena	Adel Sirhan
	11:00 a.m.	Home answering phone 696 E. Howard St., Pasadena	Adel Sirhan Trans. #52 Page 21, Lines 21 thru 22

DATE	TIME	ACTIVITY/LOCATION	SOURCE
Tues. 6/4/68	7:30 p.m.–8:45 p.m.	UNKNOWN	
	8:45 p.m.–9:00 p.m.	Standing in the Electricians Booth Adjacent to Venetian Room, Ambassador Hotel	Gonzalo Cetina,
	9:00 p.m.–9:30 p.m.	Standing at entrance to Palm Court, Ambassador Hotel	
	9:30 p.m.–10:00 p.m.	Inside the Colonial Room, Ambassador Hotel Looking at teletype machines	
	10:00 p.m.–10:15 p.m.	Standing outside rest room adjacent to Venetian Room, Ambassador Hotel	
	10:15 p.m.–11:00 p.m.	Standing in pantry area of the kitchen, Ambassador Hotel	Judy Royer
	11:00 p.m.–11:30 p.m.	UNKNOWN	
	11:30 p.m.–11:45 p.m.	Walking out of pantry door in the kitchen area	Robert M. Klase,
	11:45 p.m.–12:00-p.m.	Inside pantry area of kitchen asking questionwhether Senator Kennedy will come by there later	Jesus Perez Trans. #13 Page 3 and Page 5

DATE	TIME	ACTIVITY/LOCATION	SOURCE
Wed. 6/5/68	12:05 a.m.–12:10 a.m.	Standing on tray rack in pantry area of kitchen looking towards the stage of the Embassy Room	Martin Patrusky,
	12:10 a.m.–12:15 a.m.	Standing next to ice machine in the pantry area of kitchen, Ambassador Hotel	Barbara Rubin, Gonzalo Cetina,
	12:10 a.m.–12:15 a.m.	Standing in crouched position next to ice machine in pantry area of kitchen, Ambassador Page 8 thru 18	Vincent DiPierro, Trans #4,
	12:15 a.m.	Standing on tray rack pushing towards Kennedy reaching around Carl Uecker, and firing shots	Martin Patrusky,
	12:15 a.m.	Drew gun from his waistband and fired at Senator Kennedy	Lisa Lynn Urso,
	12:15 a.m.	Inside pantry area of kitchen firing gun	Jesus Perez Trans. #13, Page 4 and Page 6
	12:15 a.m.–12:25 a.m.	Inside pantry area being subdued by witnesses	Karl Uecker Frank Burns Roosevelt Grier, Joseph LaHive
	12:25 a.m.	Sirhan in custody of Police escorted through Colonial Room, Ambassador Hotel	

Exhibit 18
Boris Yaro Interview

TELEPHONE INTERVIEW WITH BORIS YARO,

Staff of the Los Angeles Times:

28 March 1978

(Second try after poor first connection)

Yaro: Hello.

Morrow: Mr. Yaro?

Yaro: Yes.

Morrow: Bob Morrow, again.

Yaro: Yeah. It's Yaro....Y-a-r-o.

Morrow: Oh, I'm terribly sorry, sir. I just...the reason I called is that...I can hear you a lot better, by the way.

Yaro: Yeah. Well, I was on a car telephone.

Morrow: That was obvious, after I heard the clicking. Why, you were in the pantry that day /of the RFK/ shooting...trying to get some pictures.

Yaro: Right.

Morrow: And had taken some, obviously. But, I wondered if you, by any chance, remembered seeing a young /man/, oh, I guess he'd be a Middle Eastern type or Pakistani type by the name of Ali Mohammed?

Yaro: No.

Morrow: O.K.

Yaro: No. We were....it was kind of hurry up and go /situation/, when I went back into the pantry. I had /originally/ been out in the main ballroom.

Morrow: He /Ali Mohammed/ had been to the right /interrupted/......

Yaro: /For/ all of Bobby's speech almost. The point is, when he started to wind it up, I split and went back into the pantry. So, in that length of time, god only knows how many people could have come in. The only thing I remember is that there were a couple of good looking dames and I don't even remember what they looked like.

Morrow: Well, this fellow was very unusual because he was wearing.....it was very hot in there I understand, and he was wearing a sweater.

Yaro: Well, I was wearing an /unintelligible/ suit. It was the sign of the times, you know; so, it would be difficult to even think in terms of temperature. That ballroom was jammed. I saw other people with sweaters; you know, young- sters with white shirts or blue shirts, button-downs and crew neck sweaters. It's evening time.

Morrow: Yeah. This fellow.....

Yaro: Oh, let me turn down the radio /momentary interruption./

Morrow: This fellow....the reason I'm inquiring about him. I have reason to believe that he could have been involved.

Yaro: Well, he'd have to have been standing next to Sirhan to do it.

Morrow: No. He would have been behind the Senator, on the way in.

Yaro: Well, on the way in...it would be...I don't recall seeing him at all. And, quite frankly, it would have been a hor- rible way....somebody would have had to have seen him with a gun. Do you follow me? Have you been in that pantry at all?

Morrow: Oh, I've been in the pantry /in 1976/. There was no gun as far as he /Ali Mohammed/ was involved.

Yaro: I don't recall seeing him.

Morrow: It would have been a camera.

Yaro: That I don't....Bill Eckridge was next to me taking pictures, and I didn't even see him when /he meant Senator Kennedy/ went down. I was surprised as hell, too....you know, I had ....it was a very similar photograph /Bill Eckridge's photo- graph and mine were/...made essentially from the same angle, and he had to have been side by side with me and I didn't even see him. I wasn't even aware of his presence; but that was after the shooting and the shock had set in and every- thing else. So, I did not see him. At that time, I actually

277

thought that Sirhan was a Philipino or...that /he/ was, I think, the description I initially gave the office when I came in.... /that/ he was dark complexioned, possibly a Philipino.

Morrow: Well, this fellow /Ali Mohammed/ would have been about the same complexion, but he had a rounder face. He was standing next to Jesse Unruh on the podium.

Yaro: Well, hell. There have to be pictures of him.

Morrow: We have a picture of him. That's why we think.... that's why we think he was involved. He disappeared very quickly afterwards; and was never seen from again. And, I'll be honest with you, a....what has occurred, a whole bunch of new evidence has cropped up....information we have come across in the other investigation /the John F. Kennedy/ ironically. And, it has to do with a lot of Iranians. And there were a lot of Iranians involved in the /RFK/ campaign out there /in California/ evidently.

Yaro: I'll be damned.

Morrow: And this was by design.

Yaro: In order to get them close to the man, hum?

Morrow: Yes, sir. Have you ever heard of an outfit called the Savak?

Yaro: Nope.

Morrow: The Iranian secret police.

Yaro: No. Un. S....you mean, spelled....

Morrow: S-a-v-a-k.

Yaro: That's right.

Morrow: It's pronounced and spelled in a number of different ways.

Yaro: Yeah. That's the reason the kids wore masks at the demonstrations, because they were afraid of the /Iranian/ secret police. When you said Iranian, the first thing that comes to my mind any more /is the Shah/....I've been to so many demonstrations that I can repeat it to you in their accent. 'The Shah is a murderer.' You know, it's a litany now. But, no, I didn't notice anything unusual. No one was expecting

an assassination...You're not looking for killers or anything like that. And, I....the only person that I knew at all /in the pantry/, was a photographer friend of mine, Dick Drew, and I was really surprised to see him. And I came in /the pantry/ and was waiting by the /pantry/ door, and Dicky was standing next to me ....and we /both/ went to make a picture as Bobby passed and some guy blocked it off and I started the camera up and Dick /Drew/ happened to notice and said, 'Boris, you missed him.' So I went around behind him /Dick Drew/, and the next thing I know, I ended up about three feet from Sirhan when he pulled the trigger.

Morrow: Boy!

Yaro: So, that's....it just bugs the hell out of me in one respect, when everybody says two guns. Well, it's literally impossible in that situation to fire two guns. There were too many people. In other words, somebody would have had to have seen the other gun.

Morrow: Let me say this. The information I'm going to be saying to you....may sound a little strange to you, but I used to be with the Company in Langley /meaning the Central Intelligence Agency./

Yaro: The what? The Company in Langley?

Morrow: Yeah.

Yaro: O.K.

Morrow: And we had what were known as gun cameras, which were nothing but a Nikon....

Yaro: With a 9mm slug in it....

Morrow: /No/ three .22's actually....long rifles. You could have any calibre you wanted. But in the .22 /version/ you could have three /cartridges/ of them.

Yaro: That's why they make me open my camera when I go into places.

Morrow: That's right. That's what we suspect. If there was somebody else, we think that was it /a gun camera did it./

Yaro: Well, I went through an extensive interview, which I'm sure CBS will let you have....for /the program/ Sixty Minutes, when they did the assassination thing. And I can basically account for every damn bullet, as far as the angle goes. You understand the difference between a human being and a target?

Morrow:

Yaro: Of course.

O.K. A target isn't moving. If there's any difference in where the bullet strikes, it's because you did something, not because the target moved. Do you follow me? O.K. Bobby backed up, and he bobbed and he weaved and he ducked, I mean he was really moving around trying to get away from this guy, /meaning Sirhan/. And, to top it off, Sirhan, when he fired the weapon, I mean, I have fired a lot of weapons in my life, but I've never done anything near what this fellow did. He used a weapon like I would use a knife, if I were insane. Now, he's jabbing with the weapon as he fired.

Morrow: Do you think he could have gotten as close as an inch to him? Was it possible?

Yaro: Yes, yes. Because, you know, when you're looking at it.... I can still see it. His /Bobby Kennedy's/ body if bobbing, weaving, throwing his hands up, and backing up; and Sirhan was moving forward; and, as he was moving forward, he was firing; but he was also, as you put the pistol in your hand and you bring it up so that it's in the up range /firing/ position, and then you bring it forward into firing position; and you can imagine it at a half range, O.K., with the muzzle in the air for a second and then down, down, down, boom, boom, boom, boom, boom. And at one of those things, the extension of the arm from body to body, it's not inconceivable that the weapon would have been that close.

Morrow: Le me, if I could, ask you another question.

Yaro: Yeah.

Morrow: About some of the remarks that his arm was grabbed after the second shot.

Yaro: No, no. /Well/, let's put it this way /obviously referring to the scene/. There was either one or two shots fired. O.K. And then, boom, boom, boom, boom, boom. There was a pregnant pause between those two because my initial impression was some jackass has set off fire crackers in here; because I got hit in the face with debris, you know. And, then, all of a sudden, the crowd cleared out and this son of a bitch /meaning Sirhan/ comes like gangbusters and I'm frozen. You know, I'm close enough to where I could have probably /I assumed he meant touched him/...but there was nobody between him /Sirhan/ and I. But I'm just frozen.... no guts....whatever you want to call it.

Morrow: Excuse me, but you don't see something like that every day.

Yaro: Me. And then it hit me. Oh, my God, it's happened again. And then somebody shouted something, 'get him' /meaning Sirhan/. And then all of a sudden, you know, you stop whatever it is you're afraid of. There's no more firing, and two guys went for him, and I moved; and they hit him; and pushed him kind of spread eagle on the counter; and they were trying to slam the gun loose; and the gun came loose; and I took it. I picked it up /obviously from the floor./ And I picked it up and I'm thinking the son of a bitch /referring to Sirhan's gun/ doesn't have any knurles on the grip. This gun is still warm and it.... when the gun is warm, the grip is warm. Not the barrel or the cylinder. But the grip is warm. And it's a smooth grip. And I'm thinking this. And all of a sudden, wham, and the gun goes over my shoulder. Somebody pulled it out of my hand. As it later turned out, it was apparently Rosy Grier. But the first thing I said when I came to and into our office, where I'm on a dead run, and I hollered at Bill Thomas who is now the editor of the Los Angeles Times, and I said, "My finger prints are on that gun!"

Morrow: Jesus!

Yaro: Because all of a sudden, I'm realizing I just touched evidence on this thing.

Morrow: That's a fascinating story. Because you're the most concise one I've talked to; and, the ironic part about it is that we suspect there was a camera like this used in the pantry that day.

Yaro: Uhmm. Well, that would account for why there was nothing /he obviously meant seen/....you see, I don't know that much about guns, O.K. I'm a dumb reporter, right? But, I know damn well that you cannot fire an automatic weapon in a coat pocket with a silencer on it.

Morrow: No way.

Yaro: Because the odds of even hitting the target are pretty grim unless you're right up against him. Right?

Morrow: That's right.

Yaro: O.K. And the fact that it's an automatic, the chances of the gun jamming in the clothing or whatever are also there. It's like having another barrel on a pistol /meaning a silencer/....why bother to have it? O.K. If you take it out and use it, somebody's going to see it. There's too many people around.

Morrow: There's no question about that.

Yaro: So, the other end of it was this guy would have had to take one shot. He couldn't have taken more than one shot. If he used that type of weapon. It's not inconceivable that it happened. It's just that if he did, with a moving target ....the way that target was moving, he would have either ....I don't recall seeing anybody else do it....I know there's this broad that went berserk and tried to stop me from making pictures....had a camera; but she was interviewed by the FBI and everything else.

Morrow: Well, this guy disappeared before they could get to him.... out of the country....and, forever gone; and his name was evidently....it was the wrong name he had given / I was referring to Ali Mohammed/ it's a wild story. And it's all documented in the Los Angeles police files, but no-body put it all together because they didn't have...they didn't have the Iranian connection.

Yaro: Huh. Well, this is out of the blue....I know nothing about it. If it's true, god help us all, I guess. Where do we stand with the Shah of Iran once this is out?

Morrow: Well, that's a hell of a sticky question, because you know who set him up /meaning the CIA/?

Yaro: Yeah.

Morrow: It all ties back into the JFK, which is a pretty wild story when you think about it. Well, I sure appreciate the call. And....

Yaro: Bob, do you have an office number there?

Morrow: Yeah. You can reach me; well, actually, I'm in Baltimore most of the time. I wrote the book called "Betrayal". You might have read it.

Yaro: What?

Morrow: "Betrayal". B-e-t-r....

Yaro: Yeah. I've got it.

Morrow: I was out in Los Angeles, but I wasn't on this case, when I did my book review a couple of years ago. This book will be coming out after it's cleared by the Committee.

Yaro: Let me tell you something. We got....I got Kaiser's book....

Morrow: "JFK Must Die!"

Yaro: Yeah. And, they have me quoted as /unintelligible/.... Swisher, referring to the gal who had grabbed my arm and everything else, saying 'Don't take pictures, don't take picture, I'm a photographer'....But at no point did I ever strike her. That's one. And I never said that. That I hit her. And I've got a feeling, they young FBI agent, who....I've sat there and talked to him and I typed up my own interview. He said, 'you're a newsman why don't you just type it as you talk it, and I typed the damn thing. And....I know I never hit the gal; and if I had known it, I never would have said it. Somebody rewrote it to jibe....to make things jibe. Now, if they're doing that, how much other bullshit has been done.

Morrow: Well, I'd say a hell of a lot. I know what has been done in some of these areas. And that's why we're awful care-ful....we had a hell of a time even getting the first book published; because it's a direct contradiction to most of the normal stories on the JFK thing.

Yaro: Normally....what I'm saying is, considering....was a major effort on behalf of the FBI....what was it....two hundred agents had been assigned out here.

Morrow: O.K. That doesn't mean a hell of a lot. Because Hoover hated Bobby's guts....

Yaro: Well, yeah. We know this. But I'm saying is that consid-ering the man's involvement and the possibility of discovery, what have you? The known factor that....he had a dislike for him. You'd figure he'd /Hoover/ want to cover his ass and not play around with any testimony. Now, if my testi-mony was altered....now that's one thing that I see. When they had the disclosure thing, one of our people went down and got a copy of the report. And that was the only thing that really jarred my mind, because I know I never physi-cally hit the woman, and I would not hit a woman to begin with.

Morrow: God knows whose other testimony might be involved.

Yaro: Right. And why would they alter it; unless they wanted to make something jibe. What happened? From what the man said when I was in the office, they came over to the house and then said, would you come on down to the Bureau and we'll talk. And....so, I went down to their office and sat there in this interview room, and I told him, I said, /that woman with the camera/ she grabbed a hold of my left arm and she was tugging like crazy. And....finally, I was say-ing, 'let go, let go,' and 'god damn it lady, this is history.' and I jerked my arm free. And I recall, seeing, out of the corner of my eye, this really horrified expression on her face. And as near as I could figure, I must have yanked suf-ficiently hard, because....

Morrow: She was hit?

Yaro: No. She had a camera around her neck. And I probably jolted bar hard enough that the camera came up and belted her in the mouth.

Morrow: It happens. I wouldn't worry about it.

Yaro: No. I'm not thinking of it in terms of a legal thing or anything like that, I'm just saying that that's the only way she got hit, was that she got hit by something that she was wearing, but it certainly wasn't my knee.

Morrow: Would you mind if I quoted your conversation?

Yaro: I don't care.

Morrow: I normally, as a matter of reference, I tape everything.

Yaro: Oh.

Morrow: And I won't say anything, or even refer to you if you don't want me to; but there are some of the things that I think are important. I'd like the Committee to hear this conversation.

Yaro: Yeah.

Morrow: Because the....

Yaro: Are you working with them or on it?

Morrow: In cooperation with them. I cooperated very closely with them. In fact, Tom Downing....

Yaro: In other words, the net result of this thing for you is the book?

Morrow: Well, that's right. That's why I couldn't actually work for the committee proper; but if you talk to the Deputy Director, Tiny Hutton, down there, he'll tell you who I am and one of the responsible people for getting that committee started, was me and the first book. In fact, they referenced it in the paperback done by Warner.

Yaro: Ah so.

Morrow: And Tom Downing wrote a letter of commendation and the fact that a major amount of the responsibility was the information I gave the committee to have the House of Representatives vote positively on the thing finally.

Yaro: Ah so. All righty.

Morrow: I'm a friend of Norm Kempster's. In fact, I had lunch with him a couple of weeks ago. And I'm giving Norm this whole story first in the media.

Yaro: Uh huh.

Morrow: To break before anybody else gets it.

Yaro: Ah so. Well, all right. I'm trying to think now....

Morrow: Do you have a copy of that photograph you took?

Yaro: Yeah. We do.

Morrow: I was wondering if I could pay for one and get it?

Yaro: Yeah. You can do that also. Write a letter to me....our address is 202 W. First Street.

Morrow: O.K. Now do you want my telephone number and address.

Yaro: Right.

Morrow: O.K. It's Robert D. Morrow....710 Park Avenue....Baltimore, Maryland, 21201.

Yaro: And, what's the phone number there?

Morrow: Area code (301)-728-0974.

Yaro: All right, Bob. I'll wait until I hear from you on that, and ....it sounds interesting as hell. I just....

Morrow: Well, I appreciate the call.

Yaro: Now long....just out of curiosity, if you've got a couple of seconds. You're the first person I've ever talked to, knowingly anyway, that used to work with the CIA. I just....

Morrow: Well, I disclosed it in the book. And, I was a contract agent for them working on the Cuban thing back in....in fact, I did all their counterfeiting for them of pesos and that, back during the early '60's.

Yaro: I'll be darned.

Morrow: And, when Victor Marchetti got his....you know, when they first said they can't hold you to that secrecy agreement. I said, 'holy smokes,' I'm going to exonerate myself sooner or later,' because the Kennedy Administration originally busted us for it.

Yaro: When you say busted, you mean you were arrested?

Morrow: Yeah.

Yaro: You mean you were arrested by the Kennedy Administration?

Morrow: I was arrested by the Kennedy Administration originally. And, of course, the CIA had everything taken care of, boom, boom, like that. But the one Cuban went to jail.

Yaro: Ah so.

Morrow: And he was the Cuban leader, Mario Kohly, who, as you will find out, had a very important role and was a good friend of Mr. Nixon's....a very close friend of Nixon's.

Yaro: Ah, Jesus.

Morrow: And the whole thing is so horrible that when I got into this book, I was almost terrified to write it.

Yaro: The one you're doing now?

Morrow: Yeah.

Yaro: What does a contract agent do, or do I want to ask that question?

Morrow: Well, I was a technical man originally. I did all sorts of operations. Went into Cuba the night of the Bay of Pigs, taking photographs....picking up photographs and taking electronic readings on their missile systems....capability that they were putting in. And we were using the actual landing as a cover for our operation. And, Sirhan is interesting, speaking of diversions....Sirhan, to our knowledge, was set up as a diversion. There were fellows....one was in the Embassy Room, itself.

Yaro: Let me just throw something at you. O.K. I don't know you from Adam at this point. But in Monterrey Park on ....god, I've forgotten the goddamn date....either the early part of 1963 or the latter part of 1962, there was a big knock-down drag out brawl in a house, where shots were fired. Do you know about that?

Yaro: In the city of Monterrey Park, which is a suburb of Los Angeles, in the Valley, oh, about eight or nine miles from downtown L.A.....from the center of L.A.

Morrow: I don't know it. The only person that could identify me out there is my cousin....

Yaro: No, no. Hear me out. Everybody that was....there were a lot of pictures made of the holes in the wall, in the furniture. And everybody that was arrested. You know, they were lined up....because nobody would point fingers at one another. Ostensibly, aside from the bunch of Cubans that were in this group, there was one gentleman by the name of Lee Harvey Oswald.

Morrow: Oh. I've heard about that.

Yaro: I went back there in 1967, I think it was, or....excuse me, not '67....yeah, it could have been '66, '67, somewhere in there, and tried to find the negatives. And most of these departments...Monterrey Park's a little tinky place..../change tape/. They were four by five negatives, because the photographer who worked for them.... a local newspaper type, who was tied in with the police department had a radio in his car, and when they called him, he could talk to them....he was a kind of ex-officio cop, and, he has since died, but we could not find the negatives of those people. They're all gone.

Morrow: And he claimed that Oswald was in there?

Yaro: Somebody did. And I don't know how it was....the boss that I worked for at the time, said, get your ass over there and check it out. And, I went over and checked it out and we went through this thing, and he was just nice as pie. Here they are, boom, and pulled them all out. There was such an incident, id did occur on such a date, and bingo, the negs are missing and there's no sign-out form.

Morrow: And, this was in your office?

Yaro: This was not in our office. This was in the Monterrey Park Police Department.

Morrow: Monterrey Park Police Department?

Yaro: Yeah.

Morrow: That's wild. That's a wild story. But not inconsistent with what's happened to a lot of evidence.

Yaro: Yeah. All right. I just....

Morrow: There were a couple people out in the California area, that were familiar with Oswald; and....

Yaro: Well, the fact that he was tied up with a bunch of ex-patriot Cubans....you know, Alpha 6 was out here as well.

Morrow: Alpha 66.

Yaro: 66, right.

Morrow: You know something interesting that you just....you just brought up something very interesting that....Oswald himself....was reportedly a contract man for the Company. And....not that we could ever prove it....we know he had a 201 file down here.

Yaro: Oh, really?

Morrow: Yeah.

Yaro: Military-type 201?

Morrow: He had a Company /meaning CIA/ 201 file.

Yaro: I'll be damned.

Morrow: And there was some stuff released by the KGB by accident ....Bernie Fensterwald, the attorney....got it declassified....that mentioned Oswald through the KGB, was sent over there on a mission to marry a gal....exactly what I was told back in 1961, I guess it was.

Yar: Hum.

Morrow: I've included this in my book "Betrayal". But I didn't even know this....this stuff was declassified afterwards.

Yaro: Well, it's all crazy.

Morrow: Mysteriouser and mysteriouser.

Yaro: Governments work wonderous things which....we never know what the hell's going on. I often wonder whose side we're on.

Morrow: I'm scared, to be perfectly honest with you.

Yaro: All right. Hey, Bob, I've got to run. The beeper going off, which means somebody else is trying to get hold of me, and since I'm supposed to have been out in that car a half hour ago, I'd better get moving.

Morrow: I'm terribly sorry to have interrupted you, but thanks a lot for the call.

Yaro: Right.

Morrow: I'll keep in touch. 'Bye.

Yaro: 'Bye.

Exhibit 19
LAPD Descriptive Summary of Assassination

THE ASSASSINATION   LAPD S.R.

On the afternoon of June 2, 1968, Senator Robert Francis Kennedy, his wife and four of their children arrived at Orange County Airport to begin the final two days of his campaign to win the California Democratic Party Presidential Electors being selected in the June 4th primary election.

In the course of those two days he addressed a festival in Orange County, visited Disneyland, traveled to San Francisco for a rally, returned to Long Beach for a speech and a motor-cade to Venice, flew to San Diego for an appearance and spent the day of the election at the home of a friend in Malibu. At 8 p.m., on June 4th, he was driven to the Ambassador Hotel to await the election returns and his anticipated victory. The shooting of Robert Kennedy at 12:15 a.m. that night and the subsequent events surrounding that incident is the subject of this report.

Security Provided For Senator Kennedy

The ultimate question which will be asked - the same question which is still asked about the assassinations of President John F. Kennedy and Dr. Martin Luther King - is whether law enforcement in a free society can provide the necessary security for its leaders and political candidates. Important to this question, as it should be, is the right of individuals to come and go freely whenever they wish; and to express their desires to be free from the unsolicited concern of others.

The assassination of Senator Robert Kennedy magnified the importance of this question and momentarily centered the attention of the world on the Los Angeles Police Department. This investigation, therefore, closely examined the security provided for Senator Kennedy's visit to Los Angeles and the attitude of the Kennedy staff toward police security.

This Department has a prescribed policy applicable to protection of dignitaries and their participation in public gatherings. The Department assumes a position of neutrality toward person-alities and political issues and the policy provides that the Department takes enforcement action wherever necessary.

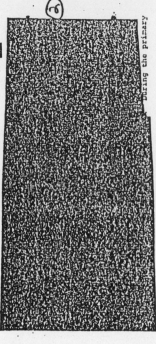

During the primary campaign of Senator Kennedy in California Department security policies and the attitude of Senator Kennedy toward security came into conflict. This conflict measurably affected the conditions which existed just prior to Senator Kennedy's assassi-nation.

Kennedy Motorcade of May 29, 1968

Department personnel became involved with Kennedy campaign

activities during a motorcade in downtown Los Angeles on May 29, 1968. On May 28th, the Department received a telegram from a Kennedy aide advising that a motorcade was planned for the next day. No request for security was made to this Department. The incidents which occurred at that motorcade illustrate the Kennedy party's attitude toward the police.

Officers of this Department were assigned to observe the course of the motorcade and to insure the even flow of traffic along the motorcade route. Several violations were observed during the motorcade as civilian motorcycle officers blocked intersections and allowed vehicles in the motorcade to drive through against red signal lights.

At one point in the motorcade, at 9th and Santee Streets, the vehicles came to a stop and Senator Kennedy was pulled from his vehicle by a large enthusiastic crowd. A Traffic Enforcement Division sergeant attempted to assist the Senator back to his vehicle when it appeared to him that Kennedy needed help. Kennedy and his aides berated the sergeant and told him that they had not asked for the assistance of the police. Several other incidents occurred along the route of the motorcade involving this Department's officers and Kennedy aides. At one point, ███████████████ shouted obscenities at several officers who were attempting to keep the crowd from becoming unmanageable and spilling onto the street. These remarks were highly inflammatory and the officers considered making an arrest ████ 'disturbing the peace.'

The identification of several persons in the motorcade was obtained for the purpose of making applications for complaints for various criminal and vehicle code violations. The applications were withdrawn in the interest of justice after the assassination.

Personal Security for Senator Kennedy

William Barry, an ex F.B.I. agent, acted as sole security for Senator Kennedy. His primary assignment was to act as personal bodyguard for Kennedy and he was responsible for liaison with local law enforcement agencies. Barry did not contact the Department to request security for the Senator for June 2/4, 1968.

After the assassination, Barry advised investigators that he had been concerned about Senator Kennedy's security. He had observed security problems at other events and had intended to speak to Kennedy on their return to New York. Barry told investigators that Kennedy was very difficult to protect because of his desire to allow supporters to be close to him.

Plans for Senator Kennedy's movements prior to the election night were made by Barry, Dutton and Richard Tuck, another Kennedy aide. Rafer Johnson had joined the Kennedy staff a few weeks prior to the assassination to assist in crowd control. Dutton advised investigators that police were not used for Kennedy's personal security except when they anticipated an unruly crowd. Dutton and Tuck arranged appointments for Kennedy and Barry and Johnson provided the sole physical security for him.

Hotel Security and Police Deployment In The Area

In anticipation of several victory parties scheduled to be held at the Ambassador, eleven regular hotel security guards were assigned to work crowd control election night. The head of hotel security, William Gardner, told investigators that no request was made to the hotel to provide personal security for Kennedy.

Gardner arranged for six additional guards, from Ace Guard Service, to work at the hotel. The total security force consisted of eighteen uniformed guards. Six Los Angeles Fire Department inspectors were assigned to the hotel for the evening to enforce fire and occupancy regulations.

Rampart Division deployed an additional eight officers, in four radio cars, in anticipation of the large crowds planning to attend festivities at the hotel. The radio cars were to be deployed normally and not specifically at the hotel. These arrangements were the total security arrangements which were made for the election night proceedings at the hotel.

Election Night at The Ambassador

By 6 p.m. on June 4th, many people were crowding in to the hotel where parties were beginning for Senator Kennedy, Democrat Alan Cranston and Republican Max Rafferty. Other guests were in the hotel for business conventions. 514 guests were registered in the hotel.

The polls closed at 8 p.m., and the public bars opened in the hotel. Volunteer workers and news media personnel were preparing for the speeches and celebrations which would come when the election results were announced.

By 8:30 p.m. admittance to the Embassy Room, where the Kennedy victory Party was to take place, was becoming difficult. Guards were having trouble restricting the flow of persons into the room which was reaching the occupancy limit. Many people were able to circumvent the guards by using unguarded entrances and service entrances. At 9:30 p.m., a Fire Department inspector ordered the main doors to be closed to all entry, except on a one-in one-out basis. Witnesses later reported that people were able to easily circumvent these measures. By 11:30 p.m., the crowd in the room restlessly awaited the anticipated appearance of Senator Kennedy.

Press Coverage At The Ambassador

The night of the assassination a large number of press personnel crowded into the Ambassador Hotel to report on the anticipated victory of Senator Robert Kennedy. Representatives of the world press were also present. More than 150 of those interviewed in this investigation stated that they were reporters who were at the hotel the night of the shooting. The Colonial Room of the hotel had been set aside for the press. The Kennedy Anchor Desk was established near this location. Several Kennedy workers stated that their specific assignments involved assisting or directing the media.

Because of the late returns of the primary, news items were slowing down by 10:30 p.m. Reporters in search of news followed Senator Kennedy wherever he went and photographed him whenever they could. It was rumored that some of the "writing press" were unhappy that they had no interviews with Kennedy and this was thought to be one of the reasons why Kennedy was going to the Colonial Room for a late night news conference. However, no newsmen reported being poorly treated by the Kennedy staff. Several newsmen actually observed the shooting and some assisted in the capture of Sirhan. Photographers took thousands of feet of film and video tape yet no one came forward with a photograph of the shooting.

The Victory Speech

Jesse Unruh, speaker of the California Assembly, spoke to the enthusiastic crowd. His legislative assistant, Jack Crose, had gone to Senator Kennedy's fifth floor suite to ask the Senator to come down to the ballroom. On the way to the elevator Kennedy told a Life Magazine correspondent to avoid the crowd and meet him in the Colonial Room after the speech. He told her that the Kennedy party was planning to go from the hotel to a private party at "The Factory," a Hollywood discotheque bar.

The small group accompanying Kennedy took a service elevator to the kitchen area at Kennedy's request so that they could avoid the crowd in the lobby of the hotel. They then walked through the employee's lunch area and Kennedy stopped to shake hands with numerous people and he autographed a poster for an admirer. Kennedy entered the Embassy Ballroom through an honor guard of Kennedy Girls, and onto the stage. The time was 12:02 a.m.

The stage area was packed as Kennedy delivered a victory message to an audience of about 1500 persons in the crowded auditorium. Lights from the news cameras heated the already hot room. As Kennedy finished his speech one of his aides said, "This way Senator," and a small group, including Kennedy, walked to the rear of the stage and through the door to an anteroom. The decision to go through the anteroom and serving pantry area was made moments before by Fred Dutton and William Barry. Both men attempted to catch up with Kennedy as he moved quickly toward the Colonial Room where the "writing press" was awaiting his arrival. Mrs. Kennedy remarked to Barry as they walked away from the stage, "stay with the Senator."

A large crowd of people surged around Kennedy as he made his way toward the pantry area. Several persons noted that Kennedy was walking "quite fast." Kennedy stopped for a brief moment to shake hands with the kitchen help. Karl Uecker, a hotel waiter captain, was with Kennedy as he walked from the stage to the pantry and took his arm to assist him toward the Colonial Room.

Vincent Di Pierro, a college student and son of the hotel maître d', was walking to the right of Kennedy and about five feet behind him. He observed a man standing on a tray rack at the east end of the ice machine. He recalled that the man had an unusual smile on his face and appeared to be bending over others thought the sounds were firecrackers. The accounts of the distance from the suspect and Kennedy varied. A hotel busboy thought the gun was three feet from Kennedy's head. Another witness thought the first shot came from point blank range. Subsequent laboratory examination placed the distance of the first and fatal shot at one inch.

The Capture

Karl Uecker swung around as Kennedy fell to the floor. Uecker seized the man by the neck and struck at his hand to push the gun away from the crowd; while several others close by reached out to control him. The man was wrestled to a nearby metal table and the gun fell from his hand for a moment. He was able to regain possession of the gun.

Roosevelt Grier, an ex-professional football player, approached the struggling group. He wrestled the gun from the man's hand and gave it to Rafer Johnson who was standing nearby. The men holding the man then pinned him to the serving table and held him there until the police arrived. During the struggle the suspect received minor injuries to his ankle and right hand. These were later treated at Homicide Division.

William Barry who was several feet behind Kennedy when the shots were fired told investigators that when he reached the suspect that no one was holding him. He stated that he took the gun from him and struck him twice in the face with his fist. He said that the suspect later retrieved the gun and others in the crowd assisted him in controlling the suspect. The investigation disclosed, however, that by the time Barry reached the suspect

holding his right hand against his stomach. Di Pierro looked away and turned toward Kennedy.

The Shooting

Kennedy stopped to shake hands with a hotel waiter and then with Di Pierro. As he let go of the hand of Jesus Perez, another hotel employee, a man moved toward Kennedy; his right arm fully extended, he fired four shots quickly at the Senator. Kennedy raised his arms over his head and two of the shots entered under his right arm. The first shot had struck him in the head behind the right ear; the second went through the padding of Kennedy's coat and struck Paul Schrade, United Automobile Workers Union official, in the head.

Witnesses' recollections of the shooting varied. One thought the man was going to shake hands with the Senator. Another saw the man raise a pistol and saw an "angry and determined" look in his face. One witness saw the man push the gun toward the back of Kennedy's head but could not identify the suspect because of the chaos that followed. A thirteen year old Kennedy worker saw the man holding the gun and then he saw a flame come from it.

Uecker immediately grabbed the man as he fired the first shots. He continued firing at Kennedy and one witness recalled that "he had a tremendous look of concentration on his face." He fired eight shots; the last four while the confused crowd tried to apprehend him. Five others were wounded in the shooting.

Many witnesses thought that they heard balloons popping and

several others had hold of him.

Medical Treatment of Senator Kennedy

Several doctors indentified themselves immediately and offerred to aid the victims of the shooting. Dr. Stanley Abo was the first to treat Kennedy. He found his heartbeat very strong, his pulse rate between 50 and 60 and his breath shallow. His left eye was closed.

When Abo told Kennedy that he thought that Stephen Smith, Kennedy's brother-in-law, had only a superficial wound. Kennedy replied, "Good." It was later learned that Smith had not been shot.

Abo found a small entry wound in back of Kennedy's right ear. At one point Abo tried to open Kennedy's left eyelid but he resisted. Later Kennedy looked around the room and recognized his wife who was kneeling near him. He called her name several times and he was able to move his hands and feet.

Abo noted that Kennedy's only apparent impairment was to his right eye. During the time that he treated Kennedy the only medical function performed was to keep the wound bleeding to prevent a clot from forming.

Dr. Marvin Esher also treated Kennedy and believed that Kennedy had sustained a cardiac arrest. He observed that Kennedy's left eyelid was closed and his right eye was open with the eyeball slightly deviated to the right. He noted that there was no visible movement in Kennedy's chest.

Removal from Hotel

A Los Angeles City Receiving Hospital ambulance was dispatched from Central Receiving Hospital at 12:18 a.m., and covered the 2.2 miles to the hotel in five minutes. The driver and attendant were directed to the pantry but due to the crowd jammed around Kennedy they were unable to open their first aid kit to provide emergency aid.

Kennedy was placed on a stretcher and carried to the ambulance. The doors to the ambulance were forcibly reopened twice by persons in the crowd who attempted to board the ambulance. William Barry and Warren Rogers, a Look Magazine editor, rode in the cab with the driver; Mrs. Kennedy, Fred Dutton, and Mrs. Stephen Smith were in the rear with Kennedy and the attendant. The ambulance left the hotel escorted by a police vehicle.

En route to the hospital the attendant attempted to stop the flow of blood from the head wound of Kennedy. [redacted] The scene in the ambulance was chaotic and tempers were very short. [redacted] Kennedy began gasping and the attendant administered oxygen. The ambulance arrived at Central Receiving Hospital at 12:30 a.m.

Treatment at Central Receiving Hospital

Preparations had been made in Emergency Room Two prior to the arrival of the ambulance containing Kennedy. Dr. Faustin Bazilauskas, a staff surgeon, met the ambulance and supervised the move of Kennedy to the treatment room. His initial diagnosis was: A comatose, weak thready pulse, in extremis, blood pressure zero over zero, heartbeat almost imperceptible, bullet wound right mastoid area with swelling, and in shock. Emergency treatment was given and decisions were made regarding the need for post-emergency treatment.

Dr. Albert Holt, of the Receiving Hospital staff, made a cursory examination of Kennedy. He found two bullet wounds and gave the opinion that Kennedy required immediate brain surgery. He recommended Dr. Henry Cueno to Mrs. Kennedy who was present in the room. Several other specialists were notified in antici- pation of injury to other areas of the Senator's body. Blood samples were sent to Good Samaritan Hospital for preparation at that location for the transfer of Kennedy.

Emergency treatment continued and a heart-lung machine was installed to assist Kennedy's respiration. Adrenalin was injected into Kennedy's arm. Kennedy was then out of shock, still comatose with hyperactive reflexes. The doctors found that the Senator had responded favorably to treatment but his condition was nevertheless critical. His blood pressure was 150/90 and he continued to receive oxygen by nasal mask and he was given serum albumen intravenously.

Transfer to Good Samaritan Hospital

Senator Kennedy was moved to an ambulance at 12:45 a.m., and the vehicle carrying Kennedy, his wife, Mrs. Smith, Barry and Warren Rogers arrived at Good Samaritan Hospital at 12:48 a.m. Kennedy was taken to the intensive care ward still unconscious and unresponsive. He showed evidence of brain injury and other symptoms indicated the need for a tracheotomy.

Dr. Paul Ironside performed the tracheotomy and his breathing improved; however, two minutes later Kennedy's breathing stopped and he was placed under a respirator.

Dr. Henry Cueno arrived at the hospital end was briefed by Dr. Holt. X-rays were taken of the head and chest area. According to all of the doctors the prognosis was extremely poor and they all agreed that they were dealing with an "absolute disaster."

The Operation

Surgery was begun at 3:10 a.m. The wound area was shaved and a small window was cut in the skull to facilitate a larger area to operate. Bone fragments, clotted blood and bruised brain tissue were removed by Dr. Cueno. Some of the lead fragments were identifiable as being from a bullet.

During surgery Kennedy's condition improved slightly and he was able to breath on his own. He was able to move his right leg but he was still comatose. Surgery was terminated at 6:10 a.m., and the respirator was reapplied when his breathing became labored.

Dr. James L. Poppen, the Kennedy family physician, arrived at 11 a.m. from Boston. He consulted with Dr. Cueno and periodic checks on Kennedy were made; the family was kept advised of Kennedy's condition. Twelve hours after the operation Kennedy's blood pressure had dropped to 80/20.

At 6:09 p.m., cardiac and kidney changes were noted and his pulse was slowing. This condition was considered terminal and only time was the remaining factor. At 8 p.m., Kennedy seemed to be stabilizing but by 1:15 a.m., on June 6th no blood pressure was noted. At 1:27 a.m., no breathing or heart sounds were recorded. At 1:44 a.m., Senator Robert F. Kennedy was pronounced dead.

The Autopsy on Senator Kennedy was conducted in the hospitals Morgue Room at 3 a.m., on June 6, 1968 and completed at 9:15 a.m. Dr. Thomas T. Noguchi, Chief Medical Examiner, Coroner of Los Angeles County, was in charge of the autopsy. The cause of death was a gunshot wound of the right mastoid, penetrating the brain.

Medical Treatment of Other Victims

Five others were wounded during the shooting. Each was in the line of fire in the crowd which was behind Kennedy.

Irwin Stroll, a Kennedy worker and student, was shot in the left leg but thought that he had been kicked. He ran into the Embassy Ballroom and realized that blood was running down his leg. He was treated at Central Receiving Hospital and discharged at 1:10 a.m. He was transferred to Midway Hospital in Los Angeles

where Dr. Nathan Cozen operated to remove a bullet from his left calf, next to the bone.

Paul Schrade, United Auto Workers Union Official, was walking directly behind Kennedy when the shooting occurred. He saw some flashes and lost consciousness. Witnesses reported observing him fall to the floor and several believed that he was dead. Schrade was bleeding profusely from a scalp wound. Dr. Abo made a quick examination of Schrade and determined that the wound appeared superficial.

Schrade was treated at Central Receiving Hospital for a bullet wound to the head and discharged at 1:27 a.m. He was treated at Kaiser Hospital in Los Angeles by Dr. Kasper Fuchs at 3 a.m. Examination revealed that the bullet entered behind the hair line and exited two and-a-half inches to the rear. Shattered bone had been forced into the skull. An incision was made and damaged tissue and bullet fragments were removed. The wound was directly over the sagittal sinus. There was small hole in the skull at the entry which would heal.

William S. Weisel, American Broadcasting Company News Director, was walking approximately six feet behind Kennedy and felt three thumps in his side but was shot only once. He did not see the shooting. Weisel was transferred with Schrade from Central Receiving Hospital to Kaiser Hospital. At 2:30 a.m., Dr. William Neal operated and removed an identifiable .22 caliber bullet from Weisel's left side at a point three inches above the waist line.

Elizabeth Evans a self employed businesswoman, was standing inside the door of the pantry surrounded by a crowd of people. she bent over to retrieve a lost shoe and she heard noises like firecrackers. She then realized that she had been shot. A bullet had entered the false ceiling of the pantry and ricocheted downward striking her in the forehead. She was assisted to the Embassy Ballroom and given emergency aid by doctors present.

After treatment at Central Receiving Hospital Mrs. Evans was transferred to Huntington Memorial Hospital in Pasadena. The bullet did not penetrate or exit and x-rays revealed that the bullet flattened itself against the skull just under the skin of the forehead below the hairline. The bullet was removed by Dr. John T. Garner at 1:10 p.m., on June 5, 1968.

Ira Marc Goldstein, a Continental News Service reporter, was struck in the upper thigh. He was attended at the scene by a doctor who found the wound to be not serious. After treatment at Central Receiving Hospital he was transferred to Encino Hospital in Los Angeles. The bullet was removed by Dr. Eugene Gettleman from the left buttocks about three inches from the point of entry. The deformed .22 caliber bullet was marked by Dr. Gettleman for identification.

Each of the five victims recovered from the shooting and participated in a reenactment of the shooting in November 1968. It was determined that Schrade was struck by a bullet which went through the padding of Kennedy's coat. Weisel and Goldstein were struck directly by bullets from the gun. The bullet which

struck Stroll ricochetted from the floor of the pantry and the bullet which struck Evans left the gun, travelled through the false ceiling and ricochetted back into the pantry, striking her in the head.

Police Department Participation

Los Angeles Police Department personnel participated fully in the activities which took place from the time of the assassination through the transportation of Senator Kennedy's body to International Airport. A section of this report chronologically recounts the various aspects of the events occurring between 12:06 a.m., on June 5, 1968 and 2:30 p.m., on June 6, 1968. These activities are described separately in sections entitled: ACTIVITIES AT THE HOTEL, CENTRAL RECEIVING, GOOD SAMARITAN HOSPITAL TO THE LOS ANGELES INTERNATIONAL AIRPORT, EMERGENCY CONTROL CENTER, FUNCTIONS OF RAMPART PATROL AND DETECTIVES AND PARKER CENTER SECURITY.

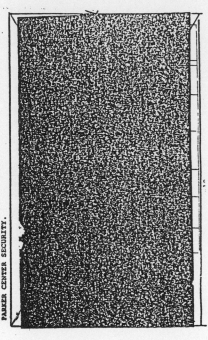

The total complement of personnel for each aspect was compiled and rosters are included in the respective section. The number of personnel deployed is reflected in the chart above.

Activities of The Ambassador Hotel

At 12:06 a.m. on June 5, 1968, a Rampart Division radio car responded to the Ambassador Hotel on a call on an illegally parked car. Within moments these officers were engulfed in the scene surrounding the shooting.

At 12:17 a.m., an unidentified caller notified the Rampart Division Watch Commander that Kennedy had just been shot. Lieutenant R. K. Sillings immediately went to the hotel to investigate the call. At 12:19 a.m., the only unit available in Rampart, Sergeant P. Sharaga, was assigned to a routine "ambulance injury" call at the hotel.

At 12:20 a.m., the emergency message that Senator Kennedy had been shot, was broadcast to all units. At 12:22 a.m., a Rampart radio car and three Metropolitan Division officers arrived at the front of the hotel. The five officers were directed by People in the crowd through a maze of hallways to the pantry area where they observed Senator Kennedy lying on the floor.

They immediately attempted to locate the suspect and observed a struggle at the east end of the crowded pantry. Two of the officers had separated from the group and were running into the pantry from the east end.

As Officer T. R. White entered the pantry he observed numerous persons struggling with a dark complexioned male near a serving table. A male in the crowd yelled to White, "Quick, he's trying to kill him." As the five officers attempted to move toward the suspect they were forced to pull the men surrounding him away.

Jesse Unruh, Speaker of the California Assembly, was on top of the serving table yelling, "This one's going to stand trial. No one's going to kill him." The officers managed to gain control of the suspect and handcuff his hands behind his back. The officers then prepared to remove the suspect from the crowded pantry to their vehicle.

The near hysterical crowd appeared to be a potential hazard to the suspect's safety and in a loud voice White ordered the others to start moving out of the room. Unruh moved toward the officers and White, fearing for the suspect's safety, pushed him away; Unruh yielded but insisted that he escort the officers from the building.

The officers formed a tight circle around the suspect and moved through the crowd. Several persons shouted obscenities at the suspect and attempted to strike out at him. The officers absorbed the brunt of these blows.

As the officers reached their vehicles they were assisted by other officers who had arrived at the hotel. The crowd around the vehicle prevented the officers from getting into their vehicles. Unruh, without permission, climbed into the front seat of the vehicle. Eventually the officers were able to drive through the crowd. The time was 12:28 a.m., six minutes from the time they arrived.

White and his partner, A. Placencia, drove immediately to Rampart Station arriving at 12:31 a.m. En route, Placencia, in the rear seat with the suspect, advised him of his constitutional rights. Unruh asked the suspect why he had shot Kennedy. He replied, "You think I'm crazy, so that you can use it as evidence against me?"

Upon arrival at the station the suspect was placed in an interrogation room; he was searched and his personal property was removed from his clothing. An officer was placed in the room to provide security for the suspect.

At the hotel measures were being taken to secure the crime scene and secure witnesses. Security measures were taken to obtain information on potential suspects who might be outstanding. Units arriving from throughout the Metropolitan area began deploying about the hotel. All available Metropolitan Division officers were deployed to the rear of the hotel. Traffic control measures were taken surrounding the hotel.

At 12:28 a.m., Sergeant Sharaga broadcast a description of a blond male Caucasian suspect which had been given to him by an unknown person. At 1:44 a.m., this description was cancelled and the suspect was no longer sought. At the same time two Juvenile Division officers broadcast the description of a male Latin and a female Caucasian wanted as suspects.

Lieutenant R. Tackaberry commanded a squad of officers dispatched to Central Receiving Hospital to provide security at that location. Officers at various locations were requesting ambulances for the other victims of the shooting. Private ambulances were enlisted to aid in this effort.

Lieutenant Sillings arrived at the Command Post which Sharaga had established at the rear of the hotel at 12:23 a.m. Sillings instructed that an outside security perimeter be established and sent Sergeant R. Rolon and J. Jones into the hotel with seven men to secure the crime scene. Upon arriving in the Embassy Ballroom they noted the complete disarray. Jones used the public address system in an attempt to calm the hysterical crowd and to advise witnesses to report to the podium. Names were taken by officers of persons stating that they had seen relevant events.

Several minor incidents occurred in the next few minutes involving hysterical members of the crowd, the press and the officers who were attempting to bring order to the confusion. Quarrels were broken up, suspicious individuals were stopped and questioned and assistance was provided to the shocked celebrants. The bars were ordered closed as soon as possible after order was restored.

A contingent of Los Angeles County Sheriff's deputies was dispatched from assignment at the nearby IBM Building where they had been providing security for ballot counting. These deputies provided assistance to Sergeant Sharaga at the Command Post.

became an information center and telephones were temporarily installed. At 8 a.m. day watch officers began relieving morning watch officers at the hotel.

For the remainder of the morning, routine security was maintained at the hotel. By 10:05 a.m., relief of all morning and mid-watch officers was completed. At 12:15 a.m., the staging area outside the hotel was deactivated and a small force consisting of sixteen officers and a policewoman commanded by a sergeant remained at the hotel.

At 2:45 p.m., the commander of the Emergency Control Center instructed Sergeant C. C. Hagele to deactivate the entire security force. By 3:10 p.m., on June 5, 1968, the detail at the hotel was completely secure.

Central Receiving Hospital

At 12:28 a.m., members of the press and sight-seers began converging on Central Receiving Hospital en masse. Officer G. F. Tinch, assigned to the hospital detail at the hospital had been informed of the shooting and was requesting assistance for security.

At 12:30 a.m., the ambulance bearing Senator Kennedy arrived preceded by two officers who had driven from the hotel. A passage way was cleared through the mob around the stretcher and Kennedy was placed in Treatment Room #2.

A large crowd began milling in the corridor outside the room. Officers W. W. Ambrecht and F. Mena were assigned to the treatment room to prevent unauthorized persons from entering. A

At 2:25 a.m., all Sheriff's personnel at the hotel were relieved by Department personnel

At 1:44 a.m., Inspector J. W. Powers contacted the Command Post and clarified the situation regarding outstanding suspects. At that time information from witnesses indicated that there was only one suspect involved in the shooting and that he was in custody. Other possible leads had been checked and found erroneous. Communications Division was instructed to cancel the broadcast on the "second suspect."

At 2:20 a.m., a Satellite Command Post was established in the Embassy Ballroom. Sergeant J. Jones supervised the activities at the location. Witnesses who had been singled out as being important were transported by bus and radio car to Rampart Station. Jones was also responsible for clearing the area of the shooting scene and preserving as much as possible for investigators and scientific investigation units.

At 3:30 a.m., Sergeant R. Rolon was assigned to clear unauthorized persons from the fifth floor of the hotel, the location of the Kennedy suite. These efforts were hampered by the presence of a crowd of young adults, many of whom were intoxicated. This incident was resolved and guards were posted in the area.

The emphasis of the event had shifted to other locations L 6 a.m., and the Command Post was moved inside at 8:40 a.m. It

Exhibit 20
Official Autopsy Report

LAPD S.R.

MEDICOLEGAL INVESTIGATION

ON THE

DEATH OF

SENATOR ROBERT F. KENNEDY

THOMAS T. NOGUCHI, M.D.

DEPARTMENT OF CHIEF MEDICAL EXAMINER-CORONER
COUNTY OF LOS ANGELES

TABLE OF CONTENTS

REPORT ON THE MEDICOLEGAL INVESTIGATION
OF SENATOR ROBERT F. KENNEDY

COUNTY OF LOS ANGELES
DEPARTMENT OF CHIEF MEDICAL EXAMINER—CORONER

HALL OF JUSTICE, LOS ANGELES, CALIFORNIA 90012
THOMAS T. NOGUCHI, M.D.
CHIEF MEDICAL EXAMINER-CORONER

File 68-5731

This is to certify that the autopsy on the body of Senator Robert F. Kennedy was performed at The Hospital of The Good Samaritan, Los Angeles, California, by the staff of the Department of Chief Medical Examiner-Coroner on June 6, 1968.

From the anatomic findings and pertinent history, I ascribe the death to:

GUNSHOT WOUND OF RIGHT MASTOID, PENETRATING BRAIN.

The detailed medical findings, opinions and conclusions required by Section 27491.4 of the Government Code of California are attached.

Thomas T. Noguchi, M.D.
Chief Medical Examiner-Coroner

TTN:etf

Robert · Kennedy
68-5731

FINAL SUMMARY

GUNSHOT WOUND NO. 1 (FATAL GUNSHOT WOUND)

ENTRY: Right mastoid region.

COURSE: Skin of right mastoid region, right mastoid, petrous portion of right temporal bone, right temporal lobe, and right hemisphere of cerebellum.

EXIT: None.

DIRECTION: Right to left, slightly to front, upward.

BULLET RECOVERY: Fragments (see text).

LESIONS IN DETAIL (NEUROPATHOLOGY)

A. Primary lesions — Caused by the bullet and further injuries — by bone and bullet fragments.

  1. Bone, dura and dural sinus.

     a. Penetration of right mastoid process.
     b. Fracture of right petrous ridge.
     c. Severance of right petrosal sinus.
     d. Metal fragments in right temporal bone.

  2. Cerebrum.

     a. Contusion-laceration and hemorrhage of right temporal lobe.
     b. Intraventricular hemorrhage due to above.
     c. Metal and bone fragments in right temporal lobe.

  3. Cerebellum.

     a. Hemorrhagic tract and cavity in right cerebellar hemisphere.
     b. Metal and bone fragments in right cerebellar hemisphere.

B. Immediate Secondary Lesions.

  1. Bone Lesion.

     a. Fracture of right supraorbital plate.

2. Meningeal Lesions.

    a. Subdural hemorrhage.
    b. Subarachnoid hemorrhage.
    c. Laceration of right supraorbital dura.

3. Cerebral Lesions.

    a. Contusion-laceration of right orbital gyri.
    b. Contusion-laceration of right occipital lobe.
    c. Contusion of contralateral (left) inferior temporal gyrus.

4. Cerebellum.

    a. Hemorrhagic necrosis of cerebellar tonsils.

5. Brain Stem.

    a. Hemorrhage in midbrain.
    b. Hemorrhagic necrosis of left inferior olive of medulla.

6. Epidural hemorrhage of C1 and C2 vertebral level.

C. Later Secondary Lesions.

    1. Edema of brain and herniations.
    2. Subdural hemorrhage.
    3. Subarachnoid hemorrhage.
    4. Intracerebral and intraventricular hemorrhage.
    5. Hemorrhagic infarction of right temporal cortex.
    6. Intracerebellar and intraventricular hemorrhage.
    7. Petechial hemorrhages of thalami.
    8. Brain stem hemorrhage and early necrosis.
    9. Herniation of cerebellum through craniotomy wound.
    10. Early laminar necrosis of occipital lobe.

GUNSHOT WOUND NO. 2, THROUGH-AND-THROUGH.

    ENTRY: Right axillary region.

    COURSE: Soft tissue of right axilla and right infraclavicular region.

    EXIT: Right infraclavicular region.

    DIRECTION: Right to left, back to front, upward.

    BULLET RECOVERY: None.

GUNSHOT WOUND NO. 3.

    ENTRY: Right axillary region (just below Gunshot Wound No. 2 entry).

    COURSE: Soft tissue of right axilla, soft tissue of right upper back to the level of the 6th cervical vertebra just beneath the skin.

    EXIT: None.

    DIRECTION: Right to left, back to front, upward.

    BULLET RECOVERY: .22 caliber bullet from the soft tissue of paracervical region at level of 6th cervical vertebra at 8:40 A.M., June 6, 1968.

EVIDENCE OF RECENT SURGICAL PROCEDURES.

    1. Craniotomy, right temporal occipital.
    2. Other, minor surgical procedures are described elsewhere.

PATHOLOGIC FINDINGS RELATED TO GUNSHOT WOUND NO. 1.

    1. Hypostatic Pneumonia.

MISCELLANEOUS PATHOLOGIC FINDINGS NOT RELATED TO CAUSE OF DEATH.

    1. Adenoma of left kidney (benign).
    2. Retention cyst of left kidney.

DESCRIPTION OF GUNSHOT WOUNDS

GUNSHOT WOUND NO. 1:

The wound of entry, as designated by Maxwell M. Andler, Jr., M.D., Neurosurgeon attending the autopsy, and more or less evident by inspection of the apposed craniotomy incision, is centered 5 inches (12.7 cm) from the vertex, about 3/4 inch (1.9 cm) posterior to the center of the right external auditory meatus, about 3/4 inch (1.9 cm) superior to the Reid line, and 2-1/2 inches (6.4 cm) anterior to a coronal plane passing through the occipital protuberance at its scalp-covered aspect. The defect appears to have been about 3/16 inch (0.5 cm) in diameter at the skin surface. The surgical incision passing through the area of the wound of entry has been fashioned in a semilunar configuration with the concavity directed inferiorly and posteriorly. The incision has been intactly sutured by metallic and other material. The arc length is about 4 inches (10 cm).

Further detailed description of the area is given elsewhere in this report.

Varyingly moderate degrees of very recent hemorrhage are noted in the soft tissue inferior to the right mastoid region, extending medially as well. There is no hematoma in the soft tissue.

In conjunction with the wound of entry, the right external ear shows, on the posterior aspect of the helix, an irregularly fusiform zone of dark red and gray stippling about one inch (2.5 cm) in greatest dimension, along the posterior cartilaginous border and over a maximum width of about 1/4 inch (0.6 cm) at the midportion of the stippled zone. This widest zone of stippling is approximately along a radius originating from the wound of entry in the right mastoid region. Moderate edema and variable ecchymosis is present in the associated portions of right external ear as well.

No evidence of powder burn, tattoo, or stippling is found in the area surrounding the wound of entry of Gunshot Wound No.1, to include an arbitrary circular zone superimposed upon the above-described stippling on the right ear.

LESIONS IN DETAIL (NEUROPATHOLOGY)

A. Scalp and Cranium.

A U-shaped recent surgical wound is present over the right temporo-occipital region of the recently shaved scalp behind the right ear. Many wire sutures are in place. About 2 cm. above the tip of the mastoid process immediately behind the pinna at about the level of the external auditory meatus, the anterior portion of the skin of the incision shows a semi-circular defect said to be a portion of the original bullet entrance wound (according to the surgeons who were present at the examination). After removing the wire sutures, the scalp is incised by the usual mastoid-to-right mastoid incision across the vertex. The incision on the right is extended into the surgical incision mentioned above. After reflecting the scalp, dark red subcutaneous and subgaleal hemorrhages are found in the right temporo-occipital region overlying and around the wound and the surgical craniotomy over an area measuring 9.5 x 10 cm. The hemorrhage ranges up to 3 mm in thickness. The right temporal muscle shows a small amount of hemorrhage along its posterior aspect.

The bony defect of the cranium included the superior portions of the right mastoid process and the adjacent temporo-occipital bones in an irregularly oval area measuring 6 x 5 cm. Gelfoam and hemorrhagic material is removed from the craniotomy site.

A circumferential cut with three notches is made in the calvarium with a vibratory saw. The calvarium is removed from the underlying dura. There is no lesion in this portion of the cranium.

The bone surrounding the craniotomy is removed in a single piece, including the posterior half of the right external auditory canal. The bullet wound in the skull appears to be located with its anterior margin 1 cm posterior to the right external auditory meatus, 2 cm superior to the tip of the mastoid process; but the original configuration is obscured by the surgical enlargement and by the adjacent craniotomy. The surgical opening of the right temporo-occipital bone measures 6 cm anteroposteriorly and 5 cm supero-inferiorly. Burr holes, saw cuts, and rongeur cuts can be seen along the margins of the bone.

The bullet wound of the mastoid extends medially to the base of the petrous portion where there is a triangular defect with the base of the triangle corresponding to the petrous ridge and measuring 8 mm in width.

A curved fracture about 1 cm long is found in the central thinnest portion of the right supra-orbital plate with intra-orbital hemorrhage beneath it surrounding the right eye. A laceration of the dura and contusion of the right orbital gyri are located above the fracture.

B. Meninges, blood vessels and cranial nerves.

In the dorsolateral aspect of the subdural space there is a

film of blood up to 1 mm thick, covering the arachnoid over both posterior frontal and parico-occipital regions and extending downward to, and in some places below the sylvian fissure bilaterally, slightly more on the left side than on the right. Similar blood clot is also found on the left middle fossa and in both posterior fossae, again more on the left side. A small amount of blood clot, about 2 cc, is found between the cerebral hemispheres just dorsal to the midbrain.

Rather diffuse subarachnoid hemorrhage is present over the parieto-occipital regions, over the dorsal and right side of the cerebellum and also over the ventral surface of the pons and medulla. All of this, however, is quite slight and the blood clot does not obscure the underlying structures.

Epidural hemorrhages are found in the following three locations:

1. Adjacent to the craniotomy defect of the right temporo-occipital region. This is minimal and extends not more than 1 cm from the surgical incision and it is less than 1 mm in thickness.

2. Above the right supraorbital plate where the fracture is present as described above. This is deemed minimal and less than 1 mm in thickness covering an area 1.5 x 1 cm.

3. Epidural hemorrhage measuring 2 cm longitudinally and 1 cm transversely is found in the dorsal aspect of the epidural space at C1 and C2 vertebral levels.

The dorsal veins which empty into the superior saggital sinus are inspected but they reveal no evidence of the source of subdural hemorrhage.

The right superior petrosal sinus is severed for a distance of 8 mm corresponding to the defect of the petrous ridge mentioned above. The remainder of this sinus adjacent to the defect has been cauterized. The tentorium which has its attachment to the right petrous ridge is lacerated where the bony defect is present. This laceration of the dura is continued laterally and communicates with the surgical defect which measures 4.5 x 2.0 cm just anterior to the right sigmoid sinus and above the transverse sinus beneath the craniotomy opening. A second surgical defect is present on the dura posterior to the sigmoid sinus and inferior to the transverse sinus and this measures 1 x 2 cm. There are areas of brownish discoloration and a minimal amount of blood clot is scattered along the margins of these dural openings.

The lateral portion of the transverse sinus and the sigmoid sinus thus traverse the craniotomy defect horizontally through its posterior portion and vertically through its inferior portion.

The tentorium cerebelli shows no defects in its central portions.

The dura was lacerated over a small area over the right supra-orbital plate where a curved fracture was present as mentioned above.

The superior saggital sinus, left transverse sinus, left sigmoid sinus and cavernous sinuses are inspected and reveal no evidence of thrombosis or laceration. The right transverse and sigmoid sinuses do not appear to be damaged in spite of their proximity to the dural openings anterior and posterior to it, but cautery marks are on and close to these sinuses which contain dark red blood clot.

Examination of the arteries of the brain stem and cerebellum reveals a right vertebral artery that is smaller than the left. The basilar artery measures 3 mm in diameter and is slightly tortuous. The anterior inferior cerebellar arteries and the posterior inferior cerebellar arteries have a normal distribution and show no evidence of traumatic injury. The left superior cerebellar artery is intact. The right superior cerebellar artery is intact throughout its main trunk but several of its superficial branches are involved in the cortical contusion and laceration of the cerebellum and many of its deeper branches have been damaged by the penetrating bullet and bone fragments.

All of the remaining blood vessels of the brain stem, cerebellum and cerebral hemispheres have normal distribution and show very slight atherosclerosis. There is no evidence of injury except for the areas of contusions and lacerations.

The cranial nerves are all intact.

C. Cerebrum.

Slight depression of the cerebral cortex is noted over both posterior frontal and parietal convexities in the areas beneath the subdural hemorrhage that is described above. The right cerebral hemisphere is slightly larger than the left with shallow tentorium grooves over both unci, slightly more prominent on the right than on the left. However, there is no evidence of herniation of the cingulate gyri beneath the falx. The gyri over both cerebral convexities are flattened.

When the brain is inspected from the ventral aspect, three areas of contusion-laceration can be seen in the cortex of the right cerebral hemisphere and a fourth area of contusion on the left. The largest one measures 4 x 3 cm. It consists of superficial and deep lacerations and contusions of the medial half of the posterior one-third of the right inferior temporal gyrus for an anteroposterior distance of 4 cm; the middle third of the right fusiform gyrus for 3 cm and the lateral portion of the hippocampal gyrus for a distance of about 1 cm. Coronal sections show that this laceration has a subcortical hemorrhage extending 1.5 cm into the subcortical white matter to the floor of the posterior part of the temporal horn of the right lateral ventricle with rupture into this cavity. The medial portions of the temporal lesion are characteristic of laceration and contusion while the lateral portions of this lesion are quite characteristic of hemorrhagic infarction.

The second largest contusion is in the middle part of the right orbital gyri and measures 1.5 x 1.0 cm with a 5 mm-curved transverse laceration within it. Hemorrhage extends into the subcortical white matter to a depth of 6 mm. This lesion overlies the lacerated dura and fracture of the right supraorbital plate.

The third contusion measures 14 x 7 mm with a linear 6 mm transverse laceration and is situated in the mesial portion of the inferior part of the right occipital cortex.

The fourth contusion of the cortex is a very small lesion in the middle of the left inferior temporal gyrus and measures 5 x 2 mm. There is no laceration in this area. This condition is limited to the gray matter.

D. Cerebellum.

In the anterior and lateral aspects of the right hemisphere of the cerebellum, there is an irregular penetrating wound. The opening measures 2 x 2 cm with irregular margins. The margins of this wound and adjacent areas are elevated to form a ring of tissue at the bony margin, 2 mm distal to the internal bone surface. This indicates herniation of the cerebellar tissue into the bony defect. On the surface of this defect and in the bone incision, there are fragments of gelfoam and soft friable blood clots.

A partially collapsed linear tract measuring 5 cm in length extends from the cerebellar cortex and subcortical white matter of the cerebellum to the vermis. The tract begins just rostral to the tegmentum of the anterior one-third of the pons, anterior to the middle cerebellar peduncle and proceeds in a superior and posterior direction. From an imaginary transverse plane between the two mastoid bones, one would estimate that this tract proceeds about 45 degrees posteriorly and medially and 30 degrees superiorly from the mastoid perforation. The tract ends in the vermis of the cerebellum where a 1 cm transverse laceration is found in the region of the primary fissure which is approximately 3 cm posterior to the anterior cerebellar notch. At the termination of the tract, hemorrhage can be seen within the cortical laceration.

The size of the penetrating wound is difficult to determine at this time since the tract is largely filled by the swollen white matter of the cerebellum and by hemorrhage. However, probing into the tract at the entrance wound indicates that it was in the order of 2 cm in width at maximum expansion.

Upon palpation and probing in the region of the laceration in the superior vermis, a metallic fragment is found just beneath the arachnoid membrane and within an area of hemorrhage. This irregular gray metallic fragment measures 6 x 3 x 2 mm and corresponds to the largest fragment that was identified in the postoperative x-ray of a radiopaque object near the midline.

In addition to the penetrating wound and the laceration of the vermis at its terminal end, an area of contusion and hemorrhagic necrosis measuring 2.5 x 2.0 cm covers most of the superior surface of the right cerebellar hemisphere and extends 5 mm over the midline. Beneath this area of contusion and communicating with the penetrating wound, a recent hematoma is found that measures 2.5 x 2.0 cm. The hemorrhage involves the region of the declive, folium, and tuber. Smaller satellite contusions and hemorrhagic necrosis are scattered lateral to the large contusion of the superior surface of the cerebellum. Both cerebellar hemispheres are markedly swollen with flattened gyri and with a cerebellar pressure cone. Two small areas of hemorrhagic necrosis, each 3 mm in diameter, are present in the cortex of the herniated left cerebellar tonsil. The right cerebellar tonsil shows a single area of cortical hemorrhagic necrosis also 3 mm in diameter.

An elliptical groove over the superior surface of the anterior lobe of the cerebellum indicates upward herniation of these structures through the incisura of the tentorium cerebelli.

Horizontal sections of the cerebellum reveal the penetrating wound and the hemorrhage described above. These lesions have destroyed much of the cortex and subcortical white matter of the right cerebellar hemisphere, the dentate nuclei and probably the roof nuclei.

E. Brain Stem.

The ventral surface of the pons and medulla is markedly flattened.

The periaqueductal gray matter contains multiple petechial

There are 31 slides divided into three groups: A, B and C. Each group is again numbered as A-1, A-2, A-3, or B-1, B-2, B-3, B-4 and C-1, C-2, C-3, C-4, etc.

Sections confirmed all the lesions described at the gross examination.

All tissue sections show congestion and some extravasation with occasional actual petechial hemorrhages, the latter being particularly noticeable in the thalami near the ventricular walls. A few mononuclear cells are present in the perivascular spaces. The ground substance of the cerebral cortex and centrum shows fine vacuolations. In the occipital cortex, there is early status spongiosus, portions of which have a laminar distribution. Some nerve cells have pyknotic nuclei and homogenization of the cytoplasm, the latter showing definite eosinophilia. The white matter of the frontal lobe shows occasional areas of pallid staining. In the ventral pons there is early necrosis in addition to the hemorrhages.

A-1, RIGHT FRONTAL LOBE:

This section shows marked congestion of the meningeal and parenchymal blood vessels. The endothelium of the blood vessels shows hypertrophy. There is no inflammatory infiltrate in the meninges. There is a diffuse rarefaction of the matrix of the cortex and white matter, but more marked in the white matter where there are actual areas of early status spongiosus. Many of the nerve cells are pyknotic. The glial and ependymal elements are swollen.

A-2, LEFT FRONTAL LOBE:

Findings are similar to A-1, except that the status spongiosus of the white matter is not obvious.

A-3, RIGHT TEMPORAL LOBE - HIPPOCAMPUS:

Findings are similar to A-2.

A-4, LEFT TEMPORAL LOBE - HIPPOCAMPUS:

In addition to similar findings as in A-3, there are several small petechiae in the cortex. This section also shows slight subarachnoid hemorrhage.

A-5, RIGHT PARIETAL LOBE:

The general findings of these sections are similar to A-2. However, some nerve cells are not only pyknotic but they are also beginning to show eosinophilia of the contracted and homogenized cytoplasm.

hemorrhages extending over an area of 8-9 mm in width on the left side and about 5 mm on the right side. In sections above the pons, the midbrain reveals several irregular hemorrhages within the tegmentum. The largest of these hemorrhages is slit-like and measures 5 x 1 mm in size and is situated in the left lateral tegmentum. Numerous petechial hemorrhages are found throughout both the tegmental and ventral portions of the rostral 3/4 of the pons on multiple horizontal sections. Section through the medulla shows an area of hemorrhagic necrosis 4 x 3 mm in diameter located in the left inferior olive.

F. Ventricular System.

The lateral and third ventricles are moderately narrowed in size. They contain a small amount of blood clot totaling about 6 cc. The source of the intraventricular hemorrhage is due to rupture into the right inferior horn of the hemorrhage of the right temporal lobe. The fourth ventricle also contains a small amount of fresh blood clots.

G. Spinal Canal and Spinal Cord.

The foramen magnum and the upper cervical vertebrae are inspected and they show no abnormalities.

The bodies of the lower cervical, thoracic and upper lumbar vertebrae are removed in a column. After inspecting the spinal nerve roots, the cervical, thoracic and lumbar spinal cord is removed in toto.

A 41-cm portion of the spinal cord extending from the high cervical region into the lumbar region is examined. The leptomeninges are thin and transparent. The anterior spinal artery is thin-walled and shows no evidence of occlusion or laceration.

The posterior aspect of the spinal cord additionally reveals thin leptomeninges and normal distribution of vessels and nerve roots. There is no evidence of pathologic damage to the spinal cord. The subarachnoid space shows faint blood staining. Multiple transverse sections of the spinal cord and nerve roots show no gross lesions.

H. Pituitary Gland.

The diaphragma sella and pituitary stalk are normal in appearance. The pituitary gland measures 1.1 x 0.8 x 0.5 cm. Section shows a pink homogeneous anterior lobe and a reddish gray posterior lobe. The bony structures forming and surrounding the pituitary fossa are all within normal limits.

A-6, LEFT PARIETAL LOBE:

This slide shows findings similar to A-2. In addition, there is subarachnoid hemorrhage.

A-7, RIGHT OCCIPITAL LOBE:

This section shows marked congestion of all the blood vessels with extravasation of blood in the white matter. The cortex shows early status spongiosus, which has a suggestive laminar pattern.

A-8, LEFT OCCIPITAL LOBE:

This section shows findings similar to A-7 above. Some of the nerve cells are beginning to show eosinophilia of the cytoplasm.

A-9, RIGHT STRIATUM:

In general the blood vessels and nerve cells show changes of the cortex similar to those described in A-2. The subependymal blood vessels show a few mononuclear cells in the perivascular spaces. There is also some extravasation of blood from these vessels.

A-10, LEFT STRIATUM:

The findings are similar to A-9.

A-11, RIGHT LENTICULAR NUCLEUS:

The findings are similar to A-9 except the extravasation of blood is not obvious.

A-12, LEFT LENTICULAR NUCLEUS:

The findings are similar to A-11.

A-13, RIGHT THALAMUS:

These sections show generalized congestion and actual petechial hemorrhages in the walls of the third ventricle. The nerve cells show pyknotic changes. Portions of the matrix show early status spongiosus.

A-14, LEFT THALAMUS:

The findings are similar to A-13 but the petechial hemorrhages are not as marked.

A-15, -16, -17, and -18, SPINAL CORD:

Sections are taken from the cervical, thoracic and lumbosacral regions. The vascular changes in the meninges and spinal cord are minimal and certainly not as pronounced as those in the cerebrum. A few of the nerve cells in the grey matter, mostly in anterior horns, show pyknotic changes.

B-1, RIGHT TRANSVERSE SINUS:

Sections show red blood cells between the laminae of the dura. The sinus contains antemortem thrombus along the vessel walls. This thrombus consists mainly of platelets. In the remainder of the blood clot, there are numerous neutrophils.

B-2, RIGHT SIGMOID SINUS:

Portions of the dura show coagulation necrosis with tinctorial changes toward basophilia. Antemortem thrombus is also found in the sinus, as in B-1.

B-3, RIGHT FRONTAL LOBE - ORBITAL GYRI:

Sections show hemorrhagic necrosis of the cortex.

B-4, RIGHT TEMPORAL LOBE - PARAHIPPOCAMPAL AND FUSIFORM GYRI:

This section shows most extensive hemorrhagic defects, both in the grey and white matter. The defect communicates with the external surface. The remaining portions of the specimen show changes similar to A-2.

B-5, RIGHT TEMPORAL LOBE:

The findings are similar to B-4.

B-6, RIGHT OCCIPITAL LOBE, MEDIAL INFERIOR ASPECT:

Sections show superficial hemorrhagic defect of the cortex.

C-1, LEFT INFERIOR TEMPORAL LOBE:

This section shows multiple hemorrhagic necrosis in the cortex.

C-2, MIDBRAIN:

Section shows multiple hemorrhages. The cerebral aqueduct is patent.

C-3 AND C-4, PONS:

Sections show multiple hemorrhage, mostly in the ventral portions, and acute necrosis. The fourth ventricle is collapsed.

C-5, MEDULLA:

Focal hemorrhagic necrosis is present in the left inferior olive.

C-6, CEREBELLUM, DORSAL ASPECT:

This shows a large hemorrhagic defect with multiple petechial hemorrhages in portions of the dentate nucleus. In another portion of the dentate nucleus, where there is no hemorrhage, there is acute necrosis.

C-7, CEREBELLUM, TONSIL:

This shows multiple petechiae in the cortex.

ADDITIONAL MICROSCOPIC SLIDES (NEUROPATHOLOGY):

The Pineal Gland shows a few corpora amylacea.

Sections of the temporal lobe reveal essentially the same histopathological findings described previously.

SLIDE LABELED GUNSHOT WOUND (GSW #1), (Entrance Wound):

The perpendicular section, stained with hematoxylin and eosin, through the wound track shows loss of epithelium and patchy areas of swollen dermis.

The area of margins of squamous epithelium shows perinuclear vacuolation and spindle form distortion.

The dermis is extensively involved with coagulation also visible in special stain. The hair follicles and sebaceous glands are partly involved also. Capillaries are dilated. There are areas of extravasation and infiltration by acute inflammatory cells. Scattered, varying-sized powder residues are found in the keratin layer and the inner surface of the wound track to a depth of 2 mm. There are also disc-like powder granules embedded in the epidermis, and the powder-embedded area is surrounded by pink-staining denatured collagen. Powder residues are in an assortment of shapes and sizes, the edges showing minute crystalloid material which is also visible on the unstained sections.

Subcutaneous tissue and muscle elements are hemorrhagic and heavily infiltrated by neutrophils.

Microscopic Diagnosis:

Entry of the gunshot wound is consistent with very close range shooting.

SLIDE FROM POSTERIOR ASPECT OF HELIX OF RIGHT EAR, INCLUDING GROSSLY DESCRIBED POWDER SMUDGING AND TATTOOING:

The sections stained with hematoxylin and eosin show patchy areas of loss of epithelium due to thermal and blast effect. The squamous epithelium between the exposed coagulated dermis shows perinuclear vacuolation and nuclear elongation, along with fragmentation at the edges.

Dark brown to black powder residues in varying sizes are embedded through the epithelium to the dermis, which is also recognizable in unstained sections. The dermis shows extensive coagulation of the collagen tissue. Sweat glands and hair follicles, together with associated sebaceous glands, are involved with changes consistent with heat and blast effect. Coagulation of the collagen tissue is also visible on sections stained by Masson's method.

TTN:ATL:etf

DESCRIPTION OF PRE-OPERATIVE X-RAYS

Anteroposterior and lateral portable films of the skull, exposed on June 5, 1968 at approximately 1:00 A.M., reveal a gunshot wound of the right temporal bone. The wound of entry is 2.0 cm above the temporal tip and approximately midway between the external auditory canal and the sigmoid sinus region, approximately 1.0 cm posterior to the auditory canal.

There are two bullet tracks. One extends slightly anterior to the vertical dimension (15 degrees). The second extends 30 degrees posterior to the vertical dimension, so that the two tracks diverge 45 degrees.

In the frontal projection, both tracks extend superiorly toward the vertex at an angle of 30 degrees to the horizontal.

In the tracks of the bullet wound are numerous metallic foreign bodies and fragments of the mastoid. The largest metallic fragment is situated in the petrous ridge and at about the arcuate eminence. This measures 12 mm in transverse dimension, 7 mm in vertical dimension, and approximately 12 mm in antero-posterior dimension.

Several metallic foreign bodies are present in the soft tissues lateral to the mastoid process. Twelve metallic foreign bodies, one millimeter or larger, are present in the mastoid process. In addition to the largest fragment described, at least thirty metallic fragments one millimeter or larger are present in the posterior fossa.

One fragment of bone and several metallic fragments projected through the orbit above the petrous ridge are, I believe, supratentorial, and in the mesial aspect of the temporal lobe posteriorly.

A fragment, 7 mm in transverse diameter, 4 mm in greatest anteroposterior dimension and vertical dimension, is situated superiorly slightly to the left of the midline and 4.0 cm anterior to the inner cortex of the occipital bone at or just below the tentorium.

The main fragments of the bullet are anterior to the sigmoid sinus as seen in the lateral projection, and this includes the major bony fragment as well.

DESCRIPTION OF POSTMORTEM RADIOGRAPHS

Postmortem radiographs exposed at 2:00 A.M. to 3:00 A.M., under the direction of the Chief Medical Examiner-Coroner, on June 6, 1968, reveal that a major portion of the petrous ridge has been removed, together with most of the metallic foreign bodies and the detached osseous fragments.

At this time, the metallic fragment most superior and posterior has shifted slightly posteriorly and to the right.

Small fragments remain in the soft tissues lateral to the temporal bone, numbering approximately eleven and very minute. Other fragments, approximately seven in number, are situated directly above the petrous apex and, I believe, supra-tentorial, in the temporal lobe. This represents the remains of the largest metallic fragment noted pre-operatively. Other minute fragments are present in the posterior fossa, numbering approximately twenty.

All of the bony fragments have been removed.

X-rays of the skull at the conclusion of the postmortem revealed that five minute metallic foreign bodies were present in the skin, and approximately twenty minute fragments remained embedded in the remaining portion of the temporal bone in the region of the semicircular canals.

DESCRIPTION OF SPECIMEN RADIOGRAPHS OF SURGICAL BONY SPECIMEN

A series of x-ray films was obtained on June 7, 1968 between 4:00 P.M. and 7:30 P.M.

The initial x-rays consisted of the fragments of temporal bone removed at surgery. These were exposed on industrial film-type M (Kodak) and reveal many more minute metallic foreign bodies than were evident on the early films. Pieces of bone identifiable as mastoid process are filled with approximately seventy individual metallic fragments. Others bearing the Rongeur marks are fragments of cortex removed at surgery from the craniotomy site. Other fragments represent petrous ridge and are also embedded with innumerable fine metallic particles.

The specimen of temporal bone removed at postmortem includes the craniotomy site and the remaining portion of the mastoid process extending posteriorly to include the lateral sinus groove and the facial canal distally. Mesially, the bone is amputated lateral to the cochlea. This contains the external auditory canal. Posterior and superior to the canal are many metallic fragments. These number at least sixty, the majority less than one millimeter in size, with ten above one millimeter.

DESCRIPTION OF SPECIMEN X-RAYS EXPOSED AT THE GOOD SAMARITAN HOSPITAL (Friday, June 7, 1968)

X-rays of the entire brain, taken initially in the vertex-base direction, reveal small metallic foreign bodies in the cerebellum and temporal lobe. There is a considerable defect of the cerebellum on the right. A small amount of residual contrast (Hypaque) is present in the arterial tree in the left temporal area.

Following the above, the individual sections were x-rayed and labeled respectively: A for the tips of the frontal lobes and successively posteriorly at 2.0 cm intervals, B; C (which includes the anterior aspect of the temporal lobes); and D; etc. E shows one metallic foreign body in the right temporal lobe, plus a defect in the mesial aspect of the temporal lobe in the region of the uncal gyrus. Residual contrast is in the choroid plexus of the lateral ventricle on the left.

Specimen labeled F consists of slice F plus the separate specimen F-1 from the temporal lobe, which contains ten minute metallic foreign bodies in one segment and three minute ones in another area. The cerebellum is also present which reveals a large defect and twenty minute metallic foreign bodies. The specimens of the brain, G and H, extending to the occipital pole, reveal no abnormality.

Separate x-rays were performed on specimen F and F-1 and the cerebellum, plus x-rays of the meninges. The meninges are tattooed with many metallic foreign bodies surrounding the defect, which is in the region of the original wound of entry.

These number fully fifty, with all but three or four under one millimeter in diameter.

TTN:RLS:etf

DESCRIPTION OF SKIN AND HAIR X-RAYS

X-rays of 68-5731 obtained at the Good Samaritan Hospital between 1:00 and 3:00 P.M., Saturday, June 8, 1968.

The right ear is portrayed in profile and en face. The profile shows the skin surface directed away from the identifying number. The larger side of the ear specimen is to the right in both projections.

Tattooed in the skin are many small metallic foreign bodies. Other foreign bodies are present in the ear which do not appear to be metallic.

Gunshot Wound No. 1 was examined in profile with the cutaneous surface directed toward the number. Two fragments of the wound are present. Both reveal metallic foreign bodies of varying size from barely visible to 1 mm in diameter in the subcutaneous tissue. Many minute foreign bodies are present in the skin superficially surrounding the wound of entry. These resemble in size the particles seen in the ear.

The skin of Gunshot Wound No. 2 and Gunshot Wound No. 3 also reveals the superficial dense metallic impregnation of the skin with several metallic foreign bodies in the subcutaneous tissue. These specimens are also arranged in profile with the cutaneous surface extending toward the identifying number.

The third examination is of the scalp hair obtained prior to surgery. In this area, many dust-like metallic particles are evident, varying in size but all extremely small and differing appreciably from the several artifacts noticed to the left of the label "scalp hair" on the superior aspect of the film.

Three metallic particles are noted in the hair obtained at autopsy. Two of these are extremely minute and one is approximately .5 mm in diameter.

TTN:RLS:etf

DESCRIPTION OF X-RAYS OF SKIN WOUNDS

X-rays were obtained of the skin wounds, which are labeled 1, 2, and 3.

GUNSHOT WOUND NO. 1:

A profile view of the skin surrounding wound of entry in the right mastoid area reveals a few metallic foreign bodies superficially and other larger foreign bodies (1 cm.) in the subcutaneous tissue.

GUNSHOT WOUNDS NOS. 2 AND 3:

A frontal projection of the axillary skin surrounding wounds labeled 2 and 3 reveals fine metallic foreign bodies in both these situations.

The wound of exit is placed in profile. Wound 2 reveals two minute metallic foreign bodies barely visible in the subcutaneous tissue below the wound.

TTN:RLS:etf

HEAD AND NERVOUS SYSTEM (Generally):

Also revealed by the reflection of the scalp is a fairly well demarcated area of non-recent hemorrhagic discoloration, about 1.5 cm in greatest dimension, in the left parietal occipital region. No associated galeal hemorrhage is demonstrated.

The cerebrospinal fluid is blood tinged.

Abundant and freshly clotted but drying blood is found at the right external auditory canal, extending outward to the lateral interstices of the external ear. No evidence of hemorrhage is found at the left ear.

The spinal cord is taken for further evaluation. At the time of removal of the cord, a small amount of cervical epidural hemorrhage is noted. There is no evidence, on preliminary inspection, of avulsion of roots leading to the right brachial plexus.

Those portions of peripheral nervous system exposed by the described dissection show no abnormality.

TTN:JEH:etf

GUNSHOT WOUND NO. 2:

This is a through-and-through wound of the right axillary, medial shoulder, and anterior superior chest areas, excluding the thorax proper. The wound of entry is centered 12-1/2 inches (31.8 cm) from the vertex, 9 inches (22.9 cm) to the back right of midline, and 3-3/4 inches (8.3 cm) from the back (anterior to a coronal plane passing through the surface of the skin at the scapula region). There is a regularly elliptical defect 3/16 x 1/8 inch over-all (about 0.5 x 0.3 cm) with thin rim of abrasion. There is no apparent charring or powder residue in the adjacent and subjacent tissue. The subcutaneous fatty tissue is hemorrhagic.

The wound path is through soft tissue, medially to the left, superiorly and somewhat anteriorly. Bony structures, major blood vessels and the brachial plexus have been spared.

The exit wound is centered 9-3/4 inches (about 24.5 cm) from the vertex and about 5 inches (about 12.5 cm) to the right of midline anteriorly in the infraclavicular region. There is a nearly circular defect slightly less than 1/4 inch x 3/16 inch overall (0.6 x 0.5 cm).

Orientation of the wounds of entry and exit is such that their major axes at the skin surfaces coincide with the central axis of a probe passed along the entirety of the wound path. No evidence of deflection of trajectory is found.

MICROSCOPIC EXAMINATION OF THE SLIDE LABELED GUNSHOT WOUND NO. 2 (GSW #2) ENTRANCE WOUND.

The perpendicular sections of the gunshot wound show cellular degeneration of the margins of the covering epithelium. The dermis shows extensive coagulation, early cell infiltration by mostly neutrophiles, and hemolyzed and relatively intact erythrocytes. The area of coagulation necrosis includes disintegration of apparently sweat and sebaceous gland. Only remnants are visualized.

Gunpowder granules embedded into the dermis and the surface of the gunshot wound track are visible on stained and unstained sections.

The subcutaneous and adipose tissue shows extensively extravasated hemorrhage.

GUNSHOT WOUND NO. 3:

The wound of entry is centered 14 inches (35.6 cm) from the vertex and 8-1/2 inches (21.6 cm) to the right of midline, 2 inches (5 cm) from the back anterior to a plane passing through the skin surface overlying the scapula, and 1/2 inch (1.2 cm) posterior to the mid-axillary line. There is a nearly circular defect 3/16 inch by slightly more than 1/8 inch overall (0.5 x 0.4 cm). There is a thin marginal abrasion rim without evidence of charring or apparent residue in the adjacent skin or subjacent soft tissue. The subcutaneous fatty tissue is hemorrhagic.

The wound path is directed medially to the left, superiorly and posteriorly through soft tissue of the medial portion of the axilla and soft tissue of the upper back, terminating at a point at the level of the 6th thoracic vertebra as close as about 1/2 inch (1.2 cm) to the right of midline.

Bullet Recovery:

A deformed bullet (later identified as .22 caliber) is recovered at the terminus of the wound path just described at 8:40 A.M., June 6, 1968. There is a unilateral, transverse deformation, the contour of which is indicated on an accompanying diagram. The initials, TN, and the numbers 31 are placed on the base of the bullet for future identification. The usual evidence envelope is prepared. The bullet, so marked and so enclosed as evidence, is given to Sergeant W. Jordan, No. 7167, Rampart Detectives, Los Angeles Police Department, at 8:49 A.M. this date for further studies.

An irregularly bordered and somewhat elliptical zone of variably mottled recent ecchymosis is present in the superior-medial axillary skin on the right, in the zones of wounds of entry No. 2 and No. 3, especially the former. The ecchymosis measures 3-1/2 x 1-1/2 inches (9 x 3.8 cm) overall with the right upper extremity extended completely upward (longitudinally).

TRIANGULATION OF GUNSHOT WOUNDS

Angles and planes refer to the body considered in the standing position, in accordance with usual anatomic custom.

GUNSHOT WOUND #1

Goniometric studies by Dr. Scanlan are described by him elsewhere in this report. Photographs of internal features of the skull are confirmatory.

GUNSHOT WOUND #2

Autopsy measurements indicate an angle of 35 degrees counterclockwise from the transverse plane as viewed frontally. Triangulation measurements from photographs give an angle of 33 degrees.

Autopsy measurements indicate an angle of 59 degrees counterclockwise from the transverse plane as viewed laterally from the right. Measurements from photographs also indicate an angle of 59 degrees.

Autopsy measurements indicate an angle of 25 degrees measured clockwise from the coronal plane (anteriorly) as viewed from the vertex.

GUNSHOT WOUND #3

Autopsy measurements show an angle of 30 degrees upward from the transverse plane, counterclockwise as viewed frontally. Photographic studies also show an angle of 30 degrees.

Autopsy measurements show an angle of 67 degrees clockwise from the transverse plane as viewed laterally from the right. Photographs indicate an angle of about 70 degrees.

Measurements indicate an angle of 5-1/2 degrees counterclockwise and behind the coronal plane as viewed from the vertex. The photographs are in agreement for this small angle.

TTN:JEH:ef

Exhibit 21
City Council News Article

THE SUN, BALTIMORE, FRIDAY MORNING, SEPTEMBER 24, 1971

Morrow Explains '64 Record

GOP Candidate Calls Role In Bogus-Peso Case Part Of Move Against Castro

By BENTLEY ORRICK

The names of presidents past, present and presumed were mingled with veiled tales of apparently amateur cold war intrigue as the Republican candidate for president of Baltimore City Council declared he was in the race to stay.

The press conference, at the Lord Baltimore Hotel, called by Robert D. Morrow, the Republican candidate who has fallen out with his running mates on the ticket headed by Dr. Ross Z. Pierpont, the candidate for mayor, had little to do with municipal politics.

The Bay of Pigs, Fidel Castro, President Nixon, the late President Kennedy, the late Senator Robert F. Kennedy, the Central Intelligence Agency, the Cuban Missile Crisis and Mr. Morrow's admission that he had helped counterfeit Cuban pesos in a patriotic attempt to battle communism, all figured prominently.

Zoning, public school costs, Council patronage, city contracts, the East-West expressway were not mentioned.

The promise of the bizarre had lured a score of newsmen into tiny Parlor A off the hotel's mezzanine. A precedent of a sort was set for a local political press conference when an amiable city patrolman, who seemed as bemused as everyone else, checked credentials at the door.

Mr. Morrow, a 43-year-old self-employed engineer, arrived with his lawyer and his star witness, Mario Garcia Kohly, who said he was named the president of the Cuban government in exile by the Cuban Underground Organization.

Mr. Kohly was convicted in the same bogus-peso plot in 1964 and served nine months of a year-long jail sentence. Mr. Morrow and his wife were allowed to plead no contest and were given a year's probation.

Several city plainclothes men accompanied Mr. Kohly, a mild-mannered man in his late 60's who said he needed police protection against the activities of Castro followers.

Approval Cited

Mr. Kohly and Mr. Morrow, as they did at their trials, said the bogus-peso plot had been given the tacit approval of Washington officials in "very high places."

These officials went on to arrange the trial on counterfeiting charges after Mr. Kohly attempted to discredit the Kennedy administration's assertion that no Soviet missiles remained in Cuba after the resolution of the missile crisis, Mr. Kohly said.

"Bobby Kennedy ... he became very angry that I had called his brother a liar," Mr. Kohly remarked.

He said his co-operation with the CIA had ended with the change of administrations in 1961. Before this, he said, he had met with Vice President Nixon on the Burning Tree Golf Course near Washington and had been recognized as a chief anti-Castro leader.

However, Mr. Kohly said
See MORROW, C14, Col. 2

MARIO GARCIA KOHLY
Cuban exiles "president" figures in city GOP hassle
Sunpapers photo—William Hotz

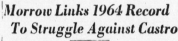

Morrow Links 1964 Record To Struggle Against Castro

MORROW, from C24 there are "many factions" of Cuban exiles, and, before the Bay of Pigs invasion, "I was secreted away by certain factions of the U.S. intelligence who were supporting another faction for the prime leadership position in the invasion."

President Nixon, while a New York lawyer, wrote a letter asking a federal judge to be lenient in the Kohly case.

"Complexities Of . . . Policy"

The Nixon letter noted, "I believe it is possible that . . . the complexities of United States policy toward the Castro regime . . . might well have created an atmosphere in which a person such as Kohly could honestly, though mistakenly, believe that actions such as those for which he was convicted were not contrary to the interests of the United States."

Mr. Kohly, who wore a pre-revolutionary Cuban flag tie clasp to complement Mr. Morrow's post-revolutionary American flag lapel pin, said he had enlisted Mr. Morrow in the bogus-peso affair.

"Technical Violation"

Mr. Morrow said he had participated because, "as I said in Federal Court in Baltimore ... I did what the dictates of my conscience, my belief in God, my country and humanity dictated to me."

Both men asserted that motives of personal profit were not involved.

He and his lawyer characterized the counterfeiting as a "technical violation of the law."

Mr. Morrow said that it "was not un-American in those days" to oppose communism and that he saw no parallel between his violation of the law for reasons of conscience and the wrecking of draft boards by anti-war activists.

Local Politics

"I don't feel I was destroying government property," he said.

Turning to local politics briefly, Mr. Morrow said that he had been thrown off the ticket, despite the original agreement, "made on July 4," to run with Dr. Pierpont.

The third member of the original ticket, Darl D. Chappell, a grocer at Cross Keys, has pulled out of the race citing embarrassment at the turn of events.

Mr. Morrow said that Dr. Pierpont was "stretching the truth" in denying that he knew all along of the bogus-peso case.

Received No Funds

"I have not received any funds and frankly, from past performances, I don't expect any from the GOP," Mr. Morrow said.

And, to further highlight his problems as an "independent Republican candidate," Mr. Morrow conceded that a court test of his eligibility to run in light of the counterfeiting case would be "very interesting."

The press conference, instead of closing with the traditional thank you's, was ended by an aside from a Morrow aide: "Security says we have to go," nodding toward plainclothes men.

The News American
Friday, Sept. 24, 1971 ★ 1

City & Counties

SECTION C

Morrow Won't Quit Despite Plot Part

By MICHAEL OLESKER

Under fire for his part in a 1963 plot against Cuba's Fidel Castro, Robert Morrow said Thursday he will continue his bid for the City Council presidency.

But doubt arose over his right to vote in the November election.

Indicted in 1963 on federal charges of illegally making plates to print counterfeit Cuban pesos, Morrow is entitled under state and federal law — to run for office.

But, according to deputy attorney general Norman Polovoy, "We just don't know if he can vote," after pleading "nolo contendere" to felony charges in 1963. Polovoy said his office would

look into the matter "with all deliberate speed" should the Board of Election Supervisors ask for a ruling. "We've anticipated a request for a ruling," Polovoy said.

CHARGES OF counterfeiting constitute a felony, and convicted felons cannot vote in the U.S. However, Polovoy said Morrow's "nolo contendere" — "no contest" — plea makes the case difficult to determine.

Morrow, a GOP candidate for president of the City Council, indicated at a press conference Thursday afternoon the he might take the case to court "as a test."

He called the conference to

Turn to Page 3C, Column 5.

Morrow to Remain in Race Despite Part in Castro Plot

Continued from Page 1C

"clear up any questions about the counterfeit plot" and had with him the president of Cuba's government-in-exile, Mario Garcia Kohly, to help explain.

In a downtown hotel room crowded with security police, detectives and press, Morrow and Kohler said they had received encouragement from high ranking government officials in their plot to overthrow Castro.

Kohly said he met with then-vice President Richard Nixon Oct. 16, 1960, at Burning Tree Country Club to discuss the plan. Kohly had been exiled from Cuba the previous year for an anti-Castro speech.

KOHLY SAID, "The Vice President had the CIA contact me. When the new administration came in, I was still working with the CIA."

He met Morrow "by accident" in Washington in 1961 and enlisted him to "install a communications network to propagandize" Cuba, according to Kohly.

Kohly said Morrow hatched a plan to print counterfeit money and then "arranged for certain government officials to review this plan."

Included in this group was Sen. Chavez, of New Mexico, then chairman of the Armed Services Committee.

Kohly said he talked with Robert F. Kennedy, then U.S. attorney general, before the Bay of Pigs invasion, and "Kennedy was very much in favor of overthrowing Castro . . . He gave us his tacit sanction to go ahead with our plan."

Kohly said he received information from Cuban underground groups, "well in advance" of the missile sightings in Cuba, but said high U.S. government officials denied the missiles' existence until their own U-2 planes detected them.

KOHLY SAID Kennedy was aware of Morrow's part in the counterfeiting scheme, which folded when Castro learned of the plot and changed Cuba's currency.

According to Kohly though, "There were differences of opinion within the administration over the plan, and in the resulting confusion (following the Bay of Pigs invasion) Mr. Morrow and myself were arrested."

Morrow received a suspended sentence, but Kohly served nine months in Lewisburg Federal Prison.

Morrow said Thursday that his aim in the plot was "nothing more nor less than the overthrow of the Castro regime. I did what my conscience, my belief in God, my country and humanity dictated to me. I do not apologize for what I did."

But, he said, given the same opportunity, he would not repeat the effort.

THE EVENING SUN

BALTIMORE, MONDAY, SEPTEMBER 27, 1971

'Could the City Use a Seasoned Counterfeiter'?

Exhibit 22
Press Statement on Watergate for CREEP

ON JUNE 2, 1972, AFTER THE MARYLAND PRIMARY, MARIO GARCIA

KOHLY, PRESIDENT DE FACTO OF CUBA IN EXILE, INFORMED ME

THAT HE HAD BEEN APPROACHED BY TWO MEN CLAIMING THEY WERE

WITH THE COMMITTEE TO RE-ELECT THE PRESIDENT.

THESE MEN WISHED TO ENLIST HIS ORGANIZATIONS' HELP TO BREAK

INTO THE WATERGATE COMPLEX TO UNCOVER WHAT THEY CLAIMED

WAS A CASTRO / DEMOCRATIC PLOT TO EMBARRASS THE NIXON

ADMINISTRATION BEFORE THE ELECTIONS.

KOHLY CAREFULLY CHECKED WITH HIS UNDERGROUND SOURCES IN

CUBA AND DISCOVERED THAT THERE WAS NO DEAL MADE BETWEEN

THE DEMOCRATS AND CASTRO BUT DID DISCOVER SUBSEQUENTLY

THAT A LARGE SUM OF MONEY WAS IN A MEXICAN BANK FOR THE

ALLEGED PURPOSE OF FUNDING THE WATERGATE BREAK-IN AND

REPUTEDLY CONTROLLED BY THE DEMOCRATIC PARTY.

BECAUSE THE STORY DID NOT MAKE ANY SENSE THAT THE DEMOCRATS

WOULD WANT TO BUG THEIR OWN HEADQUARTERS, HE DISMISSED THE

MATTER UNTIL AFTER THE ACTUAL WATERGATE INCIDENT, WHEN

HE DICOVERED THAT AN OLD FRIEND, MR. FRANK STURGIS, WAS INVOLVED.

KOHLY HAS BEEN UNABLE   UPON REPEATED ATTEMPTS TO REACH

STURGIS TO INFORM HIM OF THIS POSSIBLE DEMOCRATIC INVOLVEMENT.

I HAVE SENT COPIES OF A LENGTHY STATEMENT OUTLINING MORE

DETAILS TO THE F.B.I. AND MAILED COPIES TO U.S. ATTORNEY

BEALL FOR TRANSMITTING TO THE FEDERAL GRAND JURY IN

WASHINGTON.

Exhibit 23
HSCA Non-disclosure Agreement

<u>Select Committee on Assassinations Nondisclosure Agreement</u>

I, ████████████████████ in consideration for being employed by or engaged by contract or otherwise to perform services for or at the request of the House Select Committee on Assassinations, or any Member thereof, do hereby make the representations and accept the obligations set forth below as conditions precedent for my employment or engagement, or for my continuing employment or engagement, with the Select Committee, the United States House of Representatives, or the United States Congress.

1. I have read the Rules of the Select Committee, and I hereby agree to be bound by them and by the Rules of the House of Representatives.

2. I hereby agree never to divulge, publish or reveal by words, conduct or otherwise, any testimony given before the Select Committee in executive session (including the name of any witness who appeared or was summoned to appear before the Select Committee in executive session), any classifiable and properly classified information (as defined in 5 U.S.C. §552(b)(1)), or any information pertaining to intelligence sources or methods as designated by the Director of Central Intelligence, or any confidential information that is received by the Select Committee or that comes into my possession by virtue of my position with the Select Committee, to any person not a member of the Select Committee or its staff or the personal staff representative of a Committee Member unless authorized in writing by the Select Committee, or, after the Select Committee's termination, by such manner as the House of Representatives may determine or, in the absence of a determination by the House, in such manner as the Agency or Department from which the information originated may determine. I further agree not to divulge, publish or reveal by words, conduct or otherwise, any other information which is received by the Select Committee or which comes into my possession by virtue of my position with the Select Committee, for the duration of the Select Committee's existence.

3. I hereby agree that any material that is based upon or may include information that I hereby pledge not to disclose, and that is contemplated for publication by me will, prior to discussing it with or showing it to any publishers, editors or literary agents, be submitted to the Select Committee to determine whether said material contains any information that I hereby pledge not to disclose. The Chairman of the Select Committee shall consult with the Director of Central Intelligence for the purpose of the Chairman's determination as to whether or not the material contains information that I pledge not to disclose. I further agree to take no steps toward publication until authorized in writing by the Select Committee, or after its termination, by such manner as the House of Representatives

-2-

may determine, or in the absence of a determination by the
House, in such manner as the Agency or Department from which
the information originated may determine.

4.   I hereby agree to familiarize myself with the Select
Committee's security procedures, and provide at all times the
required degree of protection against unauthorized disclosure
for all information and materials that come into my possession
by virtue of my position with the Select Committee.

5.   I hereby agree to immediately notify the Select Committee of any attempt by any person not a member of the Select
Committee staff to solicit information from me that I pledge
not to disclose.

6.   I hereby agree to immediately notify the Select
Committee if I am called upon to testify or provide information
to the proper authorities that I pledge not to disclose. I
will request that my obligation to respond is established by
the Select Committee, or after its termination, by such manner
as the House of Representatives may determine, before I do so.

7.   I hereby agree to surrender to the Select Committee
upon demand by the Chairman or upon my separation from the
Select Committee staff, any material, including any classified
information or information pertaining to intelligence sources
or methods as designated by the Director of Central Intelligence,
which comes into my possession by virtue of my position with the
Select Committee. I hereby acknowledge that all documents
acquired by me in the course of my employment are and remain the
property of the United States.

8.   I understand that any violation of the Select Committee
Rules, security procedures or this agreement shall constitute
grounds for dismissal from my current employment.

9.   I hereby assign to the United States Government all
rights, title and interest in any and all royalties, remunera-
tions and emoluments that have resulted or may result from any
divulgence, publication or revelation in violation of this
agreement.

10.   I understand and agree that the United States Government
may choose to apply, prior to any unauthorized disclosure by
me, for a court order prohibiting disclosure. Nothing in this
agreement constitutes a waiver on the part of the United States
of the right to prosecute for any statutory violation. Nothing
in this agreement constitutes a waiver on my part of any defenses
I may otherwise have in any civil or criminal proceedings.

-3-

11. I have read the provisions of the Espionage Laws, Sections 793, 794 and 798, Title 18, United States Code, and of Section 783, Title 50, United States Code, and I am aware that unauthorized disclosure of certain classified information may subject me to prosecution. I have read Section 1001, Title 18, United States Code, and I am aware that the making of a false statement herein is punishable as a felony. I have also read Executive Order 11652, and the implementing National Security Council directive of May 17, 1972, relating to the protection of classified information.

12. Unless released in writing from this agreement or any portion thereof by the Select Committee, I recognize that all the conditions and obligations imposed on me by this agreement apply during my Committee employment or engagement and continue to apply after the relationship is terminated.

13. No consultant shall indicate, divulge or acknowledge, without written permission of the Select Committee, the fact that the Select Committee has engaged him or her by contract as a consultant until after the Select Committee has terminated.

14. In addition to any rights for criminal prosecution or for injunctive relief the United States Government may have for violation of this agreement, the United States Government may file a civil suit in an appropriate court for damages as a consequence of a breach of this agreement. The costs of any civil suit brought by the United States for breach of this agreement, including court costs, investigative expenses, and reasonable attorney fees, shall be borne by any defendant who loses such suit. In any civil suit for damages successfully brought by the United States Government for breach of this agreement, actual damages may be recovered, or, in the event that such actual damages may be impossible to calculate, liquidate damages in an amount of $5,000 shall be awarded as a reasonable estimate for damages to the credibility and effectiveness of the investigation.

15. I hereby agree that in any suit by the United States Government for injunctive or monetary relief pursuant to the terms of this agreement, personal jurisdiction shall obtain and venue shall lie in the United States District Court for the District of Columbia, or in any other appropriate United States District Court in which the United States may elect to bring suit. I further agree that the law of the District of Columbia shall govern the interpretation and construction of this agreement.

16. Each provision of this agreement is severable. If a court should find any part of this agreement to be unenforceable, all other provisions of this agreement shall remain in full force and effect.

-4-

I make this agreement without any mental reservation or purpose of evasion, and I agree that it may be used by the Select Committee in carrying out its duty to protect the security of information provided to it.

Date: July 19, 1977

I am submitting a list of material and information which has already been given to the committee, or which I intend to give the committee in the near future. I intend to publish some of this information.

LOUIS STOKES, Chairman
Select Committee on Assassinations

Exhibit 24
A Selected Chronology on Cuba (4/1/63-4/30/63)

JX 1428   THE LIBRARY OF CONGRESS
L.A. Cuba   Legislative Reference Service

                      A SELECTED CHRONOLOGY ON CUBA*
                      April 1, 1963 - April 30, 1963

April 1, 1963
        Seventeen anti-Castro raiders were arrested by British police on
a small Bahamas island last night and 16 were placed aboard a British war-
ship that was proceeding toward Nassau.
        Lincoln White, State Department press officer, said that the tip
that led to the seizure of the 17 men was furnished by U. S. authorities.
White told newsmen that "information of a Cuban exile camp on the little
cay was provided to British authorities by the United States."
        He declined to say how U. S. authorities learned of the camp or
whether it had been used as a base for raiding parties.
        White said the British were "acting on their own, collaborating with
us to prevent these hit-and-run raids."

April 2, 1963
        Cuba delivered a full apology to the United States for the attack
on the American cargo ship Floridian and the State Department said it
considered the incident closed.
        In Nassau, Bahamas, 16 Cuban exile commandos who set out last week
on a raiding mission against Cuba were sent to jail for seven days pending
investigation by British colonial authorities.
        They were charged with possessing firearms without license in
Bahamas waters.

April 2, 1963
        The United States disclosed that a Cuban rebel raiding boat was
seized in Miami just as a British force was capturing another armed vessel
belonging to an exile group.
        Apparently there was no direct connection between the expeditions.
The yacht Alisan was seized in Miami and the motor launch Violin III
was taken into custody at Norman Key in the Exuma Islands. Both of the
craft presumably were planning to attack Soviet shipping in and around
Cuba.
        A third vessel was said by rebel sources in Miami to be cruising
somewhere in the vicinity of Cuba in search of a target after escaping
the British-United States trap that caught the Violin III.

April 3, 1963
        President Kennedy said that about 1000 Soviet military personnel
have left Cuba in the last two weeks and he implied that the United
States crackdown on Cuban hit-run raids should encourage the exodus.
        From the President's figures, the number of Russians there is now
approximately 12,000 or 13,000 compared to a 21,000 to 22,000 peak
during the October crisis over Soviet missiles in Cuba.

_____
*   Unless otherwise stated excerpted from the Washington Post and the
    Washington Star; reproduced with the permission of the Washington Post
    and Washington Star.

- 2 -

President Kennedy said in his news conference that "in the last month approximately 4000 Soviets have left Cuba," 1000 more than he reported on March 21. He said the United States will continue to observe very closely in "the immediate weeks ahead whether there are going to be further withdrawals which, of course, we wish for."

Before the President spoke, the State Department, in a note to the Soviet Union, "categorically" rejected the Soviet charge that the United States "encourages and bears full responsibility for" two recent attacks on Soviet ships in Cuban ports by anti-Castro exile commandos.

Before and after those attacks, the State Department recalled, the United States declared it was "strongly opposed" to them and "in no way associated with, such attacks." Referring to a joint announcement last Saturday by the State and Justice Departments, the note added: "The United States is taking every step necessary to insure that such attacks are not launched, manned or equipped from U. S. territory."

President Kennedy re-explained the Administration's justification for its actions.

When "issues of war and peace hang in the balance," he said, "and when American territory is used," the United States "should have a position of some control in the matter."

He said he cannot see how recent raids represent "any real blow at Castro (Cuban Premier Fidel Castro)." Such an attack, he said, "gives additional incentives for the Soviet Union to maintain their personnel in Cuba, to send additional units to protect their merchant ships." He said the attacks "will bring reprisals, possibly on American ships," and this could bring American "counter-action." The end result may assist Castro in "maintaining his control," the President said, instead of undermining him.

The "cause of freedom" could be better served, said the President, by following the example of several hundred survivors of the ill-fated Bay of Pigs attempt to invade Cuba in April, 1961.

The President said that 200 of the officers and 250 of that brigade, who were ransomed with American medical and food supplies last December, have joined the United States Army.

April 3, 1963

The government used bombers and infantry in an all-out attack on Castro-trained guerrillas in the mountains of Falcon State. Unofficial reports said the guerrillas suffered heavy losses in initial clashes.

Reports from the area said 17 to 20 guerrillas were killed in opening attacks. The government, however, reported guerrilla dead at two and said it had no casualties.

April 4, 1963

Seventeen men who sailed forth to attack Cuba but wound up in a Nassau jail left Nassau today in their 35-foot motorboat with a United States Coast Guard amphibious plane trailing them.

- 3 -

The rebels had been charged with possessing firearms without license, but the charges were dropped.

April 4, 1963

Senator Kenneth B. Keating proposed a fourteen-step program of economic sanctions designed to complete the isolation of Cuba and force the withdrawal of Soviet troops and weapons from the island.

In a speech on the Senate floor, the New York Republican acknowledged that it would not be easy to implement his proposals since they would require full cooperation by the members of the Organization of American States and the North Atlantic Treaty Organization.

The first five steps he proposed involved the other American republics. They were:

1. The formation of O.A.S. inspection teams to monitor and inspect all ships and planes arriving in Latin American countries from Cuba.

2. A progressive curtailment of flights and passenger steamship routing between Cuba and other Latin American countries.

3. A complete trade boycott between Cuba and other Latin American countries, comparable to that between the United States and Cuba.

4. Denial of Latin American cargoes and fueling facilities to planes and ships trading with Cuba.

5. The withholding of United States aid to Latin American countries that furnish or strengthen the links between Cuba and the rest of the hemisphere through diplomatic relations and air and sea connections.

These steps would be the "lesser part" of his program, Senator Keating said, because "the real menace" is not Premier Castro but the Soviet Union, and the principal objective "is not merely to contain Castro but to effect the removal of Soviet troops and weapons.

Since this would require the cooperation of NATO and the entire non-Communist world, he proposed these seven economic measures:

1. Forbidding United States cargoes, Government and private, to be carried by ships or shipping lines that have supplied Cuba since January, 1963.

2. Insuring that United States shipping facilities and cargoes anywhere in the world are not available for ships or shipping lines that have engaged in trade with Cuba.

3. Initiating NATO regulations forbidding ships of the alliance to carry cargoes to Cuba.

4. Initiating NATO action to insure that no NATO cargoes will be available to ships supplying Cuba.

5. Denial of United States economic aid to any nation trading with Cuba, or providing ships or fueling facilities for Cuban trade.

6. The cut-off by NATO nations of sales to the entire Soviet bloc of all goods except food and medicine, that the bloc now supplies to Cuba.

7. Further [but unspecified] restrictions on NATO and the institution, "where possible," of a "complete free world boycott on trade with the Soviet bloc."

- 4 -

April 5, 1963

The United States is throwing more planes, ships and men into its effort to police the straits of Florida against anti-Castro raiders operating from this country.

Coast Guard headquarters announced that it had ordered six more planes and 12 more boats into the Seventh District to reinforce the patrols already assigned to the Florida-Puerto Rico area.

A frustrated little anti-Castro raiding boat slipped into Miami, but its sister craft may yet be operating against Cuba.

The Violynn III was minus fuel, machine guns and 20-millimeter cannon when it turned up, ending an extensive Coast Guard air search for the 35-foot motorboat and its crew of 17.

A crewman swam ashore and made arrangements by telephone for the little band's surrender. Immigration officials questioned all and released two soon afterward.

April 5, 1963

Pro-Castro terrorists stepped up their sabotage campaign, blowing up a radio transmitter and destroying a state garage.

The overnight violence, culminating in the predawn dynamite attack on Radio Tropical's suburban station here in Caracas, came less than 48 hours after renewed bomb attacks were made on American installations in the oil-rich Maracaibo area.

April 5, 1963

Representatives of the Central American and U. S. Governments last night recommended that their citizens be kept out of Cuba by stamping their passports "Not valid for travel to Cuba."

The United States uses the same system to bar Americans from Communist China.

Justice and Interior Ministers meeting here approved seven other recommendations for action to combat Communist infiltration from Cuba. The recommendations called for stronger crackdowns on contraband arms, cooperation in patrolling coast lines, penalties for receipt or distribution of Communist propaganda, and impounding of funds that might be used for subversion.

The conference was an outgrowth of President Kennedy's meeting in San Jose, Costa Rica, with the Presidents of Panama, Guatemala, Honduras, Nicaragua, El Salvador and Costa Rica.

April 6, 1963

Capt. Eddie Rickenbacker, chairman of the committee for the Monroe Doctrine, said President Kennedy is "underwriting continued Soviet control over Cuba with the armed might of the United States."

Rickenbacker said in a statement: "The Kennedy Administration has committed the final betrayal of Cuban hopes for freedom by its order to block the activities of exiled Cuban freedom fighters to liberate their nation from communism . . ."

- 5 -

"... For a President of the United States to utilize his functions
as commander in chief of the armed forces to actively aid in the destruction
of the Monroe Doctrine by utilizing his power to protect foreign troops
in this hemisphere is inconceivable."

Rickenbacker called on Congress "to resolve that the Monroe Doctrine
continues to be a basic plank of American foreign policy and ... to
utilize all its powers to see that the Monroe Doctrine is implemented
and that communism is removed from Cuba forthwith."

Members of the Committee include Spruille Braden, former U. S.
Ambassador to various Latin American countries; William F. Buckley Jr.,
editor of the National Review; Charles Edison, former Secretary of the
Navy and Governor of New Jersey; William F. Knowland, former Republican
leader of the Senate, and Arthur W. Radford, former Chairman of the Joint
Chiefs of Staff.

April 7, 1963
Cuban rebel sources said their movement to rid their homeland of
communism has been dealt a crippling blow both inside and outside Cuba.

Members of a small group which escaped a British-American net said
they had lost an important supply link--by air--with anti-Castro fighters
inside Cuba.

About 170 men are involved in the area where the British and Americans
have been cracking down to prevent raids on Premier Fidel Castro's Cuba,
they added.

This could mean that nearly all the raiders would eventually be
picked up. That might signal the virtual collapse of anti-Castro harassment from the outside, they said.

April 7, 1963
Sen. Barry Goldwater (R-Ariz.) gave his endorsement to Cuban exile
merchant ships even when they result in the killing of Russians.

"If they are not going to take them (Russians) out of there (Cuba)
alive," said the Arizona conservative, "maybe they are going to take them
out of there dead ..."

Goldwater presented his views in a televised interview on "Issues
and Answers."

Goldwater accused President Kennedy of "doing everything in his
power" to keep the flag of the Cuban exiles "from ever flying over
Cuba again."

Goldwater said that American leadership, rather than being "too
frightened to sustain a firm policy on Cuba," should embark on an economic
blockade of the island without fear that it would trigger all-out nuclear
war.

"Russia is not going to risk losing her world empire over a tiny
island in the Caribbean," he said. "If we don't object, she is going to
stay there because I think it is probably her most valuable possession."

- 6 -

Goldwater said that for the present he favors an economic blockade of Cuba coupled with espionage and sabotage training of exiles, rather than actual invasion.

Invasion, he added, is the "last action that we should take" and should be carried out by the Organization of American States "without our having to commit our own troops to the exercise."

April 8, 1963

Secretary of Defense Robert S. McNamara said that if an economy-minded Congress must whittle away at his 53.5-billion-dollar 1964 budget it should reduce spending in areas less critical than military assistance to foreign nations.

McNamara stated his position before the House Foreign Committee, where he testified in support of President Kennedy's 4.5-billion-dollar 1964 foreign aid program, which includes $1.4 billion in military assistance.

McNamara estimated that the Soviet Union is spending $1 billion on its support of the Castro regime in Cuba, including ship movements, economic aid and military assistance.

April 8, 1963

Manuel Urrutia Lleo, first President of Cuba under Fidel Castro, called upon the United States to help the Cuban people to overthrow the Castro regime.

At a news conference held at the International Rescue Committee's headquarters here, Urrutia indicated that Cuba was ripe for a revolution because the Cuban people were overwhelmingly against communism and Castro.

"About 90 per cent of the Cuban people are against Castro," he said. "Nobody can rule a country in the face of this opposition."

Urrutia said, however, that the struggle of the Cuban people against Castro could not succeed without the help of the United States and other friendly governments.

April 9, 1963

The row over American policy toward Fidel Castro's Cuba blew up again with an Administration charge that a Cuban exile leader had tried to serve a 50-million-dollar ultimatum on the United States Government.

Earlier news dispatches from Miami reported that Jose Miro Cardona was offering his resignation as president of the Cuban Revolutionary Council in token of a clash with the Kennedy Administration over Cuban policy.

A few hours later the State Department said publicly that while the Administration and Miro Cardona had seen eye to eye on the goal of a free Cuba they were not in accord on steps to attain that goal.

Almost simultaneously United States Government officials reported that Miro Cardona had made what they said amounted to an ultimatum to the United States: either give him $50 million to train and equip an exile army to invade Cuba or give him an intimate role in the preparation and implementation of an early invasion of Cuba by United States forces.

Both parts of the ultimatum, these officials said, were unacceptable to the Administration.

Exhibit 25
Polka Dot Dress Investigation

THE POLKA DOT DRESS INVESTIGATION

Miss ▓▓▓▓▓▓▓ came to the attention of investigators on
June 5, 1968, when she described a female running from the scene
of the assassination of Robert Kennedy. She alleged that the
female stated, "We shot him, we shot him." The person was alleged
to have been wearing a polka dot dress. ▓▓▓▓▓▓▓ allegation was partially corroborated by statements of another witness,
▓▓▓▓▓▓▓. A full-scale investigation and search for
this suspect took place as a result.

Subsequent investigation revealed that ▓▓▓▓▓▓▓ had concocted
the entire story of the female suspect. Evidence also indicated
that ▓▓▓▓▓▓▓ could not have heard or seen all of the events
that she alleged. The investigation of the "Girl in the Polka
Dot Dress" follows:

Events at the Hotel

On June 5, 1968, at 12:30 a.m., ▓▓▓▓▓▓▓ a Los Angeles
Deputy District Attorney, was approached outside the main entrance
of the Ambassador Hotel by ▓▓▓▓▓▓▓ a 20-year-old Kennedy
worker. She was obviously excited and told ▓▓▓▓ that prior to
her learning of the shooting, a man and woman walked toward her
in a hotel corridor. As they passed, the woman stated, "We just
shot him." ▓▓▓▓▓▓ asked the woman, "Who shot who?" The woman
replied, "We just shot Senator Kennedy." ▓▓▓▓▓▓ described the
man and woman as follows:

Female Caucasian, 22-26, 5-5, good figure, wearing a white
dress with black polka dots, with a bib collar, long sleeves.

324

and wearing heels.

. Male Mexican-American, 23, wearing a gold sweater.

██████████ realizing the importance of her statement, directed
her to detectives in the Embassy Room. While waiting for the
investigators, she was interviewed by Sandor Vanocur, an NBC-
TV news commentator, on a live telecast over the NBC television
network. During the interview, she stated essentially the same
information she had told ████████ but changed the location of
the encounter with the couple from a corridor inside the hotel
to an outside staircase. After her encounter and before meeting
████████ she telephoned her parents, ████████████████████████
at their home in ████████ Ohio, to tell them about the shooting.

████████████ Interviews

████████ was interviewed at Rampart Station at 2:35 a.m. on June
5, 1968. She stated that while on an outside staircase of the
hotel, she observed the female and two male companions going
upstairs. She thought she heard gunshots, but at the time
thought they were the backfires of a car. The female and one of
the males reappeared running down the stairs. The male that did
not come back down the stairs was described as Mexican-American,
23-25, 5-2 to 5-5, 130-135, wearing a light shirt, possibly
beige pants and needing a haircut. ████████ as certain that she
could identify the female and the male companion who came back
down the stairs but wasn't sure if she could identify the other
male she had seen walking up the stairs.

At 4 a.m. ████████ was reinterviewed. During this interview,
████████ statements were essentially the same as in her previous

interview. She did elaborate on the description of the polka
dot dress, stating the dress was an "A-frame" style with a "bib
collar" and "3/4 length sleeves." The dress was "white with
black polka dots approximately 1/8" in size."

▟▟▟▟▟ Corroborated ▟▟▟▟ Allegations

At 4:25 a.m. at Parker Center, investigators interviewed ▟▟▟▟
▟▟▟▟▟. During this interview ▟▟▟▟▟ stated that he is
employed at the Ambassador Hotel as a waiter. He stated that
he was in the pantry when Senator Kennedy was shot and that he
observed the shooting. He saw Sirhan on a tray stand in the
pantry area at the east end of the ice machine. He observed a
female wearing a polka dot dress standing next to Sirhan.
▟▟▟▟▟ believed the female and Sirhan were together; he
observed Sirhan turn toward the female, appear to say something
and she turned and smiled at him. ▟▟▟▟▟ described the
female as Caucasian, 20-24, well built, brunette colored shoulder
length hair, wearing a white dress with black polka dots.

As a result of receiving the information from ▟▟▟▟▟▟▟▟
the Los Angeles Police Department broadcast a teletype requesting
information for the arrest of a woman in a polka dot dress. The
teletype was sent at 11:50 a.m., June 5, 1968, and an identical
description on a supplemental teletype was sent at 12:30 p.m.
the same day. The description was as follows: Female Caucasian,
23-27, 5-6, wearing a white voile dress, 3/4 sleeves with small
black polka dots, dark shoes, bouffant-type hair.

The Follow-up Investigation

On June 7, 1968, ▟▟▟▟ reviewed colored films taken at the

Ambassador Hotel by NBC News in an attempt to identify the
suspects she had seen on the steps. She was unable to do so.

On June 7, 1968, ▓▓▓▓▓ was interviewed by F.B.I. Special
Agent ▓▓▓▓▓▓▓▓▓▓ at her home, ▓▓▓▓▓▓▓▓▓▓▓▓▓▓
▓▓▓▓▓▓▓▓▓▓, told him that on June 4, 1968, at 8:30 p.m.,
that she left the Youth for Kennedy Pasadena Headquarters with
four committee workers. At 11:30 p.m., she left the Ambassador
Ballroom and went out onto an outside stairway. She sat on the
fifth or sixth step of the stairs that lead up to the Embassy
Room. Two or three minutes later a woman and two men started
up the stairs. When the woman got near her, the woman said,
"Excuse us," and ▓▓▓▓▓ moved to the side so the three could
pass. For the next 20 to 25 minutes, no other person went up or
down past her. After hearing some noises that sounded like an
automobile backfire, one of the men and the woman ran back down
the stairs. The woman yelled, "We shot him, we shot him." "Who
did you shoot?" she asked. The woman replied, "Senator Kennedy."

▓▓▓▓▓ went inside the hallway area and asked an unidentified
guard if Senator Kennedy had been shot. The guard told her she
must have had too much to drink. She went to a public phone
booth inside the Ambassador Hotel and called her parents in
Ohio. While ▓▓▓▓▓ was in the phone booth, ▓▓▓▓▓▓▓▓▓▓▓,
a Kennedy co-worker, approached and asked her if it were true that
Senator Kennedy had been shot and she answered, "Yes." ▓▓▓▓▓
stated that she had difficulty in explaining to her parents what
had happened, because she was crying and near complete hysteria.

After leaving the phone booth, she went back to the Ambassador Ballroom and met ▮▮▮▮▮▮▮▮▮▮▮▮▮▮▮, both co-workers, but was unable to get either to understand what had happened. As she walked out of the ballroom, she met ▮▮▮▮▮▮▮, a good friend, and began walking towards the parking lot. ▮▮▮▮▮ then walked up to a man ▮▮▮▮▮▮▮ and told him what she had heard the woman say. ▮▮▮▮▮ directed her to a policeman in the Embassy Room. While she was sitting in the Embassy Room waiting to be interviewed by the police, a person asked if she were a witness and before she realized it she was being interviewed on television. ▮▮▮▮▮ was then taken to Rampart Station where she was interviewed by investigators from the Department.

On June 8, 1968, F.B.I. investigators interviewed ▮▮▮▮▮▮ and ▮▮▮▮▮▮▮▮▮▮▮▮▮▮. They verified their daughter's statement regarding a phone call to them the night of the shooting. ▮▮▮▮▮▮▮ does not recall her daughter mentioning anything about a girl saying, "We just shot Senator Kennedy." She does remember her saying, "Why would they do anything like this?"

On June 10, 1968, ▮▮▮▮▮ viewed eight assorted dress styles in an effort to pick out a dress similar to the polka dot dress. These dresses were numbered one through eight for identification purposes. After viewing each dress, she picked out dress number six and stated it looked the same as the polka dot dress except for the sleeve length.

 viewed the eight assorted dresses and selected dress

number four as most like the polka dot dress he had seen at the
Ambassador Hotel. ████████ recalled talking to ████████████
while they were waiting to be interviewed on the night of the
shooting. During this conversation, the woman wearing the
polka dot dress was mentioned but was not described by either
except for saying it was white with black polka dots.

After viewing the dress ████████ was asked if she would consent
to a polygraph examination to verify her statement. She answered
affirmatively. She was also asked to reenact the incident on
the stairs. She consented and a video tape was made of her
sitting on the outside stairway leading down from the southwest
corner of the Embassy Room.

Elements of the Investigation Conflict

On June 19, 1968, investigators interviewed Captain Cecil R.
Lynch of the Los Angeles Fire Department. Lynch stated that the
night of the assassination he was assigned to enforce occupancy
and fire regulations at the Ambassador Hotel. During the time
Senator Kennedy made his victory speech in the Embassy Room,
Lynch began checking various stairways and exits for possible
violations of fire regulations. Lynch stated that he checked
the stairs ████████ alleged to have been seated on moments before
Senator Kennedy was shot, and at that time no one was seated on
the stairs.

On June 20, 1968, 11:30 a.m., sound-level tests were conducted
at the Ambassador Ballroom. A .22 caliber Cadet model revolver
was used, with .22 caliber ammunition which matched the brand

and lot used in the assassination. The test weapon was fired in the Embassy Room pantry at the same location that Senator Kennedy was shot. The weapon was held horizontal to the floor with the muzzle pointed towards the west door of the pantry. A series of one, four and eight shots were fired. During these tests, there were no functions occurring in the Embassy Room, Sunset Room or the Boulevard Room. The tests were conducted with the exit door from the Sunset Room both open and closed. The sound-level tests indicated it would have been impossible for ███████ to have heard the shots. The sound-level meter indicated a ½ decibel change when the test shots were fired. The minimum sound-level change discernible by a person with normal hearing is 2 decibels.

███████ Polygraph Examination

Investigators invited ███████ to take a polygraph examination. The polygraph examination was given by Sgt. Hernandez #7101 on June 20, 1968. The following report of the polygraph examination was submitted by Hernandez:

███████ - Date of Examination - June 20, 1968

Allegation: ███████ stated that on the late evening of June 4, 1968, she was sitting on a rear stairway approximately half-way up between the landing connecting the Sunset Room and the Embassy Ballroom of Ambassador Hotel. She stated that shortly before midnight she observed two males and one female walk up the stairway and enter the Embassy Ballroom. ███████ described one of the men as being Sirhan and described the woman as wearing a white dress with black polka dots.

████████ stated that approximately ten to fifteen minutes after she observed these people enter the Embassy Room, she heard approximately eight to ten gunshots in succession; that a couple of minutes after the shots she observed the girl in the white and black polka dot dress and one of the men running down the stairway where she was still sitting. She noted that Sirhan was not with them. The girl in the polka dot dress was yelling, "We shot him, we shot him." ███████ asked, "Who did you shoot?" and the girl answered, "Kennedy, we shot Kennedy." ██████ stated she later identified photographs of Sirhan Sirhan as the man who entered the Embassy Ballroom, but who failed to return with the other man and the girl in the polka dot dress after the shooting.

Conclusion: Polygraph examination disclosed that ██████████ has never seen Sirhan Sirhan in person; further, that ██████ ████████ fabricated, for some unknown reason, the story about the girl in the polka dot dress. Responses to relevant questions indicate that no one made statements to █████████ telling her that they had shot Kennedy or that she heard any gunshots during the late evening of June 4 or early morning of June 5, 1968. ████████ was informed of the results of the polygraph examination.

Results: ████████ was interrogated extensively and ultimately she admitted that the story about Sirhan Sirhan, the girl in the polka dot dress and the gunshots was not true. She

stated that she had been sitting on the stairway at the time
that she had mentioned and that she did hear a car backfire a
couple of times, but she knew that the sounds did in fact come
from a car, and were not gunshots. She said that while she was
sitting on the stairway, approximately four or five people came
running down the stairway screaming that Kennedy had been shot.
She stated that no one at any time told her that "They had
themselves shot Kennedy."

██████████ stated that she had no knowledge of any polka dot
dress until after the assassination and just prior to her being
interviewed. She states that she was sitting waiting to be
interviewed when she heard a kid making reference to a girl in
a polka dot dress.

She talked to the young man and each of them inquired of the
other about the description of the dress and the girl. According
to ██████████, there must have been a mutual agreement between
them as to the description of the girl and the polka dot dress.
██████████ stated that later when she was being questioned by
the police, she felt that she should know more than she actually
did, and eventually the statements which were attributed to her
were publicized on TV and in newspapers. She said that she knew
the statements were not true; but, that she could not change
them because it would make her look like a fool.

Reinterview With ██████████

On July 1, 1968, ██████████ was reinterviewed and given
a polygraph examination by investigators. The polygraph
operator determined that ██████████ been untruthful

about what he saw at the hotel.   ████████ was advised of the
statements of ████████   he admitted that he had discussed
the polka dot dress with ████████ prior to his original interview. He stated that he had been confused the night of the
assassination and that he had not seen a girl talking to Sirhan
in the kitchen. ████████ advised investigators that he had
not seen the girl in the polka dot dress but that he may have
seen a girl somewhere in the hotel who caused him to think he
had seen the girl Serrano mentioned.

Events Occurring in Response to the News Release Regarding the
Girl in a Polka Dot Dress

On June 6, 1968, 3 p.m., ████████ discovered a
paper sack containing a gray dress with white polka dots, miscellaneous feminine undergarments and cosmetics. The sack was
found lying in the alley at the rear of ████████
████████ Los Angeles. The property was booked found evidence
at Rampart Station. Investigators interviewed ████████
████████, and the occupants of the
neighboring homes; but were unable to obtain any further
information.

On June 7, 1968, the contents of the sack containing a polka
dot dress found by ████████ were processed for fingerprints by Latent Prints Section. Numerous fingerprints were
found and photographed. These fingerprints were only adequate
for elimination purposes.

The contents of the sack containing the polka dot dress found

by ████████████ were analyzed for human hair and blood by
Scientific Investigation Division. On June 18, 1968, no human
hair or blood was found, and it was concluded that the clothing
was new and had not been worn. The stains were probably caused
by the clothing coming in contact with the lipstick and liquid
face make up. The lipstick had no top and the liquid face make
up showed evidence of leakage.

1. ████████████ was taken into custody at the County Jail at
    1:30 p.m. on June 5, 1968, as the result of an informant's
    call naming her as the then-outstanding girl in the polka
    dot dress. She was released when it was learned she was at
    home during the time of the shooting.

2. ████████████ telephonically contacted the Los Angeles
    County Sheriff's Department on June 7, 1968, and informed
    them she believed she was the girl in the polka dot dress
    wanted by this Department. ██████ told detectives she was
    at the Ambassador on June 4/5, 1968, and was wearing a
    green dress with a orange polka dot scarf around her neck.
    ██████ stated after the shooting she ran from the main
    entrance of the Embassy Room yelling, "They shot him."
    ██████ was certain that ████ was not the woman she had
    seen on the stairs after she viewed ████ in the lobby of
    Parker Center.

3. On June 7, 1968, investigators were notified that ██████
    ██████ was interviewed by the Vallejo Police Department on
    June 6, 1968, at 9:10 p.m., regarding the shooting of

Kennedy. She told the Vallejo investigator that she was
being accused by friends of being the girl in the polka
dot dress. She explained that she was in San Diego the
night of the shooting visiting her boyfriend ████████
who was aboard the U.S.S. Worden. She was described as a
female Caucasian, 38, 5', 140, hazel eyes, long black hair
with a slightly crooked nose. Due to ████████
physical description, it was apparent she was not the woman
allegedly seen by ████.

████████ (U.S. Navy) was interviewed and stated that
████████ was with him in San Diego from May 31 or June
1, 1968, until June 3, 1968. On June 3, 1968, ████ went
to sea and remained at sea June 4 and 5. He knew that ███
████ had a ticket for the return flight to Vallejo but does
not know for what date or on which airline.

4. On June 14, 1968, at 7 p.m., ████████ informed the desk
    officer at Parker Center that she thought she was the woman
    that was involved in the Kennedy assassination. Investigator
    interviewed ████ and learned that on the night of the
    assassination she was wearing a black long sleeve dress and
    a large white hat similar to a "Chef's" hat. Her physical
    description is female Caucasian, 48, 5-5½, 120, black hair,
    hazel eyes. ████ felt she might be the woman sought by
    the police because she had been in the pantry area prior to
    and after the shooting. She stated she did not run from the
    pantry yelling anything. It was determined by investigators

that she was not the woman that ▓▓▓▓ allegedly had seen
due to the totally different description of her clothing
and her physical description.

5. . ▓▓▓▓▓▓ was interviewed by investigators on June 18,
1968. She told investigators that she went to the
Ambassador Hotel on June 4, 1968, and was wearing a white
blouse with small black polka dots and a black skirt. She
stated she was coming up a flight of stairs from the
Ambassador Ballroom when Senator Kennedy was shot. Her
description is female Caucasian, 21, 5-1, 150, brown, brown.
Due to her location at the time of the shooting, her physical
description and the clothing she was wearing, she was not
the woman allegedly seen by ▓▓▓▓▓ on the steps.

6. . A telephone call was received on June 19, 1968, from ▓▓▓▓
▓▓▓▓▓ a producer for KTVU-TV San Francisco. He stated
that he had obtained information from an informant, whom he
refused to name, that a ▓▓▓▓▓▓▓ was seen the night of
the shooting. It was alleged that ▓▓▓▓▓▓ was wearing
a polka dot dress at the time.

On June 19, 1968, Ceasar Chavez, President of the Farm
Workers Union, was interviewed, and he stated that he was
at the Ambassador Hotel the night of the shooting. Chavez
knows a ▓▓▓▓▓▓ that lives in San Francisco and states
that he did not see her that night. The ▓▓▓▓▓▓ that
he knows is 60 years old and writes for the ▓▓▓▓▓▓
▓▓▓▓▓▓▓▓.

Due to the description of ███████ and her advanced age,
it was concluded that she was not the woman allegedly seen
███████.

Actual Girl in Polka Dot Dress

Though ███████ and ███████ admitted that they
did not actually see a girl in a black and white polka dot
dress; a girl with a polka dot dress was in the pantry area
when the shooting occurred. ███████ a Kennedy Girl,
was wearing a bright green dress with gold polka dots at the
Ambassador Hotel the evening of June 4, 1968. ███████
is blond and slender, and she does not fit the description
which ███████ supplied investigators in any way.

███████ was important in this investigation, however,
because she observed the shooting of Senator Kennedy. Witnesses
placed ███████ outside the pantry in the anteroom behind the
ballroom podium prior to the shooting. She walked beside
Kennedy as he went into the pantry, but she dropped behind him
as he moved quickly foreward. She was walking on one crutch
and wearing a leather support on her right leg. She was
several feet behind Kennedy when the first shot was fired.

Investigators speculated that ███████ may have seen
███████ and confused her appearance in his mind. He was also
in the kitchen at the time of the shooting. It was proven
through witnesses' statements that ███████ could not have been
close enough to Sirhan to speak to him, and it was obvious
that she was not the suspected person.

The investigation proved that a basis never existed for ██████████ allegation that there was a woman in a polka dot dress; or, that a conspiracy between Sirhan and such a woman had occurred.   Nevertheless, ██████████ coincidentally was present in the pantry area at the time of the shooting.

Exhibit 26
LAPD Background Material on Khaiber Khan

Form 15.7 (Rev. Apr 1 1962)

Los Angeles Police Department
EMPLOYEE'S REPORT

DR

SUBJECT
Progress REport: Khaibar Khan

DATE & TIME OCCURED | LOCATION OF OCCURRENCE | DIVISION OF OCCURRENCE

TO: (Rank, Name, Assignment, Division)
Lt. Higbie, PM Supervisor, SUS

DATE & TIME REPORTED

DETAILS:

Khaibar Khan (LA#835805) and family came to Los Angeles in 1953, this included his wife Talat Khan, his sons, Khosrow Khan, Amir Khan, Shahpour Khan, and his daughter Shirin Khan.

In 1959, Mr. Khan returned to Iran with an American Construction Company to take part in a business deal with the King of Iran who at that time was a personal friend of Mr. Khan. The venture fell through and Mr. Khan returned to the United States. Mr. Khan then became active in a group known as the "United Patriots for Justice". This group consisted of various leaders of tribes in Iran who don't generally favor the King.

Mr. Khan then initiated legal action against the family of the King of Iran in a lawsuit for a sum exceeding one million dollars. He also testified before the Senate Permanent Subcommittee on the investigations of The Committee on Government Operations, this committee was presided by Senator John L. McClellan (D-Ark). The committee was concerned with the mis-use of foreign aid funds in Iran. This all occurred between the years of 1959 and 1963.

Also during this time the King of Iran declared Mr. Khan a political exile. Much of the legal action that took place during the hearing before the Sub-committee brought Mr. Khan in contact with the United States Attorney General's Office and Mr. Robert F. Kennedy, who at that time was the United States Attorney General. And according to Mr. Khan this is how he became quite impressed with Robert Kennedy and which made him volunteer as a Kennedy worker.

Mr. Khan's first visit to the headquarters was on 6-1-68 at which time he registered. He again returned on 6-2-68 with Maryam Kouchan and during that time worked answering telephones and left at approximately 6:30PM. On 6-3-68 he again arrived at the Kennedy headquarters at approximately 3:00PM, with his daughter, Shirin. During this time Mr. Khan recalls seeing a male seated in a car outside the headquarters which in his mind resembled Sirhan. Also during this time Mr. Khan filled out registration cards and listed various names of individuals who are tribal leaders in Iran. The purpose of this was that in November 1968 when the presidental election takes place these various people would be in the United States and were supposedly going to help take the callers name and use his mailing address on the cards. This mailing address (10455½ Wilshire) belongs to his ex-wife Talat Khan. He also used this address on the registration cards for the tribal leaders.

DATE & TIME TYPED
7-18-68 | 1130pm | DIVN. APTG. SUS | CLEAR 1b | EMPLOYEE(S) REPORTING Sgt. P. Sartuche #10518 | SER. NO. | DIVN.

SUPERVISOR APPROVING | SERIAL NO.

Exhibit 27
Khaiber Khan Settlement Letter

ORGANISATION NATIONALE IRANIENNE
POUR LA JEUNESSE ET L'EDUCATION PHYSIQUE

Iranian National Organisation
for the Youth and Physical Education

Pars Chahr - Téhéran

TR. 00002—00009
Ad Tilp Tabinindani - Téhéra

Date .March.20............19 63
No. : ....SS00T-235-T..........

Y-11

World Athletic Sports Corp.
507 Fifth Avenue
New York 17, New York

Attention: Mr. Jacob J. Warmbrand, President

Gentlemen: RE: Your letter of March 3 ,1963

We hereby acknowledge receipt of the originals of your Certified Public
Accounting up to March 1, 1963, together with bills, vouchers, cancelled
checks, etc., through your representative in Teheran. Included was
your Final Proposal for the sports centers in Teheran and twelve other
cities in Iran with the program for the Bakhtiari regions.

According to your request for the payment through a U.S. bank, enclosed
please find check No. 124 dated March 28, 1963, drawn on the City National
Bank of Beverly Hills, Los Angeles, California, for the amount of
$1,250,000.00 signed by Her Royal Highness, Princess Fatemeh Pahlavi, and
check No. 107 dated March 28, 1963 drawn on the same bank for the amount
of $1,250,000.00 signed by His Royal Highness, Prince Mahmoud Reza Pahlavi,
totaling the amount of $2,500,000.00 issued to you according to the
instructions of His Imperial Majesty, the Shahanshah, in settlement of expenses
incurred by you on behalf of the Sports Projects up to March 1, 1963.

Your final Proposal has been turned over to General Izadpanah for review
and you will hear from him directly.

Yours very truly,

(X) _____
Gen. Mohamad Amir-Khatemi
Shahanshahi Sports Organization of Iran

(X) CAL أة
KLI أسرك

340

Exhibit 28
Khaiber Khan Press Release

SENATE PERMANENT SUBCOMMITTEE
ON INVESTIGATIONS
OF
THE COMMITTEE ON GOVERNMENT OPERATIONS

FOR IMMEDIATE RELEASE
May 16, 1963

FOR IMMEDIATE RELEASE
May 16, 1963

Senator John L. McClellan (D., Ark.), Chairman of the Senate Permanent Subcommittee on Investigations, announced today the beginning of a preliminary inquiry into certain aspects of the Foreign Aid Program. At the present time the inquiry is expected to deal primarily with the administration and the effectiveness of United States aid to Iran.

Yesterday the Subcommittee heard in executive session the testimony of The Khaibar Khan, leader of the Bakhtiari Tribe of Iran, who is temporarily living in the United States and who spoke for a group he described as "K. K. United Patriots for Justice." During the course of his secret testimony, The Kha.. described Foreign Aid operations in Iran and surrendered to the Subcom... ee voluminous documents in his possession in full substantiation of the testimony he gave the Subcommittee. These documents, if corroborated, point to gross corruption and misuse of funds in excess of $100,000,000.00 in connection with the administration of United States aid to Iran. The current inquiry will follow avenues of investigation suggested by the documents and by the ..stimony of The Khaibar Khan. Future action by this Subcommittee will be determined by the facts developed during the preliminary inquiry.

Published by or on behalf of the K. K. United Patriots For Justice. Shahpour Avenue, Khoramabahr, Iran, of which the Khaibar Khan, 341 Madison Avenue, New York 17, New York, is the United States agent. The Khaibar Khan is registered with the Department of Justice, Washington, D. C. under the Foreign Agents Registration Act of 1938 as amended as the Agent of the aforesaid principal. Copies of the Registration Statement referred to are available for public inspection in the files of the Department of Justice. Registration does not indicate approval of the contents of this publication by the United States Government.

Exhibit 29
LAPD Field Interview with Strick

INTERVIEWS

FILE # I-471

PERSON INTERVIEWED: STRICK, LARRY   DATE/TIME   7-29-68 345p

SEX   M RACE Cauc HAIR Brn EYES Hzl HT 5-8 WT 145 DOB   11-28-50

RESIDENCE ADDRESS 11930 Iredell, Studio City   PHONE   TR7-6151

BUSINESS ADDRESS   PHONE

INFORMATION: (WHO,WHAT,WHEN,WHERE,WHY & HOW)

Larry Strck a volunteer worker for the Kennedy Campaign was interviewed
in person at his home address. Larry stated that he worked at the
headquarters almost every day that it was open. Larry normally left
school at 2pm and would go directly to the campaign headquarters.
Larry normally worked at the reception desk with Elly (Eleanor) Severson
I#295.

On 6-2-68 Larry arrived at the headquarters at approx 10:30AM. Larry
was assigned to work the reception desk with Elly. While working that
day (6-2-68) at approx 2:30PM a man known as Khaibar Khan (I-216) walked
in with two other males. Larry positively identified one of these
two males as Sirhan B. Sirhan. This person ID by Larry did not walk up
to the reception desk with Khaibar Khan and the other person, but stayed
back by the main entrance. Larry asked this person (that Larry ID'd as
Sirhan) if he (Larry) could help him and this person pointed to Khaibar
Khan and stated, "No, I'm with him." Larry did not pay anymore attention
to this person (that Larry ID'd as Sirhan). Larry did take Khaibar Khan
and the person that came up to the reception desk, back into the
telephone bank area. When Larry left the reception desk with Khaibar Khan
and the other person, the person Larry ID'd as Sirhan was still standing
by the main entrance doors. Larry described the person by the door
as a male, olive complexion, longnose, bushy eyebrows, middle 20's,
wearing dark colored pants, dark shoes, white button down shirt, light
olive green button sweater. When Larry returned from the phone backs
the person by the door was gone. Approx 5 minutes after Larry returned
Elly Severson asked where Kennedy's itinerary was. Larry stated that
just prior to leaving with Khaibar Khan that the itinerary was on the
reception desk, but when Elly Severson asked where it was he couldn't
find it, so he went and got another one. Larry was shown a packet of
mugs and removed all three phots stating that he is positive that the
person he saw on 6-2-68 at the headquarters and the mugs he had removed
are the same person. Larry also removed the mug of Saidallah Sirhan
stating that it looked familiar, but he was unable to remember where
he had seen him.
On 6-5-68 at approx 5pm, he was watching a TV news cast when he first
saw Sirhan's picture, and remembered that he had seen Sirhan 6-2-68
at the headquarters. Larry immediately tried to call Elly Severson,
but her phone was busy. Larry had just hung up when Elly Severson
1b/8-5-68   continued

INVESTIGATORS MAKING INTERVIEW: APPROVED BY:
RISEN #11663

342

P-2 STRICK, LARRY   I 471

called him. Elly stated, "Did you see the News." Larry stated, "Yeah,
he's the same guy that came in with Khaibar Khan Sunday." Elly then
told Larry that she had called the FBI and wanted him to call the
FBI and verify her story. Larry called the FBI and was subsequently
interviewed by S.A. Warren. (No interview listed. Mentioned in July
1st sect#III, Page 675) Larry stated that Elly Severson has asked
him to keep her posted on whats happening.

Larry arrived at the Ambassador at 830pm 6-4-68. Larry went directly
to the Embassy Room, but couldn't get in so he went down to the
Ambassador Ballroom until approx 930pm. Larry then went back to the
Embassy Room and had David Robinson I#323 get him into the Embassy
Room. Larry stayed in the Embassy Room until approx 1130pm. At this
time he went into the lobby and watched a TV monitor until Kennedy
started his speech. Larry then went into the kitchen via the hallway
past the men's room on a hunch that Kennedy would leave that way after
the speech. Larry stated that he was at the west end of the ice machine.
(in the kitchen) when Kennedy came through the double swinging doors.
Kennedy paused a moment and at this time Roosevelt Grier passed by
Kennedy and continued walking east through the kitchen. Kennedy began
moving forward again and Larry heard one shot and then four or five
more shots in quick succession. Larry then saw somebody run by in
front of him eastbound directly into Roosevelt Grier and Geo Plimpton.
Larry believes this person was Sirhan, but never saw his face. Larry
described the clothing as light colored pants, sweat shirt light in
color possibly yellow, white or light shit collar sticking up in back.
Larry was in kitchen until after Sirhan was taken out, but didn't
see him taken out. Larry stated that there was too big of a commotion
to tell what was happening around Kennedy and Sirhan. Larry stated
that Kennedy was just inside the double swinging doors when he was
shot. Larry states that Sirhan was between he (Larry) and Kennedy.
Larry also stated he left the Ambassador at approx 330am on 6-5-68.

Opinion & conclusion:
Larry was obviously not in the kitchen when Kennedy was shot because
of the incorrect locations he gave for Roosevelt Grier, Sirhan B.
Sirhan and Robert Kennedy. Larry stated that he was very familiar
with the Embassy Room because he helped decorate it on 6-3-68. Larry was
also in the Embassy Room and the kitchen area on & 5-25-68 when Kennedy
gave his speech in the Palm Court.
Larry seemed to have information that has been released by the news and
no other details. At the time of the interview Larry acted as if he
was prepared for a third degree. Apparently Elly Severson told him to
be prepared. Larry's mother left the room during the interview, but
could be seen standing by the doorway of the room where the interview
was taking place. As Larry described the person he saw on 6-2-68 he
continually looked at the mug lying on the table as if he was using
it for the facial description. See attached Ambassador Hotel map
with marking put on by Larry Stick.

On 8-2-68 At approx. 11pm, Larry Strick was contacted by telephone. During
the conversation Larry stated he has now decided to submit to a polygraph
examination. Larry stated that he will be out of town until 8-16-68. Larry
stated that any day after 8-16-68 would be fine with him for taking the
polygraph exam. Larry stated he will call as soon as he returns.

(X)✓   INTERVIEWS   FILE # I-471

PERSON INTERVIEWED: STRICK, Larry David   DATE/TIME 8-19-68 0:45 PM

SEX _M_ RACE _C_ HAIR _brn_ EYES _hzl_ HT 5-8 WT 145 DOB 11-23-50

RESIDENCE ADDRESS   11930 Iredell, Studio City   PHONE TR 76151
BUSINESS ADDRESS   None.   PHONE

INFORMATION: (WHO,WHAT,WHEN,WHERE,WHY & HOW)

Larry STRICK was re-interviewed concerning his statements made on
7-29-68 wherein he related that on 6-2-68 he observed Sirhan Sirhan
in company with Khaibar Khan at Kennedy Campaign Headquarters, 5912
Wilshire Blvd., L.A. and further interviewed as to his observations
in the kitchen area at the time Senator Kennedy was assassinated.

When re-interviewed on 8-19-68 Mr. STRICK without hesitation
retracted his former statement and explained that he is not positive
the person he saw in the Campaign Headquarters on 6-2-68 was Sirhan
Sirhan. In fact when shown several mug shots, he was unable to
identify Sirhan's new mug shot, stating that he did not look familiar
at all.

Mr. STRICK again was questioned regarding his observations of the
kitchen area at the time of the shooting. From his interpretations
of the incident, investigating officers could only conclude that he
was either not in the kitchen at the time of the shooting or his
recollections of the incident is so vague and inconsistent with
known, established facts, that he would be of no value as a witness.

kw/8-30-68

INVESTIGATORS MAKING INTERVIEW: APPROVED BY:
     J. Ryan #5281   S/Lt. Pena

Exhibit 30
LAPD Field Interview with Isaacson

FIELD INTERVIEWS   FILE #_____

Person(s) Interviewed: ISACKSON, June (Mrs)   Date June 13, 1968

Time 5:45 PM

Business Address & Phone 5615 Wilshire Blvd (Kennedy Campaign Hqtrs) 9376300

Residence Address & Phone 1673 Malcolm Ave., WLA   GR 45239

Information (To be complete the report should include: Who,What,When,Where,Why,
& How)

Mrs. Isackson is the office manager at the Kennedy Campaign Hqtrs, at above location. She left campaign hqtrs at approx 8:00PM, election night, to go to the Ambassador Hotel. She w-as with Helena Smith (Wife of Steve Smith) and both were in the Senators suite (#582) most of the evening. Approx one half hour prior to the Senator leaving the suite to go to the Embassy room, she and Helena went down and attempte-d to ent-er the Embassy Room bu-t were refused admittance at the main doors. Both then went to the Colonial Room where Mrs. Isackson knew the volunteer guard at the door. The guard permitted them b-oth to pass and they proceeded through the kitche-n where the shooting later took place. Before they reached the doors leading from the kitchen to the Embassy room they were turne-d back. They both then returned to the Senator's suite and was at this location when the shooting took place.

Mrs. Isackson stated that subsequent to the shooting both she and Helena Smith talke d about the shooting. Helena asked her if she remembered their entering the Colonial Room and someone attempting to enter the room with them, but being turned away. Mrs. Isackson did not recall such an incident. Hele-na also asked Mrs. Isackson is she recalled seeing a dk complexioned man in the kitchen ar-ea tearing up paper. Mrs. Isackson does not recall seeing such a person and went on to state that Helena told her that she could not recall if she actually saw such a man t-earing up paper or if she had heard it from someone else

Mrs. Isackson then related what she thought was an unusual situation. On June 1,1968 and on Election day, a young man of Arab nationality, known to her as Khaibar Kahn, aka "Goody", add: 10455½ Wilshire Blvd., LA phone # 475-1849, came into the Wilshire Blvd. Hqt-rs. The first time he had been to this locati was on Memorial Day (May 30, 1968). On Election Day Khaibar Kahn came into the Hqt-rs with several young persons most of whom appeared to be of Arabic descent. Yand volunteered to help. Most of these persons were subsequently use-d to t-ransport persons to the polls (SEE PAG-E #2 FOR NAMES ETC OF THIS GROUP OF PERSONS). Mrs. Isackson reported that a woman came into the Hqtrs and asked to be taken to the polls. Mrs. Isackson approached this area wjere this group was located and obs'd a young dk complexioned boy sittigg on a desk swinging his legs. About this time Khaibar Kahn c-ame in with a blonde, dk complex-ioned young man . This young man saw the one sitting on the table and said "What are you doing here"? He seemed obviously surprised to see this fell. At this time Khaibar Kahn took the fellow sitting on the d-esk and another and left the premises. The blond then t-ransported the woman to the polls. Later, a volunteer worker, Mrs. Bernard, unk add and phone number, informe-d Mrs. Isackson that the young man that had been sitting on the desk had not done any-thing during the entire time that he had been at Hqtrs. Mrs. Isackson states that she has tried to recall the young man sitting on the desk but cannot say if he could have been Serhan Serhan or not. Other employees at Hqtrs have stat-e-d that one of the group brought in by Khaibar Kahn resembled Serhan
(SEE PAGE #3 for list of these employees)   (CONTINUE D)

Investigators making interview
R.L. SAUTER 4758   P.L. SARTUCHE 10518

Approved by: _____

FIELD INTERVIEWS   FILE #_____

Person(s) Interviewed: <u>Isackson, June</u>   Date _____

_____   Time _____

Business Address & Phone _____

Residence Address & Phone _____

Information (To be complete the report should include: Who,What,When,Where,Why,
& How)

Cont. From Page#1

Below is a list of the persons who came to the campaign headquarters with
Kaan,Khaibar as their leader. All the persons put their names on 3x5 cards
and used the same address of 104555½ Wilshire Blvd. Ph# 475-1849; Most but not
all were of Arabic descent.The date of their appearance was 6-4-68 (ElectionDay

1.Miss Lucy White
2.Miss M. Taher
3.Satar Kahn Ghashghai
4.Bro. Jesus A. Dominguez
5.Mary Khan
6.Miss Farah Kahn
7.Dr.Nosratolah Khan Brujrit
8.Abdol Hamid Taheri
9. Mr. Reza Sahanbani
10. Mr. Firouz Tabatabai
11. Mr. Nasser Ghauami
12.Mr. Alex Kachaturian
13.Mr.Nader Pakravan
14.Sheikh Abdol Azim
185 Miss Rose Khan
16.Miss Luciano Petri
17. Miss Elizabeth Bobinson
18. Miss Manijeh Esfandiari
19. Miss Pary Saleh
20. Miss Puran Ahmadi
21. M. Dajhm
22. Talat Khan
23. Mohammad Khan Kurdestani
24.Philippe Memonn

Note; Some of the cards bearing the name of the above persons appear to be in
      the same handwriting. All the cards are being retained by Mrs. Isackson.
      The FBI has already interviewed Mrs. Isackson and have also seen the
      cards.

Cont. to page #3

_____
Investigators making interview | Approved by:
. P.L. Sartuche — R.L. Sauter |

FIELD INTERVIEWS   FILE # _____

Person(s) Interviewed: ___ISACKSON, June (Mrs)___   Date _____

_____   Time _____

Business Address & Phone _____

Residence Address & Phone _____

Information (To be complete the report should include: Who,What,When,Where,Why,
CONTINUED FROZM PAGE #2........ ..   & How)

The following is a list of Hqtrs employees who obs'd and may possibly feel
that one of Khaibar Kahn's group was Serhan Serhan:

1. HARDEGE, Dorothy (Miss)
    1021 N. Doheny Drive.
    271-7308

2. SMITH, Bernice (Mrs (
    1061 Meadowbrook, LA
    931-3533
    Knows and has talked to Khaibar Kahn.

3. SWEENEY, Margarete (Mrs)
    unk address.
    DI 79910
    Volunteer worker who was in charge of the volunteer section where Khaibar
    Khan and his group were working.

4. HANABERRY or HANABRE, William
    unk add and phone number.   Can be obtained from Mrs. Sweeney.....

5. SEVERSON, Eleanor (Mrs)
    12409 Helena, Brentwood
    476-2909

6. STERN, Estelle (Mrs)
    1136 S. Wooster Ave., LA
    271-8504.....

Investigators making interview | Approved by:

INDEX

349